Joseph Karo and Shaping of Modern Jewish Law

Joseph Karo and Shaping of Modern Jewish Law

The Early Modern Ottoman and Global Settings

By Roni Weinstein

ANTHEM PRESS

Anthem Press
An imprint of Wimbledon Publishing Company
www.anthempress.com

This edition first published in UK and USA 2022
by ANTHEM PRESS
75–76 Blackfriars Road, London SE1 8HA, UK
or PO Box 9779, London SW19 7ZG, UK
and
244 Madison Ave #116, New York, NY 10016, USA

British Library Cataloguing-in-Publication Data
A catalogue record for this book is available from the British Library.

Library of Congress Control Number: 2022932205

ISBN-13: 978-1-78527-876-1 (Hbk)
ISBN-10: 1-78527-876-2 (Hbk)

This title is also available as an e-book.

CONTENTS

INTRODUCTION: METHODOLOGY, QUESTIONS, AND SCOPE

In memoriam of my late mother and father,
Yafa Weinstein (née Brenner), who taught me to cherish people and to esteem studying,
and Reuven (Romek) Weinstein, who adhered to life as a saint clings to God.

In mid-seventeenth century, the Jewish-Ottoman historian David Conforti (1618–1680) had no hesitation describing R. Joseph Karo as the contemporary leader of the entire Jewish people: "The head of that generation, the great rabbi, the master of all Israel [the Jewish people—R.W], our master and rabbi Joseph Karo son of Joseph, son of Ephraim, whose forefathers originate from the Sephardi Diaspora, [and from] a family of Sages."[1] Some two generations previously, a historian of Karo's time, Gedalya ibn Yichya (c. 1526–1587), mentioned him as merely one among several distinguished rabbis in Safed, referring to him solely as "R. Joseph Karo, a great erudite in the Torah, who left many disciples. He composed the *Beit Yosef* and *Shulchan 'Arukh* and *Kesef Mishneh* [a commentary on Maimonides's code of law—R.W.]. He died in Safed in the year 1575."[2] The difference between these two historiographical tracts, composed within a relatively short span of time, demonstrates how famous R. Karo became during his lifetime and shortly after his death. More than any of his other works, *Beit Yosef* and *Shulchan 'Arukh* were the main reasons for R. Karo's fame. He was born in Spain shortly before the mass expulsion of the Jews from the Iberian Peninsula and spent his juvenile years in Rumelia, the western part of the Ottoman Empire, where he started to compose *Beit Yosef*.[3] Moved by pietistic and mystical motivations, he immigrated to the Holy Land, where he finished this magnum opus and initiated its publication. The four different sections of Beit Yosef were printed in various Italian printing presses between 1550 and 1559.[4] In Safed, the Galilean city that would play a crucial

---

1. David Conforti, *Koreh HaDorot* (Hebrew), Pietrikow: Solomon Belchotovsky Print House, 1895, p. 63.
2. Gedalya ibn Yichya, *Shalshelet HaQabbalah* (Chain of Transmission in Hebrew), Jerusalem: HaDorot HaRishonim veQorotam, 1962, p. 149. See further reference in relation to ordination polemic in Safed, *ibid.* p. 147.
3. For an important and updated biography of R. Joseph Karo, see Mor Altshuler, *The Life of Rabbi Yosef Karo* (Hebrew), Tel-Aviv: Tel-Aviv U.P., 2016, passim.
4. Tirza Yehudit Kelman, "*I Shall Create Halakhic Ruling [...] for that is the Objective*": The Dimension of Halakhic Ruling in Joseph Karo's Beit Yosef (Hebrew), Ph.D. submitted at Ben-Gurion University (Beer-Shevah, Israel), 2018, p. 31.

part in his adult and old-age life, he later composed a short version of this work, entitled *Shulchan 'Arukh*. It was this abridged and more accessible version which gained
him immediate fame and popularity in vast areas of the Jewish Ecumene, both among
scholars and the public at large.[5] These comprehensive juridical tracts will form the
focus of my book. Other aspects of R. Karo's life and his other compositions—his book
of responsa, his rulings as halakhic arbiter, his court verdicts, his significant career as
a teacher in his religious schools, his commentary on Maimonides' *Mishneh Torah*, and
his book on Talmudic methodology—will be addressed here as secondary aspects that
can further illuminate his double codes of law. They allow us to better understand his
motivations and the vision behind their composition. A major source in this regard was
the lengthy and detailed mystical diary *Maggid Meisharim*, composed throughout his
adult life and documenting his most intimate revelations, events, and thoughts. It is a
precious and exceptional testimony in a rabbinical context, where such biographical
perspectives are rare.

The question that intrigued me and motivated the writing of this research concerned
the fact that no other Jewish code of law ever took the place of R. Karo's work, as was
the case with previous codes of law. How is it that R. Karo's work was followed by four
hundred years of intensive rabbinic scholarship in which impressive Talmudic scholars
enjoyed great authority, and yet no text filled the same role as *Beit Yosef* and *Shulchan
'Arukh*? Given this apparent anomaly, how should we assess the role of these massive
legal tracts, with their highly juridical, formalistic, and technical character? What is
their cultural sense, beyond offering normative instructions? How is legalistic literature
in general to be read and understood?

This book is dedicated to books of law. Both *Beit Yosef* and *Shulchan 'Arukh* added
to a long list of rabbinic rulings; they are highly technical and formal in nature and
offer professional guidance in Jewish legality and halakhic tradition. Their fundamental contribution to the centuries-long tradition of rabbinic scholarship could in itself
justify the writing of the present book. Yet my interest relates not to law by itself, and
certainly not to positive law, but rather to the role of law in the formation of modern
Jewish society and the political-cultural vision standing behind this double codification project. For this reason, I will avoid entering technical or legalistic ("positivistic")
discussions of their content. Such a discussion has been undertaken in contemporary
and later exegetical literature and in modern academic research, as will be referenced
extensively in the following pages. My main interest concerns the role of law in a changing environment and the significant role that legal traditions, rulers, and "experts of the
law" played in shaping those changes. I will also examine the geographical and cultural
contexts, including the question of contact and exchange between different areas, such
as Europe, the Mediterranean Basin, Islam, or East versus West. The role of law as
formal instructions and judicial institutions will be regarded as less significant than the
forging of political and social institutions enabling the formation of a common politeia,

---

5. Meir Benayahu, *Yosef Bechiri* ('Joseph, My Chosen One' in Hebrew), Jerusalem: Yad HaRav
Nissim, 1991, passim.

or common life, alongside other domains with which law stands in constant interaction. Accordingly, the introductory chapter will be dedicated mainly to a presentation of the methodological tools used in the subsequent chapters, such as the anthropology of law, global history, or a proposed new reading of the social history of Halakhah. I intend to offer three fronts—or perspectives—in order to illuminate the contributions and innovations of R. Karo to Jewish culture and tradition, and, further, to consider the Jewish case study of legality and codification in a global context. Each of these perspectives opens diverse vistas and queries, as is clear from what follows.

The first relates to the place of these codes in the long sequence and history of Halakhah. These texts make sense primarily as part of a long heritage of Talmudic scholarship and the functioning of the rabbinic milieu since late antiquity. When reviewing the history of halakhic erudition and literature, how far back should we go, and what parts are more pertinent to this discussion? What new dimensions did Karo's codes add to previous codification projects? Do these texts reflect a geographical or cultural bias, or were they intended to serve the entire Jewish Ecumene?

The second concerns the concrete historical circumstances in which these codes were composed, read, disseminated, and later accompanied by rabbinic glosses. Why did they incite a mostly enthusiastic response from so many rabbinic authorities, and in which geographical settings, in particular? Any discussion of such queries is directly connected to the passage of Sephardi tradition from the Spanish-Catholic-European domain to the Sunni-Muslim arena under the rule of the Ottoman Empire. To what extent did the formation of a Sephardi diaspora in Northern Europe and along the Mediterranean Basin in the early modern period affect their composition and role in Jewish culture?

In the third and last perspective, it is assumed that the Jewish context as well as the halakhic heritage are not sufficient players when reading both *Beit Yosef* and *Shulchan 'Arukh*. Non-Jewish traditions also shaped the motivations of both the Sephardi Diaspora and their ruling elites, including the rabbinical elite. The immediate sphere of reference is obviously Ottoman civilization, within which both these codes of law were composed. Life under the prosperous and innovative Ottoman civilization of the Early Modern period surely required a Jewish response, but this was not a new or an unprecedented issue. The encounter between Jewish communities and vibrant cultures had evoked lively responses in various earlier periods in the Jewish past. Again, the question arises as to how far we will enlarge this context. Should we confine ourselves to Rumelia, where the vision and writing of *Beit Yosef* began, or to the Arabic lands under Ottoman rule, given that he completed his project in the Galilean city of Safed in the area of *Bilad a-Sham*, before adding the further stage of the composition of the *Shulchan 'Arukh*? An alternative perspective might follow the geographical and historical trail of Sephardi tradition between Catholic (and partially Calvinist) Europe and Muslim traditions. In other words, we would now require a much broader historical perspective of global dimensions. Returning to the Ottoman settings that played such a dominant role in R. Karo's work, is it advisable to sever these from their wider roots and cultural history relating to eastern traditions in Persia and Turkish nomadic tribal patterns or to ignore the impact of the Mongol past? In other words, an Eurasian perspective may also be relevant to the following discussion. Extending our gaze to include the broad Eurasian space not only expands our perspective beyond the European or even the Mediterranean settings but draws into our discussion centuries-long processes that affected Jewish communities and culture in very concrete ways, as part of Ottoman civilization. As we shall see in the following chapters, the Ottomans in their turn were part of a wide cultural and political network, expanding far to the east, to Safavid Iran, Mughal India, and even beyond.

History of Halakhah: Suggesting a Sociological Turn

To a large degree, the modern research of Halakhah and history of Halakhah still stands under the shadow of the founding fathers at the Hebrew University, such as Ephraim Urbach, Jacob Katz, Menachem Elon, and Israel Ta-Shma, and their inspiring successor Hayim Soloveichik.[6] Essential to their important and still fundamental writings is the presupposition that halakhic tradition is unique and follows its own intrinsic paths, as transmitted in the inner circle of its bearers—the Talmudic scholars and rabbinic authorities. Non-Jewish traditions, especially of a legalistic character, supposedly play only a minor role in this particular legal tradition and are regarded as an external "infiltration" into internal Jewish Talmudic discourse. No less important, it is implicitly assumed that, unless proved otherwise, the Jewish public followed the rabbinical instructions and conducted its life according to halakhic norms. No wonder that in their works most of the discussion is dedicated to Talmudic literature, the legalistic issues, and its internal evolvement. Another affiliated domain of Halakhah studies is dedicated to the philosophy of Halakhah, the presuppositions, and the implicit *Weltanschauung* behind the juridical debates.[7] These discussions focus on classical and recurring questions of "general" philosophy and refer only tangentially to the cultural, religious, and political context of the texts discussed.

Fortunately, a new research perspective has emerged over the last two decades that emphasizes the significant weight and contribution of the nonhalakhic context for

---

6. See for instance, Efraim E. Urbach, *The Halakhah – its Roots and Evolvement* (Hebrew), Jerusalem: Yad LaTalmud, 1983; Jacob Katz, *The "Shabbes Goy". A Study in Halakhic Flexibility*, tr. by Yoel Lerner, Philadelphia: JPS, 1989; Menachem Elon, *Jewish Law: History, Sources, Principles*, tr. by Bernard Auerbach and Melvin J. Sykes, Philadelphia and Jerusalem: JPS, 1994, Vols. I–IV; Israel Ta-Shma, *Talmudic Commentary in Europe and North Africa* (Hebrew), Jerusalem: Magnes Press, 2004, Vols. I–II; Haym Soloveichik, *Collected Essays*, Oxford: Littman Library of Jewish Civilization, 2013-2014, Vols. I–II. See also the articles published in the leading professional journals concerning history of Halakhah *Shnaton Ha-Mishpat Ha-'Ivri* (*Annual of the Institute for Research in Jewish Law*) and *Dinei Israel. Researches on Halakhah and Jewish Law*.

7. Avi Sagi, *The Open Canon. On the Meaning of Halakhic Discourse*, tr. by Batya Stein, London and New York: Continuum, 2007; Idem., *'It is not in Heaven'. Themes in the Philosophy of Halakah* (Hebrew), 'Ein Tzurim: Jacob Herzog Center, 2003; Moshe Halbertal, *Maimonides: Life and Thought*, tr. by Joel A. Linsider, Princeton: Princeton U.P., 2014; Aviezer Ravitzky, and Avinoam Rosenak (eds.), *New Streams in Philosophy of Halakhah* (Hebrew), Jerusalem: Magnes Press, 2008.

our understanding of the concrete functioning of Halakhah in historical conditions.[8] Halakhah is related not only to juridical-Talmudic and post-Talmudic debates but also to additional factors. The rabbinical milieu is examined not only as the sanctified bearers of the divine heritage but also as a social group with its own history, social, and economic constraints, affecting its conduct and study institutions, as well as the literary products themselves. These fresh avenues of halakhic research include the study of new kinds of material and documentation—such as the Cairo Genizah or various court records—that shed light on daily interactions between the Jewish public and its halakhic norms, point to the fascinating gap between formal instructions issued by halakhic authorities and their partial implementation.[9] The rabbinical milieu is also discussed as part of the community texture, highlighting the deep commitment of premodern rabbis and Talmudic scholars to the wellbeing of their communities—the "consumers" of their instructions. No less than the rabbinical carriers of Talmudic heritage, the public regarded itself as the sovereign or "owner" of this tradition. The formality of the law always engaged in some form of interaction with social needs. The bias of the rabbinical sources is also increasingly being taken into consideration, given that the rabbinical elite constituted a small minority within the general public, with a cultural, behavioral, and professional ethos of its own. Most of the documents at our disposal reflect a rabbinical bias, as they were produced by this erudite milieu, and it is questionable to what extent this milieu sought to reflect public life in its writing or was alternatively preoccupied with shaping an internal discourse addressing itself and composing the Halakhah for its own needs. The extent to which the resolutions and instructions of this elite were binding and enforceable on the general public is another issue that has not yet received sufficient attention in research. In other words, the question to what extent the rabbinical literature reflects reality and implies that the Jewish public followed its rabbinical authorities—for instance in the Responsa literature, or alternatively that Responsa documents a predominantly internal discourse confined to rabbinic milieu—remains open. Other groups within the Jewish communities, competing with the rabbinical elite, are still designated in current research as "secondary elites," following the perceptive suggestion of Jacob Katz. Are these indeed secondary in their importance and effect on Jewish life or do they constitute alternative and competing channels? Again, the scarcity of documents in this respect is due to the fact that rabbinical elite dominated the arena of writing and publishing (in manuscript and print) until late in Jewish history.

---

8. See especially the various works of Judah Galinsky, Tirtza Kelman, Elchanan Reiner, Rami Reiner, Pinchas Roth, Jay Berkovitz, and Moti Zalkin.

9. See for instance, Oded Zinger, *Women, Gender and Law: Marital Disputes according to Documents from the Cairo Genizah*, Ph.D. submitted at Princeton University, 2014; Gideon Libson, *Jewish and Islamic Law: A Comparative Study of Custom in the Geonic Period*, Cambridge, MA: Harvard Law School, 2003. Regarding the European context, see especially Jay Berkovitz, *Law's Dominion: Jewish Community, Religion and Family in Early Modern Metz*, Leiden and Boston: Brill, 2020.

The anthropology of law, an entire domain that is barely used in modern scholarship on the history of Halakhah, will also contribute to my work.[10] This discipline underlines the informal procedures used in oral societies for achieving justice and maintaining social peace. The anthropological perspective is relevant to the Jewish case study in spite of Judaism's long literary tradition. Several alternative channels for achieving justice functioned alongside each other in noncentralistic and fragmented communities, such as the Jewish medieval and early modern communities. These relied mainly on social institutions and informal control to pacify contentions and lower the level of confrontations. The formality of legal proceedings and the use of professional "experts of the law" were one option, but not necessarily the more desired or practiced one. Most of these internal processes of pacification have left no trail of written documentation. Yet even the archives of court records testify to the effectiveness of legal plurality and authority of the community, in Jewish, Muslim, and Christian courts.[11] An exemplary work on the nonlegalistic channels was conducted by Dan Smail regarding court cases in late medieval Marseille, under the Angevin rule.[12] Smail's work demonstrates the importance and relevance of the suggestions and writings of anthropology of the law to understanding judicial processes in premodern Europe and to understanding legal literature in general. The rich local archives enabled Smail to trace the community mechanisms behind the legal formalities:

> Reading cases such as these, one is forcefully reminded why the history of justice in late medieval Europe cannot be written from the perspective of procedural manuals, juristic commentaries, anecdotal observations, or even case summaries alone. Case records are punishing sources: often fragmentary, difficult to get at, hard to read. But cases complement the learned sources nicely, for they offer the perspective not of those who designed the courts but of those who used them, the consumers of the law who invested both financially and emotionally in the procedural apparatus of late medieval justice. It is easy to understand why kings, princes, and communes chose to invest in courts of law—this was a key element of the state-building process. Our histories of law and justice in medieval Europe, was written largely from the perspective of rulers.[13]

---

10. Laura Nader, *Le forze vive del diritto. Un'introduzione all'antropologia giuridica*. Edizioni Scientifiche Italiane, 2003; Sally Falk-Moore (ed.), *Law and Anthropology: A Reader*, Malden, MA: Blackwell Pub., 2005; Idem., *Law as Process: An Anthropological Approach*, London and Boston: Routledge & K. Paul, 1978.

11. Silvana Seidel Menchi and Diego Quaglioni (eds.), *I processi matrimoniali degli archivi ecclesiastici italiani*, Bologna: Il Mulino, 2000–2006, Vols. I–IV; Charles Donahue, *Law, Marriage, and Society in the Later Middle Ages. Arguments about Marriage in Five Courts*, Cambridge: Cambridge U.P., 2007. Regarding Ottoman courts, see for instance Metin Coşgel and Boğaç Ergene, *The Economics of Ottoman Justice Settlement and Trial in the Sharia Courts*, Cambridge, Cambridge U.P., 2016; Leslie Peirce, *Morality Tales. Law and Gender in the Ottoman Court of Aintab*, Berkeley, Los Angeles and London: University of California Press, 2003.

12. Daniel Lord Smail, *The Consumption of Justice: Emotions, Publicity, and Legal Culture in Marseille, 1264–1423*, Cornell U.P. Ithaca 2003.

13. *Ibid.*, p. 4.

Like many members of premodern societies, the residents of Marseille resented formal court procedures and considered them an act of aggression by their rivals. Informal pressure was exerted by other community members to use the mechanism of compromise or nonformal channels conducted by arbiters.[14] When one of the contending parties, or both, were constrained to be involved in court procedures, they used these as a theatrical arena to publicize their status within the community; legal language and terminology were merely a means to this end.[15] Smail noted that "family, faction, and neighborhood remained very prominently in view as institutions of coercion, and public retaliation and vengeance remained the conceptual norm throughout the fourteenth century, despite Angevin efforts to delegitimize such practices."[16]

These assertions regarding the nonformal channels for achieving justice and the dominant role of the community are valid not only in the case of Marseille but also in premodern Europe in general, and for that matter, for the concepts of justice in the premodern world.[17] Manlio Bellomo, Paolo Prodi, and Diego Quaglioni, leading Italian historians of law in medieval and early modern Europe, each in his own way, presented the major shift in the modern concepts of law leading from an ethos of law-as-justice to the legalistic perspective. Modern life is suffused with legalism, unlike the premodern approach of justice intimately affiliated to natural law or divine order as the foundation for human law and justice mechanisms. The discipline of legal knowledge and science—of both medieval *Ius commune* and Canon law—reflects the best human effort to approach this eternal level of justice.

I have so far concentrated on research into legal history in the European context but the religious-cum-legal tradition closest to the project of R. Karo and to his halakhic perceptions in general was that of Islam. What the late Shahab Ahmed wrote in his insightful book *What is Islam?* might equally apply to Jewish religious and legal notions. In both cases, religion was primarily what a believer does, how he conducts his life and follows the religious practices rather than adherence to a set of preconceived ideas and religious credos. The relatively minor function of credo is directly related to the lack of any centralistic institution—like the Christian Church—charged with deciding and enforcing the defining lines of Muslim belief: "The fact that there is no Church in Islam means that there is no institution invested with the epistemological authority to affix the imprimatur of religious truth upon a statement and send it forth as such into society. As Wadad al-Qadi has simply put it, 'The entire community bore the burden of interpreting the revelatory-prophetic legacy.'"[18]

---

14. *Ibid.*, pp. 6, 8.
15. On the "performative nature of late medieval justice" see, *ibid.*, p. 28.
16. *Ibid.*, pp. 162–163.
17. Diego Quaglioni, *La giustizia nel Medioevo e nella prima età modern*, Bologna: Il Mulino, 2004; Paolo Prodi, *Una storia della giustizia: dal pluralismo dei fori al moderno dualismo tra coscienza e diritto*, Bologna: Il Mulino, 2000; Manlio Bellomo, *The Common Legal Past of Europe, 1000–1800*, translated by Lydia G. Cochrane, Washington, DC: Catholic University of America Press, 1995.
18. Ahmed Shahab, *What is Islam? The Importance of Being Islamic*, Princeton and Oxford: Princeton U.P., 2016, p. 192.

The law and the tradition of *Shari'a* contributed, following Ahmed, heavily to the notion of what is Islam, but it had to compete with other alternatives, no less crucial in premodern Islam, discussed in this book, such as mystical Sufi traditions,[19] the ethical literature [*Akhlaq*],[20] philosophy,[21] literature,[22] or even state law as legislated by political authorities.[23] The notion that law is the defining axis of Islam is mistaken, and projects backward the centrality of legalism in the modern Muslim states, including modern Arab states. Modern Muslims and scholars alike read Islamic tradition through state-oriented eyes. This approach identifies so-called authentic and normative Islam with one aspect, the law, while marginalizing other dimensions of Islamic tradition over the centuries.[24] In allocating a central role to law in Islamic life and identity, this reading of the Islamic tradition relegates to the margins other cultural perspectives.[25] Ahmed's insightful critique will resonate later in relation to the Halakhah and the work of R. Karo.

The cultural pluralism within Islamic legalism was clearly shown in the rise of various competing schools of law (*Madhhabs*). As we shall see in the forthcoming chapters, these schools evolved within the scholastic community, which constantly attempted to stay aloof from political authorities and maintain its independence. This process is similar to the Jewish case, where law evolved regardless of political power and establishment. Considering Muslim legality as the defining parameter of Islamic life and tradition from its early history would imply the adoption of the perspective of the same legal scholars. In fact, Ahmed asserts that the life of large groups within Islam stood in contradiction to formal law. For many Muslims, law was merely one part of Islam, alongside others guiding the believers' lives, such as philosophy, Sufism, ethics, and aesthetics. All these facets had their own institutions, practitioners, and legitimacy within Islam: "Evidently, to these Muslims *normative Islam* was elaborated through complex lived-and-thought-and-spoken negotiation and assimilation both individual and social—between these different modes of ordering, expressing and valorizing that were available to them. And for these Muslims, this multidimensional, multivocal construction and practice *made sense and held true* as *Islam*."[26] Paraphrasing Ahmed, "it is not only categorically wrong, but is reductionist nonsense to say that law defined not only the Jewish way of life, but also the culture and psyche of Jews throughout the Middle Ages and the early modern era." In both cases, the community, its needs and wellbeing, and its customs and oral traditions—carried on within social institutions such as family, tribe, professional groups, cities or ethnic groups—provided a basis for Muslim solidarity and a sense of belonging to the same religious heritage no less than the religious law. This identity is

---

19. *Ibid.*, pp. 94–99.
20. *Ibid.*, pp. 127, 462–463, 470, 503.
21. *Ibid.*, pp. 128–129.
22. *Ibid.*, p. 494.
23. *Ibid.*, esp. pp. 475–484.
24. *Ibid.*, pp. 117–118, 125.
25. *Ibid.*, p. 537.
26. *Ibid.*, pp. 120, 122, 93.

rooted in a sense of human solidarity and connectedness across geographical space and historical time. In this sense, the *ummah muslimah* (literally, "Muslim community") and each individual community are the carriers and "owners" of the law and legal tradition no less than professionals of the law.[27] If law is not the factor bolting the entire community of believers, then the sense of belonging to the same faith collective is an agent of no less importance. Again, what characterized Islam before the establishment of modern states may prove to be applicable in the Jewish case as well.

The Sephardi Dominance

In his will from 1654, a former *Converso* (an Iberian Jew constrained to convert to Catholicism) left his property to various branches of his family, living in Aleppo, Cyprus, Florence, Gibraltar, Marseille, Venice, and Western Europe.[28] Such a dispersion of Sephardi families over wide geographical territories and beyond religious borders was not exceptional. The Sephardi Diaspora, formed mainly after the general expulsions from Spain (1492) and Portugal (1497), was indeed global in its extent. It stretched from Western Europe to the entire Mediterranean basin, in between Catholic and Protestant Europe and Ottoman Empire and the Arab lands, and even beyond, to the "New World" of southeast Asia and the Americas. The close family and business ties between those who fled Spain and Portugal and those who remained and converted to Catholicism constrained some of them to return occasionally—under disguise obviously—to Iberia.

The Sephardi tradition developed its own special approach before the expulsions.[29] The local communities were numerous and incorporated a sizable number of members. Prominent members of the community were politically connected with the Spanish king. A strong and well-organized elite led Spanish Jewry, combining political experience, economic power, and cultural erudition. A small group of courtiers had its own cultural traits and maintained control over Jewish communities, thanks to tight connections with the king or with feudal lords, combined with a strategy of intracommunal marriage. Occasionally, they managed to overcome the habitual tendency of Jewish communities in the Middle Ages toward localism and create supra-local organizations under their control. The rabbinic elite functioned hand in glove with the political elite to protect their mutual interests of enforcing community control and religious heritage. The Spanish rabbis carved their own particular patterns of Talmudic traditions and halakhic rules. The unique political, economic, and cultural traits of Sephardi communities—alongside their demographic superiority in respect to other medieval Diasporas—resulted in a sense of self-confidence and superiority that they sought to guard.

---

27. *Ibid.* pp. 140–141. On the importance of community wellbeing as motivation for maneuvering religious law, see *ibid.*, 505. See also, *ibid.*, pp. 471, 485–486.
28. Jacob Barnai, *Smyrna, the Microcosmos of Europe: The Jewish Community of Smyrna in the 17th and 18th Centuries* (Hebrew), Jerusalem: Carmel, 2014, p. 55.
29. Haim Beinart (ed.), *Moreshet Sepharad: The Sephardi Legacy*, Jerusalem: Magnes Press, 1992, Vols. I–II.

This tradition reached new places in the early modern period, where the Sephardi newcomers enforced upon the local Jewish population their particular traditions in the political, religious, sociological, and cultural domains. The mystical corpus *Book of Splendor (Sefer Ha-Zohar)*, considered part of their own particular patrimony, became the prime book of Jewish mysticism during the early modern period and condemned other traditions of medieval Kabbalah to oblivion. The Sephardi and Portuguese Jews designated themselves as a *Nacion* or *Naçao* (in Spanish and Portuguese, respectively), that is, a distinct and superior subgroup within the Jewish collective. Their domineering attitude, especially the arrogance of ex-Castilian Jews who formed the backbone of this Jewry, was noticed by contemporary Jewish observers. An Italian rabbi David Messer Leon, who headed a community in Vlora (Albania), plainly and explicitly commented on the Sephardi component of the local population: "They [the Portuguese Jews—R.W.] are truthful and generous, and not covert and secretive and proud as the Castilians [Castilian Jews—R.W.]."[30]

Arriving in the Ottoman core lands in Rumelia and Anatolia, the Sephardi former refugees managed to establish several exceptionally large communities (by Jewish standards) in Istanbul, Salonica, and later in Izmir. The sultans offered incentives to encourage this immigration, and Istanbul became a center of Jewish life. The newcomers came to serve a mediating role between various Jewish communities and the Ottoman sultans and high officials. By the mid-sixteenth century, Istanbul was eclipsed by the new community of Salonica, with its sizable Jewish population, to the point that the city was later nicknamed the "Jerusalem of the Balkans."[31] The internal institutions and cultural life in Salonica inspired many other Sephardi communities in the Balkans. In a way, it functioned as a corollary Jewish capital city in the Ottoman Empire.[32] Salonica became a center of religious erudition and schooling and spawned famous Talmud scholars. Its cultural institutions were supported by rich local families and included public libraries, advanced Talmudic schools, and modern schools serving the young male population. Extensive literature was composed during the sixteenth and seventeenth centuries by Salonican sages, addressing readers beyond the restrained rabbinic milieu through the composition of popularized halakhic works. Scholars initiated in local *Yeshivas* later moved from this central city to smaller communities in the Ottoman territories, disseminating the local patterns of Salonica to the periphery. A common methodology of study, established some decades before the expulsion but enjoying growth later in their new places of settlement, enabled the formation of an intensive network of Talmud scholars in various Sephardi communities around the Mediterranean Basin. This

30. Yehuda Messer Leon, *Kevod Chakhamim* (Honor of Sages/Rabbis)], ed. and introduction by Shimon Bernfeld, Berlin: H. Itzkowski Print, 1899, pp. 5–6.
31. Joseph Hacker, "The Intellectual Activity among Jews in the Ottoman Empire during the Sixteenth and Seventeenth Centuries" (Hebrew), *Tarbiz* 53, no. 4 (1984), pp. 569–604; Yaron Ben-Naeh, "City of Torah and Study: Salonica as a Torah Center during the Sixteenth and Seventeenth Centuries" [Hebrew], *Pe'amim: Studies in Oriental Jewry*, 80 (1999), pp. 60–82.
32. Ben-Naeh, "Salonica as a Torah Center during the Sixteenth and Seventeenth Centuries," p. 68, regarding the cultural and trade networks woven around Salonica.

mode of study served as a cultural *lingua franca* among scholars. Aided by the printing of books, it encouraged the exchange of scholarly messages among the Jewish members of this "Republic of Letters."[33] The wide network of human connection, relative ease of communication, and the need to form a common ground for scholars and communities also paved the way for standardization and unification in the halakhic domain. This was the fertile terrain on which *Beit Yosef* and *Shulchan 'Arukh* began to be composed.

Next to these political-economic-cultural centers was added another virtual Jewish capital: the city of Safed.[34] During the sixteenth century, Safed became the arena for a Jewish mystical Renaissance that radiated out to almost the entire Jewish world. The city hosted the most senior scholars in various domains of Jewish culture. For the first time in Jewish history, mysticism/*Kabbalah* were not confined to small esoteric circles but filtered out to the wider public. The main channels of this dissemination were ethical literature, guiding the devotees in their correct beliefs, religious acts, and mystical conduct. New rituals were invented by the great Kabbalistic masters (such as conventions for religious singing or night vigils), and mystical confraternities provided the institutional channel for their dissemination.

The Global Ottoman Setting and its Legal System

The conquest of Constantinople (1453), the capital city of the Byzantine Empire, was a crucial and turning point in the construction of its successor, the Ottoman Empire. Further conquests of Arabic lands over the succeeding decades, including the holiest cities of Islam, Mecca, and Medina, led to the emergence of the largest and longest-lasting empire in Islam. The ethnic variety, the geographical extent, the numerous religious traditions of local populations, the diversity between Sunna- and Shi'a-inclining groups, the dominance of Persian culture, and the heritage of Turkish tribes originating from the Asian steppe all contributed from the outset to the global character of the Ottoman Empire beginnings. It is to be considered as part of a wide cultural continuum:

> The boundaries of modern nation-states [...] have tended to obscure both important areas of shared experience and significant systems of connection between the Middle East and South Asia. If this is true of the structural characteristics of the Ottoman, Safavid, and Mughal empires, and if this is also true of their commercial organization and techniques of trade, it is no less true of the content of their systems of formal learning, of the nature of their major sources of esoteric understanding, and of the ways in which they were linked by the connective systems of learned and holy men.[35]

---

33. Francesca Trivellato, *The Familiarity of Strangers. The Sephardic Diaspora, Livorno, and Cross-Cultural Trade in the Early Modern Period*, New Haven, CT: Yale U.P., 2009.

34. On the rise and impact of Safed on the entire Jewish world, see Roni Weinstein, *Kabbalah and Jewish Modernity*, London: Littman Library of Jewish Culture, 2016, passim. The book includes rich bibliography on "The Safed phenomenon."

35. Francis Robinson, "Ottomans-Safvids-Mughals: Shared Knowledge and Connective Systems" *Journal of Islamic Studies* 8, no. 2 (1997), pp. 151–184. Citation from *ibid.*, p. 151.

The Ottoman Empire confronted mighty powers both from the West and the East.[36] The Habsburgs presented a political and military challenge to Ottoman expansionist goals on the European front after their wide conquests in the Balkans and the Slavic territories. They confronted Charles V, a ruler who had his own aspirations for universal rule and was motivated by a messianic vision:

> To appreciate the excitement and the foreboding that the young Habsburg prince [Charles V—R.W.] awakened, we need to remind ourselves of the current mental outlook that allowed men to experience themselves as participants in a prophetic scheme of history. It is well known that medieval religious and political prophecy had received its ultimate stamp under the influence imparted by the twelfth-century Calabrian abbot, Joachim of Flora. Here was to be found the idea of that progressive trinitarian elaboration of world history, culminating in the Age of the Spirit with its profound sense of *renovatio*, renewal. The Joachimite pattern looked to an outstanding ruler, a monarch of the whole world, a second Charlemagne, repeatedly identified either with a current French *Rex Christianissimus* or with a German *Rex Romanorum* who would renew the church, chastise its ministers, conquer the Turk, and—like David—gather all sheep into one fold. Some expositors of the Joachimite tradition believed that an angelic pope, a *pastor angelicus*, shunning temporal goods and collaborating with the Savior-Emperor, would rule the Holy See [the papacy—R.W.].[37]

In the East, they confronted at sea the new European colonial powers,[38] especially the Portuguese fleet, and the trading companies, but above all, the Safavid state, with its equally ambitious vision of universal rule. The contest for power, once again, had religious roots, as the Safavid polity solidified around the Shiʻa tradition, which was soon adopted as the official state religion.

Hüseyin Yılmaz and others have shown how rulers across the Eurasian domain shared common concepts of a universal rule of sanctified character, charged with the mission to reform and renovate the religious traditions. Their sources of inspiration were often the Sufi traditions, rather than ones based on juristic canon. This is true of the Ottoman case, where the Ottoman sultan was held to be the deputy of God on earth, in both the temporal and spiritual domains:

See also, Kaya Şahin, *Empire and Power in the Reign of Süleyman. Narrating the Sixteenth-Century Ottoman World*, Cambridge: Cambridge U.P., 2013, esp. pp. 7–8.

36. The double front challenging the Ottoman Empire is illuminatingly presented in Şahin, *Empire and Power in the Reign of Süleyman*, esp. pp. 4, 62, 226.

37. John M. Headley, "The Habsburg World Empire and the Revival of Ghibellinism," in: David Armitage (ed.), *Theories of Empire, 1450–1800*, London and New York: Routledge, 2016, pp. 45–79. Citation from *ibid.*, p. 46. I wish to thank Tijana Krstić for drawing my attention to this article. See also Franz Bosbach, "The European Debate and the Revival of Ghibellinism," *Theories of Empire, 1450-1800*, pp. 81–98. In relation to Spain political Messianism, see Geoffrey Parker, "Messianic Visions in the Spanish Monarchy, 1516–1598," *Calíope: Journal of the Society for Renaissance and Baroque Hispanic Poetry* 8, no. 2 (2002), pp. 5–24.

38. Şahin, *Empire and Power in the Reign of Süleyman*, pp. 27, 214.

Among others, Cornell Fleischer, Kathryn Babayan, Mercedes García-Arenal, and Azfar Moin masterfully demonstrated how rulers of the postcaliphate Islamicate world from Morocco to India constructed colorful visions of rulership by decorating themselves with mystical imageries and posing themselves as caliphs, lords of conjunction, renewers of religion, Mahdis, and saints [...] Sufi-minded scholars put Islamic sources to a new scrutiny to discover divine revelations regarding the Ottomans, which resulted in constructing an elaborate eschatology in which the Ottomans were specifically foretold to rule. The Ottoman rulership was depicted to be the seal of the caliphate.[39]

As the inheritor of both the post-Mongol and classical traditions of Islam,[40] reverting back to the period of the Caliphs, the ruler legitimized his domination not only by virtue of direct military power and the use of force, but also on the basis of justice and law. Obedience to imperial law, and to a larger degree religious law (*Shari'a*), added a fundamental element of legitimacy to the dynastic rule of the House of Osman. These positions were repeatedly stated in the *Adaletnameler* (Decrees of Justice) sent to provincial officials to remind them that the protection of the taxpaying *re'aya* from any kind of illegal financial and physical oppression was one of their foremost responsibilities of rulership.[41]

Guy Burak convincingly showed how the main innovative components of Ottoman justice system were tightly controlled by the state:[42] the establishment of a state-appointed official (the *Şeyḫülislâm*) charged with controlling the entire legal domain from the center; control over the religious schools in which the new generation of legal scholars pursued their studies;[43] the transformation of the Hanafi school of law (*Madhhab* or *Mezheb* in Arabic and Turkish, respectively) into a quasi-formal state position; domination by a group of religious scholars (*'Ulama* in Arabic);[44] a hierarchic network of schools

39. Hüsein Yılmaz, *Caliphate Redefined. The Mystical Turn in the Ottoman Political Thought*, Princeton: Princeton U.P., 2018, pp. 1, 2, 5, 199. See also Şahin, *Empire and Power in the Reign of Süleyman*, passim. On similar political concepts in the Safavid and Mughal contexts, see A. Azfar Moin, *The Millennial Sovereign. Sacred Kingship and Sainthood in Islam*, New York: Columbia U.P., 2012.

40. David Morgan, "The Great Yasa of the 'Great Chinggis Khan' Revisited," in: Reuven Amitai and Michal Biran (eds.), *Mongols, Turks, and Others. Eurasian Nomads and the Sedentary World*, Leiden and Boston: Brill, 2005, pp. 291–308. On the Ottoman context, see Guy Burak, *The Second Formation of Islamic Law. The Hanafi School the Early Modern Ottoman Empire*, Cambridge: Cambridge U.P., 2015, pp. 17, 215–220.

41. See also Hasan T. Karateke and Maurus Reinkowski (eds.), *Legitimizing the Order: The Ottoman Rethoric of State Power*, Leiden and Boston: Brill, 2005.

42. Burak, *The Second Formation of Islamic Law*.

43. Shahab Ahmed and Nenad Filipovic, "The Sultan's Syllabus: A Curriculum for the Ottoman Imperial Medreses Prescribed in a Fermān of Qānūnī I Süleymān, Dated 973 (1565)," *Studia Islamica* 98–99 (2004), pp. 183–218.

44. On the increasing dependency of law scholars in Islam, especially under the Ottomans, see Zouhair Ghazzal, "The 'Ulama: Status and Function" in: Youssef M. Choueiri (ed.), *A Companion to the History of the Middle East*, London: Blackwell, 2005, pp. 71–86. See especially *ibid.*, pp. 75–76.

(*Madrasa*s in Arabic) controlled by the state; the abiding authority of legal rulings issued by the Şeyḫülislâm and their prioritization over the opinions of other schools, so that they were regarded as binding by state-nominated judges; the formation of a professional and hierarchic legal guild in control of teaching and adjudication functions; and the increasing use of documents and the establishment of professional state archives. Some aspects of increasing state control over justice mechanisms continued Mameluke precedents, as shown by Yosef Rapoport, but these had never achieved the intensity of Ottoman control.[45]

The roots of these changes can be traced back to the period of Mehmet II, the conqueror of Constantinople, but their impact was much stronger in the period of Sultan Süleyman (ruled 1520–1566), remembered by later generations as *Kanuni*, the legislator. It would not be superfluous to draw the attention at this point that R. Joseph Karo is contemporary of this ruler. In his classical article on Sultan Süleyman, Cornell Fleisher pointed on two distinct phases of his long and successful rule, the first one suffused with apocalyptic connotations and universalistic dreams, while the second after 1550 was associated with

a new gravity of tone and a formalizing impulse to establish consistency of imperial style [...] It is only in the last segment of the reign, from about 1550, that those phenomena normally associated with the image of a Süleymanic system of a universalized dynastic law, institution and standardization of central and provincial bureaucratic structures, stabilization of expectations and obligations of the nominally meritocratic elite service orders emergence of a distinctive imperial culture shared by a newly corporatize elite, and visual and literary formulation of an imperial iconography based equally on dynastic glory and dynastic commitment to upholding the legitimating principles of order and justice begin to take palpable form [...] After the execution of Ibrahim Pasha, Süleyman employed a far less personal, and therefore more awesome, surrogate persona: The dynastic law, *kanun*, which represented and implemented sovereign authority, in written and oral form, over tremendous distances. It is in this period, the late 1530s and 1540s, that we see an energetic compilation, codification, and modification of imperial ordinance, its regularization, universalization, and reconciliation with the dictates of the Holy Law, and also the rapid expansion and deepening of the machinery of government based on newly articulated principles of hierarchy, order, meritocracy, regularity, and replicability of basic structures based on function rather than on persons.[46]

In establishing a centralistic legal system, the Sultan cooperated closely along many years with his nominated Şeyḫülislâm Ebu Su'ud.[47] Ebu Su'ud is a significant person in Ottoman legal and political history, and crucial to tracking its impact on Jewish life

45. Yossef Rapoport, "Royal Justice and Religious Law: *Siyāsah* and Shari'ah under the Mamluks," *Mamluk Studies Review* 16 (2012), pp. 71–102.

46. Cornell H. Fleischer, "The Lawgiver as Messiah: The Making of the Imperial Image in the Reign of Süleymân," in: Gilles Veinstein (ed.), *Soliman le Magnifique et son temps*, Paris: La Documentation Française, 1992, pp. 159–177. Citations from *ibid.*, pp. 159–160, 167, 171.

47. Colin Imber, *Ebu's-su'ud. The Islamic Legal Tradition*, Edinburgh: Edinburgh U.P., 1997.

and to the life project of R. Karo. Colin Imber described the important aspects of their mutual cooperation, when Ebu Suʿud managed to establish a balance between state and religious law, form an efficient machinery, responded to urgent legal questions in his vast fatwas, instructing judges, and innovating the legal procedures.[48]

The codification of Ottoman law demonstrated the increasing role of law in imperial policy. These law codes (*kanunnames*) depended on Sultanic authority and were imposed on the entire Ottoman realm. Ottoman sultans and officials became involved in the codification of Sunni Hanafi law as the official law, and imperial decrees specifically commanded the imposition of this law in the courts:

> The dynastic law, *kânûn*, which represented and implemented sovereign authority, in written and oral form, over tremendous distances. It is in this period, the late 1530s and 1540s, that we see an energetic compilation, codification, and modification of imperial ordinance, its regularization, universalization, and reconciliation with the dictates of the Holy Law, and also the rapid expansion and deepening of the machinery of government based on newly articulated principles of hierarchy, order, meritocracy, regularity, and replicability of basic structures based on function rather than on persons.[49]

This policy was applied in the core lands of the empire, but also accompanied the annexation of newly conquered areas, including the Arab territories. Timothy Fitzgerald termed this process "ceremonies of possession." Occupation by Ottoman soldiers implied the application of various measures such as taxes, land surveys, and in the legal sphere codification and restructuring of the local legal system according to Ottoman standards. This process resonates with similar developments following the conquest of the "New World" by European powers.[50] Baki Tezcan suggested that the monetization of the Ottoman economy also encouraged the composition of codes of law in response to the rise of elite families benefitting from these changes. These families increasingly established a monopoly over judicial posts in the state mechanisms: "In the late sixteenth and the early seventeenth centuries the high-ranking Ottoman judges and professors of law, the *mevali* (sing. *mevla*, lord), came to constitute a privileged social group, a nobility of sorts, the members of which could pass on their social status to their sons. These legal developments were led by a socio-economic transformation towards a more market-oriented society in the Ottoman Empire of the sixteenth century."[51] The

---

48. *Ibid.*, esp. pp. 14, 24, 51, 107, 109.
49. Abdurrahman Atçıl, *Scholars and Sultans in the Early Modern Ottoman Empire*, Cambridge: Cambridge U.P., 2017, pp. 129–131.
50. Timothy J. Fitzgerald, "Rituals of Possession, Methods of Control, and the Monopoly of Violence: The Ottoman Conquest of Aleppo in Comparative Perspective," in: Stephan Conermann and Gül Şen (eds.), *The Mamluk-Ottoman Transition Continuity and Change in Egypt and Bilad al-Sham in the Sixteenth Century*, Bonn: Bonn U.P., 2016, pp. 249–273. Citations from *ibid.*, pp. 249–250, 263.
51. Baki Tezcan, "The Ottoman *Mevali* as 'Lords of the Law'," *Journal of Islamic Studies* 20, no. 3 (2009), pp. 383–407. Citations from *ibid.*, pp. 383, 387. A fuller discussion, see idem., *The Second Ottoman Empire: Political and Social Transformation in the Early Modern World*, Cambridge:

Ottoman legal system cast its long shadow over all the religious and ethnic groups living under its yoke, both the Muslims and certainly the non-Muslim minorities, including obviously the Jews.

The intricate power balance between the Ottoman center and the Arabic periphery will be a constant element throughout this book. This balance was continually renegotiated in different places and times, including with regard to the Jewish minority. It is not superfluous to recall that the city of Safed, as part of the *Bilad a-Sham* area (including Modern Syria, Lebanon, and the Holy Land), was subject to the impact of these changes. The non-Muslim minorities maintained a limited scope of legal autonomy so that they needed to function under the unmistakable hegemony of the Ottoman justice mechanisms. Non-Muslim Ottoman subjects not infrequently preferred the state justice of the *kadi* over their own communal courts of law. The local magistrates were bred and educated in the religious *medreses*, and then spent time retraining in order to gain expertise in secular and regional law. Later they were sent out into the provinces and cities of the empire as representatives of the Ottoman Empire and sultanic law. These officials embodied the unity between center and periphery.[52] Written documents played an increasing role, at the expense of oral agreements. Their credibility relied on the establishment of central state archives and stricter control of court archives throughout the empire—a process Guy Burak termed "Archival Consciousness."[53]

Next to the legal elite of the empire—the *Şeyḫülislâm*, the two military judges of Anatolia and Rumelia (*Kâdîasker*s in Turkish), the professors of law, judges, jurisprudents, and families who increasingly monopolized the high-ranking positions[54]—stood in close synergy with the bureaucratic elite in charge of running a huge empire. One of the senior figures among them during the sultanate of Süleyman was Celal Mustafa, whose contribution was discussed by Kaya Şahin. Secretaries and state bureaucrats were essential for running a wide empire, acting in such functions as land surveys, tax collection, systematic registration and documentation, as well as in the composition of

---

Cambridge U.P., 2010, Ch.1. For a further discussion, see Michael Nizri, *Ottoman High Politics and the Ulema Household*, London: McMillan and Palgrave, 2014.

52. Karen Barkey, "Aspects of Legal Pluralism in the Ottoman Empire," in: Lauren Benton and Richard J. Ross (eds.), *Legal Pluralism and Empires, 1500–1850*, New York and London: New York U.P., 2013, pp. 83–107. See especially *ibid.*, pp. 84, 90. See also Hakan T. Karateke, "Opium for the Subjects? Religiosity as a Legitimizing Factor for the Ottoman Sultan," in: Karateke and Reinkowski (eds.), *Legitimizing the Order*, pp. 111–129. See *ibid.*, p. 126: "The assistance provided by Mahmud II on his tour of Rumelia may be cited as an example." In a speech he had Vassaf Efendi read in Shumla, a city in today's Bulgaria, he said: "You Greeks, Armenians, Jews, you are all servants of God, and you are all my subjects—just as good as the Muslims. Your beliefs are different, but you all obey the laws and my imperial orders."

53. Guy Burak, "'In Compliance with the Old Register': on Ottoman Documentary Depositories and Archival Consciousness,' *Journal of the Economic and Social History of the Orient* 62 (2019), pp. 799–823. See esp. *ibid.*, pp. 810, 813, 819.

54. Tezcan, "The Ottoman *Mevali* as 'Lords of the Law'," pp. 383–384.

law codes. As mentioned previously, the annexation of new lands was followed by the composition and imposition of state laws, as in the famous case of Egypt (1516).[55]

The third pillar in stabilizing the Ottoman Empire—alongside the legal establishment and the administrative bureaucracy—consisted of the immensely varied Sufi and Dervish orders that spread during this period and enjoyed increasing cooperation and protection from the Ottoman state following:

> the rapprochement that had been forged between the Ottoman ruling elites and the "mainstream" sufi orders in the second half of the sixteenth century. After decades of Sunnitization, many sufis had also come to conform more closely to the social, political and cultural norms that were now being favored by the ruling elites, and even to act as agents of Sunnitization themselves [...] In the first half of the sixteenth century, various Ottoman scholars and statesmen steeped in the sufi intellectual tradition also made use of this mystical conception of rulership to justify Ottoman claims to the caliphate and to counter the claims of the Shii Safavids as well as of various potentially unruly sufi groups within the Ottoman realms.[56]

Sufi traditions made an important contribution to the process of change undergone by Ottoman state and society, a process referred to by Derin Terzioğlu, Tijana Krstić, and others as Sunnitization. Krstić characterized it as a "marked shift in Ottoman religious politics in the beginning of the 16th century from one comfortable with 'confessional ambiguity' to one increasingly concerned with defining and enforcing a particular understanding of correct belief and practice."[57] The reasons for this change are still debated among scholars and include the rise of the Shiite Safavid Empire and the religio-political challenge this posed to the Ottoman dynastic legitimacy, as well as factors relating to state building, particularly urbanization, monetization of the economy, institutionalization, and bureaucratization, followed by the rise of an increasingly self-confident class of Ottoman scholars who sought to assert their vision of Islam and sharpen the boundaries of belief. The empire's rulers showed an increasing interest in the religious positions of their subjects. The sixteenth century appears to have brought intensified discussions regarding unorthodox positions, including the persecution of individuals and groups considered heretical. A person suspected of heresy needed to pass rituals of "renovation of belief" in order to be reintegrated in the community of

---

55. Şahin, *Empire and Power in the Reign of Süleyman*, see esp. pp. 3, 4, 57, 190, 214.

56. Derin Terzioğlu, "Sunna-Minded Sufi Preachers in Service of the Ottoman State: the Naṣīḥatnāme of Hasan addressed to Murad IV," *Archivum Ottomanicum* 27 (2010), pp. 241–312. Citations from *ibid.*, pp. 245, 250. See idem., "Sufis in the Age of State-Building and Confessionalization," in: Christine Woodhead (ed.), *The Ottoman World*, London and New York: Routlege, 2012, pp. 86–99. See esp. *ibid.*, pp. 86, 96.

57. Tijana Krstić, "State and Religion, 'Sunnitization' and 'Confessionalization' in Süleyman's Time," in Pál Fodor (ed.), *The Battle for Central Europe*, Boston and London: Brill, 2019, pp. 65–91. Citation from *ibid.*, p. 66. See also Nir Shafir, *The Road from Damascus: Circulation and the Redefinition of Islam in the Ottoman Empire, 1620–1720*, Ph.D. submitted at University of California, 2016, passim.

believers.[58] Mosques needed to be constructed in every city, and, in the case of large cities, in every quarter, and Muslims were required to explain nonattendance at Friday prayers. A vast guidance literature (*'Ilm-i Hal*) was composed in Turkish and Arabic, and some texts in this genre achieved impressive popularity through dissemination.[59] These tracts supplied a comprehensive guidance for right belief, proper conduct, and Sufi-oriented traditions. In the late sixteenth century and in the seventeenth century, the legal aspect of these *'Ilm-i Hal* compositions appears to have become increasingly dominant. To conduct a proper Muslim life was regarded as synonymous with obedience to the law/*Shari'a*.

As we shall see below, the Jews in the Ottoman core lands, and those dispersed in the Arabic-speaking territories, not only absorbed important elements of Ottoman civilization into their life fabric and culture[60] but also had a deep acquaintance with the Ottoman legal system. This is apparent in the responsa of the sixteenth-century leader of the Jewish community in Cairo and its chief Rabbi David ben Zimra (known by the acronym *Radbaz*, fl. 1513–1573), regarding for instance the use of written documents and archives in Ottoman courts and the exact terminology of the *sicil*. Ben Zimra expressed a clear trust in these non-Jewish courts.[61]

The following chapters offer my reading of a formal legalistic text—the *Beit Yosef* and *Shulchan 'Arukh*—based on the shifting of the focus of discussion from the nature of the text as positive law. The three modes of readings or perspectives suggested above illuminate these codes of law and intersect with one another. The first one explores how the Halakhah functions in concrete circumstances of Jewish life. It expropriates the Jewish legal and normative tradition from the rabbinical monopoly and shares it with the community and Jewish public at large. Following historical research on legal mechanism in premodern societies and the perspective of the anthropology of law, I will seek to position the codification of R. Karo primarily as a response to his historical settings, no less than an adherence to precedent post-Talmudic traditions and past codifications. Karo's work directly responded to two major aspects of early modern

58. Guy Burak, "Faith, Law and Empire in the Ottoman Age of Confessionalization" (Fifteenth–Seventeenth Centuries): The case of "Renewal of Faith," *Mediterranean Historical Review* 28, no. 1(2013), pp. 1–23.

59. See the inspiring works of Derin Terzioğlu, "Where 'Ilm-I Hal Meets Catechism: Islamic Manuals of Religious Instruction in the Ottoman Empire in the Age of Confessionalization," *Past and Present* 220, no. 1(2013), pp. 79–114, and Krstić, "State and Religion, 'Sunnitization' and 'Confessionalization' in Süleyman's Time."

60. Yaron Ben-Naeh, "Urban Encounters: The Muslim-Jewish Case in the Ottoman Empire," in: Eyal Ginio and Elie Podeh (eds.), *The Ottoman Middle East. Studies in Honor of Amnon Cohen*, Leiden and Boston: Brill, 2014, pp. 177–197. For an overall review of this issue, see idem., *Jews in the Realm of the Sultans. Ottoman Jewish Society in the Seventeenth Century*, Tübingen: Mohr Siebeck, 2008, pp. 412–414; Aryeh Shmuelevitz, *Ottoman History and Society. Jewish Sources*, Istanbul: The Isis Press, 1999, esp. pp. 9–19, 55.

61. Burak, "On Ottoman Documentary Depositories and Archival Consciousness," pp. 808–809. See further Minna Rozen, *A History of the Jewish Community in Istanbul: The Formative Years, 1453–1566*, Leiden: Brill, 2002.

Jewish life: the importance and dominance of the Sephardi tradition and the passage from a Catholic to an Ottoman–Sunni civilization. The geographical, no less than the cultural, horizon support a global reading of these works, as the Jewish case study adopted concepts of law, rulership, and renovation shared by Catholics, Ottomans, Safavids, and Mughals.

The following chapters will discuss various aspects of the codification project of R. Karo, following the methodology presented in the introduction. Chapter one is dedicated to canonization, specifically in the legal domain, and presents the main parameters of codifications of the law. The circumstances and cultural-communal-political settings leading to the formation of codification will form the center of our examination rather than the textual final product of "codes of law." A comparative history of codifications in all three monotheistic religions, inseparable in their legal history, exposes the minor role of codification in the Middle Ages and the dramatic change in the early modern period, especially in the Ottoman Empire. This is the principal arena in which R. Karo sought to contend in composing *Beit Yosef* and *Shulchan 'Arukh*. The preambles, especially to *Beit Yosef* but also to *Shulchan 'Arukh*, are discussed in Chapter Two. Karo's insistence on printing these repeatedly in various versions of his codes indicates the importance he ascribed to them. The preambles certainly correspond with introductions written by rabbinical figures to their Talmudic compositions, such as the codes of law of Maimonides and R. Jacob ben Asher. However, their content reveals a layered message. Behind the usual rabbinical rhetoric, Karo's preambles also clearly respond to the preambles composed by Ottoman bureaucrats and legal experts for their own codifications, delineating the ruling policies and political ethos of the Ottoman dynasty. Chapter Three focuses on the title *Maran*, which by the mid-seventeenth century was used to refer to R. Joseph Karo. This title had no precedent in Jewish tradition, and for many centuries, Karo was the only person referred to as Maran. Accordingly, the title became almost synonymous with him and was even more dominant than his personal name. Following the long honorary and titular history in Jewish context, it becomes clear that this innovative appellation responded mainly to titles in Ottoman civilization, particularly regarding two eminent Sufis, Ibn 'Arabi and Rumi. The polemic on rabbinical ordination (*Semichah* in Hebrew) is the main theme of Chapter Four. The debate involved the major Talmudic persons in Safed confronting Jerusalem rabbis who refused to accept their initiative to reinstate formal rabbinic *Semichah*. The classical rabbinic argumentations masked an underlying intention to set hierarchy and order within the rabbinical professional milieu, a process that interacted clearly with changes in the functioning of law and legal experts in the Ottoman Empire. The years that made R. Karo a famous figure in the Jewish Ecumene came during his second part of his life, living in the city of Safed where he played his part in the ordination event. Chapter Five follows the rise to importance of this city in the religious and cultural history of Jewish communities around the Mediterranean Basin and beyond. The death of the dominant local rabbi R. Jacob Beirav left a great vacuum. In the battle for his place, R. Karo appears to have been the clear winner, proving resourceful in using a strategy of several parallel channels. Chapter Six concerns one of the most fundamental traits for understanding Karo's life and projects: the fusion of Talmudic legal erudition with an intense mystical life. This theme connects him to the Muslim and Ottoman traditions, where such a combination had been known since the beginnings of Islam. In the early modern period, the close link between law and mysticism enhanced the fundamental role of Sufi traditions in the Ottoman Empire, increasing control over the religious beliefs of regular believers, the image of the Sultan as a saintly figure, and the role of law—in both Jewish and Muslim contexts—in renovating and reforming religion. Chapter Seven discusses a seemingly technical issue in court procedures: the obligation to provide reasoning for court verdicts. This theme already had its roots in Talmudic debates and continued to be discussed throughout the Middle Ages and into the Early Modern period without ever reaching a clear resolution. The dominant tendency among rabbinical scholars, however, argued against providing any explanations for the court's decisions, particularly in the case of prestigious courts or Talmudic scholars of renown. R. Karo discussed this issue against the background of the leading court of law functioning in Safed. He absolutely rejected requests by any of the litigating parties to provide reasoning and considered it an act verging on a religious sin. His strict position is related to the functioning of Ottoman justice system across the empire and the functioning of the person standing at its head—the Şeyhülislâm—who was absolved from justifying his legal positions. The concluding discussion in Chapter Eight illuminates another innovative aspect of Karo's activities during his Safed years: the construction of a "Jewish International Court of Law." Like some of the leading scholars in Safed, Karo maintained his own court of law which transcended the subethnic group comprising the population in the city. Later the court was redefined in such a way as to serve the entire Jewish Ecumene living under the Ottoman Empire in the Mediterranean Basin and in eastern Arab lands, and even in European Jewish communities under Christian domination, particularly Catholic. This intention runs counter to long Jewish medieval traditions that favor local rabbis and fragmentary authorities rather than supra-local institutions. Again, this shift reflects both the Ottoman legal system that was moving toward standardization in the entire wide Empire and parallel changes in European law, inspired by the discussions of the "Second Scholastics" and the rise of international law as a balancing factor between the colonial states.

No new documentation of importance regarding the life and work of R. Joseph Karo has been added in recent years. I will offer a new synthesis of the existing materials, and in so doing the book progresses along two parallel channels: the Jewish tradition and the non-Jewish setting in Europe and particularly in the Ottoman Empire. I will refer to the latter as functioning in a wide cultural-political-religious context of both Sunni Islam and the Eurasian space. This approach requires the reader to skip from one track to the other and back again, and I apologize for this in advance. The "Ottoman perspective" is present by reference to current research, either through short citations—when needed—or by a summary of the modern research relevant to my arguments. My basic assertion is that it makes little sense to understand the Jewish cultural world—including the codification project of R. Joseph Karo—and its early modern shift without reference to the history of the Eurasian, and especially the Ottoman world, with its diverse legal, political, cultural, messianic, and religious aspects.

Chapter One

THE IMPORTANCE OF BEING CANONIZED

The canonization of sacred texts has accompanied Jewish history from its beginning: the Bible, the Mishnah, the Jerusalem and Babylonian Talmuds, Gaonic monographs, and the medieval "Books of Rulings" (*Sifrei Pesiqah*). At first glance, R. Karo's codes of law *Beit Yosef* and *Shulchan 'Arukh* might seem to be no more than two more names in this long list. Even if we take into consideration the high value of Talmudic erudition in Jewish culture, was this enough to motivate R. Karo to dedicate so many years of his life to this project? Moreover, in what sense were these double codes of law canonical; how did they differ from other Talmudic and post-Talmudic compositions, especially of the early modern period?

Legal canons, or codifications, were common to all three monotheistic religions. Codification implied an attempt to standardize law and legal discussions around several books of major importance. This chapter will shift the main focus of discussion from the textual aspect—that is the content and legalistic assertions—to the social and cultural scene in which they crystallized. More concretely, in respect to R. Karo, beyond the issue of the legalistic-halakhic components of his works, I wish to discuss their function and their response to both Jewish and Muslim surroundings. As we will see, codification is a dynamic process that does not halt once the composition of a text has been finalized. It is rather a product negotiated between legal experts and their "lay" community; between central political authorities and the legal-professional milieu; and between the text and the interpretations woven around it. Clarifying the use of the term codification, its main characteristics, and their history in all three monotheistic religions will provide the starting point for this chapter and indeed this entire book.

Canon: History and General Meaning

The term canon refers to texts of exceptional importance, especially of a religious character, serving as a source of inspiration and emulation for the group considering them as canonical.[1] The semantic history of canonization and modern research on the term in Western civilization have revolved around major religious texts, such as the New and Old Testaments, examining their evolvement, philological aspects, the crystallization

---

1. See, for instance, various suggestions in the online edition of Merriam-Webster Dictionary, s.v. "Canon": "An authoritative list of books accepted as Holy Scripture, the authentic works of a writer, a sanctioned or accepted group or body of related works, an accepted principle or rule, a criterion or standard of judgment, a body of principles, rules, standards, or norms."

of their final form, the historical processes and institutional mechanisms behind the textual fixation, and their deep impact on cultural heritage. Focusing on the textual aspect has long historical roots, dating back to the Renaissance period. This emphasis further intensified during the early modern period due to religious competition between Catholics and Protestants over the interpretation of the sacred texts and their religious implications, and it has left a deep imprint on the modern preoccupation with philology. In recent decades, the examination of canon has been expanded to further domains, such as literature and poetry (still textual aspects, though not necessarily of a religious character), esthetical canons, and even the domains of technology or know-how.[2] Non-Western cultures have also attracted the attention of scholars regarding alternative modes of canonization, especially in oral societies, or in relation to material culture as the keeper of the collective (canonical) memory. An emblematic work in this respect is the magisterial project of Pierre Nora about "places of memory" in the sense of cultural institutions, rituals, monuments, habits, and so forth.[3]

Works on various aspects of canonization are extremely numerous; I chose to refer those that are both insightful and pertinent to the forthcoming discussions, and especially related to the history of law in the monotheistic religions. As will become clear, the codification of Jewish and Muslim law (*Halakhah* and *Shari'a/Fiqh*, respectively) had many common traits, so that recent works on canonization in Islam contribute greatly to understanding the project of R. Joseph Karo. The interaction between Jewish, Christian, and Muslim traditions across many centuries affected their legal patterns and canonization. I will use the term "codification" to refer to the consolidation of canons in the legal domain. Since the topic of this book is the codification project of R. Karo—in other words, printed books—our discussion will focus on written texts as the end products of canonization. At the same time, however, I will claim that the textual aspects are meaningless without taking into consideration the process that lead to their formation. In the following paragraphs, I will discuss the major parameters or elements of canonization; key terms and concepts appear in italics.

The fundamental importance of texts was noted by Moshe Halbertal in his insightful book on Jewish Canons, where he contributed important suggestions on the phenomenon of canonization in general. Religious tradition could be constructed around *shared commitment* to certain texts, endowing this tradition with coherence.[4] A canonical

2. Frank Kermode, *The Classic*, New York: Viking Press, 1975; Gülru Necipoğlu, "A Kanun for the State, a Canon for the Arts: The Classical Synthesis in Ottoman Art and Architecture during the Age of Süleyman," in: Gilles Veinstein (ed.), *Soliman le Magnifique et son temps*, Paris: La Documentation Française, 1992, pp. 195–215; Andrew Plaks, "Afterword: Canonization in the Ancient World: The View from Farther East," in: Margalit Finkelberg, Guy G. Stroumsa (eds.), *Homer, the Bible, and Beyond. Literary and Religious Canons in the Ancient World*, Leiden and Boston: Brill, 2003, pp. 267–275; Matteo Valleriani (eds.), *The Structures of Practical Knowledge*, Berlin: Springer, 2017.
3. Pierre Nora, (sous la direction de), *Les lieux de la mémoire*, Paris: Gallimard, 1984–1986.
4. Moshe Halbertal, *People of the Book. Canon, Meaning, and Authority*, Cambridge (Mass.) and London, Harvard U.P., 1997, esp. p. 1 – The canonical text not only reports sacred events of

text is not merely another item on a list of books but acquires a special status, and thus is *read differently.* Canonical texts are read with special commitment and expectations: "In other words, canonization affects not only the status of a text but the *way it is perceived and read.*"[5] The process of the formation and acceptance of canon is often slow and may even take several generations. It relies on the heritage of generations; to use the felicitous expression of Ahmed El Shamsy, it serves as a storehouse of *the collective memory,* offering successive generations an encounter with their cumulative heritage. It encourages a commitment to previous traditions and makes it more difficult to forget or ignore uncomfortable ideas. Such inconvenient remnants of the past need to be explained (or explained away) by creative exegesis.[6] The canon provides a cultural repertory from which people can draw *allusions, citations, points of reference,* referring to their mutual heritage as they attempt to discuss and resolve internal conflicts. This explains why familiarizing the young with the cultural canons often forms part of schooling and early education.[7] The canon is *shared by the erudite elite and common people alike.* So much so that changing circumstances and new situations lead to *re-reading of the shared canon,* so that the novel occurrences may be reflected in the old canon.[8] Since the canon is charged with providing the highest and most valid *measure for truth and authority,* it is often *memorized by heart,* or used in rituals and public performances, in order to present its special and sanctified value.[9] The text of the canon, that is the *material object,* is often treated with awe and respect, as a form of sanctified religious object, regardless of its verbal content.[10]

These factors were applied and persuasively discussed in the work of Jonathan Brown on the formation of the Hadith Canon in Islam. His discussion is important and highly pertinent to our study of the work of R. Karo, since both evolved within Islamicate civilization—in the case of Karo under the Ottomans and in the area of *Bilad a-Sham.* When a text is considered an authentic expression of God's will, its very *ontological status is raised.* Due to their need for exemplary literature, the readers make the books "more than the sum of their pages, endowing them with *a new authority and significance* [...] Study

---

the part, its reading "becomes a religious drama in and of itself." God is present in the sacred text and in its studying (*ibid.,* pp. 8, 91–92).

5. *Ibid.,* p. 11.

6. Ahmed El Shamsy, *The Canonization of Islamic Law: A Social and Intellectual History,* New York: Cambridge U.P., 2013, esp. p. 183.

7. Moshe Halbertal, "What is *Mishneh Torah?* On Codification and Ambivalence," in: Jay M. Harris (ed.), *Maimonides after 800 Years. Essays on Maimonides and his Influence,* Cambridge, MA and London: Harvard U.P., 2007, pp. 81–111, esp. p. 101. See also Halbertal, *People of the Book,* p. 90, the way canons are studied, taught, transmitted, rehearsed, performed, and reflected upon, and affects many domains, including attitudes, beliefs, judgments, sensitivities, aspirations, ideals, language and self-identity.

8. *Ibid.,* p. 93.

9. *Ibid.,* p. 12; Margalit Finkelberg, "Homer as a Foundation Text," in: Idem. and Stroumsa (eds.), *Literary and Religious Canons in the Ancient World,* pp. 75–96, esp. p. 91.

10. António Manuel Hespanha, "Form and Content in Early Modern Legal Books. Bridging the Gap between Material Bibliography and the History of Legal Thought," *Rechtsgeschichte. Zeitschrift des Max-Planck-Instituts für europäische Rechtsgeschichte* 12(2008), pp. 12–50, esp. p. 17, in regard to medieval and early modern law books.

of the canonical text is itself *an act of devotion* urged upon all." The text influences and shapes *the boundaries of a community*, often entailing the twin phenomena of *canon and heresy*, the latter constituting alternative components of the past defined as unacceptable and dangerous.[11] To paraphrase Brown, making sense of a canon—a textual product—is impossible without its "Canonical Culture," that is to say, the non-textual dimensions that preceded its formation and shaped the unique modes of its reading.

We should resist the temptation to define a canon as a well-defined and final text that allows no further changes or editing. The sacred texts of the various religions (Bible, New Testament, Koran) supposedly reaching a final textual content and forbidding any further changes became paradigmatic models for canonization, but they are the exception to the rule. Canon rigidity is to a large extent a cultural myth; canons are often negotiated among their users and appear as *a process rather than a sealed text*. El Shamsy argues that Islamic law was not canonized in the same way as the Uthmanic codex of the Quran. Islamic law was a project in constant change: "It was constituted by a continuing, open-ended process of interpretation and debate taking place within the disciplinary realm of legal theory. This could rightfully be called a *canonizing discourse*," intended to provide a *shared understanding* of the sources of religious normativity among ordinary believers and professional jurists.[12] The term "canonizing discourse" coined by El Shamsy will inform the following chapters, even when not mentioned explicitly. The elasticity of canons and their cultural impact are further enhanced by the fact that once they are sealed, they incite a *wave of exegesis*, conveying their message in various and changing directions.[13] Halbertal further pointed to the distinction between *closed canons* and *open canons*; the text of the latter continues to evolve over successive generations.[14] This observation is highly significant in the Jewish case, since the rabbinical ethos relied on a chain of transmission of the common heritage, dating back to the formative moment at Mount Sinai. It presented *pluralism* as an immanent trait of Jewish culture: The Torah was handed down in several "voices," and no *Urtext*, primeval version, or ultimate canon could be constructed.[15] The interface between *oral canon* and *written canon* (or even a printed one) is porous and not always clear.[16] Even if a strictly oral canon is transformed into a written one, the traits of orality and its elasticity in passing on the

11. Jonathan Brown, *The Canonization of al-Bukhari and Muslim. The Formation and Function of the Sunni Hadith Canon*, Leiden and Boston: Brill, 2007, pp. 20, 29–30, 33, 34, 44.

12. El Shamsy, *The Canonization of Islamic Law*, p. 224.

13. *Ibid.*, p. 147. See also Halbertal, *People of the Book*, pp. 32–33. The battle over the control of religious truth is diverted from the canonical texts to their interpretation, see Brown, *The Canonization of al-Bukhari and Muslim*, p. 41.

14. Halbertal, *People of the Book*, p. 16. The applicability of this analytical distinction in relation to R. Karo's *Shulchan 'Arukh*, see *ibid.*, p. 77.

15. *Ibid.*, p. 53. Later I would mention the comprehensive and important work of Richard Hidary. See also Peter Schäfer, "Research into Rabbinic Literature: An Attempt to Define the Status Quaestionis," *Journal of Jewish Studies* 37,2 (1986), pp. 139–152.

16. Finkelberg and Stroumsa (eds.), *Literary and Religious Canons in the Ancient World*, passim.

heritage are still maintained.[17] *Canons may be opposed*, rejected or simply ignored, so that their presumed dominant impact on collective life and culture must be reexamined in each specific historical context. Lastly, it was observed that some cultures, even one as complex as the classical Greek, could function well *without any clear canon*.[18] Canon, seen as an ongoing process rather than a sealed text, is a juncture or meeting point of various social and cultural processes.

The Community Settings of Canons

Canons require a gradual process of sharing and absorption by both the erudite, in charge of shaping it, and by the wider circles of its "consumers." Canonization is therefore a social phenomenon, no less than a textual product, since it relates to processes of consensus formation. The act of authorizing certain texts requires the *exclusion of others*, and accordingly the formation of a canon is intelligible in a context of conflicting claims to control the accepted version and later its interpretations.[19] The element of exclusion and censorship was mentioned above, but no less important in this respect is the formation of consensus around the canons: "Canons can also emphasize *inclusion and agreement* more than exclusivity. They can function as a tool of reconciliation, a medium for communication or for creating common ground between adversaries[...] we must take care to consider the emergence of the Sahihayn [two fundamental books of Hadith—R.W.] canon as an inclusive effort to force various sects to recognize a common medium for discussing the Prophet's legacy."[20] The social context was excellently demonstrated and discussed in the works mentioned previously, especially in Jonathan Brown's study of the canonization of Hadith traditions in the famous works of Bukhari and Muslim and in Ahmed El Shamsy's exploration of codification in Islam prior to the modern period. El Shamsy considered the shaping of new canon as a significant indication that the religious community was changing its perspective on its own cultural heritage. In the case of classical Islam, it signified the passage of the *"lived practice of the Muslim Community"* to a *"written, clearly demarcated canon,"* in the sense of marking certain texts as a source of religious norms.[21] This perspective will serve as a guide for this chapter and the following ones, supporting our focus not on the textual aspect but on the social and cultural settings to which the text responds.

A crisis of identity, or a fear that the collective memory is jeopardized and may even be lost during a crisis period, activates a process of canon formation. In the case of Islam, this sense of crisis stemmed from the rapid spread across wide territories, massive

---

17. El Shamsy, *The Canonization of Islamic Law*, p. 165; Finkelberg and Stroumsa (eds.), *Literary and Religious Canons in the Ancient World*, passim.

18. Robert Lamberton, "The Neoplatonists and their Books," in: Finkelberg and Stroumsa (eds.), *Literary and Religious Canons in the Ancient World*, pp. 95–211, esp. p. 196.

19. Brown, *The Canonization of al-Bukhari and Muslim*, p. 39. See also the wise comment in Hespanha, 'Form and Content in Early Modern Legal Books', p. 38.

20. Brown, *The Canonization of al-Bukhari and Muslim*, p. 40.

21. Shamsy, *The Canonization of Islamic Law*, pp. 3–4.

converts from diverse backgrounds, the emergence of new and localized Muslim subcultures, and the dissolution of tribal ties and ethnic homogeneity:

> "*This social and cultural upheaval undermined confidence in the authenticity of the essentially mimetic normative tradition of the Muslim community*, which was predicated on the perception of unbroken continuity with the prophetic age<...> Canonization offered a solution to this dilemma by enshrining revelation in a fixed category of textual sources—the canon—that could then be subjected to systematic analysis by a professionalized group."[22]

In Egypt, codification happened in tandem with the formation of the *Shafi'i* school of law (*Madhhab*); it was affected by immigration waves, the loss of power of the local elites, and the sense that oral traditions secured thus far by local transmission were threatened and must be secured in a structured and written form.[23] Less dramatic changes contributed to and accelerated the process of canonization, including *increasing literacy* in the Arab world or the use of *written documents* as a valid legal testimony. *Technological aspects*, such as the discovery and expanding use of paper, also influenced this process.[24]

Codification: Rejection of the State Model

Historians of the law in previous generations shared the idea that significant codification projects were related to the rise of modern state, with its increasing capability to enforce law by institutional/police means. This approach also drew on new political and Enlightenment ideas concerning law and the regulation of reality.[25] Nils Jensen presented the focusing of modern research on the state codification of law, such as 1734 in Sweden, 1756 in Bavaria, 1794 in Prussia, 1804 in France, and 1811 in Austria, but much later in 1896/1900, in the German *Reich*.[26] This thesis of a state monopoly of codification, according to Jensen, does not withstand historical test, for four main reasons. First, some important codes of law were established on a non-state basis or began as a private initiative and only later became recognized as canonical and binding. The professional guilds of legal experts were no less responsible for the rise of legal tradition, its evolvement, and juridical practice than state authorities. The significance of codification as a factor in the history of law (at least in the European context, until very late) has been exaggerated, since legislation and the legal domain continued to evolve even

---

22. *Ibid.*, pp. 5, 9.
23. On the historical background for the increasing dominance of Hanafi School of law in pre-Mameluk Egypt, see *Ibid.*, p. 132.
24. *Ibid.*, p. 35, also underlines the decreasing role of memory and memorizing the sacred texts.
25. Manlio Bellomo, *The Common Legal Past of Europe, 1000-1800*, translated by Lydia G. Cochrane, Washington D.C.: Catholic University of America Press, 1995, esp. pp. 74–75, 98–101, 165–166, 173, 186. His book is an illuminating analysis of the legal foundations of Western law since the Middle Ages, and their contribution to future codifications in eighteenth and nineteenth centuries.
26. Nils Jensen, *The Making of Legal Authority. Non-legislative Codifications in Historical and Comparative Perspective*, Oxford: Oxford U.P., 2010, p. 14.

after grand projects of state codification. And lastly, legal pluralism in Europe changed little after the formation of modern codification. Establishing one law was a long process that only ended, if at all, when the centralistic hand of the state became a significant factor in legal reality.[27]

Premodern Codifications in the Monotheistic Religions

The story of R. Joseph Karo, as we shall shortly see, is intimately related to the fate of the Sephardi Diaspora and its passage from the Iberian-Catholic to the Ottoman-Muslim setting. Both these domains left a deep imprint on his life and work, especially his legal *summae*. The circumstances and motivations for their composition are inseparable from the history of law in the Muslim and European settings. This section will present a very concise history of codification in Islam and Christianity prior to the eighteenth century, followed by the Jewish case. Only major phases relevant to the subsequent discussion will be presented.

Codification in Europe

The legal tradition in Medieval Europe leans heavily on the late Imperial Roman laws, in its content, the fundamental books in use, the motivations, and the intention to provide a comprehensive code for the entire Catholic world. As Bernard Stolte noted, the sources for Roman imperial legislation were both state officials and "experts of the law" (*iuris periti*) acting as private individuals. Many of their opinions have been preserved in Justinian's *Digest* and are valuable for its interpretation.[28] The Emperors Theodosian and, especially, Justinian labored to bring order to the cumulative traditions of Roman law and to impose rules regarding the various layers of juridical tradition and contradicting opinions of private legal experts, in favor of legal monopoly by the state. The *Codex Justinianus* (529–534) was intended to order the law, set definitive positions, and marginalize the non-codified positions.[29] The power of imperial law remained limited, since the text itself was circulated primarily among private and professional jurists not necessarily affiliated to the state mechanism; neither is it certain to what extent it was applied in real cases in court.[30] The Byzantines, the former eastern and Greek-speaking part of the Roman Empire, continued this tradition, shifting the linguistic infrastructure of imperial legal tradition from Latin to Byzantine Greek.[31] Stolte rightly asserts that it was the West, evolving Catholic Europe, which was the true inheritor of imperial

---

27. *Ibid.*, pp. 4, 17–18, 20, 44.
28. Bernard H. Stolte, 'Codification in Byzantium. From Justinian to Leo VI', in: John Hudson, Ana Rodríguez (eds.), *Diverging Paths? The Shapes of Power and Institutions in Medieval Christendom and Islam*, Leiden and Boston: Brill, 2014, pp. 59–74. See esp. p. 59.
29. *Ibid.*, pp. 60–61.
30. *Ibid.*, p. 68.
31. *Ibid.*, pp. 64–65.

law rather than the Byzantines. It continued through the tradition of *ius commune*, which absorbed its terminology and legal tools.[32]

The Catholic Church was the main agent for reviving interest in Roman law during the early Middle Ages.[33] The prominent role of the papacy was aided by the rise of centralistic legislation and papal decrees or decretals (*decretales*). Several compilations of the expanding amount of decretals and councils' resolutions were made during the twelfth and thirteenth centuries, including one initiated by Pope Innocentius III. Yet its applicability was highly limited:

> In contrast with Justinian's legislative programme as outlined in the constitutions *Deo auctore*, *Tanta* and *Cordi nobis*, this text was not intended to displace other sources of law nor even older texts from forensic or educational argument; neither did it assert finality—these decretals were never intended by Innocent to be the last word. Even when viewed against its immediate background of the early thirteenth century, Innocent's decretal collection emerges in some respects as a typical contribution to a tradition of scholarship and practice already well-established wholly independently of governmental initiatives. In fact, this first officially promulgated "codification" of papal letters was intended to become a part of but not to replace the law taught by the standard-setting law schools.[34]

Again, the real authority of this and later codificatory collections of Canon Law was rather limited: they were mainly copied and used by law schools; no formal and definitive version was determined; and there was no mechanism for their distributions in various European areas. Those in charge of ordering the Canon Law were persons belonging to the juridical milieu of the Catholic Church, who often worked as private scholars rather than church agents. The most important among them was Gratian, whose glosses on Canon Law became quasi-official among experts of the law.[35]

The deep interest of the church in the Roman legal heritage was one of the factors behind the rise of the "Science of Law" in lay contexts as well, especially under the lead of Italian universities. This process constituted a further step toward unification and homogeneity in legal domain. The intellectual tools—both glosses around the text and the study of law in universities—were proposed and elaborated as "private" initiatives. Gratian composed his famous *Concordia Discordantium Canonum* in the mid-twelfth century as a private agent rather than a person nominated by the Pope. His major contribution to the long process of codification in Europe was manifested not only in the production of a sealed text but also in the development of working

---

32. *Ibid.*, p. 73.

33. Emanuele Conte and Magnus Ryan, 'Codification in the Western Middle Ages', in: Hudson and Rodríguez (eds.), *The Shapes of Power and Institutions in Medieval Christendom and Islam*, pp. 75–97. See *ibid.*, p. 82: "On this matter, of course, the most important model for the Church was Justinian, the legislator *par excellence*. Gregory presented himself as a kind of Emperor of the Church, even if there is no evidence that he ever thought of promulgating a great codification on the model of Justinian".

34. *Ibid.*, p. 85.

35. *Ibid.*, pp. 83–84.

tools that eventually promote unification and *increasing consensus* among professional jurists. The *Ius commune* (the science of "non-religious law" as taught in universities) was certainly not a state tradition, as it evolved in the highly fragmented political context of the Italian communes. Manlio Bellomo, one of the most insightful scholars of medieval European legal history, demonstrated how this legal tradition provided a common language and working tools all over Europe.[36] *Ius commune* hardly served as concrete guide for law enforcement in various parts of Europe nor did it replace the enormous scope of legal pluralism and local institutions. Yet it provided a common ground for jurists all over Europe. When attempting to set order and unity in legal traditions, it would serve as a leading factor, such as in forming feudal codes of law or in the composition of Saxon law (the German *Sachsenspiegel*) in the late Middle Ages. The dominant role of *Ius commune* was later weakened as a result of the harsh criticism of Renaissance humanists and the nascent rise of modern and centralized states.

The new form of sovereignty of modern states was accompanied by expanding national legislation, in the vernacular rather than in Latin, designed to serve the needs of the local (national) population rather than to manifest universalistic concepts of justice, as in the past. One of the products of these modern concepts was the codification projects of the nascent centralistic state:

> The late sixteenth century and the seventeenth witnessed the appearance of codes, first in Portugal (Ordenações alfonsinas, 1467; Ordenações manuelinas, printed 1512), and later in France (collections of *coutumiers* in shortened and harmonized versions, the project of Antoine Loisel), in imperial Germany (the Carolina of Charles V), and in Spain (Leyes de Montalvo, the edict of Philip II regarding the criminal law). Padoa-Schioppa persuasively describes how the state moved from putting limits on local/particular laws to a phase of producing the law, and presenting itself as the source of law and legality, a source from which all other legal traditions of corporate bodies were derived. It took the place of God as a source of justice, and legitimized positive law on relativist and lay or national grounds, serving community and political utility.[37]

Codification in premodern Islam

Codification in Islam never played an important role as it did in Western legal tradition. The first compilations of normative literature in Islam relate to the Hadith tradition rather than legal compilations: "Using different interpretative methodologies, jurists (*fuqahā*) produced a number of manuals or text-books, some of which enjoyed almost

---

36. Bellomo, *The Common Legal Past of Europe*, esp. p. 186. See also *ibid.*, p. 213: "The emperor, the pope, and lesser rulers made use of well-known *doctores* [experts of *ius commune* – R.W.] to arbitrate quarrels or to help avoid foreseeable controversies".

37. Roni Weinstein, 'Jewish Modern Law and Legalism in A Global Age: The Case of Rabbi Joseph Karo', *Modern Intellectual History* (Cambridge University Publications On-line), 2018, pp. 1–18. Citation from *ibid.*, p. 12.

exclusive authority at least for certain periods or regions."[38] An attempt to establish one law for the entire Muslim population under the same regime was made during the Abbasside reign, with limited success:

> The possibility of preparing an "imperial" codification had earlier been proposed by Ibn al-Muqaffa' (d. 139/756), who in his *Risālat al-ṣaḥāba* suggested to the 'Abbāsid Caliph al-Manṣūr (r. 136/754-158/775) that he could strengthen his legitimacy and his government by preparing a codification of laws and legal decrees and by uniting under his authority the different opinions of the jurists.[39]

Two other significant steps in the same direction were taken by rulers with clear Shiite affiliations, and both enjoyed only limited impact: under the Shiite (Ismā'īlī) dynasty of the Fāṭimids (fourth to tenth century) and later under the Almohads (sixth to twelfth century).[40]

The slow progress toward unity and homogeneity of Islamic law within Sunni Islam owed little to state authorities and was inspired predominantly by the formation of several schools of law. It was conducted by professional scholars ('*Ulama*), and not by political authorities and rulers. Over the centuries, these scholars exerted their best efforts to maintain their independence from lay rulers. These schools evolved an internal scholarly legal consensus, each following its own course and attached to its own geographical contexts. It revolved around the common literature typical of each *Madhhab*, the ethos of the eponymous founding figure, the methods of rulings, and the legitimate ways to conduct internal disputes in a way that would not destroy internal cohesion. For instance, in the Hanafi School, no sole text was recognized as binding, yet its followers shared a common legal and textual heritage of al-Shaybani and Abu Yusuf, the principal students of the eponymous founder Abu-Hanifa.[41] The need to produce a more coherent and systematic literature in writing radiated to nonlegal domains, and also inspired the mystical Sufi tradition well.[42]

The most effective codification of normative literature relevant to the entire community of Sunni believers (the *Umma*) concerned the Hadith literature. Though bereft of structured and thematic organization, and far from user-friendly for those wishing to draw clear legal rules, the Hadith served all the leading law schools in

---

38. Maribel Fierro, 'Codifying the Law. The Case of the Medieval Islamic West', in: Hudson and Rodríguez (eds.), *The Shapes of Power and Institutions in Medieval Christendom and Islam*, pp. 98–118. Citation from *ibid.*, pp. 100–101.
39. *Ibid.*, p. 102. See also El Shamsy, *The Canonization of Islamic Law*, pp. 31–32. On the main phases of this process and its deep affiliation to non-Muslim legal tradition, especially the Byzantine law, see Benjamin Jokisch, *Islamic Imperial Law. Harun Al-Rashid's Codification Project*, Berlin and New York: Walter de Gruyter, 2007.
40. Fierro, 'Codifying the Law. The Case of the Medieval Islamic West', p. 103.
41. El Shamsy, *The Canonization of Islamic Law*, pp. 173, 176.
42. Erik S. Ohlander, *Sufism in an Age of Transition. 'Umar al-Suhrawardi and the Rise of the Islamic Mystical Brotherhoods*, Leiden and Boston: Brill, 2008, esp. pp. 34, 187–188.

Islam. In his meticulous and perceptive work on the codification process of Hadith literature in the canonical works of Bukhari and Muslim, Jonathan Brown presented several elements and phases of this long process. Though depicting the Muslim religious tradition, they are highly relevant to understanding the codification project of R. Joseph Karo:

- Both books of Hadith collections represented the Prophet himself and his copious heritage.
- They attracted veneration from both regular believers and professional Hadith and law professionals.
- Both books defined the boundaries of Islamic orthodoxy during the Umayyad and Abbasside periods and continued to do much later.
- Their composition marks a watershed line of passage from oral to written traditions regarding the Prophet and his heritage.
- Once accepted as canonical and binding, scholars of Hadith and law (*Fiqh*) claimed that it was forbidden to raise any criticism in their regard.
- The life and biography of their composers increasingly became an important issue, so that their presentation as "orthodox" Muslim, beyond any suspicion of heresy, contributed to the legitimacy of the works.
- They defined more clearly the borders and content of Hadith and the methodology of discussion.
- These works set the standard of truth and offered a set of well-defined and representative texts.
- The myth that they were accepted by the entire community of believers.
- Historically, the books encountered severe criticism after their publication and over several generations. The entire project was castigated at first as an insolent innovation and a deviation from tradition.
- In spite of the intention to shift the Hadith heritage from the oral realm to writing, the oral transmission of Hadith continued.
- The books, each in its own way, contained methodological guidance in relation to measuring reliable traditions, alongside substantive and direct instructions.
- All the law schools that evolved in tandem, following the crystallization of Hadith, leaned heavily on these books. Canonical literature in one domain left its imprint on other domains and encouraged further phases of canonicity.
- The acceptance of these books as canonical and binding took a long time and was far from a linear process.
- Once accepted, a rich and variegated exegetical literature followed, intended to illuminate their various aspects: methodology, chains of transmission, various versions of the books, or internal inconsistencies.
- The books served as models for important Hadith books composed in subsequent centuries.
- The dissemination of the books was carried by a specific network of scholars with its distinct geographical affiliations and religious agenda.

- These compositions are formative texts, serving as a common forum for community members, to express their own relationship with the source of authority in their tradition.[43]
- Their standards enabled later Hadith scholars to extend the range of this literature.
- They clearly intensified the legalistic character of Islam and the dominant role of law scholars as providers of epistemological certainty and communal consensus.[44]
- The common use of Hadith provided scholars from diverse schools of law with a common measure of authenticity and common ground, despite their differences.
- A certain school of law, the Shafi'i, was the main agent of disseminating these books after their composition. They were the main agents of their acceptance among Muslims in the first generations.
- The need for molding in writing the oral traditions was justified as a response to internal crisis in Islam, after its emergence as large civilization. It was mainly intended as a correction to the decaying chains of transmission.
- Alongside the comprehensive and long versions of these books, new popular and shortened versions were composed. These were meant to serve the entire population and young scholars of Hadith, initiated to this domain.
- Scholars of Hadith disseminated the claim that nothing more should be added to these books.
- The demand that professional jurists should make use of these books, lest their resolutions would be considered as invalid.
- The books served in public events and rituals, including public readings of some sections. The books, as material objects, were considered sanctified and regarded as a kind of channel for the conduction of divine grace (*Barakah*).
- The Hadith canonization provided a unifying axis for Muslim society as a whole, in its search for direct contact with its heritage, and was connected to the standardization of other fundamental texts in Islam. Sunnism of the eleventh century engaged in a process of minimizing "sources of contention." For the sake of internal consensus, it demanded "loyalty to the community and its acknowledged symbols <...> even at the expense of all other values."[45]
- The books are products of cosmopolitan elite, a network of people on the move, and weaving contacts of wide geographical extent. Codification currents were formerly presented as related to the internal processes of each religion. Yet recent research has illuminated unexpected interactions between these histories of law, considered until recently distinct. In a comprehensive and stimulating work, Benjamin Jokisch pointed to the deep imprint of Byzantine law and codification on the Abbasside project of codification.[46] Maribel Fierro suggested that the grand project of codification of the Normans in southern Italy echoed Islamic traditions

---

43. *Ibid.*, p. 105.
44. *Ibid.*, p. 154. See also *ibid.*, p. 206.
45. *Ibid.*, p. 371.
46. See Jokisch, *Islamic Imperial Law*, pp. 484–485.

of the Fatimid. The codification project of the Spanish King Alfonso El Sabio, *Siete Partidas*, shows the influence of the Almohads.[47]

Jewish codification during the Middle Ages and early Modern Period

The codification project of R. Karo was not the first of its kind. It was preceded by Halakhic compilations, books enumerating the various religious commandments (*sifrei mitzvot*), collections of legal rulings (*sifrei pesiqah*), monographs on specific themes, and full-fledged codes of law. The classical works of Chaim Tchernowitz and Menachem Elon still provide the most useful and comprehensive information in this regard.[48] The attempt to synthesize the Talmudic positions on specific issues, to provide a structured perspective on Talmudic discussions and to offer clear-cut conclusions and guidance began in the Gaonic literature. It echoed the interaction of the Jewish elite with their colleagues of law in Islam, especially during the Abbasside period.[49] This trend continued in the historical extension of the Babylonian and Gaonic tradition in the Sephardi Diaspora, through the works of various eminent Talmud scholars, such as R. Isaac Alfasi (the "Rif") Maimonides, R. Solomon Aderet (the "Rashba"), and R. Jacob ben HaRosh.

It would seem that as the halakhic literature evolved in its themes and methods of discussion, and as the associated literary products expanded in their size and content, there was a growing need to bring order and unity to the vast heritage and lay a common ground for various and contradicting positions. Yet although codification remained an option to organize and provide a systematic frame for the vast pool of halakhic material and books, in most of the rabbinic centers this option was not utilized. Of the two dominant halakhic traditions of the Medieval Jewish world, it was followed by the Sephardi path, but almost completely rejected in the Ashkenazi tradition.[50]

---

47. Fierro, 'Codifying the Law. The Case of the Medieval Islamic West', pp. 117–118.
48. See Chaim Tchernowitz (Rav Tza'ir), *Toldot ha-Poskim* [Hebrew], New York: Jubilee Committee, 1947, Vol. III, pp. 73–137; Menachem Elon, *Jewish Law*, Philadelphia: Jewish Publication Society, 1994, Vol. III, pp. 1367–1422.
49. Robert Brody, *The Geonim of Babylonia and the Shaping of Medieval Jewish Culture*, Yale: Yale U.P., 1998, passim.
50. On the particular traits of Ashkenazi Halakhic tradition and its variance from Sephardi Halakhah, see Moshe Dovid Chechik, *The Struggle over Ashkenazi Legacy in Poland: The Printing of Shulhan 'Aruch in Poland and the Reactions to It* [Hebrew], M.A. thesis submitted at the Hebrew University (Jerusalem), 2018. Further important discussion on the Ashkenazi tradition and its later literary products, see Tamara Morsel-Eisenbert, *The Organization of Halakhic Knowledge in Early Modern Europe. The Transormation of Scholarly Culture*, Ph.D submitted at Pennsylvania University, 2018. Both these works rely on the inspiring research of Elchanan Reiner. See also Shlomo Glicksberg and Shlomo Cassirer, 'The Halakhah and Meta-Halakhah Codification Debate: Rabbi Chaim ben Bezalel and the Maharal of Prague' [Hebrew], *Jewish Studies* 49(2013), pp. 157–191.

The Ashkenazi Talmudic mentality was characterized by a quasi-unanimous opposition to written codes of Talmudic law. Indeed, throughout the entire Middle Ages, no
comprehensive codification was suggested by eminent Ashkenazi scholars. Instead the
literary products focused on a dialectical and innovative exegesis of the Talmud—the
famous *Toseftot* literature—or on compilations of instructions on well-defined themes
and documentation of customs and local habits (*sifrut minhagim* or *liqutim*).[51] Leading
Ashkenazi rabbis, such as R. Jacob Moeln (the "Maharil"), actively objected to composing halakhic literature addressing the public at large, on the grounds that it would
reduce the regular people's need to consult with rabbis on halakhic issues. The rabbinic
elite considered itself the locus of living tradition or the personification of Torah and
religious heritage; tradition was regarded as living through people, not through texts.
In such a context, which would change radically during the early modern period,[52] a
comprehensive code of law seemed a superfluous and even threatening proposition.[53]

The codification in Sephardi context was consistent not only with the nature of its
rabbinical and Talmudic scholarship but also with sociological aspects of Jewish-Iberian
culture in general. Looking backward, R. Joseph Trani, the chief rabbi of Istanbul in
the early seventeenth century, commented that the general expulsion from Spain and
Portugal had indeed been disastrous, yet had provided an unexpected opportunity to
shift the Sephardi heritage to new and wider horizons. Rather than catastrophe and a fis-
sure with the past, he saw continuity and promising prospects for the Sephardi heritage:

> Right after the sunset of Torah in Castile, due to expulsions and tribulations, commenced
> the sunrise of Torah in the Maghreb, and Egypt, and the Holy Land, and in all the Ottoman
> Empire [*Malkhut Togarma* in the original text—R.W.] thanks to the Sages of Castile, who
> came from there [Castile—R.W.] and established Torah in all the lands of the Lord.[54]

One channel of continuity, relevant to our discussion, explaining the welcoming attitude to codification was the particular Sephardi methodology of Talmud study, which
evolved in the pre-expulsion years and was disseminated more widely thereafter.[55] The
method of *'iyyun* attributed to R. Isaac Canpanton (1360–1463) absorbed elements from

---

51. Moshe Halbertal, 'Nahmanides' Conception of the History of Halakhah and the Minhag'
[Hebrew], *Zion* 67(2002), pp. 25–56; Solomon Havlin, *Rabbi Abraham Halevi (Author of Responsa
"Ginath vradim") and the Scholars of his Time and Place* [Hebrew], Ph.D. submitted at The Hebrew
University (Jerusalem), 1983, pp. 8, 15, 119, 374–377; Morsel-Eisenbert, *The Organization of
Halakhic Knowledge in Early Modern Europe*, passim.

52. See the various works of Elchanan Reiner.

53. Meir Rafeld, *The Maharshal and the "Yam Shel Shlomo"* [Hebrew], Ph.D. submitted at Bar-Ilan
University (Ramat-Gan, Israel), 1990, passim.

54. Joseph Hacker, 'The Intellectual Activity among Jews in the Ottoman Empire during the
Sixteenth and Seventeenth Centuries' [Hebrew], *Tarbiz* 53, no. 4 (1984), pp. 569–604.
Citation from *ibid.*, p. 569.

55. Haim Bentov, 'Methods of Study of Talmud in the Yeshivot of Salonica and Turkey after
the Expulsion from Spain' [Hebrew], *Sefunot: Studies and Sources on the History of the Jewish
Communities in the East* 14 (1971–1978), pp. 7–102.

medieval scholasticism and claimed to provide a logical system for considering the entire scope of Talmudic discussion. This method was later absorbed by leading scholars in the Sephardi Diaspora in the Mediterranean Basin. *'Iyyun* provided a common language for the entire community of Talmudic scholars, just as the *Ius commune* offered common tools of debate across Catholic Europe. The scholarly lingua franca encouraged a formation of legal summa. It reached the city of Safed and was practiced by its leading scholars, including R. Karo.[56] Other aspects enhanced the suitability of canons in the Sephardi Diaspora.[57] Rabbis and scholars took a positive view of the dissemination of halakhic literature among the general public, in contrast to the firm opposition to such a possibility in the Ashkenazi world.[58] Sephardi scholars in local Yeshivas formed a kind of "Republic of Letters" as they dispatched to each other their comments on the Talmud and engaged in epistolary discussions. This network encouraged the need for a common textual center, and eventually sustained the dissemination of R. Karo's books after their printing. Some prosperous centers of Jewish life increased the sense of self-assurance and security. The large Jewish community in Salonica was emblematic and functioned as a focus of inspiration and imitation for smaller Sephardi communities around the Mediterranean Basin under Ottoman rule. Books and rabbis were dispatched from the Jewish metropolis in Salonica to serve in smaller communities and spread its religious, cultural, and political messages. The power and wealth of this community enabled it to sustain institutions that noticeably increased the need for authoritative books. The Salonica community hosted a printing house that published the works of contemporary authors. The local rich Maecenases provided generous support for a modern education system that reached larger parts of the population. Some benefactors even established public libraries open to scholars and erudite laypeople. Literature of both a sacred and lay character attracted unprecedented interest and stimulated the publication of popular works. Sephardi writers faced the new challenge of producing accessible and attractive books and of responding to the taste of their potential readers. Writing in a harmonistic and encyclopedic mode became more popular. Joseph Hacker noted that this cultural fermentation was not restricted to an elite group of sages nor to any specific location.[59] The double codes of law composed by R. Karo should be viewed as part of this cultural pattern.

R. Karo and the Muslim Setting

R. Karo was inevitably indebted to previous precedents of Jewish codification, especially the two major ones, composed by Maimonides and R. Jacob ben HaRosh, both in the Sephardi domain. Their impact can be felt on almost every page of his twin

---

56. See below Chs. 4, 5.
57. Hacker, 'The Intellectual Activity among Jews in the Ottoman Empire', passim.
58. Yoel Marciano, *Sages of Spain in the Eye of the Storm - Jewish Scholars of Late Medieval Spain* [Hebrew], Jerusalem: Bialik Institute, 2019, pp. 259–260.
59. Hacker, 'The Intellectual Activity among Jews in the Ottoman Empire', pp. 580–581. The characteristics mentioned above were discussed in this article as well.

codes of law. In the early modern period, the Sephardi legal tradition reacted to a new arena, the Ottoman/Sunni Islam world. This legal tradition provided a setting that was far more responsive to the Halakhah and its codification than the European domain. Considering the major aspects of codification in Islam, prior to the establishment of the Ottoman Empire, the codification of Hadith as presented above in the work of Jonathan Brown offers the most relevant point of reference. The points of phenomenological similarity are various and significant:

- His books are addressed to the entire community of Jewish believers.
- It encompasses legal traditions of various origins that are woven together into a single fabric.
- The codification project was assisted heavily by new technology (the print revolution of the early modern period).
- The dissemination of the books and Karo's plan relied on a network of his close students.
- The more R. Karo's books established their canonical position, the more nonscholars began to regard open opposition to their content as illegitimate.
- The texts, once printed, inspired almost instantly the flourishing of interpretations.
- The long version of *Beit Yosef* was accompanied by the shorter *Shulchan 'Arukh*.
- The books were intended to serve practical goals, such as Talmudic rulings in concrete cases or use during court proceedings.
- The codification project interacted with a general and grand vision of reforming the Jewish collective and Jewish religion.
- It molded later halakhic literature so that this pattern shaped the structure of major halakhic tracts.
- The personality of the composer played an important role in the dissemination process. R. Karo was hallowed as a unique, saintly, and exceptional figure.
- It enhanced the legalistic aspect of Jewish tradition.
- Law, legality, and normative behavior were infused with mystical dimensions of religious tradition.[60]
- The books explicitly attempted to disseminate one tradition—the Sephardi—at the expense of the variety of local traditions in the Jewish Ecumene. It embodied the Sephardi superiority of the early modern period.

These parameters not only associate Karo's project with Islamicate civilization. They also make Karo an exceptional figure in the Jewish context. The twin codification project may seem at first glance to be a continuation of the long chain of Talmudic erudition. Yet it suggests a major turn in halakhic history and a paradigmatic shift in the way law and legality were to play within Jewish tradition from the sixteenth century onward. In this respect, too, it was clearly related to the Islamicate tradition, and this time specifically to Ottoman civilization. This was the arena in which the most dramatic change

---

60. See the discussion on Ch. 6.

regarding codification in Islam occurred, distinct from the previous ones (as mentioned above in §1.4). This is the setting that provided R. Karo with new perspectives regarding law, legislation, and codification and to which he responded.

Codification in the Ottoman Empire

As noted above (§1.4.2), codification in Islam was restricted mainly to the professional circles of law scholars (*'Ulama*) from the various law schools. These scholars strove to maintain their independence from the political authorities, who were often of foreign origin and were not considered as representing the local population or correct standards of religious traditions.[61] The result was a sparse number of codification projects initiated and supported by the political regimes. This trait of Islamic history began to change during the Mamluke reign, but a more significant shift followed the establishment of the Ottoman Empire. I follow here the analysis of Guy Burak, as presented in his various works. It was the dynastic Ottoman state that organized and supervised the composition and the enforcement of the legal Canon, the *Kanuname*:

> Unlike the canonization of texts in the pre-Ottoman and Arab lands, canonization within the Ottoman learned hierarchy was more formal and followed strict procedures. Upon its approval, the text entered circulation, which means that it was taught in the imperial *medrese* system and jurists could make use of it, or—if certain restrictions and limitations were imposed—of parts of it.[62]

The expansion of the Ottoman state into large territories in a relatively short time led to encounters between Ottoman and Arab legal traditions and required a unique response. This reality resulted in the tighter organization and definition of the particular traditions of Ottoman *'Ulama*.[63] The inclusion of texts in the formal canon was controlled by the leading state-nominated jurist of the Empire, the Şeyḫülislâm. Burak elegantly depicts this functionary as the gatekeeper of the canonization procedure, in charge of introducing any tract to an *official list of "texts."* Once included, these would become part of a reliable or authoritative textual corpus in circulation:

> From the sixteenth century onward, references to the reliable texts became quite frequent in jurisprudential works compiled by members of the *imperial learned hierarchy*, in collections of legal opinions issued by the chief imperial jurisconsults, and in imperial edicts [...] It is worth dwelling on the *role the sultan played in the Ottoman canonization procedures*.[64]

---

61. See the various important works of Wael Hallaq.
62. Guy Burak, 'Reliable Books: Islamic Law, Canonization, and Manuscripts in the Ottoman Empire (Sixteenth to Eighteenth Centuries)', in: Anthony Grafton and Glenn Most (eds.), *Canonical Texts and Scholarly Practices: A Global Comparative Approach*, Cambridge: Cambridge U.P., pp. 14–33. Citation from *ibid.*, p. 29.
63. *Ibid.*, p. 18.
64. *Ibid.*, p. 20.

Once canonized, these texts were later subject to the reading and interpretation of the juridical elite, and especially the person standing at its head. The legal canon was not a one-time event of fixing textual limits, but an *ongoing process*. Further, jurisprudential works were not necessarily canonized in their entirety, and their use required the constant updating of juridical expertise.[65] The promulgation of codes of law went hand in hand with the establishment of a distinct and self-assured professional milieu of state-jurists, confident in the validity and importance of the legalistic literature at its disposal, accompanied by a *relatively standardized law across the empire*. The Hanafi school of law was practically declared the dominant tradition over other legal schools, and Ottoman Hanafis benefitted from clear advantage over their Arab Hanafi colleagues. To follow Burak, jurists affiliated with the Ottoman regime inculcated "establishment consciousness," secure in their position relative to their colleagues in Arab lands, and certainly in relation to non-Hanafi scholars. Their collective esprit also relied on a centralized hierarchy and the important service they provided to the Ottoman Empire.[66] The inclusion of texts in state-supported canon implied the exclusion of other legal traditions—mainly from the Arab (non-Ottoman) Hanafi law school and various traditions of Arab 'Ulama. It also implied the functioning of a censorship mechanism, surprisingly similar to the European mechanism concerning printed books.[67] The credibility and trust the Ottoman elite placed in its legal texts enhanced their role in the legal institutions across the empire. This was augmented by surveillance mechanisms intended to ensure that only these texts were consulted and to regulate the reading of members of the imperial learned hierarchy. It was customary to mention these texts explicitly, so as to demonstrate adherence to the imperial jurisprudential canon of "texts of high repute" and to enable their superiors, as well as those who solicited their opinions, to inspect their use of the texts.[68] The incorporation of newly conquered territories was accompanied by the composition of *Kanuname*s, considered more valid and authoritative than local traditions and juridical heritage.[69] This process also aimed to integrate the legal traditions of non-Muslims, under the hegemony of Ottoman law.[70]

---

65. *Ibid.*, p. 27.
66. *Ibid.*, pp. 21, 33.
67. Guy Burak, 'Reflections on Censorship, Canonization and the Ottoman Practices of *Imza* and *Takriz*', published on www.acacemia.edu site.
68. Burak, 'Reliable Books: Islamic Law, Canonization, and Manuscripts in the Ottoman Empire', esp. p. 22. On the domination of the Ottoman center over judges and legal procedures in the Arabic lands, see also idem., 'According to His Exalted Ḳânûn: Contending Visions of the Muftiship in the Ottoman Province of Damascus (Sixteenth-Eighteenth Centuries)', in: Dror Ze'evi and Ehud R. Toledano (eds.), *Society, Law, and Culture in the Middle East: "Modernities" in the Making*, Berlin and New York: De Gruyter, 2015, pp. 74–86, esp. 75, 80.
69. Guy Burak, 'Evidentiary Truth Claims, Imperial Registers, and the Ottoman Archive: Contending Legal Views of Archival and Record-Keeping Practices in Ottoman Greater Syria (Seventeenth–Nineteenth Centuries)', *Bulletin of SOAS* 79,2(2016), pp. 233–254; Colin Imber, *Ebu's-su'ud. The Islamic Legal Tradition*, Edinburgh: Edinburgh U.P., 1997, pp. 41, 44.
70. Karen Berkey, 'Aspects of Legal Pluralism in the Ottoman Empire', in: Lauren Benton and Richard J. Ross (eds.), *Legal Pluralism and Empires, 1500–1850*, New York and London: New York U.P., 2013, pp. 83–107. See *ibid.*, esp. p. 84.

The canonization of law became an obligatory and fundamental component in the management of the large empire, alongside the formation of an efficient bureaucracy with clear standards:

> Secretaries were necessary for the creation and deployment of *technologies and instruments of control such as land surveys, law codes, and various registers recording* expenses, the distribution of land grants (*tımar*), the decisions of the imperial council, and so forth.[71]

The increasing standardization in imperial mechanisms implied greater use of written documents and trust in the imperial archives.[72]

The trend toward standardization and unification in the Ottoman Empire had repercussions not only in the political, legal, and bureaucratic levels. It was motivated by religious causes, characterized by Derin Terzioğlu as the "Sunnitization" of Ottoman society:

> Demonstrating how the process of state identification with Sunnism had roots in the eleventh and twelfth centuries, Terzioğlu presents a narrative of the gradual strengthening and centralization of frontier polities in the fourteenth and fifteenth centuries that drew on the knowledge of urban and migrant scholars to mold religious practice and belief. As Terzioğlu points out, much of this process had begun well before the Ḳızılbāş revolts flared and the Safavid threat appeared, though imperial expansion and Safavid rivalry was surely one motor that consistently drove the dynasty to claim a Sunni, and Hanafi, identity for both itself and its subjects. *The legal codes of the empire were systematized and reconciled with the shari'a and an ambitious program of congregational mosque building in every town and city in the empire was undertaken in the mid to late sixteenth century.*[73]

Gülru Necipoğlu demonstrated a parallel and contemporaneous process in the crystallization of an esthetic canon under the tight supervision of state authorities.[74] Finally, Helen Pfeifer showed an aspect of cultural canonization taking place in various literary salons, where Ottoman and Arab scholars met on equal terms. This "Republic of Letters" and personal encounters contributed to a common taste and the emergence of a

---

71. Kaya Şahin, *Empire and Power in the Reign of Süleyman. Narrating the Sixteenth-Century Ottoman World,* Cambridge: Cambridge U.P., 2013, p. 3. See also *ibid.,* p. 174, the bureaucratic perspective of the Ottoman Empire, and the need for classification (including legal classification, obviously). See also the important observations in Abdurrahman Atcil, *Scholars and Sultans in the Early Modern Ottoman Empire,* Cambridge: Cambridge U.P., 2017, p. 126 on changes in the size and sophistication of the centralized bureaucracy.

72. Burak, 'Evidentiary Truth Claims, Imperial Registers, and the Ottoman Archive', pp. 233–234. See also Atcil, *Scholars and Sultans in the Early Modern Ottoman Empire,* p. 124.

73. Nir Shafir, *The Road from Damascus: Circulation and the Redefinition of Islam in the Ottoman Empire, 1620-1720,* Ph.D. submitted at University of California, 2016, pp. 44–45.

74. Necipoğlu, 'A Kanun for the State, a Canon for the Arts', esp. pp. 197, 205.

consensus around literary and religious compositions.[75] It adds an important dimension to canonization, beyond the control of the central authorities of the Ottoman Empire.

Codification, It's Not All about Texts: A Summary

Paradoxical though it sounds, the text is not necessarily the focus of canonization. The canonical text is the final product of an intricate encounter of several factors, such as the formation of community identity, an authority capable to compose a canon and impose its special status, the crystallization of an interpretative community around the canonical text, its reading according to changing circumstances, a dissemination network, new technologies (such as the expanding use of paper, codes instead of scroll, and the print revolution) initiating its composition, the aggrandizement of the figure of the canon's composer, the special mode of reading a canon, its ritual and public use, and other factors mentioned in this chapter.

Put differently, the canonical text as a literary and material object (book or manuscript) is but one of a number of components that imbue canons with special status in cultural and social history. To quote the insightful phrasing of El Shamsy, a canon is "constituted by a *continuing, open-ended process* of interpretation and debate taking place within the disciplinary realm of legal theory. This could rightfully be called a *canonizing discourse*, because its core purpose was to establish rules for connecting lawmaking rigorously to the sacred sources." The canonical text, and in our case legal codification, is an inextricable player in the complex game of unification and standardization proposed by legal schools with their particular methodological approaches, alongside mechanisms for reaching consensus within society at large or among law experts, the projection of previous cultural-religious canons on new canonization (in the Islamic case, the radiation of the Hadith canon on legal compilations and codes) or general interest in compositions of an encyclopedic nature.

Canon is a trustworthy observer on the collective in which it was shaped and crystallized. It embodies an intention to set limits to collective identity, be it religious or "ethnic," in apposition to external or internal rivals. The myths that justify codification often reveal a sense of challenge or danger to the cultural heritage and community regulative patterns. The law codes encourage the construction of consensual space and offer common language and a cultural reservoir that can serve the consumers of this code. Simultaneously, it excludes other potential positions and condemns them to oblivion.

A cursory review of the history of law codes in the three monotheistic traditions shows that until the early modern period, the role of states or centralized political authorities in this regard was short-lived and minimal. The main codification projects in Sunni-oriented Islam took place among the Abbasids, with very limited success. The Catholic Church was the main promoter of codification of Canon Law,

---

75. Helen Pfeifer, 'Encounter after the Conquest: Scholarly Gatherings in 16th Century Ottoman Damascus', *International Journal of Middle East Studies* 47,2(2015), pp. 219–239. See esp. *ibid.*, pp. 220, 229–230.

yet did not even publish a formal and approved text until the early modern period. The various Jewish Diasporas lacked any central authority capable of enforcing a law code, even after the composition and publication of *Beit Yosef* and *Shulchan 'Arukh*. In all three cases, a clear change took place during the sixteenth and seventeenth centuries. The significant context was the Ottoman and not by chance Jewish codification that evolved and disseminated in the interstice between the traditions of Islam and Christianity, between Catholic Spain and the Ottoman Empire. In the Jewish case, this process was initiated by a scholar of Sephardi origin, who fused in his life course and in his work the traditions of the European/Catholic domain (related to the Sephardi Talmudic methodology of *'Iyyun*) and those of the Islamicate/Ottoman domain in which he spent his adult years. Yet observing the main traits of R. Karo's codification project, it is apparent that the Muslim codes of previous generation and the contemporary Ottoman *Kanunames* left a deeper imprint on his work. In both cases, the codes derive from the sacred scripture of the respective tradition (Bible and Talmud, Koran and Hadith); the law is presented as the heritage of past generations; it confronts the challenge of homogenizing various schools of religious and civil law; and legal guidance and regulation is never limited to the earthly realm, but aspires to guide the believer toward proximity to the divine. Further traits were mentioned in regard to Jonathan Brown's book on the canonization of Hadith literature in Islam.

Karo's codification project is unique in respect to previous canonizations and standardization processes in the history of Halakhah. It offered a grand and unprecedented fusion of Ashkenazi and Sephardi Talmudic traditions, albeit with a clear Sephardi dominance. R. Karo implicitly presented his vision in the famous introductions to both *Beit Yosef* and the *Shulchan 'Arukh*. He considered the double codes as essential agents in religious renovation and reform—under his own leadership, needless to say, alongside that of other eminent sages in the city of Safed, as a new center or capital of the Jewish world. He cultivated a generation of young scholars charged with the task of disseminating his perspective and works. The universalistic vista was apparent in Karo's initiative to establish an international court of law, encouraging Jewish communities in the Jewish Ecumene to address his court. His image was constructed as uniquely prestigious, as reflected in the myth that he was ordained by two hundred rabbis. The twin codes enhanced the legalistic character of religion. Karo's work echoed the parallel elements of contemporary Ottoman codification. All these aspects will be discussed in depth in the following chapters.

Avriel Bar-Levav suggested another perspective, and one that is highly pertinent for understanding the broader context of our subject, although it does not directly address Karo's work. Bar-Levav characterized the passage from medieval to early modern culture as a paradigmatic shift toward a model of comprehensive knowledge, to be found in an imaginary-virtual library containing all the books of Jewish culture.[76] The ideal

---

76. Avriel Bar-Levav, 'The Religious Order of Jewish Books: Structuring Hebrew Knowledge in Amsterdam', *Studia Rosenthaliana* 44(2012), pp. 1–27.

of the perfect library is apparent in the work of R. Karo, especially in his introductions (see Chapter Two). It certainly resonates with the Sephardi traditions of Talmudic study and precedent codifications, yet it became more pertinent and relevant with the advent of the printing press in the Jewish world. Sensitive both to his immediate and distant surroundings, R. Karo understood perfectly the advantages of print technology:

> The *Shulhan 'Arukh* embodies many aspects associated with the advent of print, such as unification, distribution, the rise of new codes, new communities of readers, and the standardization of textual traditions and praxis. Karo was an obvious, albeit exceptional example of "a new author" who was well aware of the advantages and restrictions of print. The explicit purpose of the book was popularization—namely to make the law available to both scholars and lay people—and the author was well aware that it would be quickly disseminated throughout the Jewish world, and hoped that it would bring unification and consensus.[77]

The printing of both codes of law during R. Karo's lifetime joined the contemporary printing of practically the entire "classical" Jewish canon, such as the mystical corpus *Sefer Ha-Zohar*, the Bible, the Babylonian Talmud, liturgical books, rabbinical Midrash, and the large mystical Summa *Pardes Rimonim* by R. Moses Cordovero, a contemporary of Karo in Safed. It contributed to the cultural flourishing of Sephardi communities around the Mediterranean Basin, especially in Istanbul and Salonica, and the composition of religious literature of a popular character, including popular halakhic works.

---

77. Amnon Raz-Krakotzkin, 'Persecution and the Art of Printing. Hebrew Books in Italy in the 1550s', in: Richard I. Cohen, Natalie B. Dohrmann, Adam Shear, and Elchanan Reiner (eds.), *Jewish Culture in Early Modern Europe. Essays in Honor of David B. Ruderman*, Pittsburgh (PA) and Cincinnati (OH): University of Pittsburgh Press and HUC Press, 2014, pp. 97–108. Citation from *ibid.*, p. 104.

Chapter Two

THE PREAMBLE TO *BEIT YOSEF*: MANIFESTO OF A JURIST

The preamble to *Beit Yosef,* and to a lesser extent the complementary and shorter one to *Shulchan 'Arukh,* are among the constitutive Jewish documents of the early modern period. Even during his own life, R. Karo clearly considered the preamble an important manifesto for his entire codification project. He insisted on attaching it to all four parts of his books, printed at various times and in different printing presses. The introduction indicates how deeply these double codes are inserted in the rabbinical and post-Talmudic fabric, preserved in a growing number of past books and writings, expanding even further following the deep impact of the print revolution on Jewish culture. The perception of Karo's preamble as exclusively rooted in this Jewish past has come to be taken for granted in Jewish erudition. I seek to show here that this traditionalist perspective leaves too many gaps and cannot by itself explain the full scope of Karo's life project. It is no less essential to examine his text against the background of Ottoman legal history. The important codes introduced by the Ottomans in various parts of their expanding empire included detailed preambles in which they defined the role of law for political control, the Sultan as guarantor of justice and just law, and the contribution of legal mechanisms to the bureaucratic system needed to sustain the empire's ongoing functioning. These preambles reaching the entire empire essentially constituted an Ottoman manifesto of law and rule. As the Jewish minority had a profound acquaintance with the Ottoman law and its courts, they were exposed to these messages, conveyed in the preambles to codes of law (*Kanunnameler*).

Reading a Preamble to a Legal Code

The attempt to explore the personal world of rabbinical figures throughout the Middle Ages is a frustrating task for contemporary historian.[1] The individual composers hide themselves behind the collective "we" of the chain of past generations and their literary productions. The wide rabbinical literature at our disposal is saturated with paraphrases and allusions to previous compositions or to the canonical literature. One of the channels that allow us to delve beyond this collectivist screen is found in the introductions

---

1. On the lack of biographical, and even more so autobiographical, aspects in rabbinical writings until the early modern era, see Chapter Six.

to books, where authors often propose their motivations for writing or reveal their personal circumstances.

This channel might seem superfluous in the case of R. Karo, since we have a surprising amount of knowledge about his personal and intimate life, including the thoughts, sentiments, and motivations that accompanied him both at important moments and in the course of his everyday life. His mystical diary *Magid Meisharim* follows his entire adult life and provides rich information enabling us to reconstruct his self-image and unique role as an innovator of Jewish religious life.[2] It further reveals that the composition of both codes of law was part of a divine master plan for a comprehensive reform of religion, pietism, and re-shaping of Jewish religion, and underscores Karo's own dominant role in these future changes. It presents two deeply connected courses of activity—as jurist and halakhic arbiter (*poseq*) and as a mystic drawing on an unbroken chain of revelation. Although Karo believed that he was under divine orders not to stop writing his diary, it was primarily intended to remain secretive and not to reach the public at large. Another channel of personal communication, entirely diverse from the mystical diary in its discourse mentality, will form the focus of this chapter: the double preambles for his codes of law. These were intended from the outset to publicize *Beit Yosef* and *Shulchan 'Arukh* and to establish their place in the long chain of rabbinic and post-Talmudic precedents.

Tirza Kelman rightly noted the importance of the preamble to *Beit Yosef*, which was composed and published while *Beit Yosef* itself was still a work in progress. R. Karo continued to update the versions in various printings of his work and appended it to other sections of his work. He declared in a later part of *Beit Yosef* that reading the preamble was essential for understanding the composition itself. Once he decided on the final version, it was the only one printed in later editions. This stands in stark contrast to the various preambles composed by R. Jacob ben Asher (or *HaRosh*— R.W.) to his *Turim*, bearing distinct differences, which caused their distinct and repeated printings.[3]

How does one read or make sense of these preambles? Do they contribute in any significant way to our understanding of R. Karo's life project? An introduction by its very nature is a kind of publicizing act intended to enhance the special qualities and contributions of a contemporary work in respect to past works. It inherently tends to reiterate commonplaces typical of the literary genre. It will likely refer to the circumstances of composition, the place of the composer in his professional milieu, concepts of justice and legality in contemporary community, or finally its affiliation to theological concepts of law, obedience to God, or religious practices.

The reading of the preambles would immediately tackle the immersion of the individual voice within the collective "we" of the long chain of transmission,

---

2. See the discussion in Chapter Six.
3. Tirza Yehudit Kelman, *"I Shall Create Halakhic Ruling… for that is the Objective": The Dimension of Halakhic Ruling in Joseph Karo's Beit Yosef* (Hebrew), Ph.D. submitted at Ben-Gurion University (Beer-Shevah, Israel), 2018, esp. pp. v, 36.

considered in rabbinical tradition much more significant than the individual composer. But a more difficult hurdle to overcome is the "culture of quotations," whereby it is expected that almost any assertion will be anchored in the endless repertory of the Jewish canon and past works. It is no easy task to extract unique and historical elements from such referential writing. Yet Karo's insistence on repeatedly printing his introduction clearly shows that he had very specific messages to convey to his potential readers. The elements of innovation were cloaked, as customary in contemporary writing in all three monotheistic traditions, under the mantle of references to classical rabbinical literature and traditional rhetoric. The reassuring message is that nothing new is being suggested, merely the continuation and evolvement of past precedents.

If the rhetoric is indeed used to mask the concrete assertions, then it is clearly vital to distinguish various levels of rhetorical messages. The most obvious of these is the familiar and reassuring rabbinical rhetoric that would position *Beit Yosef* and the *Shulchan 'Arukh* as the continuation of past Talmudic scholarship. This assertion is correct, of course: these texts constitute no more than another super-commentary on a previous code of Talmudic law—the fourteenth-century *Four Columns* or *The Columns* (*Arba'ah Turim* and *Ha-Turim*, respectively) of R. Jacob ben HaRosh. The important and inspiring scholarship of recent years on Karo's Talmudic works offers new readings of his twin preambles. Yet common to them all is a literal acceptance of his assertions.[4] The motivation for composing the *Beit Yosef*—and later his abridged version the *Shulchan 'Arukh*—was the crisis in Jewish life in his times and ensuing fears that the Torah and its study might dwindle. An emergency situation—following R. Karo and his modern readers—demands a significant response, in this instance the composition of his magnum opus. Such a rhetorical claim is commonplace in rabbinic writing from late antiquity, throughout the Middle Ages, and well into the early modern period. A claim of crisis, real or imaginary, provides the motivation for change or renovation and reform of religious traditions. In a cultural ethos that dislikes and rejects blunt expressions of innovation, any new step should be always camouflaged under the old. An alternative mode of justification is that under circumstances of duress or crisis it is legitimate—following this rhetoric—to change the old and the traditional. But was there really a crisis in R. Karo's time entailing the dwindling of scholastic and religious traditions? Sixteenth century witnessed the establishment and flourishing of Torah centers across the Eastern Mediterranean; some of the eminent Sephardi halakhic figures left a most impressive patrimony of writings and printed compositions. If no real crisis took place, what was the message behind Karo's rhetorical assertion? I shall claim now that though the legitimacy of a supposed crisis was false, the explicit message was that his project intended to reshape Jewish tradition and the halakhic domain.

---

4. See the studies of Yaron Durani, Maoz Kahana, Tirza Kelman, and Mor Altshuler, mentioned along the various chapters of this book.

Ottoman Preambles to *Kanuname*s

How, then, are we to read Talmudic scholars' introductions to their works? One per-spective, just mentioned and further elaborated in the introductory chapter, turns our attention to rabbinical rhetoric, in general, and its modes of response to changes. Historical writing was not considered an important component of rabbinic heritage. Historical changes were taken into consideration (in writing) primarily insofar as they affected the professional milieu of traditional institutions and Talmudic scholars—the prime literary class in Jewish tradition, responsible for written material available to us in the Middle Ages and into the early modern period. The evolvement of Jewish culture was mostly considered *sub specie aeternitatis*, as obeying some grand divine plan, and accordingly the more somber or concrete details of history were barely documented unless they constrained rabbis to follow a new cultural course. To complicate things even further, any modern reading that extracts historical and reality-oriented elements from rabbinical writings is forced to confront the dominance of quotations and refer-ences to past literature. It is alluring to settle for this apparent exterior message (the traditional emphasis on allusions and quotes). I would designate this textual layer as "rabbinical rhetoric" and argue that behind this screen stand further layers and internal messages that need to be decoded.

A second methodology of reading a preamble is to contextualize it in relation to previous ones belonging to the same literary genre of halakhic and rabbinical writing. In our case, it is clear that R. Karo was paraphrasing and responding to the preambles of the preceding codes of law composed by Maimonides—the *Mishneh Torah*—and by R. Jacob ben HaRosh—*Ha-Turim*.[5] The interaction of R. Karo's preamble to *Beit Yosef* with these two famous introductions has been discussed by previous modern scholars, and I need not add to their insights. Yet the differences are noticeable, since the goal of Maimonides in composing the first Talmudic code of law was actually to relegate law and Talmudic norms to second place, thereby creating space for philosophical musings, and particularly for moral amelioration and personal devotion to God. Law provided the frame for religious life and practices, but was not inherently essential.[6] The intro-duction to the *Four Columns* presented Talmudic law and Halakhah, in general, as a unique corpus that distinguishes the Jewish collective from the rest of humankind. It did not offer any political or cultural vision of law beyond standard and traditional sayings.[7] From the outset, this code evolved gradually, so that it remained basically a literature addressed to professional jurists and scholars acquainted with Talmudic and post-Talmudic literature, and less to the public at large.[8] Unlike these two preambles,

---

5. Kelman, *The Dimension of Halakhic Ruling in Joseph Karo's Beit Yosef*, pp. 40–41.
6. Isadore Twersky, *Introduction to the Code of Maimonides (Mishneh Torah)*, Yale: Yale U.P., 1982, passim.
7. Kelman, *The Dimension of Halakhic Ruling in Joseph Karo's Beit Yosef*, pp. 40–41, 51.
8. See the elaborate discussion in Yehuda D. Galinsky, *The Four Turim and the Halakhic Literature of 14th Century Spain. Historical, Literary and Halakhic Aspects* (Hebrew), Ph.D. submitted at Bar-Ilan University (Ramat-Gan, Israel), 1999.

the one composed by R. Karo considers law as fundamental tool of religious innovation, so that its message is addressed to the entire public.

The third axis or methodology for interpreting Karo's vision as presented in his preamble is to consider its interaction and response to historical circumstances beyond the Jewish milieu. In this context, we may begin by wondering whether the contribution of Karo's *Beit Yosef* and *Shulchan 'Arukh* make to halakhic literature or to a renewed commitment to the study of Torah (*Talmud Torah*) offers sufficient justification for Karo dedicating 35 years of his life to this project. And even if this is the case, was this project entirely disconnected from what R. Karo, as well as other intellectuals of his generation, saw around them? It is hardly plausible to suggest that this is the case, since the major changes in the history of Halakhah— such as the codification of the Mishnah, the composition of the Babylonian Talmud, the diversification of Talmudic literature during the Gaonic period, the innovative exegesis on the Talmud in medieval France and Ashkenaz (contemporary Germany), and the flourishing of Talmudic studies in the Mediterranean Basin and central-eastern Europe in the early modern period—were all related to political-cultural changes in the non-Jewish domain that had an impact on the Jewish minority. The case of R. Karo was no exception in this long chain of various phases of the history of Halakhah. In Karo's case, the external influence was that of the thriving Ottoman Empire and civilization and its unique role in Islamicate tradition during the early modern period.

Starting from early sixteenth century, the Ottomans expanded their territories into Arab lands, establishing an impressive empire—the largest in territory and the longest-enduring in the history of Islam. The annexation of the new territories necessitated much more than mere military control and the use of naked violence. The conquest of the eastern part of the Mediterranean Basin—Egypt and shortly thereafter Greater Syria (*Bilad a-Sham*)—was accompanied by significant administrative measures, such as rules concerning land control and tax collection. For our purposes, the innovations in the legal domain are more relevant. The dominant role of the Ottomans in regard to the local population and its customs was manifested by the publication of Ottoman sets of laws (*Kanunameler*). The authors of these texts, such as Ibrahim Paşa or Mustafa Celalzade, were the top-ranking professionals in managing the imperial administration, and not soldiers of the *Askeri* milieu. The Sultan was the incontestable head of the expanding empire, but its presence and authority were delegated to the mechanisms that sustained the empire. Crucial among these were Ottoman laws and the institutions charged with enforcing justice and maintaining public prosperity, which explicitly manifested the nexus between the political and legal domains. *The Preamble to the Kanuname*, following the conquest of Egypt, was the first official document that embodies the specific ideological tenets of Ottoman sovereignty under Süleyman and Ibrahim Paşa, his grand vizier. It develops a new "political theology," depicting the Ottoman ruler as a divinely ordained sultan and caliph who reigns over both the spiritual and temporal realms. The support offered for this claim ranges from a mainstream reading of Sunni Muslim political theory to astrology and apocalyptic musings. The preamble signifies the dawn of a new era in which the global program it outlines would be put into action. Ibrahim was described as the ideal grand vizier whose unconditional devotion to the sultan, together with his moral and intellectual capacities, made him the perfect instrument of the ruler's will. Buzov characterized it as "the young Suleyman's manifesto."[9]

In her seminal work on the Ottoman preambles to the *Kanunames*, Snjezana Buzov noted how they publicized the political ethos of the empire and the measures of control that soon legal, administrative, and military officials would exert:

> In this document [the preamble] the chief chancellor (nişanı) Celalzade appears as the consolidator and systematizer of the Ottoman kanun law, and the translator of the religio-cultural sentiments of the time into the new imperial ideology. The sultan is no longer the peer of his soldiers and commanders, distinguished for his wisdom, courage and leadership, but an invisible overarching figure that shapes and puts into motion the imperial scenery. As the young sultan was removed from the position of primus ante pares, a young and capable slave, Ibrahim, was placed in that position [...] The Egyptian preamble glorified the Ottoman kanun law as a consistent system of law, that were in harmony with the divine law, and also superior to the law of the newly conquered regions.[10]

The violent disappearance from the public scene of talented administrators Celalzade Mustafa and Ibrahim Paşa paved the way for the emergence of another major figure, from the juridical milieu, flourishing for long years under Sultan Süleyman: the Şeyḫülislâm Ebu Su'ud. The messianic aspirations and plans for universal rule during the first half of Süleyman's reign were abandoned in favor of consolidating the great empire. This shift opened an era of intensive legislation and codification projects, each preceded by its own preamble. Following the classical tradition of just rulers from early Islam, Ebu Su'ud cooperated closely with Süleyman to expand the interface between state law and *Shari'a* and to depict the sultan as the fifth Caliph and as a sacred ruler. The sultan is the one

> who makes smooth the path for the precepts of the manifest *shari'a* and the exalted words of God. The Sultan has powers not only of *siyasa* (state law and order—R.W.), but also of interpreting and executing the *shari'a*, bearing the title of Caliph, which go far beyond the strict limits which the Hanafi jurists originally prescribed.[11]

These law collections were later presented to the various provinces of the expanding empire, from the Arab world, the core land of Rumelia and Anatolia, and to professional guilds and occupations. Many of them included preambles that publicly declared the intentions and purposes of the codes of law, and especially the fundamental role of

---

9. Kaya Şahin, *Empire and Power in the Reign of Süleyman. Narrating the Sixteenth-Century Ottoman World,* Cambridge: Cambridge U.P., 2013, esp. p. 57. On the high titles conferred upon Süleyman and on his roles as caliph and messianic figure, see *ibid.*, p. 189.

10. Snjezana Buzov, *The Lawgiver and his Lawmakers: The Role of Legal Discourse in the Change of Ottoman Imperial Culture,* Ph.D. submitted at Chicago University, 2005, esp. pp. 5, 9.

11. Colin Imber, *Ebu's-su'ud. The Islamic Legal Tradition,* Edinburgh: Edinburgh U.P., 1997, esp. p. 98. On the spiritual qualities of Süleyman, see Buzov, *The Lawgiver and his Lawmakers,* pp. 35–36.

law in establishing peace and justice for all subjects of the Ottoman Empire. The proximity of Safed to Egypt, and especially the fact that it belonged to the district (*Eyalet*) of
Damascus, make Buzov's observations of these two preambles—given shortly after the
military conquest, during the ruler of Sultan Süleyman— highly relevant to what Karo
later wrote.

These preambles include several key components: justification for the imposition of
law on new territories; the centrality of law for the legitimacy of Ottoman rule; the connection between state law (*Kanun*) and divine law (*Shari'a*); the superiority of Ottoman
law and rules over the local legal traditions; the policy of respecting local traditions
while at the same time framing these within Ottoman law; the special role of the sultan
in providing and enforcing these laws; and last but certainly not least, the need for the
systematization and codification of contemporary laws.[12]

The fact that these preambles were composed in Arabic, rather than Turkish, indicates that their publication and dissemination among the local Arabic-speaking populations was part of formal Ottoman policy. The large number of extant manuscripts
of these emblems provides further indication that they reached audiences beyond the
inner circle of professional jurists.[13]

Reem Meshal aptly showed the impact of Ottoman law on areas adjacent to the
Holy Land (and to Safed), Egypt, and *Bilad a-Sham*. Before the conquest rumors spread
that Sultan Selim planned to abolish all the legal schools in Syria, which fell in 1516,
and these were partially confirmed when the sultan suspended all but the Hanafi
school in Damascus (*abtala min al-Sham al-madhabib al-thalatha*), as per the "custom in his
[Selim's] lands" (*'adatih fi biladihi*). Some local judges were persecuted by the Ottomans
and given an ultimatum to rule according to the Hanafi rite or to forfeit their office or
even their life.[14] Still, the Ottoman conquerors had to take into account the power of
local elites, as much as their control stabilized along the sixteenth century, especially
its second half. Now that no new territories were appended to the Ottoman Empire, a
new balance of power regarding political, military, and administrative aspects required
the cooperation with local elites in the periphery. This shifting balance is an alternative
perspective to the famous decline thesis in regard to the sixteenth-century Ottoman
Empire, suggesting that the period saw "an ongoing process of dialogue, negotiation,
conflict, and conflict management between different actors and interest groups from
the imperial through the regional and provincial down to the local levels."[15] The preamble to the *Kanuname* indicated well the new Ottoman control of Egypt. The local

12. Buzov, *The Lawgiver and his Lawmakers*, pp. 28–34.
13. Buzov, *The Lawgiver and his Lawmakers*, esp. pp. 127–128, 130–133.
14. Reem Meshal, 'Antagonistic Shari'as and the Construction of Orthodoxy in Sixteenth
    Century Ottoman Cairo', *Journal of Islamic Studies*, 21, no. 2(2010), pp. 183–212, esp. *ibid.*,
    pp. 193–194.
15. Astrid Meier, 'Patterns of Family Formation in Early Ottoman Damascus: Three Military
    Households in the Seventeenth and Eighteenth Centuries', in: Peter Sluglett, Stefan Weber
    (eds.), *Syria and Bilad al-Sham under Ottoman Rule. Essays in honour of Abdul-Karim Rafeq*, Leiden
    and Boston: Brill, 2010, pp. 347–369. Citations from *ibid.*, pp. 347, 351.

elites in Damascus and its surroundings were gradually "ottomanized" and adopted the Ottoman way of life, esthetics, housing, and political worldview.[16] The "Rumi" tradition gradually infiltrated and reshaped the eastern Mediterranean. Obviously, the Jewish minority was exposed to the impact of Ottoman civilization, including its legal aspect.

A further front of this progressive osmosis of Ottoman civilization into the Arabic-speaking areas was the adoption of the Ottoman Kanuname as a model of law and legislation in the Arab provinces.[17] In conclusion, the preambles to the important *Kanuname*s publicized Ottoman law as the mode of ruling the local population. The sultanic political ethos was diffused across the empire, including the Arab lands. Safed and its people—both Jews and Muslims—were not exempt from this propagandistic rhetoric.

The Preamble to *Beit Yosef*: An Ottoman Reading

Suggesting an Ottoman "reading" of the opening words of *Beit Yosef* relates to our recognition above that codification projects were particularly pertinent to the time and place of R. Karo—those same Ottoman settings, alongside similar contemporary projects in large states and empires in Western Europe and the colonial regimes in the New World. This reading cannot be severed from other aspects of R. Karo's life project, as we shall see in the coming chapters. I will propose now an "Ottomanized" perspective on some of the major elements in his preamble to *Beit Yosef* and secondarily to *Shulchan 'Arukh*.

The centrality of the law

As in the introductions to the important codes of law imposed on places annexed to the Ottoman Empire, the role of law and legality is stated by R. Karo not in some theoretical or general context, or in relation to Talmudic discussion, but as the opening words to *Beit Yosef*, a professional work on law.[18] It states the motivations and intentions behind its composition:

> Due to His love of His people, He [God] drew us nearer at Mount Sinai, and bestowed by means of the supreme among humankind, that is Moses of blessed memory, righteous teaching and commandments, law and regulations, to benefit us, so that we might follow His ways and find favor.[19]

---

16. *Ibid.*, pp. 348–349.
17. Buzov, *The Lawgiver and his Lawmakers*, pp. 128–129.
18. Moshe Dovid Chechik, *The Struggle over Ashkenazi Legacy in Poland: The Printing of Shulhan Aruch in Poland and the Reactions to It* [Hebrew], M.A. thesis submitted at the Hebrew University (Jerusalem), 2018, p. 120.
19. In this section I am using the regular and modern printed version of *Beit Yosef* (and *Shulchan 'Arukh*).

Before discussing the content and message of these lines, it is no less important to note their remarkable presentation. From the outset, Karo states his position with complete self-assurance, as if delegating an indisputable authority.

R. Karo was not innovative in saying that the fundamental role of law owes its constitutive moment to God's revelation at Mount Sinai, through His greatest prophet Moses, leading to the bestowal of the Torah on an entire collective. Both the biblical story and later the Midrash (the narrative hermeneutic of the Pentateuch—R.W.) are somewhat unclear as to what exactly was delivered during these precious moments. The content of the Ten Commandments was too meager to sustain the entire oral tradition as it evolved over the centuries.[20] In the classical rabbinical ethos, these revelatory moments were constructed as fundamental for the transmission of Jewish heritage in its entirety, beyond its juridical and halakhic aspects. This view was stated by his contemporary and long-standing colleague and rival in Safed, R. Moses di Trani:

> Everything was passed to Moses on Mount Sinai in an ordered mode, that is, the Bible, the Mishnah, the Talmud, and the Aggadah [similar to the above-mentioned Midrash—R.W.], as said: "And God spoke all these words, saying [...]" (Exodus 20:1), implying that every question posed by a disciple to his rabbi-master was mentioned by God, blessed be He, to Moses on Mount Sinai.[21]

For Karo, the content is very precise and specific: law, and only law.

By positioning law as the core message of the Sinaitic revelation, R. Karo implies that a very specific and identifiable content of the law was bestowed on the "People of Israel" or the Jewish collective. This underscoring of positive law certainly echoes Maimonides' introduction to his code of law *Mishneh Torah* and Sephardi tradition in general. It represents a notion that during this specific event the Law in its original and divine version was conferred. The coming generations witnessed the decline of this authentic version, leading to increasing legal plurality. The difference between these two towering Talmudic scholars is that in the case of Maimonides halakhic law relates to a broader ethical, historical, and philosophical perspective, while in R. Karo's case, it is entirely filtered through the eyes of a legal expert and his mode of fashioning a mythical past. This Sinaitic history is reconstructed in such a way that it could legitimize the functioning of contemporary legal mechanisms and justice institutions, as well as his own unique contribution. There happened a one-time event of having an authentic version of the law, and this is approximated once more by the magnum opus *Beit Yosef*. R. Karo bluntly ignores important options within Jewish heritage regarding the multiversional aspects of Torah, even during the moments at Mount Sinai. Leading thinkers of previous generations and his contemporaries underlined the fluidity of Talmudic traditions. To mention two alternative positions, the Sephardi

---

20. Roni Weinstein, "Jewish Modern Law and Legalism in A Global Age: The Case of Rabbi Joseph Karo," *Modern Intellectual History* [Cambridge University Publications Online], (2018), pp. 1–18, esp. P.14.
21. Moses di Trani, *Kiryat Sefer*, Venice: Aldo Bragadin Publishing House, 1551, p. 7a.

Kabbalist R. Meir ibn Gabbi (1480–1540) claimed that *Torah*—as a metonym of various aspects of Jewish heritage and a particular way of life—is being given constantly at every minute, and not only during the Sinaitic event. Only as an ongoing moment could it preserve its vitality and freshness. The important Talmudic scholar R. Hayim ben Bezalel (1520–1588) considered the various options in the Torah as an immanent element in its nature and as a great advantage.[22]

The opening lines in Karo's introduction constitute what it may not be overly dramatic to term a watershed moment in Jewish culture. They define the identity of the Jewish collective as intimately related to legality, law, and a specific corpus of positive law (his own work, naturally). This excludes other options—such as pietism, devotions, messianic visions, or the community as bearer of collective identity—and focuses on law. Other elements are acknowledged, certainly, but law provides the fundamental axis uniting them all. As mentioned previously, the preambles positioned Ottoman laws and justice mechanisms as the platform for establishing the Sultan's rule, the legitimacy of Ottoman dominion over large areas of Islam, and served as a uniting element for the rich ethnic and cultural texture within the empire. This was a core mechanism that enabled the empire to prosper and insure its role alongside other competing forces from the West (Holy Roman Empire) and the East (the Safavids).

Rejection of variety in law

R. Karo states bluntly that he considers legal variety or "legal pluralism" to be a negative trait of the Halakhah of his times: "The Sages' sagacity was lost and Torah and its scholars became powerless, so that the Torah has become not two Torahs but endless Torahs." This comment reflects the same position Karo expressed in his mystical diary *Magid Meisharim*: "Due to the multitude of judges, controversies will increase, and as a result the Torah becomes a thousand Torahs"—hence the need for a central authority.[23] R. Karo again echoes the introduction of Maimonides, which was dominated by severe criticism and rejection of what he considered the indecisiveness of the Talmudic laws and practical instructions of his time. Legal variety was the fruit of long centuries of unfortunate historical circumstances, reflecting a fall from grace and deviation from the original and authentic version of the Law.[24] As we shall further on see Karo's motivation was very different and centered on an allegation of the overabundance of knowledge, rather than any dwindling of Torah study.

---

22. Avi Sagi, "'Both These Version are Words of Living God'—On the Possibility of Multiple and Contradictory Halakhic Rulings" [Hebrew], in Moshe Koppel and 'Ali Marzbach (eds.), *Sefer Higayon. On the Thinking Modes of Rabbis*, Alon Shevut: Machon Tzomet, 1995, pp. 113–141, esp. 135.
23. Joseph Karo, *Magid Meisharim*, Wilnius: Judah Leib Lipman Metz Print, 1875, p. 43a.
24. A somewhat similar position, though relying on a completely different motivation, is expressed by the great Polish Talmudist R. Solomon Luria [known as *HaMaharshal*]. See Chechik, *The Struggle over Ashkenazi Legacy in Poland*, pp. 118–119.

Karo again stated as a matter of fact that this situation is to be considered a negative aspect of contemporary Jewish culture and life. He flatly disregarded the opposite view that constitutes a no less legitimate and respected strand in rabbinical ethos and Jewish tradition. Important Kabbalistic figures of his time, R. David ibn Zimrah (1479–1573) and R. Chayim Vital (1542–1620), living in proximity to him in Safed, cherished the pluralism in Halakhah and the variety of Jewish traditions as a reflection of the endless and mysterious affluence within divinity. An infinite Torah with multiple options projects the infinity and sublimity of God.[25] Turning to the halakhic milieu, rabbis from various cultural contexts in time and place have suggested that Halakhah is not a well-confined text, or an amalgam of instructions, but rather a heritage in a constant process of change and negotiation in each generation and by every rabbi of import. Legal variety reflects the ongoing and ceaseless search for consensus among contemporary rabbis and halakhic arbiters.[26] Seen from a somewhat metaphysical angle, it was proposed that the Torah as it existed in the divine domain, before its passage to the human realm, contained many options rather than one "authentic" version.[27]

The roots of these two optional modes in relation of legal pluralism were persuasively presented by Richard Hidary, as rooted in the Talmudic period.[28] He wisely follows the suggestions of Robert Cover about "paideic" and "imperial" notions of legality and justice. The paideic approach approximates the social world created by community narratives; members are personally educated into a common set of narratives and particularistic principles that embody the group's vision for an ideal society and its goals for the future. This normative world obliges its members to create a strong community where members actively engage one another. The imperial model, on the other hand, approximates the strictly legal order of precepts. It ensures that many paideic worlds can coexist by imposing universal principles on its members. This second model maintains order but does not inspire or create community. Following Cover, prominent examples of paideic and imperial orders in the modern world are, respectively, religious communities and the nation-state.[29] Community-oriented law responds to diversity and changing circumstances as legitimate sources for legal and juridical norms. This approach suited the fragmentary nature of the Jewish Diaspora, including the communities living under the Ottoman Empire in the Mediterranean Basin. Jewish communities lacked

---

25. Maoz Kahana, "A Universe Made of Words. The Self-Image of R. Joseph Karo as Composer of Halakhah" (Hebrew), *Hebrew Law Annual (Shnaton HaMishpat Ha'Ivri* in Hebrew) 30 (2019–2020), pp. 79–127, see especially pp. 84–85; Eyal Davidson, *Safed's Sages between 1540–1615, Their Religious and Social Status* [Hebrew], Ph.D. submitted at the Hebrew University, 2009, p. 77.

26. Avi Sagi, "The Dialectic of Decision-Making and Objective Truth in Halakhah: Some Considerations Regarding the Philosophy of Halakhah," (Hebrew) *Dine Israel* 15 (1989–1990), pp. 7–38.

27. Sagi, "On the Possibility of Multiple and Contradictory Halakhic Rulings," pp. 114–115.

28. Richard Hidary, *Dispute for the Sake of Heaven. Legal Pluralism in the Talmud*, Providence (RI), Brown Judaic Studies, 2010.

29. *Ibid.*, p. 10.

any centralized institutions or substantial authority to enforce law.[30] The "imperial" approach represented, to a large extent, the cultural world of Sages and rabbis—legal experts belonging to a social and professional milieu of small numbers and confined to their internal discourse and language. Further, the two analytical terms mentioned by Hidary, following Robert Cover, reflect the differences between the two centers where Talmudic tradition was shaped in Late Antiquity and later in the Middle Ages: The Holy Land (*Eretz Israel*) and Babylonia. The tendency of the Jerusalem Talmud to ordered law and codification echoes the Late Antiquity laws of the Roman Empire and their increasing codification by Justinian and Theodosius, and later the Christian Church in tandem with clear lines of belief in the ecumenical councils. The appreciation of Babylonian Talmud for a variety of opinions reflects a similar attitude in Sassanian tradition, where it was shaped until the arrival of Islam.[31]

Between these two options, R. Karo clearly preferred the imperial over the paideic approach rooted in and legitimized by community tradition. The imperial approach favors a centralized vision determined by a single authority (himself). Its political character is reflected in the complete silence it imposes on alternative positions within Jewish thinking. Given his opposition to legal pluralism, we would expect that R. Karo would produce a code featuring unequivocal assertions, yet this is not the case. *Beit Yosef* contains impressive post-Talmudic erudition, including contemporary compositions, yet it is replete with countless unresolved discussions. Put differently, a clear gap exists between the declaratory level of the emblem and its partial implementation. The declaration is important in itself. It is the vision of his code that matters no less than the content of positive law.[32] If law is to function across large territories, and serve varied Jewish ethnic traditions, it must be presented as decisive and devoid of too many legalistic intricacies. This inspires a further step, so that the core rabbinical ethos of Talmudic discussion and disputation is relegated to a secondary position. It is superseded by a professional ethos of a juridical nature. The end result was that Karo's codifications were constructed as a commentary on a previous legal tract *Ha-Turim*, a legal Summa, and not as a commentary on the Talmud. Thus, the center of gravity is shifted to the internal discussion of legal literature— understanding the position of previous professional experts—rather than the study of Talmud. The messages of the Ottoman preambles are clearly applied in the context of the Jewish minority. The impact is present in defining law under the control of professionals, the need for governmental and legal unification,

---

30. See the discussion on Ch. 7. See also, Hidary, *Legal Pluralism in the Talmud*, p. 12: "As a historical precedent for this imaginary world, Cover points to Talmudic law: 'The Jewish legal system has evolved for the past 1900 years without a state and largely without much in the way of coercive powers to be exercised upon the adherents of the faith [...] there had been no well defined hierarchy of law articulating voices in Judaism.'"
31. *Ibid.*, pp. 77–80.
32. See the wise comment of Meshal, "Antagonistic Shari'a and the Construction of Orthodoxy," p. 193: "While the preamble to the Qanunname Misr [of Egypt–R.W.] is an innovative and important document, the legal code itself, its method of compilation and substantive arrangement are not."

the prioritization of one specific legal heritage over others, codification, and the need for hierarchy in legal mechanism, headed by a single and unique person.

Methodology of halakhic decision-making (Pesiqah)

Any elaborate legal system, such as the Talmudic-rabbinical tradition, that reaches maturity after centuries of intense discussions must confront the challenge of forming a basic consensus. This mutual understanding among the professional milieu is a prerequisite for the smooth functioning of the legal heritage and for its capacity to provide workable solutions in concrete cases. The rabbinical tradition was no exception in this respect and it provided similar channels to reach basic consensus. For instance, it discussed mechanisms for balancing the opinions of senior rabbinical jurists relative to those of others, less senior but outnumbering them. Another challenge concerned the importance of overcoming internal discord that continues to rage even after consensus has been reached.[33]

The mechanism determining Jewish law was stated by R. Karo from the outset as a constitutive component in his justification of his work:

> And so I have decided that, since there are three pillars upon which the house of Israel stands due to their rulings—that is, the *Rif* [R. Isaac AlFasi (1013–1103)], *Maimonides*, and the *Rosh* [acronym of R. Asher (1250–1327)] of blessed memory—where two of them share the same position, I would rule according to them.

The first and most fundamental phase of the halakhic ruling, then, is presented as the simple counting of votes: R. Karo as an arbiter needs only to examine the opinions of these three dominant and exceptional scholars and make a simple calculation of votes. In a juridical heritage as intricate and diverged as the Talmudic, with its long tradition dating back to the Second Temple period, this assertion verges on the implausible. Yet modern scholars have pointed out that R. Karo was not completely innovative in this respect. Prior to the general expulsion from Spain in late fifteenth century, several attempts were made to declare these three halakhic figures of major authority and prestige in Sephardi tradition as Pillars of Halakhah.[34] This position was stated openly by an important Sephardi Rabbi, David ibn Zimrah (1479–1573):

---

33. Sagi, 'The Dialectic of Decision-Making and Objective Truth in Halakhah', passim; Shlomo Zalman Havlin, 'On Literary Canonization as Constitutive for Time Division in the History of Halakhah' [Hebrew], *Studies in the Talmudic Literature. In Honor of Saul Lieberman on His Eightieth Birthday*, Jerusalem: The Israeli Academy of Sciences and Humanities, 1978, pp. 148–192. See Davidson, *Safed's Sages between 1540–1615, Their Religious and Social Status*, pp. 89–90, a precious testimony that confrontations stand at the core of Halakhah, so that it is impossible to point at some 'authentic' Halakhah; It is shaped rather by ceaseless debates within the rabbinic milieu, having its own modes for reaching a consensus. In case of impasse, the unavoidable solution would be to count votes.

34. Yaron Durani, *Three Pillars of Guidance in the Halakhic Ruling of R. Joseph Karo* [Hebrew], M.A. thesis submitted at Bar-Ilan University (Ramat-Gan, Israel), 2006, pp. 26, 33, 36; Kahana,

So is the opinion of the most prominent Talmud scholar, and R. AlFasi, Maimonides, and R. Asher whom we follow, all the more because they carry credible tradition [...] All the more so, since the inhabitants in all these regions [in Spain, and later their descendants – R.W.] have accepted the authority of R. AlFasi, Maimonides, and R. Asher, to follow their rulings, either to be lenient or strict, either to absolve or to bind [...] we must not deviate to the right nor to the left from what prominent Talmudic scholars said and R. AlFasi, Maimonides, and R. Asher wrote, only adhere thereto.[35]

Two reasons substantiated this choice from R. Karo's perspective. First, these three scholars essentially represented mostly the Sephardi halakhic tradition, especially Maimonides, yet at the same time included important elements from the Ashkenazi heritage, since R. Asher—a great scholar of Ashkenazi Talmudic methodology—migrated from Germany to Spain and carried his Ashkenazi heritage with him. The second, and even more pertinent, reason was that these three scholars were presented as exceptional since they ruled on all domains of Halakhah and discussed or interpreted the Talmud in its entirety.[36] Every aspect of Jewish tradition was present in their works, interwoven into an all-inclusive unity.

In declaring his reliance on specific and prominent figures, R. Karo joined a current that was becoming increasingly prevalent in Sephardi communities. This approach cherished the authority of a dominant rabbi—be he Maimonides, R. Asher, or R. Solomon ben Aderet (known as *HaRashbah* 1235–1310]])—as binding across large territories, and not only on a restricted and local basis.[37] Standing behind a sole authoritative figure made sense in the political circumstances of late medieval Spain. The Spanish king imposed on local communities the position of "Court Rabbi" (*Rab de la Corte*) as a central figure for a large territory. Yet as much as Karo's declared methodology seems to be a continuation of preexisting patterns, it was primarily innovative, based on his own strategic and personal choice.[38] Yaron Durani and Maoz Kahana have persuasively outlined the innovative elements in his proposal. It was stated as a binding assertion intended to apply to the entire halakhic tradition rather than a merely descriptive testimony of current Sephardi tradition. Furthermore, Karo's voting method was to serve in all domains of life, and not only in those originally applied in Spanish communities, as a lever in reshaping the halakhic tradition and as a prime methodological tool. As openly claimed in *Beit Yosef* and in the mystical diary *Magid Meisharim*, this mechanism

---

'A Universe Made of Words. The Self-Image of R. Joseph Karo as Composer of Halakhah', pp. 86–87.

35. Durani, *Three Pillars of Guidance in the Halakhic Ruling of R. Joseph Karo*, p. 33.

36. *Ibid.*, p. 3

37. Durani, *Three Pillars of Guidance in the Halakhic Ruling of R. Joseph Karo*, pp. 24–25, 29, 30–31

38. Kahana, "A Universe Made of Words. The Self-Image of R. Joseph Karo as Composer of Halakhah," pp. 107–108: "The decision to use the Jewish Catalan tradition of Halakhah ruling for this universalistic cause is indeed very innovative, and Maran's rhetoric ('I made up MY mind' [*veHiskamti beDa'ati* in Hebrew]) does not conceal the personal dimension of this use, uncorroborated by any precedent or similar pretension for such a precedent."

generates valid and applicable law for the entire Jewish collective.[39] Once again R. Karo was borrowing customary and traditional patterns and redirected them to untrodden and innovative paths.

The innovative aspects of his suggestion were reflected in the criticism it soon evoked. The great Talmudic scholar in Poland, R. Moses Isserles (1530–1572), a contemporary of R. Karo whose Ashkenazi glosses were inserted next to Karo's text in printed editions, ironically commented that R. Karo was attracted to "big names," as if their publicity and prestige constituted an almost automatic guarantee for their halakhic claims.[40] A Sephardi scholar, R. Moses ElAshkar (1466–1542), rebuked Karo for using the vote-counting methodology out of its proper context, since it was only meant to apply to figures from the distant Talmudic period.[41] R. Isserles further criticized R. Karo for failing to adhere to his own methodology, and in practice regulating Halakhah according to other criteria.[42] This assertion—originating from a major Talmudic scholar yet a rival of Karo due to his intentionally ignoring Ashkenazi distinct tradition—was further corroborated by modern scholarship: R. Karo rarely uses this methodology in his current rulings in *Beit Yosef*, and when he does so he often rules contrarily.[43]

Even more puzzling is R. Karo's complete disregard for the methodology of Talmud studies that typified Sephardi scholarship two generations before the exile, and later spread across the Mediterranean Basin among the Ottoman-Jewish schools.[44] The method of *'Iyyun* (which might be translated as "deep reading") was molded by the famous R. Isaac Canpanton (1360–1463) and extended to further schools and halakhic compositions by his close disciples, especially R. Isaac Aboab (1433–1493). It implied a close reading of every Talmudic discussion (*sugiyah*) by itself and as an independent unit of discussion, ascribing a specific message to every expression or word and applying the

39. *Ibid.*, p. 108: "This formula claims for the first time a universal validity. The three Halakhah decisors are depicted as 'Pillars of Knowledge', 'that all the house, House of Israel [*Beit Yisrael* in Hebrew] leans on their instructions'. 'The House of Israel' is the entire Jewish collective, regardless of distinctions between Ashkenaz and *Sefarad*/Spain, or between various 'Sephardi' regions."

40. Kelman, *The Dimension of Halakhic Ruling in Joseph Karo's Beit Yosef*, pp. 204–205. On the Jewish-Polish context of this assertion, see Chechik, *The Struggle over Ashkenazi Legacy in Poland*, pp. 70, 89. See Durani, *Three Pillars of Guidance in the Halakhic Ruling of R. Joseph Karo*, p. 89, regarding the objection to this mechanism, raised by the Ashkenazi eminent Talmudic scholar R. Jacob HaLevi of Moelln [known as *HaMaharil* (1360–1427)], claiming that it is not really a valid method for ruling law. Every issue needs to be examined by its own terms and decided according to the accumulated heritage of past generation and the insights they contributed to the discussion. An automatic mechanism empties the Talmudic erudition of its passion.

41. Durani, *Three Pillars of Guidance in the Halakhic Ruling of R. Joseph Karo*, p. 78.

42. *Ibid.*, p. 70

43. *Ibid.*, pp. 43, 48, 58, 77; Kahana, "A Universe Made of Words. The Self-Image of R. Joseph Karo as Composer of Halakhah," pp. 109–112; Kelman, *The Dimension of Halakhic Ruling in Joseph Karo's Beit Yosef*, pp. 215–218.

44. Kelman, *The Dimension of Halakhic Ruling in Joseph Karo's Beit Yosef after the Expulsion from Spain*, passim; Haim Z. Dimitrovsky, "Rabbi Yaakov Beirav's Academy in Safed" ([Hebrew], *Sefunot: Studies and Sources on the History of the Jewish Communities in the East* 7 (1963), pp. 41–102.

tools of logic. In Safed, this approach became the leading method, due to the dominant position of R. Jacob Beirav and his yeshiva. It is clear that the methods of counting votes and the *'Iyyun* scholastic-oriented tradition are incompatible. Although R. Karo's Yeshiva followed this method, as did most schools in Safed, he does not hint at its importance in the preambles.

Despite the widespread criticism of his method, and Karo's avoidance of applying it in practice, it carried a strong message. The law was a proper and distinct domain, established not by personal whim or individual bias but through a quasi-automatic mechanism. In Weberian terms, this approach reveals an aspiration to form a systematic domain, with its own rules and expectations, both for its consumers and for professional actors. Moreover, Karo's proposal fuses the consensuses of past generations into a single conclusive position. Facing past debates and ceaseless arguments and counter-arguments, and the unwieldy scope of discussions and books to peruse, it offers a workable pattern. The voting methodology reflects a yearning for consensus and for a common ground among all those committed to Jewish law. It places the arguments and debates of past scholars next to a conclusive point. And finally, this mechanism indicates the variety of halakhic traditions of different Jewish ethnic diasporas, as well as their fundamental unity, by positioning one former Ashkenazi scholar next to two Sephardi rabbis. In practice, this ostensible legal pluralism submits to Sephardi dominance, as most of the rulings tend to accept Maimonides' assertions. The periphery—as seen from the Sephardi perspective in Safed—is expected to accept the authority of the center, be it the leading Sephardi yeshivas of the Eastern Mediterranean under Ottoman rule or more specifically the imaginary "capital city" of Safed.[45]

Gradations and hierarchy among Talmudic scholars

Shortly after presenting his vote-counting method, R. Karo adds an important proviso of a restrictive character:

> And so I have decided that, since there are three pillars upon which the house of Israel stands due to their rulings—that is, the *Rif*, *Maimonides*, and the *Rosh* of blessed memory— where two of them share the same position I would rule according to them, UNLESS a majority of rabbis and scholars disagree with this position, and the contrary custom has already spread. Where one of the three pillars mentioned above does not express his opinion, and the other two pillars disagree, then I would turn to Ramban, and Rashbah, and the Ran, and Mordechai, and the Semag, [all] of blessed memory. We would turn to the opinion indicated by the majority, so we will rule on Halakhah.

Should the three pillars of Halakhah not provide a halakhic rule, then, a secondary instantiation of legal scholars is evoked. Their position is assured not only due to their merit by virtue of their erudition, but no less due to their membership of the category

---

45. On the special role of Safed, as presented by R. Karo and his contemporaries, see Ch. Five.

of "Last Generations Scholars" (*Acharonim* or *Batraei*, in rabbinical parlance, in Hebrew and Aramaic, respectively). The rule that Halakhah follows the positions of the "Last Generations' Ruling" (*Hilkhetah keBatraei*) was discussed among Talmudic scholars throughout the Middle Ages and into the early modern period. It evolved as a partial answer to the challenge of the increasing volume of Talmudic literature and the need to reach an endpoint for concrete legal instruction.[46]

It is clear that these two methods are not compatible: the second diminishes the authority of the three leading scholars. It expands the range of Talmudic study and increases the range of discussions and uncertainty rather than diminishing it in favor of a concluding point. Approached differently, Tirtza Kelman rightly noted that the second methodology paradoxically tips the balance of discussion in favor of these "Last Generations Scholars," since the procedure of judging in court or studying in yeshiva becomes weightier as more persons of prestige are involved.[47]

Why, then, begin with a strong declaration of methodological clarity, only to enfeeble its commanding rule by adding a second, incongruent method? Asked differently, why not settle for the second option, so customary in the rabbinical ethos of Talmudic study, of encouraging diversity and disagreement along the path of understanding God's words? Again, despite this inherent inconsistency, R. Karo conveys an important message regarding the urgent need to structure an inclusive and virtual community of rabbinical scholars in a strictly gradated hierarchy. This hierarchy extends across the entire scholarly chain, from its starting point in Jewish tradition at Mount Sinai, conveyed by Moses, through Karo's early modern present. Each of the scholars mentioned on this long list is a "big name" of his generation and milieu, ranked alongside his peers from throughout the ages; while above them all stand the towering figures of Rif, Maimonides, and HaRosh.

At the summit of this scholarly chain stands R. Karo himself, legitimized by the very work he is engaged in introducing. As seen in Chapter 6, on his heavenly journeys he ascends to the "Divine Yeshiva," where he meets the various generations of scholars—only the very elite, of course. This is not merely an intellectual or academic discussion, but a face-to-face encounter, and one that often grants post-factum approval for Karo's concrete halakhic resolutions in Safed. These long-dead scholars are mentioned by their generational affiliation and their rank in the history of halakhic scholarship. This hierarchy related not only to past generations, but also to the contemporary study institutions, where scholars of various levels engaged in personal context. The Sephardi yeshivas of the Mediterranean Basin under the Ottomans, including those of both R. Beirav and Karo in Safed, were organized in a hierarchical manner. In this aspect, they did not differ from the other center of Sephardi Talmudic learning in Salonica, no less prestigious that the Safedian center, under the ruling of R. Taitatzak.[48] The

---

46. The distinction between various generations of scholars relates directly to issues of rabbinic authority. See the discussion on Chps. Four and Six.

47. Kelman, *The Dimension of Halakhic Ruling in Joseph Karo's Beit Yosef*, p. 205.

48. Meir Benayahu, "R. Joseph Taitatzak from Salonica, Head of Sephardi Diaspora" (Hebrew), in: Zvi Ankori (ed.), *Then and Now. Annual Lectures on the Jews of Greece (1977–1983)*, Tel-Aviv:

famous Safed schools applied a three-way distinction: beginners—passing the initiation course—next to advanced scholars, and above them persons holding their own yeshiva.[49] The schools of both R. Beirav and R. Karo assembled on special days of the week all the grades of scholars. The participants attending these meetings maintained a strict order of sitting and role in discussion. The lively, energetic, and confrontational mood of discussion united all those present, while at the same time allotting each of them his distinct place in the hierarchy.

The need to shape some form of basic consensus had well-known precedents in the history of Mediterranean and Middle Eastern law. Hidary recognized the impact of Roman law on Jewish scholarship during late antiquity regarding codification activities. This process also entailed a mechanism for achieving consensus through reference to a hierarchy of contending legal positions, based on the "Law of Citations."[50] A similar challenge in reaching juridical consensus also confronted Islamic legal tradition. The *Ijma'*, which could be considered an Arabic parallel of the Latin term *Consensus*, was presented early in the history of the legal schools (*Madhhabs*) as one of the fundamental pillars of law and legal tradition in Islam. The evolvement of several parallel schools of law in Islam necessitated internal cohesiveness in respect to other schools of law. It encouraged the formation of a strict internal hierarchy around the figure of the founding figure, his close disciples, and later generations of scholars.[51] The rank of an individual scholar was defined by his ability to provide an independent opinion and respond to changing circumstances. A scholar could position himself in regard to previous generations—obviously the most conspicuous among them—as a faithful imitator (*Muqalled*) or as someone tending more to innovation (*Mujtahid*), a position granted to a very few; he thereby joined the ongoing chain of transmission and added his part to the accumulated heritage. All these elements could faithfully apply to R. Karo, his construction of past learning, and especially his particular role within this chain of legal erudition.

The Ottomans took these traits of Muslim tradition much further, establishing a hierarchic mechanism of law, state-controlled curriculum, nomination of judges to state courts and as professors in state *Madrasas*, and finally declaring one legal school—the Hanafi—as the quasi-official state school of law. The Şeyḥülislâm stood at the top of the legal guild and his rulings were defined as binding. The encounter between Ottoman Hanafi scholars and their Arab counterparts, particularly Arab Hanafi scholars in the

The School of Jewish Studies, Tel-Aviv University, 1984, pp. 21–34.

49. Kelman, *The Dimension of Halakhic Ruling in Joseph Karo's Beit Yosef*, pp. 39–40, 44; Yoel Marciano, *Sages of Spain in the Eye of the Storm - Jewish Scholars of Late Medieval Spain* [Hebrew], Jerusalem: Bialik Institute, 2019, pp. 75–77, 140; Dimitrovsky, "Rabbi Yaakov Beirav's Academy in Safed," passim.

50. Hidary, *Legal Pluralism in the Talmud*, pp. 78–79.

51. Guy Burak, *The Second Formation of Islamic Law. The Hanafi School the Early Modern Ottoman Empire*, Cambridge: Cambridge U.P., 2015, esp. p. 7, on reaching internal consensus among scholars of the same legal school, and regarding the distinction between followers of legal tradition within a school and the innovators.

provinces, accelerated the formation of internal gradations within this tradition. Guy Burak described marvelously the impact of these changes, which were reflected in the expansion of the literary genre devoted to the biographies of the Ottoman jurists and their respective rank, the *Tabaqat*. This genre canonized certain positions and texts by virtue of their mere inclusion in these genealogical lists of authorized and important figures. It added to the construction and legitimacy of a state canon, as well as contributing to the professional cohesion of the Ottoman Hanafi school. Not by chance the *Tabaqat* corresponded to the conquests of Arab lands and the encounter with their legal traditions.[52] It includes divergent enumerations of generational grades within the scholastic community, but all these share the notion that each succeeding grade possesses less authority and prestige than its predecessor, with which it cannot therefore openly disagree.

Abundance of printed books

A substantial part of R. Karo's preamble is devoted to a discussion of the works that served him in his composition. The list sounds very much like a library catalogue, specifying the extent of books at his disposal:

> This is the book's content, to clarify the norms as presented in *Arba'ah Turim* (basing itself on various books), be it *Mishnah*, or *Beraita*, or *Tosefta*, or an expression in the *Babylonian* or *Jerusalem Talmud*, or the *Safra*, or the *Sifra*, or the *Mechiltah*, and if it is agreed upon or leading to argumentation between *Tannaim* or *Amoraim*, and the composer followed one of them and for what reason. Should the composer present contradicting views of arbiters, I would enlighten the reasons behind each position and its roots and background in the Talmud [...] The consequence is that whoever possesses my book would have—in an organized manner—the sayings of the *Talmud* with the exegesis of *Rashi*, and the *Tosafot*, and the *Rules of the Rif*, and the *Rosh*, and *Mordechai*, and *Maimonides* and its annotated notes, and *Magid Mishneh*, and *R. Yerucham*, and *Sefer HaTerumah*, and *Shibolei HaLeqet*, and the *Roqeach*, and *Sha'arei Durah*, and *Sefer HaTashbetz*, and *Sefer HaItur*, and *Nimuqei Yosef*, and *Semag*, and *Semaq*, and *Orchot Chayim*, and *Torat HaBayit*, and *Hagahot Asheri*, and *Sefer Hamanhig*, and *HaAgur*, and *Sefer Ba'alei HaNefesh* by the *Raavad*, and the *Responsa of HaRosh*, and *HaRashbah*, and *R. Isaac Bar-Sheshet*, and *R. Shimon bar Zemach Duran*, and *R. Yosef Qolon*, and *Terumat HaDeshen*. All their sayings are well interpreted. And in some places the sayings of the *Zohar* [...].

In her meticulous study on these aspects of R. Karo's work, Tirza Kelman noted the importance of the print revolution and its impact on the content of *Beit Yosef*.[53] The compositions that served Karo most in his legal rulings, and were thus canonized for centuries to come, having a greater impact on the future Halakhah, were those that

---

52. *Ibid.*, pp. 12, 125.
53. Amnon Raz-Krakotzkin, *The Censor, the Editor and the Text. The Catholic Church and the Shaping of Jewish Canon in the Sixteenth Century*, tr. Jackie Feldman, Philadelphia: University of Pennsylvania Press, 2007.

reached his desk as printed books.[54] The rendition in print within just a few decades of the entire Jewish canonical literature—the Bible, its major commentaries, Mishnah and Talmud, major Midrashic books, the Zohar, prayer books, key halakhic works, and responsa—had a dramatic impact on early modern Jewish culture. In a relatively short period of time, these works became available to much larger sections of Jewish population. They encouraged the unification and standardization of Jewish texts at the expense of the impressive local variety typical of the Jewish medieval period. The faster channels of communication and transport of books created an international Jewish book market. Its direct result was an encounter (and confrontation) between various Jewish ethnic traditions, so that the differences could no longer be ignored. The impact of this almost unbearable variety—or "Too much to know,": as elegantly phrased by Ann Blair—was an increasing search for a unifying substratum that could serve the entire collective or community of believers. In a seminal work, Avriel Bar-Levav examined the need of leading Jewish intellectuals, rabbis, and Talmud scholars to define some kind of "universal library" that would unite this sudden flow of new information available in print and provide some common frame in order to unite the printed canon.[55] In Sephardi communities in the major cities in the Ottoman core lands, important "public" libraries were founded under the patronage of rich individuals. These institutions housed an impressive number of books that stood at the disposal of erudite persons unable to purchase them themselves.[56] Kelman followed his work and persuasively showed the deep impact of a "library consciousness" on the halakhic work of R. Karo. Anxiety at the over-abundance of knowledge and consciousness of the comprehensive library are two sides of the same coin. The expansion of the library was enabled by print technology and global channels of distribution. This created a sense of an uncontrollable ensemble, with no beginning or end, beyond the capacity of human study and memory.[57] Again, despite his promise to include "all books of Halakhah, none to be missing," and despite the detailed bibliography he provided, Karo's choice of books was highly selective, excluding those he did not deem proper for his project. Yet in practice, the books he used were much more varied than those he specified:

Undoubtedly, R. Karo was acquainted with a richer literature that he intended to include in *Beit Yosef*. The promise "none will be missing" does not concern the entirety of Torah literature, but what he defined as the entirety Halakhic literature relevant to his project.

---

54. Kelman, *The Dimension of Halakhic Ruling in Joseph Karo's Beit Yosef*, p. 20.
55. Avriel Bar-Levav, "Between Library Awareness and the Jewish Republic of Letters" (Hebrew), in: Yosef Kaplan, Moshe Sluhovsky (eds.), *Libraries and Book Collections*, (Jerusalem: Shazar Center, 2006), pp. 201–224.
56. Joseph Hacker, "The Sephardi *Midrash* – A Jewish Public Library" (Hebrew), in: Idem., Yosef Kaplan, Binyamin Z. Kedar (eds.), *From Sages to Savants. Studies Presented to Avraham Grossman*, Jerusalem: Shazar Center, 2010, pp. 263–292.
57. Kelman, *The Dimension of Halakhic Ruling in Joseph Karo's Beit Yosef*, p. 107.

The traces of those exegetes that R. Karo could have chosen, yet he did not, are spread all along *Beit Yosef.* Similarly various other books of import in other issues flash here and there. These deviations [from the declared master plane—R.W.] enable us to chart the lines of the corpus R. Karo considered pertinent to his Halakhic composition. As declared, the book is about to offer its reader a total and all-inclusive Halakhic inventory. According to the author thirty two books are mentioned by their name in a dense list, offering a comprehensive treasure of knowledge. A meticulous examination of Maran Karo's writing, as started by Judah Lavi, quadruples the number of his sources, reaching the number around hundred and fifty various tracts, in manuscripts and printed books. Out of the large treasures Karo chose to offer a short and concise list of Halakhic ruling books included in his code, the very same list with thirty-two renowned Halakhah books, to which he added "in some places sayings of the Zohar." [58]

Having said all this, the obvious question is to what extent was it relevant to the Ottoman surroundings, where the "print revolution" only began to have an impact in the nineteenth century? Ottoman Jews, including those in *Bilad a-Sham* and the inhabitants of Safed, benefitted from the advantages of Jewish printing houses in Europe, as well as those—more limited in capacity—established in the Ottoman heartland.[59] R. Karo composed, *pace* Raz-Krakoztkin, the first modern book to be disseminated from the outset in print, and not in manuscript format.[60] As in many aspects of his work, he was perfectly aware of the changing circumstances and the benefits of the circulation of materials in print. Yet what benefit could he draw from this paradigm of a "universal library" or encyclopedic vision of pan knowledge in the Ottoman civilizational context?[61] As we shall see in the next section, the surplus value lies in the connection of the bibliographical project to court procedures.

58. Kelman, *The Dimension of Halakhic Ruling in Joseph Karo's Beit Yosef,* p. 143; Kahana, 'A Universe Made of Words. The Self-Image of R. Joseph Karo as Composer of Halakhah', pp. 95–96.

59. Joseph Hacker, 'Authors, Readers and Printers of Sixteenth-Century Hebrew Books in the Ottoman Empire', in: Peggy K. Pearlstein (ed.), *The Myron M. Weinstein Memorial Lectures at the Library of Congress,* Washington: Library of Congress, 2012, pp. 17–63.

60. Amnon Raz-Krakoztkin, 'From Safed to Venice: The Shulhan Arukh and the Censor', in: Chanita Goodblatt, Howard Kreisel (eds.), *Tradition, Heterodoxy and Religious Culture: Judaism and Christianity in the Early Modern Period,* Beer Sheva: Ben-Gurion University of the Negev Press, 2007, pp. 91–115.

61. Kahana, 'A Universe Made of Words. The Self-Image of R. Joseph Karo as Composer of Halakhah', the important observation on p. 104: "The utopia of 'one Law', a universal law, is incorporated in the 'bibliographical turn': Maran's concept of meticulous bibliographical assembly, required to legitimize a 'true' and valid Halakhic-ruling project, is the one that constitutes a sharp crisis in his concept of knowledge. R. Joseph Karo does not wish to write A Halakhic book, but 'Thy Halakhic Book', to solve the chaos in favor of 'one Law', a global law, whose validity is not confined to one territory or to a certain Jewish public".

"One Torah, One Law"

The goal of *Beit Yosef* is succinctly stated as to ensure "One Torah, One Law."[62] This is not a mere declaratory statement, lacking any concrete repercussions. The legal instructions were to set the normative infrastructure for religious, community, and individual life. Halakhic law provides the fundamental axis for collective Jewish life. In their important studies on the content of *Beit Yosef* and its internal halakhic mechanisms, Durani and Kelman lucidly presented the parallels between Karo's halakhic reasonings and the procedures of Jewish courts. Durani suggested that the model Karo had in mind in proposing a single halakhic text capable of uniting the entire Jewish people was the "Supreme Court" (*Beit Din HaGadol*) in Jerusalem.[63] His "assumption," as Durani modestly designates it, is backed by several indications he soon mentions: the term "pillars of instruction" (*'Amudei Hora'ah*) borrowed from Maimonides' code of law and referring to the supreme court in Jerusalem, dispatching his books to the entire Jewish collective; choosing three major halakhic arbiters, paralleling the basic quorum required in Jewish courts; modeling his court of law at Safed as the Jerusalemite supreme court or *Sanhedrin*;[64] and finally the attempt to reinitiate rabbinic ordination (*Semikhah*).[65] For her part, Kelman aptly presented the modes and mechanisms of halakhic ruling in *Beit Yosef* reflecting court procedures. These include the importance attached to reaching majority opinions, or the notion that once an halakhic position was accepted, even the opposing minority of sages joins this position.[66]

The disciples attending the major yeshiva of R. Karo in Safed, and others studying under R. Jacob Beirav and later under Beirav's disciples, followed a study curriculum that prepared them to function later as rabbis in local ethnic communities and officiate as judges in courts of law.[67] The study of the Talmud as a religious and sacral act was deeply linked in Sephardi heritage to practical aspects, including the future functioning of yeshiva graduates as judges or halakhic arbiters. Karo's heritage combined all of them. His codes of law provided a textual background for his function as yeshiva head and teacher and for his work in preparing his young disciples for their later independent roles. The code was designed to serve as a legal reference text for court procedures and the regulation of Jewish life, and also for responsa literature. More than once, R. Karo criticized rabbinical authorities when they failed to consult his halakhic code, an omission he regarded as a grave mistake verging on religious sin.[68] All these elements mentioned above—yeshiva studies, textual reference, instructing the public or

---

62. The full phrasing is: "It occurred to me that after all these stages I would offer the Halakhic decision, among the various and contradicting positions, as this is the final aim, to have One Torah and One Law" [*Mishpat Echad* in Hebrew].
63. Durani, *Three Pillars of Guidance in the Halakhic Ruling of R. Joseph Karo*, p. 15
64. See below Ch. 5.
65. See below Ch. 4.
66. Kelman, *The Dimension of Halakhic Ruling in Joseph Karo's Beit Yosef*, p. 93. See also *ibid.*, p. 92.
67. See below Chs. 4, 5, 7.
68. Kelman, *The Dimension of Halakhic Ruling in Joseph Karo's Beit Yosef*, pp. 79–82.

the community, and court procedures—pointed to a single person and text as a focal point radiating its authority to the Jewish Ecumene.

An ambitious project of this size turned Safed into a virtual halakhic center (see further in Chapter Five) that disseminated its innovative massages to the Jewish periphery. The interaction between center and periphery echoed in a restricted Jewish context an important problematics in the management of the Ottoman Empire. The imposing dominance of the center on the periphery could not be ignored in the Ottoman Empire. This included the right to compose the law, issue legal and normative instruction carrying special weight due to their sultanic stamp, and the monitoring of the legal mechanism through the appointment of judges from the center in the capital city.[69] The Jewish reflection of this Ottoman approach can be seen in the positioning of Safed as a spiritual capital city, the search for a person to lead the rabbinical hierarchy, and the important affiliation of R. Karo as "legislator"—by virtue of his composition of the double codes—to legal practice. It showed either in his role as judge and respondent, next to his role in his own schooling system in Safed, and in his function as a loyal patron supporting his disciples when they competed for posts as community rabbis and as judges.

A Jewish Preamble, an Ottoman Vision: Summary

Rabbinical authorities of the past and modern scholars have noted the continuity and interaction between R. Karo's preamble to *Beit Yosef* and previous preambles composed by Maimonides and *HaRosh* to their impressive codes of law, *Mishneh Torah* and *Arba'ah Turim* (respectively). Not only are the literary and religious formulae similar, but the narrative that stands behind their composition, establishing their legitimacy, and the structure of their composition form a single sequence. They all allude to situations of crisis in Torah study and Talmudic erudition, the exile of the Jewish people, the immense extant of current legalistic debates and ceaseless disputations among rabbinic authorities, and legal pluralism due to various Jewish ethnic traditions. No doubt, R. Karo's words owe much not only to these famous preambles, but to the Jewish halakhic heritage in general.

Yet when rabbis task themselves with presenting their opinions in relation to issues that do not relate directly to their professional expertise as juristic figures—as occurs in preambles—they must comply with the "rules of the game" and follow what I called rabbinical rhetoric. Above all, this implies the presentation of all their positions as the mere continuation of past patterns; they anchor their assertions in citations from the sacred canon. Most of the medieval and early modern introductions of important compositions sound as a mélange of citations from the classical literature and convey the sense of nausea and repetitiveness. Yet it is precisely here that the story becomes interesting; This "Culture of Citations" is nothing but a screen, obscuring further assertions of often innovative and concrete nature, quite often diverse from the front rhetoric.

---

69. Burak, *The Second Formation of Islamic Law*, esp. pp. 48, 55.

The fact that R. Karo persisted on printing his preamble to *Beit Yosef* in all four parts of his composition, all printed within a time span of 10 years and in various printing houses, strongly supports the contention that he had specific messages to convey to his future readers, beyond the routine reference to the preambles of previous halakhic codes. Living under Ottoman rule in the Damascus district of *Bilad a-Sham* in the second half of the sixteenth century, he was well acquainted with the mechanisms of Ottoman law and justice. These state laws (*Kanunnameler*), including that given to the population of Damascus, were publicized and presented to the subjects of the empire through several channels, including through their important preambles. Snjezana Buzov and others have discussed the content and role these texts played in disseminating the messianic visions of the period. They were later replaced by more institutional visions of imperial rule and of justice and security for all subjects abiding by the Ottoman rules. The preambles presented law and legality as a pillar in the Sultan's rule and in the efficient management of the empire by professional administrators and jurists. Their grand vision, sometimes presented in florid literary style, made the preambles more innovative than the laws they preceded.

In this last sense, Karo's introduction integrates well with its Ottoman parallels. His opening words are also more innovative than the juridical content of *Beit Yosef*. His preamble ostensibly reiterates the classical narratives in the Jewish rabbinical repertory of crisis, the need to present a coherent legal corpus in response, references to previous halakhic compositions, and legitimizing codification. Yet his arguments do not seem to stand the test of reality. The sixteenth century was not a period of crisis for Talmud and Torah studies; it actually witnessed an almost unprecedented renaissance in all fields of Jewish tradition; Karo's reliance on three "Pillars of Scholarship" (*'Amudei Hora'ah*) is not a dominant criterion in his halakhic ruling; his bibliographical list does not reflect his actual use of sources in the text—many works are used but remain unmentioned, while *HaRashbah* is mentioned as just another rabbinical authority, though its presence in *Beit Yosef* is far more dominant; the long and short versions of these codes of law do not provide concise and clear-cut legal rulings, but offer an impressive repertory of past debates; the legal assertions are not always consistent (a fact marked already by his contemporaries); the universality of the halakhic assertions often gives way to local traditions, considered legitimate when they are consistent with rabbinical traditions.

It would be mistaken to adhere to a modernistic perspective and present his claims as false or insincere. The preambles do not claim to provide a legalistic characterization of the succeeding items but rather to present a manifesto regarding the role of law under new circumstances and the urgent need to adapt and reform. References to a crisis situation are a key instrument in the rabbinical arsenal as a rhetorical tool to justify the call for innovation. What is indeed impressively innovative in this respect is that a figure of a public position and scholarly stature such as R. Karo declares law to be the foundation of Jewish identity. It is not shared heritage, family or community sense of sanctity, a common vision of the messianic future, or liturgical patterns that form the backbone of Jewish tradition, Karo implies, but legality in its strictest sense, as defined in *Beit Yosef* and *Shulchan 'Arukh*. This marks a watershed moment in Jewish religious history, shifting the multifocal perspectives toward a single, central point. The halakhic literature and legalistic tradition were charged with the task of providing concrete lines of demarcation between "us" and "them," between inclusion and exclusion.

The circle within the Jewish collective responsible for bearing this task is obviously the rabbis and Talmudic scholars. It is no coincidence that the two previous codes of law were independent compositions, whereas Karo's project is presented as a commentary on *Arba'ah Turim* by Jacob ben HaRosh. Rabbinical juridical literature is thus presented as the leading thread in ongoing Jewish tradition, ensuring its future continuation. This book is not chosen as the closest approximation to halakhic truth, but for an institutional reason: "And so I based it [*Beit Yosef*] on the 'Four Columns' (*Arba'ah Turim*) composed by R. *Yaacov ben HaRosh*, as it includes most of the halakhic arbiters' opinions." Both these books would shape a chain of transmission and represent rabbinical consensus within internal debates ("most of the Halakhic arbiters' opinions"). Throughout his introduction, Karo's tone is decisive, silencing other options in Jewish rabbinical traditions.[70]

The role of the rabbinical milieu as a professional guild and its new ethos will be discussed in later chapters.[71] This certainly reflected the international, or at least Mediterranean, character of the Sephardi rabbinical network, whose members exchanged letters and books or turned to distant colleagues for juridical comments in scandals or affairs that transcended local limits. The major yeshivas along the eastern Mediterranean Basin shared a common methodology of study (*Iyyun*) that had evolved prior to the expulsion in 1492, and was later disseminated across the major schools of the Ottoman Empire, including Safed. This methodology encouraged advanced students to propose their reading of especially challenging discussions in the Talmud to other scholars affiliated to the network. As in the Ottoman context, it contributed to an increasing sense of a "Republic of Scholars" with its own cultural, esthetic, and professional tastes.[72]

The methodological choice of an almost mechanistic procedure for halakhic ruling sets the law as a *sui generis* domain, with its independent course and claim for sovereignty. At the same time, it accentuated the role of dominant figures in the Jewish legalistic tradition, in a surprisingly similar mode to the description of Muslim *Madhdhhab*s by later generations; later, under Ottoman rule, this developed into the perception of the Grand Mufti, or Şeyḫülislâm, as the dominant head of all the juridical institutions. In the Jewish instance, this approach led to a search for authority around the leading

---

70. Chechik, *The Struggle over Ashkenazi Legacy in Poland*, p. 120, regarding the position of the Ashkenazi R. Solomon Luria and the original Ashkenazi tradition, which considered the Talmud alone as the authoritative source.

71. See especially Chs. 4, 7.

72. Gülru Necipoğlu, 'A Kanun for the State, a Canon for the Arts: The Classical Synthesis in Ottoman Art and Architecture during the Age of Süleyman', in: Gilles Veinstein (ed.), *Soliman le Magnifique et son temps*, Paris: Actes du Colloque de Paris, Galeries Nationales du Grand Palais, 1992, pp. 195–215. On the sense of distinctiveness of Ottoman jurists in regard to other professions, see Burak, *The Second Formation of Islamic Law*, esp. Ch 2 – 'Genealogies and Boundaries: Situating the Imperial Learned Hierarchy within the Hanafi Jurisprudential Tradition'.

figures of each generation. Commenting from faraway Poland, R. Moses Isserles ironically criticized R. Karo for his fascination with "big names." Karo was certainly not alone in this attitude: contemporary Sephardi historiography focused on the "great names" of rabbis along the long chain of transmission, while almost completely ignoring other aspects of Jewish life.[73]

R. Karo's preamble to *Beit Yosef* was not devoid of internal inconsistencies within the text, let alone contradictions with his other writings. These begin with his indecisiveness regarding the general law applicable in the Jewish Ecumene, followed by his acknowledgment that centuries-old traditions of various localities were too deeply entrenched to be displaced. Throughout his life, he was perfectly aware of his very limited capacity to enforce his vision, even in his close vicinity in Safed. Again, this mirrored the gap between the intention of the center in Istanbul to impose the Ottoman way and its recognition of the power and traditions of local elites. The conclusive aim of R. Karo's legal Manifesto was "One Nation, One Law," highlighting the urgent need for the legal unification of the entire Jewish collective. The word he used in the Hebrew original was *Torah*, conveying the double sense of law/*nomos* as well as religious tradition. As in the Ottoman context, the task of Jewish law was to define the religious community as a political unit. Buzov cogently noted the important role of preambles in the Ottoman codes of law as an instrument for political propaganda and a tool for introducing the new Turkish rule over vast Arab territories. A no less important function was the role of the preambles in marking the passage from legal pluralism to unity following the encounter between various legal traditions. The ruling center in Istanbul played a dominant role in producing law and enforcing it in court. These messages were concretized by the figure of the person heading a centralistic system, and oftentimes directly involved in the compositions of various *Kanunameler*, radiating the dominance of one legal tradition. Law served as one of the main vehicles for legitimizing political control. All these elements were reflected well in the various preambles. R. Karo's preamble joins those Kanunames and preambles published in the same century across the Ottoman Empire. Maoz Kahana noted the double levels of his work; next to the traditional aspect as rabbi and Talmudic scholar, addressing his colleagues and a real audience, another aspect of utopian vision is present:

> Maran writes in two distinct genres to serve two different modes of Halakhah ruling. In the first genre (Responsa) he faces his real audience, concurring with local tradition of Halakhah ruling, while in the second canonical one (*Beit Yosef* and *Shulchan 'Arukh*) he intends to promote a futuristic and different one, of unifying and utopian character.[74]

This utopia is lucidly presented in his double preambles.

---

73. Next to this theme it included stories of major political and community events.
74. Kahana, 'A Universe Made of Words. The Self-Image of R. Joseph Karo as Composer of Halakhah', p. 88.

Chapter Three

"MARAN" [OUR MASTER] JOSEPH KARO

By the seventeenth century, the fame of R. Joseph Karo was already well-established. When people referred to his fundamental double codes of law, and to his responsa, they did not refer to him in the customary manner in the rabbinical milieu, as Rabbi or *Chakham* (literally "sage," a common title for rabbis in the Sephardi tradition). Karo bore the title *Maran* ("our Master" in Aramaic), sometimes without even adding his surname "Karo."

In the early modern world, and in the geographical location where R. Karo lived, on the seam between Catholic Europe, the Ottoman Empire, and the Jewish Mediterranean Diaspora, titles mattered a lot. They distinguished their bearer from other members of his collective (such as a professional guild); they endowed a specific position within a hierarchy; they marked the boundaries between various ethnic and religious collectivities; and they delineated a professional identity. They shaped self-perceptions and inspired honor and respect from others. This was equally true regarding the Islamic and Catholic majority societies and the Jewish minority living among them. Jewish community leaders bore certain titles and insisted on a suitable response from others. The same was true in relation to the rabbinical milieu in regard to honorary and professional titles, continuing a centuries-long tradition.[1] However, "Maran" was a unique title of Joseph Karo, related to no other rabbinical, Talmudic, or post-Talmudic persona. The circumstances leading to its use and its semantic and cultural affiliations are the main themes of this chapter.

Jewish Titles

As the rabbinical tradition of learning was progressively institutionalized in schools (the *Yeshiva* or *Beit Midrash*) during late antiquity in the Holy Land, and further east in Babylonia under Sassanian and later Islamic rule, Jewish tradition witnessed an impressive growth of various titles. These included: *Rav* (rabbi), *Chakham* (sage, the default term for a rabbi in Sephardi tradition), *Yachid Mumcheh* (legal expert), *Mufla shel Beit-Din* (expert judge), *Rabban* or *Rabbenu* (our Master/Rabbi), *Qatzin* (prominent leader), *Dayan* (judge), *Mar* (Master in Aramaic), *Mari* (my Master), *Qadosh* (saintly), *Chasid* (pious), *Navi* (prophet), *Morenu HaRav* (the Rabbi our Master) alongside *Morenu HaRav HaGadol* (the great Rabbi our Master), *Marana veRabana* (our Master and Rabbi),

---

1. Yochanan Breuer, "Rabbi is Greater than Rav, Rabban is Greater than Rabbi, The Bare Name is Greater than Rabban" [Hebrew], *Tarbiz* 66, no. 1(1997), pp. 41–59.

Mofet HaDor (exemplum of his generation), *Gaon* or *HaGaon* (the extraordinary one),[2] *Mara deAtra* (Master of Territory),[3] *Gedol HaDor* (the major in his generation), *HaMaor HaGadol* (the great luminary), *Gaon Castiliya* (the senior Rabbi in Castile), *Nagid* (a Jewish leader in Muslim lands), *Nasi* (head or Leader), *Gevir* (authoritative person), and *Manhig* (leader, in general).

A quick glance at this list, which is far from exhaustive, reveals several subcategories: rabbinical versus political titles; professional versus nonprofessional; Hebrew versus Aramaic titles; and finally, titles confined to certain Diasporas versus general Jewish titles. Some of them were used only when fulfilling a temporary role (such as judge), while others attached to personal names and created a new nominal unit, or even replaced the personal name; important rabbis would never be called by their name, only by their attached honorary title. Some titles appertain solely to pietistic persons, or later to those affiliated with Jewish mysticism (Kabbalah).

No less significant in the variety and subcategories of this semantic titular tradition is its role in molding and preserving hierarchy within the Jewish scholastic milieu. In a letter dispatched by sages in Kairouan (in modern Tunisia) to the famous R. Sherira Gaon (died c. 987), the community members raised a query regarding the use of different titles of Talmudic sages. His answer, reflecting the common position along medieval sages, was that such titles construct a hierarchy among the sages: Rabbi is "greater" than *Rav*, *Rabban* is greater than Rabbi. Yet towering above them all is a person bearing no title at all and referred to by his bare name, as he is universally known and respected (*Gadol miRabban Shemo*, literally: his [bare] name is greater than the title *Rabban*).[4] The personal prestige of R. Sherira and the prominent position of Babylonian *Gaonim* in early Islam legitimized and encouraged the use of hierarchical titles in various Jewish Diasporas. The persons heading the hierarchy were marked by a distinct semantic term. As leaders of the Jewish minority, they commonly functioned under political constraints either within Islam or Catholicism and were required to adapt to contemporary political rulers in order to expand their direct control over local communities. In medieval Spain and France, the kings nominated supra-local rabbis to supervise the functioning of the limited Jewish legal autonomy and to represent the Jewish minority as a political and financial entity.[5] In Spain, such an official carried the title of "Court Rabbi" (*Rab de la corte*). External circumstances beyond the

---

2. *Gaon* was the typical title of Babylonian Sages during the Gaonic period (roughly sixth to tenth centuries), later spreading to other Jewish Diasporas during the Middle Ages. See Robert Brody, *The Geonim of Babylonia and the Shaping of Medieval Jewish Culture*, New Haven, CT and London: Yale U.P., 2013.

3. "'Master of Territory" in the sense of holding a juridical authority over specific area. See the discussion on Chapter Four.

4. Breuer, "Rabbi is Greater than Rav," pp. 41–42.

5. Yom-Tov Assis and Mark Meyerson, "The Iberian Peninsula," in: Robert Chazan (ed.), *The Cambridge History of Judaism*, Vol. VI: "The Middle Ages: The Christian World," Cambridge: Cambridge U.P., 2018, pp. 129–184; Crespo Álvarez, Macarena, "El cargo de Rab Mayor de la corte durante el reinado de Juan II: el camino hacia la centralización," *El Olivo; documentación y estudios para el diálogo entre judíos y cristianos* 61–62 (2005), pp. 51–64.

control of Jewish communities were only one factor in encouraging the hierarchy of Jewish rabbinical titles. The prestigious medieval Talmudic tradition in Ashkenaz and France espoused the distinction between "First Generations" and "Last Generations" scholars among the Talmudic chain of transmission (*Rishonim* and *Acharonim*, respectively), as value-laden titles. In structuring their own heritage, the Ashkenazi scholars inadvertently echoed the parallel European scholastic distinction between *Antiqui* and *Moderni*.[6] The Sephardi Talmudic study evolving in their particular *Beit Midrash* or *Midrash* (parallel to the Ashkenazi *Yeshiva*) was structured as a three-level course: the beginner students or *Talmidim*; above them the advanced scholars *Chaverim*; all headed by the great school master—the *Rav*.[7] As such, a hierarchy endorsed competition and antagonism among aspirants for the top, it is no wonder that it enticed the young to compete for professional and honorary titles, and even to acquire them by money, as a kind of symbolic asset.[8] Structuring the internal rabbinical milieu in graded and hierarchical patterns suited the early fifteenth century. It responded to a progressive enfeeblement of local traditions in favor of supra-local organization, hence the need to accentuate and publicize differences. The centuries-old traditions, which wavered during the Middle Ages between locality and communal autonomy, on the one hand, and the formation of large territorial and cultural units, on the other, tipped in favor of the last one. The rabbinical guild reflected this change toward unification and homogeneity by forming internal gradations and by a search for dominant and imposing figures.[9] Dominant figures, in their turn, demanded impressive and (at times) new titles.[10]

Appearance and Sense of the Title Maran

Taking into consideration the variety and constantly evolving repertory of titles in Jewish culture since late antiquity, the title *Maran* attached to R. Joseph Karo is all the

---

6. Israel Yuval, 'Rishonim and Aharonim, Antiqui et Moderni (Periodization and Self-Awareness in Ashkenaz)' [Hebrew], *Zion* 57, no. 4 (1992), pp. 369–394. For a general medieval setting of these concepts, see Albert Zimmermann and Gudrun Vuillemin-Diem, *Antiqui und Moderni Traditionsbewusstsein und Fortschrittsbewusstsein im späten Mittelalter*, Berlin and New York: Walter de Gruyter, 1974.

7. Haim Bentov, 'Methods of Study of Talmud in the Yeshivot of Salonica and Turkey after the Expulsion from Spain' [Hebrew], *Sefunot: Studies and Sources on the History of the Jewish Communities in the East* 13 (1971–1978), pp. 5–102, esp. p. 40.

8. Mordechai Breuer, "The Ashkenazi Semichah" [Hebrew], *Zion* 33, no. 1–2 (1968), pp. 15–46, esp. pp. 24–25.

9. On the "quest for center," see Elisheva Carlebach, *The Pursuit of Heresy: Rabbi Moses Hagiz and the Sabbatian Controversies*, New York: Columbia U.P., 1990, passim. On the Ashkenzi context, see Joseph Davis, 'The Reception of the Shulchan 'Arukh and the Formation of Ashkenazic Jewish Identity', *AJS Review* 26, no. 2 (2002), pp. 251–276. On the organization patterns of Sephardi communities in the Ottoman Empire, and their internal organization in Safed, see Introductory Chapter, and Ch. Four.

10. See for instance the description of Maimonides in David Conforti (1618–1690), *Koreh Ha-Dorot*, Piotrikow 1895, p. 20.

more conspicuous. It was not used in connection to other rabbis or Talmudic scholars beforehand or in later centuries. This situation changed only in the late twentieth century, when scholarly titles within Orthodox circles were popularized and their value lowered. Some important figures—certainly not of the same stature and erudition as R. Karo—are now hailed by their admirers as *Maran*.

Why *Maran* and no other title? Why was Rabbi Karo the first and (for centuries) the only one to carry this title? The rabbinical search for an explanation did not rely on historical or philological considerations, but attempted to provide reasons that integrate with rabbinical exegesis and rhetorical puns. The early testimony was provided by the great bibliophile and scholar R. Hayim Yosef David Azulai (known by the acronym *HaChidah*; 1724–1806):

> And now I would state the truth, as I heard it from the mouth of sacred rabbis, as they heard it from the mouth of the great rabbi, exceptional in his generation, Rabbi H. [Hayim—R.W.] Abulafia of blessed memory, [who in his turn] received it from the glorious ones of the generation. They consented that whatever halakhic ruling Maran would state, it is as if ruled by two hundred rabbis. Those are the statements of him, of blessed memory [*ki kol asher ya'aseh Pesaq Maran 'avid ke-maatan rabbanan. Elu devarav*].[11]

During his itinerant years around the Mediterranean Basin, inspecting books and manuscripts, especially rare ones, R. Azulai devoted much of his time to documenting meticulously what he found of interest. His writings provide rich and reliable references about contemporary and previous rabbinical traditions, some of which have since been lost. This particular testimony relies on the writings of R. Hayim Abulafia (the First),[12] who in turn testifies that former scholars held this tradition. His testimony seems highly reliable and provides no reasons for suspicion. Of more significance is his suggestion that R. Karo[13] was sustained by two hundred rabbis around the Mediterranean Basin in regard to all his major halakhic positions. In concomitance with this early tradition, the unprecedented title Maran acquired a precise etymology: as an acronym, it supposedly stood for the expression "provided with *Semikhah*[14] by two hundred Rabbis" (*Ma'atayim Rabbanim Nismakh*). This popular etymology, verging on the folkloristic,

---

11. The citation appears in HaChidah, *Birkei Yosef*, Livorno 1774, vol. II, Section – "Choshen Mishpat," §29, pp. 55b–56a. On rabbi Hayim Yosef David Azulai see Yaakob Dweck, "A Jew from the East meets books from the West," in: Richard I. Cohen, Natalie B. Dohrmann, Adam Shear, and Elchanan Reiner (eds.), *Jewish Culture in Early Modern Europe; Essays in Honor of David B. Ruderman*, Pittsburgh [Pa] and Cincinnati [Oh]: University of Pittsburgh Press and HUC Press, 2014, pp. 239–249.
12. HaChidah refers to Hayim Abulafia the first (d. 1670), rather to his homonymous grandson (1660–1744), since the tradition about Maran is ancient.
13. R. Karo is current in contemporary Hebrew use, and henceforward I shall refer to him thus.
14. *Semichah* is a formal rabbinic permit to teach and adjudicate, very similar to the Islamic *Ijaza*. See Chapter 4 dedicated entirely to this issue.

became dominant from the seventeenth century and aroused no reservations by rabbinical or even modern scholars.[15]

The title Maran became the customary hallmark of R. Joseph Karo, as it related to several semantic domains. The concomitant presence of the title *Rav*/Rabbi (in Hebrew) or *Mar* (its Aramaic parallel) in the rabbinical milieu may provide another setting for the name, as may the use of the term *Marana* ("Our Master" in Syriac Aramaic) among Christians in the eastern Mediterranean. Yet none of these semantic contexts can offer a convincing explanation to a seemingly simple question: What necessitated the invention of a new title, when the Jewish titular repertory, enriched along the centuries, provided so many options? The key to the enigma lay not in the linguistic domain but in historical circumstances. The new title implied a distinct echelon of superiority on the part of its bearer, unique and hence requiring a titular neologism. It is a clever innovation, since it plays between the new and the old. It corresponded to the well-known semantic heritage of the rabbinical milieu, through the core term *Mar*, yet added a twist which made it completely new and unprecedented.

Like some other Semitic languages, Hebrew lacks a morphological structure for comparative and superlative adjectives. In order to create such forms, linguistic constructions of doubling are employed, such as *Song of Songs*—in order to convey the sense of special song or poetry or *God of Gods* (the double form *Melekh Ha-Melakhim* or even the triple *Melekh Malkhei Ha-Melakhim*) to underscore the utter supremacy of God.[16] There are additional linguistic channels to construct distinctness and superiority. One such is conferring a certain title upon a very limited number of persons, such as "the Saint" (*Ha-Qadosh*)—bestowed on Rabbi Yehudah *Ha-Nasi* (*Rabbenu Ha-Qadosh*), R. Isaac Luria (*HaAri Ha-Qadosh*, "the Sacred Lion"), and R. Isaiah HaLevi Horowitz (known under the title of his famous book as *Ha-Shelach Ha-Qadosh*). Again, this title *Qadosh* suffered value diminution following the eastern European Hassidic movement in the eighteenth century.

In the case of R. Karo, the title *Maran* overpowered its bearer's first name and surname. During the seventeenth century, it became sufficient to mention simply the title *Maran* when referring to Karo's works or expressing admiration for his life projects. The title became the person, and the person was absorbed in and by the title. Yet *Maran* contains another element: collective possession. He is OUR Master (literally: our *Mar*/ Master), without specifying who is this collective "we." This anonymity relates to a collectivity in the widest sense, the Jewish Ecumene. In other words, the title is also unique in the way it glorifies and designates Karo as the master or rabbinical authority of the entire Jewish Diaspora.

---

15. Even a fine modern scholar as Meir Benayahu reiterated this popular etymology without casting any doubt. See Meir Benayahu, "The Renovation of Rabbinic Semichah in Safed" [Hebrew], in: S.W. Baron, B. Dinur, S. Ettinger, I. Halpern (eds.), *Yitzhak F. Baer Jubilee Volume. On the Occasion of his Seventieth Birthday*, Jerusalem: The Historical Society of Israel, 1960, pp. 248–269. Contemporary Jewish Orthodox books and internet sites continue to adhere to this popular etymology as a given fact.

16. I wish to thank Nathan Wasserman for drawing my attention to this semantic fact.

Once again, this usage employs a dialectical play between old and new: borrowing from the semantic heritage of glorification kept for special persons (*Mar* of *Rav*), while concurrently generating a new titular turn. Basing on the wide-scale Database of the *Responsa Project* of Bar-Ilan University, Israel, it emerges that the use of the term *Maran* was confined to the Sephardi communities along the eastern Mediterranean Basin under the Ottomans, and only later by extension to certain Sephardi centers in northern Europe, such as Amsterdam. The title *Maran* essentially echoed a Sephardi titular tradition. Shortly before the 1492 general expulsion of the Jews from Spain, the leading Talmudic scholar R. Isaac Aboab (the Second), "was named merely 'The Rabbi' (*HaRav*) in all Spain, a name that only the famous R. Moses ben Nachman [Nachmanides] had borne in the past."[17] R. Aboab was the master of R. Yaakov Beirav, the dominant rabbi in Safed during R. Karo's time, whose imprint on the life and works on Karo is undeniable.[18] The master of R. Aboab was R. Isaac Canpanton, considered the founder of the particular Sephardi methodology of Talmudic studies of '*Iyyun*, "was named [alternatively: bore the title of] 'the Major Scholar in Entire Castile' [*Gaon Castiliya*]," again a title not accompanied by any personal name.[19] The Sephardi tradition thus constructed a chain of four generations—R. Canpanton, R. Aboab, R. Beirav, and R. Karo—all bearing glorifying superlative-like titles that largely replaced their individual names and surnames. All these dominant figures adhered to the characteristic Talmudic methodology of the Spanish Diaspora around the Mediterranean, and all related to one another through paradigms of master–disciple or master–colleague.

There was another source of inspiration for the title *Maran*. In a world on the move, as reflected in the personal fate of R. Karo, Sephardi and Ashkenazi scholars became acquainted with new traditions and were exposed to the rabbinical titles of foreign origins. Glorifying titles were practiced in other Jewish contexts. The contemporaneous Polish R. Moses Isserles (1530–1572), who added his Ashkenazi, Eastern European glosses to the *Shulchan 'Arukh*, was hallowed by his admirers as the "Leader of His Generation" (*Gedol Ha-Dor*) and "the Great Luminary" (*Ha-Maor Ha-Gadol*).[20] In previous generations, the title "Our Master/Teacher" (*Morenu*) had become common in Ashkenazi medieval communities as a designation for the most conspicuous Talmudic scholars; it generally preceded the person's name.[21]

17. Yoel Marciano, *Sages of Spain in the Eye of the Storm - Jewish Scholars of Late Medieval Spain* [Hebrew], Jerusalem: Bialik Institute, 2019, p. 108.
18. See the discussion on Chapter 4.
19. Conforti, *Koreh HaDorot*, p. 25a.
20. Elchanan Reiner, "Rabbi Ya'akov Pollack of Cracow: First and Foremost among Cracow's Scholars" [Hebrew], in: Idem. (ed.), *Kroke – Kazimierz – Cracow. Studies in the History of Cracow Jewry*, Tel-Aviv: Publications of the Diaspora Research Institute – Tel-Aviv University, 2001, pp. 43–68, esp. pp. 45, 66–67.
21. Breuer, "The Ashkenazi Semichah," p. 25.

Honorific Titles in Ottoman and Arabic Islam

Honorific titles in Islam are a rich and diverse domain that still awaits a detailed study. The Jewish communities of the Babylonian Diaspora under the *Geonim* and those across the Mediterranean Basin, and as far west as the leading Sephardi communities, were all deeply immersed in the Islamicate tradition. The Muslim titulature was part of this contact and it was either adopted by local Jews or imposed by local Muslim rulers. A short sample of Jewish-Arabic titles: Maimonides was addressed as *Mufti* by those seeking his Responsa;[22] Important persons in leadership positions were called *Sheik El-Yahud* and *Ra'is El-Yahud* in Arabic, and later *Çelebi* in Turkish.[23] It infiltrated even the religious domain, when the renowned liturgist Israel Najara (1555–1625) used a Turkish political title *Beğler beği* (ruler of rulers) to refer to God as dominating this world.[24]

The need to consolidate Islam within immense geographical territories and to establish permanent institutions in the political, administrative, religious, and cultural domains was reflected in the expansive use of titles, especially ones with a hierarchic character. Hierarchy served first and foremost to mark and differentiate the leading person, or the *primus inter pares*, standing at the head. This pattern expanded from the original political context to other significant domains, such as the Ottoman bureaucracy *Rais el-Kuttab*.[25] In the important domain of translation, forming a bridge between Ottoman officials or merchants and European diplomats and businessmen, the *Baş Tarcuman* served as head of the *dragomans*.[26] Even an outstanding poet was lauded as the "Sultan of the Poets."[27] Several important titles resonated deeply with Islamic history, such as *Khalifa* (or *Khalifat Allah*), *Mahdi, Imam, Mujaddid, Amir,* and *Sultan.*[28] Alongside these designations, the doubling structure mentioned above became

22. Gideon Libson, "Maimonides Halakhic Writings in their Muslim Background" [Hebrew], in: Aviezer Ravitzky (ed.), *Maimonides. Conservatism, Originality, Revolution*, Vol I – "History and Halakhah," Jerusalem: The Zalman Shazar Center for Jewish History, 2009, pp. 247–294, esp. p. 273 n. 83.

23. Martin Jacobs, "An Ex-Sabbatean's Remorse? Sambari's Polemics against Islam," *JQR* 97, 3(2007), pp. 347–378, esp. 350; Jacob Barnai, "The Status of the 'General Rabbinate" in Jerusalem in the Ottoman Period' [Hebrew], *Cathedra: For the History of Eretz Israel and Its Yishuv* 13(1979), pp. 47–69, esp. 49; Joseph R. Hacker, "The Rise of Ottoman Jewry," in: Jonathan Karp and Adam Sutcliffe (eds.), *The Cambridge History of Judaism*, Vol VII – "The Early Modern World, 1500–1815," Cambridge: Cambridge U.P., 2017, pp. 77–112, esp. 97.

24. Najara is rebuked by another important liturgist, due exactly to his use of this poetical metaphor, considered as degradation of God and for not placing him in a distinct position. See Yosef Yahalom, "Hebrew Mystical Poetry and Its Turkish Background" [Hebrew], *Tarbiz* 60 (1991), pp. 625–648, esp. 639–640.

25. Tijana Krstić, "Of Translation and Empire: Sixteenth-Century Ottoman Imperial Interpreters as Renaissance Go-betweens," in: Christine Woodhead (ed.), *The Ottoman World*, London and New York: Routledge, 2012, pp. 130–142.

26. See the previous note.

27. Walter G. Andrews, Mehmet Kapaklı, *The Age of Beloveds: Love and the Beloved in Early-Modern Ottoman and European Culture and Society*, Durham: Duke U.P., 2005, p. 340.

28. Patricia Crone, *God's Caliph: Religious Authority in the First Centuries of Islam*, Cambridge: Cambridge U.P., 1986; Wael Hallaq, "Was the Gate of Ijtihad Closed?" *International Journal*

increasingly prevalent in titles in various domains: *Shaykh el-Shuyukh* (the Head/Leader of All Leaders); the political-military position of *Amir el-Umara* carried by the Ottoman governor in sixteenth-century Aleppo;[29] *Qadi el-Qudat* (Judge of Judges) in the legal domain;[30] *Kahlifat el-Khulafa* in Safavid Iranian;[31] and in the Sufi context, the *Qutb el-Aqtab* (Pole of Poles), who headed the hierarchy of all the living saints and "Friends of God" (*Awliya*) in Islam.[32] The consolidation of political power and of religious canons— both Hadith and Law (*Shari'a* or *Fiqh*)—during the long Abbasside period witnessed the dissemination of the important title *Shaykh el-Islam*.[33] This title, implying prestige and domination, was current in both Sunni and Shi'ite traditions under Timurid rulers from the end of the fifteenth century, referring to judges who both served as chiefs of legal colleges and issued fatwas.[34] The polysemic Arabic word *shaykh* could refer to an old man, a person of authority, or the head of some collective or institution. The title *Shaykh el-Islam* glorified a person and marked him as unique in his religious and professional domain.

In the Ottoman context, the *Shaykh el-Islam* (Turkified as *Şeyhülislâm*) acquired unprecedented significance. He exercised broad jurisdiction as the state-appointed overseer of the legal system. Consulting with the Sultan and his chief *vezir*, he had the authority to appoint jurists to various positions within the evolving hierarchy. According to the Ottoman understanding of this office, only the mufti who holds official state

---

of Middle East Studies 16,1(March, 1984), pp. 3–41; Mercedes García-Arenal, *Messianism and Puritanical Reform. Mahdis of the Muslim West*, Brill: Leiden & Boston, 2006.

29. Timothy J. Fitzgerald, "Rituals of Possession, Methods of Control, and the Monopoly of Violence: The Ottoman Conquest of Aleppo in Comparative Perspective," in: Stephan Conermann & Gül Şen (eds.), *The Mamluk-Ottoman Transition. Continuity and Change in Egypt and Bilād al-Shām in the Sixteenth Century*, Bonn: Bonn U.P., 2017, pp. 249–273, esp. p. 258.

30. Yosef Rapoport, "Royal Justice and Religious Law: *Siyāsah* and Shari'ah under the Mamluks," *Mamluk Studies Review*, 16 (2012), pp. 71–102.

31. Willem Floor, "The Khlifeh al-kholafa of the Safavid Sufi Order," *Zeitschrift der Deutschen Morgenländischen Gesellschaft* 153, no. 1 (2003), pp. 51–86; Roger M. Savory, "The Office of Khalîfat al Khulafâ under the Safawid," *Journal of American Oriental Society* 85, no. 4 (1965), pp. 497–502.

32. See for instance, Derin Terzigolu, "Sunna-minded Sufi Preacher in Service of the Ottoman State: The NAṢĪḤATNĀME of Hasan Addressed to Murad IV," *Archivum Ottomanicum* 27 (2010), pp. 241–312, esp. p. 244, on the invisible hierarchy of saints, presided by the Pole (ḳuṭb) or Pole of Poles (ḳuṭbü'l-akṭāb) as the highest spiritual authority in the world, and was also believed to be the ultimate sovereign over worldly affairs.

33. , See Guy Burak, *The Second Formation of Islamic Law. The Hanafi School the Early Modern Ottoman Empire*, Cambridge: Cambridge U.P., 2015, p. 188, on this title in Mameluke period, prior to the Ottoman conquest of the Arab lands, occasionally attached to jurists, next to fairly wide range of honorific titles that organized an informal scholarly hierarchy.

34. Rula Jurdi Abisaab, *Converting Persia. Religion and Power in the Safavid Empire*, London and New York: I. B. Tauris, 2004, esp. pp. 8, 10, 23, 28, 32. The titles 'Imam' and 'Mujtahid' are mentioned in *ibid.*, pp. 17–18. The head Vizier of 'Abbas II carried the title 'Sultan el-'Ulama', see Moojan Momen, *An Introduction to Shi'i Islam. The History and Doctrines of Twelver Shi'ism*, New Haven and London: Yale U.P., 1985, p. 113. On the title and role of 'Shaykh al-Islām' in Shi'i context, see *ibid.*, p. 112.

appointment has the right to issue enforceable legal rulings within the imperial legal system. In his role as the chief imperial jurisconsult, the *Şeyhülislâm* carried a "canonizing authority," providing instructions on how to apply and interpret certain passages and texts.[35] The *Şeyhülislâm* functioned as the de facto head of the Hanafi School of law, defining its positions. His ruling carried much weight on court proceedings in specific cases due to his official position. This aspect was shown in signing imperial edicts, and the dispatching of *Fetva* (responses to legal queries) to all corners of the Empire.

An equivalent set of terminologies designating prominence and superiority within the hierarchy in Ottoman civilization was deeply related to its political ethos. It derived from a Semitic root r.b.b that carries association of authority in Arabic, Aramaic, and Hebrew. In the Ottoman case, its cultural roots were connected to much broader horizons, stretching as far as the Persian culture. This was noted by Hüseyin Yılmaz in his important work on the mystical dimensions of Ottoman political ethos. Due to the importance of his observations for understanding the semantic and cultural network of contemporary titles, I shall quote him at length:

> Rulers, who are endowed with proper qualities and manifest God's attribute as *Rabb*, for being part of God's *rubūbiyya*, are capable of ruling over His creation and enact laws that are based on divine wisdom. Although the term *rubūbiyya* does not appear in the Qur'an or hadith, the word Rabb, derived from the same root, is among the most commonly mentioned names of God in both sources. Rubūbiyya, the act of being a Rabb, had been widely used in mystical theology. Different from other designations referring to God's rulership, such as Malik, which implies ownership and sovereignty, Rabb implies a relational *rulership* between the servant and the master. A sixteenth-century lexicographer, Ahteri (d. 1579), defined *Rabb* as possessor (*mālik*), owner (*sāhib*), and master (*seyyid*), and provided its root meaning as to feed (beslemek), to complete (tamām itmek), to increase (ziyāde eylemek), and to accumulate (cem eylemek). This lexicographic definition of the term alone clearly indicates that Rabb referred to a specific concept of rulership rather than a mere authority, pointing to the status of the ruler and the functions of rulership. Bidlisi's contemporary, Şeyh Mekki, defined Rabb as owner (*sāhib*) and possessor (*mālik*) with the implications of subjugation (tahakkum) and authority (saltanat). With this corollary, while referring to the unity of sovereignty, Bidlisi also pointed to a moral high ground for political authority. With *rubūbiyya*, Bidlisi argued that caring for subjects and providing guidance are indispensable for *good rulership*. In tandem with his definition, Ahteri also provided an illustration for one of the derivatives of Rabb in full agreement with Bidlisi's usage of the term: "In current usage," Ahteri pointed out, "*rabbānī* refers to a knower of God (*'ārif bi-Allāh*) who turns his knowledge into practice (*'ilmiyle 'āmil*)." Bidlisi called these scholars with such traits as godly scholars (*'ulemā'-i rabbānī*). When applied to government, one of the favorite constructs Bidlisi used to depict ideal political authority was *khilāfat-i rabbānī*, by which he stated that rulership had to be in full accordance with divine ordains. He defined the true rulership, which he commonly dubbed as *khilāfat-i rahmānī*, as endowing oneself with godly traits (*avṣāf-i rabbānī*). In framing worldly rulership in comparison to that of God's, Bidlisi

---

35. Burak, *The Second Formation of Islamic Law*, pp. 41, 48, 64, 79, 88, 134, 137, 163, 167, 170, 172, 180, 190, 210, 212.

further stated that what made *divine government* (*rubūbiyyat*) manifest was God's combination of two attributes: knowledge ('*ilm*) and prowess (*qudrat*). For him, these two were the most conspicuous attributes for the perfection of *rulership* on Earth. He then stated that true rulership (*khilāfat-i rahmānī*) was an exemplar (*numūdār*) of God's authority (*iqtidār-i subhānī*) on Earth. But true rulership, called the vicegerency of the Truth (*khilāfat-i Ḥaq*), could only take place (*haqq-i khilāfat*) when the above attributes became manifest in the ruler [emphasis added—R.W.].[36]

Jews living in all parts of the Ottoman Empire—in its Turkish, Arabic, and Slavic-speaking zones—could not ignore the "rabbinical" echoes of this word in its new context,[37] especially when the term Rabb in the Muslim context and rabbi (*rav* in Hebrew) derived from the same root, as noted. A further point of similarity is that both terms pinpoint a person standing at the peak of hierarchy. As Yılmaz states, "*Rabb* implies a relational rulership between the servant and the master"—a master in need of no other title. As mentioned previously, *Maran* is actually the exact Aramaic semantic corollary of the Arabic/Ottoman *(Our) Rabb*, and it replaced the name of its carrier, Joseph Karo.

"Our Masters": Ibn-'Arabi and Rumi

Living under Ottoman rule in the core lands, and beyond into the Arabic world after the spread of the Ottoman Empire, no one could ignore the increasing presence and weight of the various Sufi *Tarikas*. With the formation of more durable empires by the Ottomans, Safavids, and Mughals, Sufism became truly popularized, and the organizational features of Sufi communities were also transformed. This process was intimately connected with Ottoman state-building and with Confessionalization, that is, the initiatives taken by Ottoman religious and political authorities during the sixteenth century to refashion the attitudes and behaviors of the empire's Muslim subjects in conformity with the principles of Sunni Islam.[38] In this immensely rich Sufi tradition within Ottoman civilization, two figures towered above others and left a deep imprint on future generations: Ibn 'Arabi and Rumi. Regarding the first, Ibn 'Arabi became tremendously influential in Ottoman society. Among mystical writers, he was matched only by Jalal al-Din al-Rumi, the great Persian mystical poet (d. 1273). Later, many viewed him as a *patron saint of the Ottoman dynasty* and attributed to him a treatise in which he had allegedly predicted the rise of the Ottomans and their conquest of the

---

36. Hüseyin Yılmaz, *Caliphate Redefined: The Mystical Turn in Ottoman Political Thought*, Princeton: Princeton U.P., 2018, citations from pp. 184–185. See also, *ibid.*, pp. 113, 116, 122–123, 133, 139.
37. On the Jewish sensitivity to non-Jewish linguistic ambient in the Ottoman Empire, see Roni Weinstein, "Languages of Jews in Early Modern Ottoman Empire," [forthcoming].
38. Derin Terzioğlu, "Sufis in the age of state-building and confessionalization," in: Woodhead (ed.), *The Ottoman World*, pp. 86–98, esp. pp. 86–87. See also, Francis Robinson, 'Ottomans-Safavids-Mughals: Shared Knowledge and Connective Systems', *Journal of Islamic Studies* 8, no. 2 (1997), pp. 151–184.

Arab lands. Under Sultan Süleyman *Kanuni* (the law-giver) the Magnificent (reigned 1520–1566), the doctrine of Ibn 'Arabi became official state policy. The *Şeyhülislâm* Ibn Kemâl Pasha, the mufti of Istanbul (d. 1534), issued a fatwa declaring the Shaykh "a great *'arif* (gnostic), who had many disciples whom the ulema approve. Anyone who does not understand [him] must be silent. Those who deny this will be reprimanded by the sultan." Indeed, Ottoman officeholders who opposed Ibn 'Arabi's views could lose their posts.[39] After conquering Damascus, the Ottomans hastened to repair his tomb, and its importance grew to such a degree that it was claimed that they intend to divert the classical pilgrimage from the two holy cities to this site.[40] His works of poetry and rich mysticism spread despite resistance and sharp criticism by traditional 'Ulama in the Arab world. Distinguished mystics in the eastern Mediterranean Basin—such as Gulşani (d. 1534), and later Niyazi (d. 1694)—were deeply inspired by Ibn 'Arabi's heritage; they associated their activities and writings with his heritage, or even presented themselves as his successors.[41] The *Tarika* evolving in the wake of Gulşani stretched from Anatolia to the Balkans and Egypt—the very same places where important Sephardi communities prospered. Following Ibn 'Arabi's tradition, Gulşani accepted the hierarchical scaling of Sufi saints, designating himself (and his master Ibn 'Arabi) by ultimate and glorifying titles, such as *shaykh al-mashāyikh* (the sheikh of all sheikhs), the vicegerent (*khalīfa*) of God, and the true *imām*—a term denoting a leader, prophet, and successor to Prophet Muhammad; a lieutenant of which there are two at any given time; a leader and pole of mystical saints of God on earth; the protector of people; and the saint of God.[42]

The impact of the second towering mystic—Jalal a-Din Rumi—was highly felt during the late sixteenth and seventeenth centuries, especially through his *Mathnawi*, known throughout the Turkish- and Persian-speaking world. The Mevlevi order, institutionalized by Rumi's son Sultan Veled, spread Rumi's word and music through the just-emerging Ottoman Empire, where the Mevlevi order became intimately connected to the Ottoman court. Its leader was called by the honorific titles *Molla Hünkar* (Master Sovereign) and *Çelebi*. During the early modern period, many smaller *tekkes* of

---

39. Michael Winter, "Egyptian and Syrian Sufis Viewing Ottoman Turkish Sufism: Similarities, Differences, and Interactions," in: Eyal Ginio and Elie Podeh (eds.), *The Ottoman Middle East. Studies in Honor of Amnon Cohen*, Leiden and Boston, Brill, 2014, pp. 93–111, esp. pp 98–99. See also Robinson, "Ottomans-Safavids-Mughals," pp. 165–166.

40. Nir Shafir, *The Road from Damascus: Circulation and the Redefinition of Islam in the Ottoman Empire, 1620-1720*, Ph.D. submitted at the University of California (Los Angeles), 2016, pp. 198–199, 201.

41. See Derin Terzioğlu, *Sufi and Dissident in the Ottoman Empire: Niyazî-i Mısrî (1618-1694)*, Ph.D. submitted at Harvard University, 1999, passim; Side Emre, "A Preliminary Investigation of Ibn 'Arabi's Influence Reflected in the Corpus of İbrahim-i Gulsheni (d.1534) and the Halveti–Gulsheni Order of Dervishes in Egypt," *Journal of the Muhyiddin Ibn 'Arabi Society* 56 (2014), pp. 67–111. See also Winter, "Egyptian and Syrian Sufis Viewing Ottoman Turkish Sufism," p. 99, mentioning some of the famous partisans of ibn-'Arabi among the Arab Sufis, such as the Egyptian 'Abd al-Wahhab al-Sha'rani (d. 973/1565), the moroccan 'Ali b. Maymun al-Fasi (d. 917/1511) and the Syrian 'Abd al-Ghani al-Nabulusi (d. 1144/1731).

42. Emre, "A Preliminary Investigation of Ibn 'Arabi's Influence," p. 102.

the Mevlevis were found across the Ottoman Empire, as far away as Egypt and Syria, although the order never crossed the Ottoman borders.[43]

The titles of both these great Sufis were unique and particular, associated with them alone. Ibn 'Arabi was called *Shaykh el-Akbar* ("the Great Sheikh"), while Rumi was known as *Mevlana*, ("Our Master" in Turkish, or much less commonly the cognate *Mawlana*). In both cases, the titles were generally more in use than their bearers' personal names. They designated supremacy in relation to the long chain of preceding Sufi saints. Both Ibn 'Arabi and Rumi were considered eponymous figures of Sufi heritage, and even of a specific institutional Sufi school (*Tarika*) in the case of *Mevlana* Rumi. In this last case, the linguistic meaning of *Mevlana* is completely parallel to the title *Maran*: both signify *Our Master*, in the sense of the founder of a new authoritative religious path whose authority is willingly obeyed by the professional milieu and by the entire assembly of believers.

Conclusion: The Semantic Fusion of Titles

By the mid-seventeenth century, whenever writings, court decisions, or books of halakhic decisions (*Sifrei Pesiqah*) mentioned the word *Maran*, this invariably referred to Rabbi Joseph Karo. As mentioned, he was very often referred to solely by this title, without adding his surname. No one before him bore this title, and no one after him would do so for centuries, until the late twentieth century, as part of a broader phenomenon of devaluation in rabbinical titles.[44] The title is derived from the Aramaic word *Mar* or its Hebrew equivalent *Rav*, both implying dominance and control. In their semantic or grammatical variations, they had been common in the rabbinical milieu since late antiquity, but no figure had previously borne the specific form *Maran*. This clearly indicates that R. Karo set a category of its own, supreme in the rabbinical hierarchy. It undeniably defines him and his position within the traditional semantic field, yet at the same time delineates a quantum leap for a new scale. This is corroborated by the collective first plural nature of the title: he is *our* master/*Mar*, whose authority is universal and extends, or was at least intended to extend, to the entire Jewish Ecumene.

What did the invention or allocation of a new honorary title for a single person imply? Alongside its basically egalitarian nature, the Jewish world of learning was sensitive to titles, to the honor and position they confer, and to the internal hierarchy

---

43. AnneMarie Schimmel, *Mystical Dimensions of Islam*, Chapel Hill: The University of North Carolina Press, 1975, p. 324. On Rumi's biography, see John Renard, *Friends of God. Islamic Images of Piety, Commitment, and Servanthood*, Berkely, Los Angeles, London: University of California Press, 2008, pp. 21–22, 38–39. See also, Aslı Niazioğlu, *Dreams and Lives in Ottoman Istanbul. A Seventeenth-Century biographer's Perspective*, London and New York: Routledge, 2017, esp. p. 100, noticing the widespread of Rumi's teachings in seventeenth century Istanbul, especially his *Mesnevi*, attracting the interest of major Sufis and inspiring the composition of commentaries.

44. This process actually started in the early modern period. See, for instance, the titles conferred upon the Sephardi Rabbi Joseph Escapa as presented in Jacob Barani, "R. Yosef Escapa and the Rabbinate of Izmir" [Hebrew], *Sefunot: Studies and Sources on the History of the Jewish Communities in the East* 3(1985), pp. 53–81.

that they imply. This sensitivity intensified during the Middle Ages and in the early Modern period. In late tenth century, R. Sherira Gaon explicitly stated the various grades in rabbinic titles, from the highest degree—that of bearing no title, an honor reserved for very few—down to the title *Rav*. This statement became a cornerstone for later rabbinical writing throughout the Middle Ages. As we shall see in the coming chapter about rabbinic *Semikhah*,[45] titles were worth waging a battle along the sixteenth and seventeenth centuries, as they defined positions of prominence in a changing Jewish society. This reality was accentuated following the arrival of Sephardi exiles in new places around the Mediterranean Basin, bringing with them their Spanish (mainly Castilian) sense of honor—a sensitivity that tessellated with parallel traditions in both Catholic and Muslim societies. It was no coincidence that the title *Maran* disseminated among the rabbis and community members of the Sephardi Diaspora along the Mediterranean since the seventeenth century and remains in use to the present day among Jews originating from Arab lands.

When Maimonides was asked to state his position in a rabbinic responsum and was addressed by Jews as *Mufti*, this testified to the sensitivity and acquaintance with the Islamicate culture in general and its particular traditions of honorary titles. The consolidation of Islam during the "Classical Period" was reflected in a parallel construction of rich titulatory semantics. This began with the classical titles, such as *Caliph* or *Emir el-Mu'minin*, and later evolved toward various "biggest-of-them-all" titles in political, religious, or scholarly domains, and very often in all three combined. In the legal domain, the founding fathers of the various schools (*Madhhabs*) were increasingly described as saintly figures possessing comprehensive knowledge in various religious domains, and endowed with special inspiration. Often the writings and innovations of their direct successive disciples were attributed to them, as incomparable fonts of comprehensive knowledge. Those heading the hierarchy received distinct titles, such as *Mujtahed*, *Imam*, and *Shaykh el-Islam*. Alternatively, the doubling structure was used, as in *Shaykh el-Shuyukh* or *Qutb el-Aqtab* in Sufi tradition. The Sufi context is highly pertinent to the Jewish context for two main reasons. First, most of the leading Sufi scholars were involved in, and knowledgeable of, juridical aspects of Islam.[46] The second aspect is the significant role played by various mystic traditions and formal or semi-formal institutions, and their deep impact on the religious life of the population in early modern Ottoman Empire. Ibn 'Arabi was admired among large sections of the Ottoman ruling elite and his mystical cosmos pervaded the thoughts and writings of leading mystics. His title *Shaykh el-Akbar* conveyed the sense of "the biggest among the [Sufi] sheikhs (or masters)." The title *Maran* resonates exactly this sense. It stands in even tighter proximity with the title of another towering figure in the Ottoman-Turkish tradition, Jalal a-Din Rumi, called by his admirers simply *Mevlana*, Our Master. The title *Maran* has no exact and full corollary in rabbinical semantic tradition, yet we see here its full partner the Ottoman–Muslim context. On this semantic level, there is a surprisingly similarity between the

---

45. See the extensive discussion on Ch. 4.
46. See chapter 6, on the link between law and mysticism, in both Jewish and Muslim traditions.

title *Maran* and the titles of Ibn 'Arabi (*Shaykh el-Akbar*), a superlative pointing at the peak among Sufi masters, and of Rumi (*Mevlana*), adding the collective nomination—"Our Master." Both these terms gained high popularity, especially in the Ottoman world, and—with all the reservations—in the Arab territories as well, in the very same places inhabited by Sephardi communities around the Mediterranean Basin.

The invention of titles or nicknames does not have a specific point in time; they evolve, disseminate, become popular, crystallize, and at some time are permanently attached to persons. It is impossible to reconstruct the first moment or moments when Joseph Karo was cloaked in the title *Maran*. It is however clear that by the mid-seventeenth century this was an established practice, at least in the Sephardi Diaspora in the Mediterranean. This context is significant as it reflects the close cultural osmosis between Jewish and Ottoman or Islamicate traditions, in the semantic domain as in others. It reflects how a classical Jewish-rabbinical term *Mar*—in the sense of Talmudic scholar—served as a basis, but acquired a semantic twist when Ottomanized as "Our Mar" or *Maran*. The uniqueness of this term activated a traditional Jewish mechanism of charging new names or terminologies with "Jewish" sense—a practice exemplified in relation to the city of Toledo, written in Jewish sources as *Tolitula*, so as to reflect the Hebrew verb *le-taltel* (to toss), thereby providing a metonymy for the Jewish people's being tossed from one place to another in his exile. The same process played out in the case of the name *Polaniya* (Poland), explained as *Po-Lan-Yah* ("here stayed the Lord" in Hebrew), as badge of prominence for Torah scholarship among Polish rabbis. The same mechanism was activated in regard to the title *Maran*. It was interpreted as the acronym of "Approved by Two Hundred Rabbis" (*Ma'atayim Rabbanim Nismakh*), as if every statement of R. Karo is supported and approved in retrospect by two hundred rabbis. It seems improbable that the mobilization of hundreds of rabbis to sign the same document of consent would have left a scant trail of documents, and we may conclude that this explanation for the title *Maran* is no more than popular etymology. One wonders if this legend of two hundred rabbis standing behind the authority of R. Karo may not echo the stories surrounding Rumi and his saintly family, as they disseminated in the important hagiography composed by Eflaki, the *Manāqib al-'Ārifīn*. Eflaki refers to Baha Veled (the son and successor of Rumi) as the Sultan of Scholars (*sultān al-'ulemā*), an epithet confirmed by other contemporary sources, a title of stature with a claim for authority:

As the chosen one for the mission, it was no other than the Prophet who grants this position to the scholar-saint: In Balkh, 300 muftis, all jurists, see a dream simultaneously in which the Prophet, having Baha Veled on his side, commands them to call him the sultan of scholars from then on. Waking up with awe and astonishment, the muftis rush to Baha Veled to submit their loyalties and become his disciples (*murīd*). The dream not only establishes the primacy of intuitive knowledge over that of discursive but also unifies the two distinct forms of piety [the Sufi alongside the legal – R.W.] and their adherents in one body. [47]

---

47. Yılmaz, *Caliphate Redefined: The Mystical Turn in Ottoman Political Thought*, p. 116.

The title *Maran*, attached inseparably and solely to the name of Joseph Karo, implied that he stood at the head of the rabbinical hierarchy. It echoed the vision of organizing and institutionalizing the rabbinical milieu. In turn, this vision reflected a form of virtual competition and interaction with Islamicate tradition in the Ottoman settings, even on the relatively trivial level of semantics and titles.

Chapter Four

SEMIKHAH POLEMICS IN SAFED:
ESTABLISHING A GUILD OF JURISTS

In one of the most condensed revelations in his mystical diary *Megid Meisharim*, R. Karo was addressed and promised thus:

> It is I, the *Mishnah*, speaking through [or: in] your mouth, the mother castigating her sons [or: children], the one embracing you. And you shall often adhere to me, I shall return to you[1] and you shall return to me. I shall raise you to become master and leader [*sar ve-nagid*] over the entire Jewish diaspora in *Arabistan*.[2] Since you have profoundly devoted yourself[3] to reinstating *Semikhah*, you shall be honored to be ordained by all the Sages of the Holy Land, and by the Sages abroad [i.e. beyond the Holy Land]. Through you, I [the Mishnah, i.e. the mystical speaking figure] would re-establish the glory of *Semikhah*, and I would benefit you by enabling you to finish your major corpus [both codification books: *Beit Yosef* and *Shulchan 'Arukh*]. And later you would burn on the stake for my name's sanctity and would earn [the honor] of rising from the dead, and you shall become one of those of whom it is said that they were awarded with a place in heaven [while alive—R.W].[4] And so, peace be upon you.[5]

This is a highly charged revelation, encompassing the major themes of R. Karo's intellectual and public activities: leadership over the entire Eastern Diaspora (*Arabistan*), the composition of *Beit Yosef* and *Shulchan 'Arukh*, constant expectations of martyrdom, daily ecstatic contact with the divine figure, and, finally, all these as a reward for his commitment to re-establishment of *Semikhah*.

This last theme provoked a lively and highly charged polemic in late sixteenth-century Safed. The competing parties were the local rabbis, headed by the dominant and prestigious R. Jacob Beirav, versus a Jerusalem rabbi, R. Levi ben-Haviv. Accordingly,

---

1. In the sense of: "I will reveal myself to you."
2. The geographical extent of "Arabistan" and the wider sense of this message will be discussed on chapter 5.
3. Alternatively: "you martyred yourself."
4. More concretely: having a completely reliable knowledge of gaining a place in Paradise while still alive. This is a typical echo of Islamic tradition, in relation to several exceptional figures among the "Company of the Prophet" in the famous Hadith known as "The Ten with Glad Tidings of Paradise."
5. Joseph Karo, *Magid Meisharim*, Wilnius: Judah Leib Lipman Metz Print, 1875, p. 29a.

this polemic has hitherto been discussed in the literature as an internal affair between scholars and experts of Talmudic law. While this dimension is fundamental to illuminate some aspects of the affair, it disregards the Ottoman setting and the urgent considerations that motivated both parties as they shaped Jewish life under Ottoman rule. The non-Jewish context relates further to the grand vision of R. Karo establishing a Jewish legal guild.

Semikhah in Classical Rabbinic Tradition

Semikhah basically denotes a formal authorization to be numbered among the members of the rabbinical professional milieu and to participate in legal procedures in courts of religious law. Referring to the European context, it could easily be translated by the Latin *ordinatio* or its modern English term *ordination*, while in the Islamic legal context, it would be labeled *Ijaza*. I will consider below the extent to which both these terms are pertinent to the Jewish context. In order not to charge the discussion with semantic bias from the outset, I will use the Hebrew rabbinical term *Semikhah*, due to its Halakhic particularity, rather than any term borrowed from other languages. Only toward the conclusion of the discussion I will present a case for considering the term to be closer to the Islamic *Ijaza* rather than to the European *ordinatio*.

The city of Safed formed the setting for an acrimonious rabbinical polemic surrounding the issue of renewing rabbinical Semikhah during the second half of the sixteenth century. This debate involved major rabbinical figures—mainly local ones, but also some from Jerusalem, and in later years, even individuals based outside the Holy Land. The antagonism involved deep personal emotions as well as a geographical clash between Safed and Jerusalem. The discussions left an impressive trail of documentation. R. Karo did not play a leading role in the events, yet his presence was not insignificant, and it is certainly crucial to understanding his codification project (as seen in the opening citation). Was the *Semikhah* polemic really so different from other rabbinical antagonistic debates in that period, particularly in the Sephardi Diaspora? Considered from a wider comparative standpoint, for example, how different was it in respect to the clashes among rabbis in Ashkenaz, Italy, or Mediterranean communities throughout the early modern period? It was essentially an internal debate among rabbinical figures; although highly contentious, it was barely revealed to the public at large. On the other hand, it was meticulously documented, to a degree uncommon in the contemporary Sephardi milieu, and was even included in the printed responsa books of its contestants. The tone was so harsh that the printed text presented the discussion in a censored and softened manner.

The *Semikhah* polemic revived cultural memories dating back to the classical rabbinical period of late antiquity, and even beforehand. A preliminary general remark: It is common in rabbinical discourse, especially in the halakhic domain, to present innovation (or the adaption of religious heritage to changing circumstances) as nothing more than a further reading or interpretation of the preexisting literary heritage. The debate surrounding the reinstatement of pure *Semikhah* was no exception to this rule, and the participants resorted to classical rabbinical sources, alluding in turn to two mythical origins of this institution, considered of equal authenticity and legitimacy.[6] The first regards Moses "Our Rabbi" (*Moshe Rabbenu*) as the originator of the chain of rabbinic ordination. The second links this procedural formality to the figure of R. Yochanan ben Zakkai, the founding father of the rabbinical tradition following the destruction of the Second Temple. These two opposing suggestions never led those involved to raise any doubt which one is more correct and for good reason. They were interpreted as embodying two alternative roles of *Semikhah*.[7] The first one was judicial: the bearer of *Semichah* was empowered to adjudicate in important city courts in the Holy Land. In the rabbinical ethos, this function was related to the sanctified institution of the Sanhedrin, located alongside the Holy Temple. It served as the core of rabbinical learning, inspired by the sanctity of the temple and the divine presence (the *Shekhinah*).[8] As a Supreme Court and a centralistic institution, its instructions and rulings, following the discussions of its authoritative members of scholarly elite, were considered binding on the entire Jewish population. The second suggestion for the origins of *Semikhah* was related to the function it filled within the community of sages (*Chakhamim*) in the Holy Land. *Semikhah* in this context mainly implied the maturation of a scholar and hence his ability to teach and participate in legal adjudication. These two alternative connotations of *Semikhah*—the institutional-judicial versus the scholarly—merged after the destruction of the Second Temple and the re-establishment of the Sanhedrin in the Galilee. The rabbinical sages competed for the right of *Semikhah* and official rabbinical nomination on the grounds of scholastic excellence. This construct embodied the continuity of the chain of transmission going back to Moses and the giving of the Torah on Mount Sinai. These sages competed with a prominent family of scholars who combined academic distinction with their political contacts with the Roman authorities.[9] Due to their title "the Overlord" (*Nasi* or *Beit HaNasi*), the descendants of this family considered themselves the political and cultural-religious leaders of the local Jewish population within Roman Palestine, and hence entitled to a monopoly over rabbinical *Semikhah*.

The claim of the household of the Nasi family to a monopoly over *Semikhah*, and its attributed link to the Jerusalemite center of the Sanhedrin in vicinity to the Holy Temple, spawned the halakhic rule that the *Semikhah* procedure could only be activated within the confines of the Holy Land and not abroad—even in the prosperous Babylonian diaspora. This rule, testified in both the Jerusalem and Babylonian Talmuds, was later accepted as definitive. Yet it was far from reflecting legal reality. The Babylonian diaspora, which following the destruction of the Holy Temple became increasingly dominant in political, demographic, cultural terms, practiced *Semikhah* procedures no less than the

---

6. Hayim D. Mantel, "Ordination and Appointment in the Days of the Temple" [Hebrew], *Tarbiz* 32, no. 2 (1963), pp. 120–135, esp. pp. 122–123.

7. *Ibid.*, pp. 123–124.

8. Hugo [=Hayim] Mantel, *Studies in the History of the Sanhedrin*, Cambridge, MA: Harvard U.P., 1961, passim.

9. Hanoch Albeck, "Semichah, Nomination and Court of Law" [Hebrew], *Zion* 8 (1943), pp. 85–93.

sages of the Holy Land.[10] This pattern continued until the Arab conquest of Iraq in the seventh century and suited the self-image of Babylonian Talmudic scholars—the *Geonim*—as leaders of the Jewish Ecumene. Their version of *Semikhah* was consistent with the general policy of imposing "legal monism and centralism."[11] The rabbinical mythicizing of the golden times (in this case, the Temple era) underlined another element: the dominant position of rabbis in directing Jewish life. Recent research has demonstrated the limited scope of the legal autonomy granted to the Jewish communities under the Roman Empire in the Holy Land.[12] The Sanhedrin—wandering from Jerusalem to the Galilee after the destruction of the Temple in 70 AD—and the local sages could barely impose their traditions and rulings without Roman consent. To sum up, classical rabbinical lore was indecisive about the authority, validity, and origins of *Semikhah*. It left much to be decided in the coming generations, which thus shaped it in their turn according to their own needs. It also kept alive dreams of wider Jewish autonomy through centralist institutions—aspirations to be fully accomplished in a messianic era.

Maimonides' Writings on *Semikhah*

The heritage of the rabbinical sages was mediated to medieval and later generations most succinctly in the writings of Maimonides (1138–1204).[13] His halakhic writings, and particularly his magnum opus, *Mishneh Torah*—the first halakhic code of law— established his status as a prestigious post-Talmudic authority. His position as a leader of Egyptian Jewry, physician, great philosopher, composer of rabbinical responsa, and commentator on the Mishnah further increased his fame in contemporary and later generations. He presented his positions regarding the re-establishment of *Semikhah* in two different works. The first was his commentary on the Mishnah, the summary of the Sages' erudition as it evolved in the Holy Land, and canonized by R. Yehudah Ha-Nasi around the second to third centuries.[14] Maimonides' commentary offered the most elaborated vision for any future initiative by Talmudic scholars to reinstate *Semikhah*. Like the rest of this commentary, it was composed in Judeo-Arabic and not in Hebrew:

10. Yochanan Breuer, "Rabbi is Greater than Rav, Rabban is Greater than Rabbi, The Bare Name is Greater than Rabban" [Hebrew], *Tarbiz* 66, no. 1 (1997), pp. 41–59, esp. pp. 47–53.
11. Yishai Kiel, "Reinventing Yavneh in Sherira's Epistle. From Pluralism to Monism in the Light of Islamicate Legal Culture," in: Michael Satlow (ed.), *Strength to Strength. Essays in Appreciation of Shaye J. D. Cohen*, Providence [RI], Brown Judaic Studies, 2018, pp. 577–598. The expression appears in *ibid.*, p. 580.
12. David Goodblatt, "The Political and Social History of the Jewish Community in the Land of Israel, C. 235–638," in: Steven T. Katz (ed.), *The Cambridge History of Judaism*, Vol. IV – "The Late Roman Rabbinic Period," Cambridge: Cambridge U.P., 2008, pp. 404–430.
13. Moshe Halbertal, *Maimonides: Life and Thought*, tr. by Joel Linsider, Princeton: Princeton U.P., 2014; Sara Stroumsa, *Maimonides in his World: Portrait of a Mediterranean Thinker*, Princeton U.P., 2009.
14. On the composition of the Mishnah and its cultural settings, see David Kraemer, "The Mishnah," in: Katz (ed.), *The Cambridge History of Judaism*, Vol. IV, pp. 299–315.

I am convinced that when all the scholars would reach a consensus to nominate a scholar within the Yeshivah as their head, on condition that it would take place in the Holy Land, as said previously, then the Yeshivah would be officially established and he would eventually carry *Semikhah*, and this man could confer *Semikhah* upon whomever he wishes. Should you [the potential reader—R.W.] reject this proposition, a supreme court of law would never be established, due to the requirement that each of its attending members should carry an official *Semikhah*. More so, God has promised its return [the supreme court's—R.W.], by saying "I will restore your magistrates as of old" [Isaiah 1,26]. Should you claim that the Messiah would nominate them, even though they did not carry a formal *Semikha*, well this is utterly denied, as we already expounded that [...] the Messiah would not add nor subtract anything from the written or oral Torah, and this would provide one of the signs of its verity [...] It would undoubtedly happen when God will ameliorate people's hearts, and their goodness and passion for God and for Torah would increase, and they would follow the straightway, prior to the coming of the Messiah, as proposed in the biblical verses.[15]

The Mishnah commentary was composed in Maimonides' early years, yet it already reflects his fundamental positions on Halakhah and Jewish heritage in general.[16] The rabbinic sages were the circle that bore the primary responsibility for sustaining and defending the Jewish way of life and religious practices. Their authority is not personal, but essentially institutional, leaning backward on a chain of transmission of oral law and erudition: The Mosaic Torah revealed at Mount Sinai provides a fundamental channel of legitimacy and sanctity. The conviction in the validity of this event is so firm that even in the Messianic age the sages clarified that the instructions of Talmudic Halakhah would not change and would certainly not be abrogated. Jewish legal heritage, following this ethos, reached its peak in the Second Temple period, with the establishment and functioning of the Sanhedrin as a supreme court of law. The court benefitted from its proximity to the Temple, the inspiration of the Holy Spirit, and the erudition of the leading scholars. The proposed vision suggested by the young Maimonides sought to revitalize all these elements—including the reinstatement of the Sanhedrin and of *Semikhah*—in a future Messianic era not by the Messiah but by Talmudic scholars.

Straightforward though his words were, they left much to be clarified. The Mishnah, unlike the Jerusalem and Babylonian Talmud, lost its status as an independent authoritative text during late antiquity and medieval period, and was studied not for its own sake or as independent text, but as a starting point for further Talmudic discussions. It no longer served as a legitimate basis for Halakhic legal decision-making (*Pesiqat Halakhah*) to be applied in court discussions or in rabbinical responsa. What then was the hermeneutic status of Maimonides' assertions in his Mishnah commentary? Were they meant

---

15. The citation and its discussion, see Gerald J. Blidstein, "The Suggestion of Maimonides to Renovate the Semichah" [Hebrew], *Dinei Israel. Researches on Halakhah and Jewish Law* 26–27 (2009–2010), pp. 241–252, esp. p. 242.
16. Idem., "On the Institutionalization of Prophecy in Maimonidean Halakhah" [Hebrew], *Daat: A Journal of Jewish Philosophy & Kabbalah* 43 (1999), pp. 25–42.

to further an academic elucidation of a text, or were they intended to serve as binding instructions for the future? This important point was left unresolved by Maimonides, certainly not by coincidence. Unlike his resolute phrasing in other contexts, in this commentary he casted doubt on his own suggestions, introducing them with the phrase "I am convinced [...]" The dubious legal validity and applicability of these assertions were further strengthened by the allusion to a prophetic verse as a basis for the renewal of *Semikhah*. This was a highly exceptional act in Talmudic discourse, which centuries earlier had ceased quoting biblical, and certainly prophetic, verses in order to substantiate normative rulings.

Semikhah was also discussed twice by Maimonides in his code *Mishneh Torah*, mainly in regard to Sanhedrin rulings. These remarks represent the perspective of a mature scholar offering his comprehensive view on halakhic heritage:

> It appears to me that if all the wise men in *Eretz Yisrael* [Holy Land] agree to appoint judges and convey *Semikhah* upon them, the *Semichah* is binding and these judges may adjudicate cases involving financial penalties, and convey *Semikhah* upon others. If so, why did the Sages did not exert themselves over the institution of *Semikhah*, so that the judgment of cases involving financial penalties would not be nullified among the Jewish people? Because the Jewish people were dispersed, and it is impossible that all could agree. If, by contrast, there was a person who had received *Semikhah* from a person who had received *Semichah*, he does not require the consent of all others. Instead, he may adjudicate cases involving financial penalties, for he received *Semikhah* from a court. The question whether *Semichah* can be renewed requires further resolution.[17]

Again, this was accompanied by the formulaic expression "The question requires further resolution" (*ve-ha-davar tzarikh hakhra'ah*). What was it that needed to be resolved? This issue has been discussed by rabbinic sages over the centuries, as well as by modern scholars, without yielding any conclusive answer. This vagueness, so untypical in Maimonides' halakhic writings, opened the gate to disagreements among the participants in the *Semikhah* polemics in late sixteenth-century Safed. There was another unresolved query, too: if *Semikhah* indeed depended on a chain of past generations, from a master to his direct disciple, how could it possibly be renewed after it had been dormant for many centuries? What would be the concrete benefit of a re-established *Semikhah* for Jewish life and legal proceedings? The mechanism for renovating this institution remained vague. But even more vague was the link between rabbinical *Semikhah* and the messianic era—a prominent theme in Maimonides' Mishnaic commentary, but much less so in the *Mishneh Torah*. Was *Semikhah* part of the comprehensive process of salvation or was it a precondition for the coming of the Messiah? In other words, is it an integral part of Jewish legal renaissance, and, as such, applicable in any generation, depending on concrete historical circumstances and serving as an element in constituting a just society or is it rather a prerequisite for a revolutionary Messianic scenario? In another

---

17. Maimonides, *Mishneh Torah*, section "Hilchot Sanhedrin," §4,11. Translation taken from the website www.chabad.org.

part of the *Mishneh Torah*, the "Rules regarding Kings" (*Hilkhot Melakhim*), Maimonides asserts that the construction of a just society is not a precondition for the Messianic era and concluded that "All these things will remain unknown until they happen" (*Kol eilu ha-dvarim lo yeda' ha-adam eikh yihyu 'ad she-yihyu*).[18]

Medieval Discussions of *Semikhah*

To a large extent, the purported monopoly of the Holy Land sages over *Semikhah* was an historical myth, serving the yearning of the Jewish Diaspora for legal and political autonomy in its historical homeland. During the Late Antiquity period, the Babylonian center eclipsed the classical and sanctified center in the Holy Land; a sure indication of this was that the Babylonian Talmud became the canonical book for guiding religious life rather than the Jerusalem Talmud. In fact, the *Semikhah* procedure was practiced in Babylon during the Gaonic period (roughly the sixth to tenth centuries).[19] Scholars were nominated to positions as teachers and official judges, and carried an official and honorary title *Rav*, paralleling the Holy Land title *Rabbi*. In some instances, the *Semikhah* was restricted to certain domains of law, as a kind of expert certification. As late as the twelfth century, R. Samuel ben 'Ali, head of the Baghdad Yeshivah, wrote:

> It [the *Semikhah*] was shifted from one generation to the succeeding one, among whom [those entitled to *Semikhah*—R.W.] heads of *Yeshiva*s or heads of courts of law. Each one of them summons the worthy one among the Yeshiva [students] and confers *Semikhah* upon him. Should one claim that many years passed without the institution of *Semikhah*, considering that *Semikhah* is not valid beyond the Holy Land, I could calm him down, for this rule regards penalty procedures by courts, but *Semikhah* is applicable in cases of admittances [*Hoda'ot*, i.e. admitting legal commitments] and loans. Regarding this issue there are plenty of evidences, I would not cite them in this epistle.[20]

As in other cases, it is claimed that Babylonian *Semikhah* does not equate to the original Holy Land version of the concept, and the process is apologetically presented as functioning beyond the Holy Land. Yet in practical terms, it fulfills the same function of maintaining the rabbinical chain of erudition, adjudication, and the cooption of new members through a formal procedure.

Another major center of Jewish life and Talmudic scholarship, where *Semikhah* was practiced, was medieval Ashkenaz (the north European communities beyond the Alps).[21] The practice began relatively early, reaching its full scope by the time of the famous R. Meir of Rothenburg (d. 1293). Ashkenazi *Semikhah* was reinstated by the scholarly milieu as a formal confirmation of scholarship and as a mechanism for regulating the interaction between masters and their direct disciples. Toward the end of the Middle

---

18. See the discussion in Blidstein, "The Suggestion of Maimonides to Renovate the Semichah."
19. Breuer, "Rabbi is Greater than Rav," pp. 47–48.
20. *Ibid.*, p. 48.
21. Mordechai Breuer, "The Ashkenazi Semichah" [Hebrew], *Zion* 33, no. 1–2 (1968), pp. 15–46.

Ages, the holders of such a document, and especially their masters, came into conflict with local communities when rabbis sought to impose their own nominations on local communities by granting *Semikhah*. In his detailed article, Mordechai Breuer noted that the dissemination and structure of this form of *Semikhah* were not derived from halakhic and valid rulings, but motivated by historical reality, and aroused halakhic and social criticism.[22] Lay individuals not associated with the rabbinic milieu claimed that unworthy students acquired *Semikhah*, or even bought it as an investment for future posts in communities, or to elevate their social status and personal honor. From Ashkenaz, *Semikhah* migrated to other European communities, following the establishment of new Ashkenazi communities in the Balkans and Italy. This latter location attracted immigrants from northern Europe and the Mediterranean Basin and produced new patterns of Jewish life. The Italian form of *Semikhah* was certainly influenced by urban life and the academic titles conferred in local universities.[23] It was similar to the Ashkenazi pattern of constructing hierarchical relationship between masters and their long-term disciples and maintaining a balance of power between the rabbinical milieu and local communities. The communities insisted on their own legal sovereignty when they confronted a rabbinical determination to nominate *Semikhah*-entitled rabbis. Italian *Semikhah* had a peculiarity of conferring two distinct and hierarchic titles: *Chaver* and *Rav*. Following large-scale waves of Jewish immigrations and expulsions in the early modern period, various Jewish traditions of *Semikhah* confronted one another in Italy. The Sephardi exiles raised sharp criticism on the Ashkenazi-Italian patterns of *Semikhah*, contending that these lacked any substantial halakhic foundation (again, the claim that there could be no *Semikhah* outside the Holy Land was raised); it was further suggested that this mechanism actually reflected "non-Jewish" formalities, as practiced in lawyers' guilds or in the Italian universities.

This confusing phase of interethnic encounters, necessitating a new cultural and institutional balance, was vividly reflected in a tract composed in early sixteenth century by the Italian Rabbi David Messer Leon, head of the Sephardi community of Vlora (Albania).[24] As customary in rabbinical writings, concrete events rather than any theoretical interest provide important testimonies on rabbinical attitudes. In this instance, a clash erupted concerning Messer Leon's rabbinical authority, exacerbated by an assault on his honor by the Castilian component of the community. The incident provoked Leon to compose a long and detailed tract regarding the roots of rabbinical authority in general. Once more a personal affront provided the initial drive for staging such an exceptionally detailed statement. The wider context was the need to redefine rabbinical functions within the dynamic and changing communities of the Sephardi

---

22. Idem., "The Ashkenazi Semichah," p. 29.

23. Robert Bonfil, *Rabbinate in Renaissance Italy* [Hebrew], Jerusalem: Magnes Press, 1979, pp. 23–66, 173, 213–217, 234.

24. Yehuda Messer Leon, *Kevod Chakhamim* [Honor of Sages/Rabbis], ed. and introduction by Shimeon Bernfeld, Berlin: H. Itzkowski Print, 1899. On the life and writings of Messer Leon, see *ibid.*, Introduction, pp. vii–xxiii.

exiles across the Mediterranean Basin.[25] Many pages were dedicated to presenting the roots, legitimacy, and roles of rabbinical *Semikhah*, not as a theoretical and scholarly subject but within the concrete historical settings of Jewish life. Messer Leon acknowledges that *Semikhah* of the classical type could not formally continue in the Diaspora. Yet in practice it did and had already been an integral part of Jewish rabbinical and communal traditions for generations:

> Basing myself on clear evidence from their Sephardi sages, who are our sages as well [...] I showed that *Semikhah* is possible even at the present. For we implement some acts as if we are entitled to genuine *Semikhah* [...] All the more so given that this *Semikhah* of ours is not genuine for it carries the title *Rav* and not *Rabbi*, which would have shown that it is genuine [...] Our *Semikhah* is not genuine, since it lacks the real element, which is the title Rabbi. In my humble opinion, it should be named Interim *Semikhah* [*Semikhah Emtza'it*], as on the one hand it resembles the genuine type, with the written items [included in the *Semikhah* document of his time], but on the other hand it is not genuine, since it lacks the title [and authority of] Rabbi. To the objections posed by the Sephardis in their books, that we have borrowed it from the Gentiles' conferring of doctorate titles, we would respond that, God forbid, we do not follow the Gentiles' manners [...] It is all due to the fact that we the *Italiani* [sic] obtained it from our French and Ashkenazi masters/rabbis, the roots of Torah, from whose mouth we live [...].[26]

The rhetoric here is fascinating in several respects. The concept of "Interim *Semikhah*," clearly a neologism of R. Messer Leon, is supposed to justify the hazy status of concrete practices: current *Semikhah* could not rely on past requirements, yet required some form of halakhic legitimacy. Therefore, it is an "as if" *Semikhah* ("we implement some acts *as if we are entitled to* genuine *Semikhah*.") The major difference is that the original title was exchanged for a different one.[27] The tract further asserts that, despite their official claim, the Sephardi rabbis and communities are accustomed to using their own kind of *Semikhah*, albeit without naming it explicitly:

> It seems that implied *Semikhah* carrying the title *Rav* is customary everywhere, even in Spain [...] It was generally agreed that scholars would be summoned to read from the Torah by the title *Rav*, for they practice the *Semikhah*, and the Sephardi [rabbis, be called to read the Torah] by the title *Chakham*, since they did not practice it [the Ashkenazi-Italian version]. This caused the Sephardi duress [due to disrespect], but later on the [Sephardi] community members agreed [to use the title *Rav* among their member rabbis].[28]

---

25. The crisis in Rabbinic functioning was discussed by David Ruderman, *Early Modern Jewry: A New Cultural History*, Princeton and Oxford: Princeton U.P., 2010, Ch. IV – "Crisis of Rabbinic Authority," pp. 133–158.
26. Messer Leon, *The Honor of Sages*, pp. 62–63. See also, *ibid.*, pp. 53–56, 61, 64.
27. Breuer, "Rabbi is Greater than Rav," pp. 52–58.
28. Messer Leon, *The Honor of Sages*, p 64.

Leon was not mistaken nor biased in stating that *Semikhah* extended to the Sephardi tradition during the early modern period.

The Safed *Semikhah* Polemics

Toward the mid-sixteenth century, a leading scholar in Safed, R. Yaakov Beirav (1474–1541), initiated a formal procedure of *Semikhah*. As asserted above and discussed later in this chapter, informal *Semikhah*-like procedures had been practiced from the Gaonic period through the sixteenth century, but the Safed initiative was different in its intended publicity and in the role it was to play in the innovative Safed arena. R. Beirav was formally chosen by his Yeshiva scholars as head, henceforward bearing a formal *Semikhah* title. The plan went beyond the personal title of R. Beirav and was intended to apply to his direct students and colleagues and to later generations:

> God turned angry on his people [...] there is no king nor leader, or someone fighting the Torah war [significant scholar] [...] and God's people are dispersed, as a lost flock [...] For this reason we [Safed sages] chose the excellent one—in years and erudition—the omniscient rabbi R. Jacob Beirav, to have the *Semikhah* title [*she-yihyeh samukh*] and head of Yeshivah, and be nominated as Rabbi. He would nominate the most erudite among us as Rabbis, imbued with Semikhah in perpetuity, so that they would truthfully and justly carry the laws of Torah in court, adjudicate the mighty, and smite the evil-doer [...] He in His mercy would grant mercy on our deeds and make true his words "I will restore your magistrates as of old, and your counselors as of yore. After that you shall be called a city of righteousness, a faithful city" [Isaiah 1:26], end of quotation. Undersigned by twenty five rabbis, the distinguished ones first, followed by the rest of the scholars and disciples.[29]

R. Beirav was indeed the initiator and forerunner of this innovation, but it was far from a one-man-show: He was enthusiastically supported by the leading scholars in Safed, including R. Joseph Karo. Since the halakhic legitimacy for this project relied predominantly on Maimonides' writings, a rabbinical consent or "consensus" of Holy Land rabbis [*haskamah*] was a precondition. An envoy was sent to Jerusalem to obtain the local rabbis' consent for the initiative, especially from their leading scholar, R. Levi ben-Haviv (c.1480–c.1541) (known by the acronym Ralbach). Both were scholars of great renown and position, both came from renowned Sephardi scholastic families, and both expressed their opinion in unequivocal terms. These shared characteristics served only to aggravate the tone of the polemics, once it started.

The polemics over formal rabbinic *Semikhah* was documented by R. Levi ben-Haviv, who collected the major documents and arranged them according to his editorial narrative, including them as an appendix in his printed responsa. Further documents have

---

29. Levi ben-Haviv, *Responsa*, Jerusalem: Keren Re'em Institute, 2018, §147, p. 2. The following references to this Responsa relate to §147.

been discovered and published by modern scholars.[30] Very scant material remained in the writings of disciples of R. Beirav, Ralbach, and later rabbinical scholars.[31] Any reconstruction of the events sequence thus owes much to the material accumulated by R. Levi ben-Haviv and published in his responsa under the title "The *Semihhah* Booklet" (*Quntres Ha-Semikhah*). Modern scholarship disagreed about the reconstruction of consequential phases of the *Semikhah* polemics, even regarding its opening and the concluding moments. Did it begin with the abovementioned "Declaration of *Semikhah*" or was this merely a reaction to earlier moves? Was the second epistle of R. Beirav to R. Levi ben-Haviv his last one, hence indirectly noting his despair at the entire *Semikhah* project or was there another epistle, expressing his energetic commitment to grant *Semikhah* to his chosen disciples? The contradictory modern readings are unsurprising, given that some of the documents that could have shed light on the entire sequence of events were later lost and were not included in Ralbach's material.[32] Some aspects of the modern reconstruction are hypothetical, but the overall sequence of events, pertinent to our discussion, is accepted by scholars. It includes the plan by Safed scholars—headed by R. Beirav—to reinstate *Semikhah*, and its public declaration. No concrete act had as yet been taken, but at some point, a messenger named Israel Hazan was sent to Jerusalem to secure consent for such an act, proposing to include their leading scholar, R. Levi ben-Haviv, among the persons bearing the *Semikhah* title. One of the local scholars (in Jerusalem), R. Moses di Castro, a former disciple of R. Beirav, politely but firmly opposed the entire project. His response sparked the ire of R. Beirav, who responded with an uncharacteristically furious and offensive letter. At some point—it is not completely clear whether before or after this letter—the sages of the "Major Yeshiva of Safed" convened and conferred the title of *Semikhah* on R. Beirav. His offensive tone incited a response by the Jerusalemite Rabbi Levi ben-Haviv. Once this letter reached the hands of the Safed sages, and later R. Beirav himself, the confrontation between these two figures progressively escalated as they exchanged three rounds of letters and counter-letters. As Ralbach did not withdraw from his opposing position, at one point a personal threatening letter was sent to him by the Safed court of law ordering him to respect the decision reached by major scholars of Talmudic law, as customary in Jewish tradition. It was signed by R. Karo, who was probably in charge of this act. The main counter-argument of R. Levi ben-Haviv was that the terms for rabbinical consensus, as

30. Haim Z. Dimitrovsky, "New Documents Regarding the Semichah Controversy in Safed" [Hebrew], *Sefunot: Studies and Sources on the History of the Jewish Communities in the East* 10 (1966), pp. 113–192; Meir Benayahu, "The Renovation of Rabbinic Semichah in Safed" [Hebrew], in: S.W. Baron, B. Dinur, S. Ettinger, I. Halpern (eds.), *Yitzhak F. Baer Jubilee Volume. On the Occasion of his Seventieth Birthday*, Jerusalem: The Historical Society of Israel, 1960, pp. 248–269. Dimitrovsky pointed out that there are some differences between the printed and manuscript versions of the polemic documentation, *ibid.*, p. 16, note 9.

31. Dimitrovsky, "New Documents Regarding the Semichah Controversy in Safed," p. 115, footnote 2.

32. See the list of documents exchanged along the polemics, of which some important ones are lacking, in Jacob Katz, "The Controversy on the Semichah (Ordination) between Rabbi Jacob Beirav and the Ralbach" [Hebrew], *Zion* 16, no. 3–4 (1951), pp. 28–45, esp. 29–30.

required by Maimonides, the great authority offering legitimization for a future rabbinical *Semikhah*, had not been fulfilled. Pressed by some unclear urgency to leave Safed and by internal rabbinic opposition,[33] R. Beirav hastily conferred *Semikhah* on four rabbis, one of whom was R. Joseph Karo. At this point, the granting of *Semikhah* ceased temporarily, and no other rabbi was claimed to be *Semikhah*-worthy in R. Beirav's life. The third wave of *Semikhah* conference took place in later years and will be discussed below.

The modern reading of this entire event—as suggested by leading scholars such as Katz, Dimitrovsky, Benayahu, and more recently Davidson, Kelman, Kahana, Ben-Naeh, and Marciano[34]—has focused on the sharp antagonism of the parties, as reflected in their exchange of letters and in the court decision, including their unusual defamatory and disrespectful rhetoric.[35] Their second areas of focus have included the formalistic legal and halakhic arguments of both sides, the order of the various phases of the entire event, and the rabbinical precedents in halakhic argumentation regarding *Semikhah*, the messianic vision behind the project, and finally the personalities and motivations of both rabbis Beirav and Ralbach. According to this historical narrative, the severity of the polemic was due to the concrete intention to establish an autonomous legal center in Safed that would regulate the professional and legal status of worthy scholars of Talmudic law and contribute to the empowerment of their legal guild. This guild would serve first in the city of Safed and later across the entire Jewish Diaspora. Following my suggestions in the Introduction, I will seek here to offer a more diverse reading, shifting the focus away from legalistic arguments and presenting them as a rhetorical screen for other implicit assertions.

My objection to the current interpretations starts with the assertion— common among historians—that Beirav actually advocated a messianic vision in which the reinstallation of *Semikhah* played a decisive part, as a precondition for his apocalyptic scenario. The so-called messianic motivation remains unclear if it is not explicitly stated what "Messianism" implies in this particular historical context. Is it, as assumed in the abovementioned works, a reference to the classical mainstream vision of the political salvation of the Jewish people, the establishment of sovereignty and military force headed by the messiah, the construction of the Holy Temple (hence the need for a Sanhedrin), and the massive return of the Jewish people to its homeland? It is far from clear that this was the intended vision of the innovators of the *Semikhah* procedure, especially R.

---

33. Ben-Haviv, *Responsa*, pp. 6, 13, 22–23, 38–39, 52, 79.

34. Eyal Davidson, *Safed's Sages between 1540–1615, Their Religious and Social Status* [Hebrew], Ph.D. submitted at the Hebrew University, 2009; Tirza Y. Kelman, *"I Shall Create Halakhic Ruling... for that is the Objective": The Dimension of Halakhic Ruling In Joseph Karo's Beit Yosef* [Hebrew], Ph.D. submitted at Ben-Gurion University, 2018; Maoz Kahana, "A Universe Made of Words. The Self-Image of R. Joseph Karo as Composer of Halakhah" [Hebrew], *Hebrew Law Annual* [Shnaton HaMishpat Ha'Ivri in Hebrew] 30 (2019–2020), pp. 79–127; Yoel Marciano, *Sages of Spain in the Eye of the Storm - Jewish Scholars of Late Medieval Spain* [Hebrew], Jerusalem: Bialik Institute, 2019; Yaron Ben-Naeh, "Rabbi Joseph Karo and His Time" [Hebrew], in: *Rabbi Joseph Karo. History, Halakhah, Kabbalah*, Jerusalem: Zalman Shazar Center, 2021, pp. 103–123.

35. This aspect would be discussed later in section "The Safed *Semikhah* Polemics".

Beirav. Other messianic options were rampant in early modern Safed, the cradle of the impressive mystical-Kabbalistic renaissance of Jewish religiosity, and these had very little to do with political-historical or activist messianism.[36]

Moreover, the fundamental problem with all these works is that they hardly include any reference to the historical context in which the *Semikhah* was to take place, namely Safed as part of the Ottoman Empire, after its expansion to the entire Arab world in the early sixteenth century. Reading rabbinical sources out of their temporal frame is a tempting and almost irresistible lure, as the documents themselves barely refer to concrete reality and present their arguments mainly in respect to precedent discussions within the rabbinical post-Talmudic literature, and certainly not as a response to material reality. For instance, reaching a halakhic verdict (*Pesiqah*) is regularly presented as a reliance on immanent rules of halakhic discourse. The "Declaration of *Semikhah*" issued by the Safed sages in the early stage is a good case in point. History is to be found nowhere in the vague background ("God turned angry on his people [...] and God's people are dispersed, as a lost flock"), while the internal rabbinical precedents take front stage,

Were the participants unaware of the historical circumstances in which they lived, in the Arabic parts of the Ottoman Empire? I would later claim that the opposite is true. Yet as members of the rabbinical milieu, they were constrained to follow the rules of the game and present all their claims under rabbinical terminology and arguments, without referring directly to their temporal motivations or exposing their overall intentions. The arguments in the *Semikhah* polemics construct a front-screen to serve behind-the-scene intentions and motivations.

The choice to anchor the *Semikhah* on the sayings of Maimonides, both in his Mishnah commentary and in the *Mishneh Torah*, was a deliberate strategic choice by R. Beirav. The prominent colleagues in his Safed "Major Yeshiva" followed suit, as did the opposing figures in Jerusalem. Ever since the sixteenth century, all the rabbinical discussions and proposals to reinstate rabbinical *Semikhah* rely on Maimonides' suggestions as an axial point of reference.[37] At first glance, this may seem an almost inevitable choice, since Maimonides was virtually the only one figure who discussed this issue in the post-Talmudic legal literature. What is more, shortly after the composition of the *Mishneh Torah*, he became a leading halakhic figure. His sayings became authoritative in several Jewish Diasporas and he became the declared halakhic leader of eastern Diasporas (*Mara de atra* or "master of the place" in Aramaic rabbinical parlance, is the term mentioned).[38] Yet this choice was less inevitable than it might seem. The discussion

---

36. Roni Weinstein, *Kabbalah and Jewish Modernity*, Littman Library of Jewish Culture, London, 2016, passim.

37. See the attempts of R. Israel of Shklov in early nineteenth century, and a second wave following the establishment of the State of Israel in the mid-twentieth century and the establishment of a formal state-rabbinate (*Rabbanut Rashit*).

38. Yaron Durani, *Three Pillars of Instruction in the Rulings of R. Joseph Karo* [Hebrew], M.A. Thesis submitted at Bar-Ilan University, 2006, passim; Aviezer Ravitzky (ed.), *Maimonides: Conservatism, Originality, Revolution*, Vol I – "History and Halakhah," Jerusalem: Zalman Shazar Center, 2008.

of *Semikhah* was not an academic or textual matter, but a political one, in the sense that it aimed to organize Jewish collective life and justice within given historical circumstances and restraints. The choice by Beirav and his supporters was a typically political one, intended to provide the legitimating cover of rabbinical-halakhic discourse. This becomes all the more clear when we recall that his main source of choice among the Maimonidean writings was the exegesis on the Mishnah. As mentioned previously, the Mishnah had long ceased to serve as an independent canonical reference for rabbinical verdicts and was merely used as the starting point for further Talmudic discussions. Could an exegesis of such a text even be regarded as legally relevant and binding? Rabbis Beirav and Ben-Haviv diverged sharply on this issue; the former asserting boldly that this source is a legitimate halakhic source, while the latter refuted its relevancy to the debate.[39]

Further, a short perusal of Maimonides' proposals, cited previously, reveals several differences of content and tone between the suggestions in the Mishnah commentary and the *Mishneh Torah*. No discussion could simply ignore these differences, and Ralbach seized on this theme, rhetorically asking which of them should be regarded as the ultimate conclusion. His answer was crystal clear, and quite reasonable: the Mishnah exegesis was composed by Maimonides as a young man, while the *Mishneh Torah*—the first binding code of law—was the product of a mature scholar and hence obviously more binding.[40] The Mishnah-related expressions provide no more than a "soft" base of suggestions and potential readings and cannot mandate any broader vision or historical narrative. Another unavoidable barrier to tackle was the hesitant language used by Maimonides in presenting his position in both texts. In the Mishnah exegesis, composed in Judeo-Arabic (essentially Arabic written in Hebrew letters), he used the verb اعتقد, which means "I am persuaded," rather than an overt expression of a clear-cut ruling. In his code of law, he ended his words by casting doubt on himself, as noted, by means of the expression "The question whether *semikhah* can be renewed requires further resolution." To which part of his previous sayings does this expression apply? Does it relate to certain point (and if so, which one), or does it extended to the entire feasibility of the *Semikhah* issue? Again, both rabbis were at odds in this regard.[41] And lastly, when Maimonides referred to the need for unanimous consent among the Holy Land rabbis, what did this imply? Did it suggest a need for the complete and full consent of all the participants or would an impressive majority suffice, so that the opposing minority could be considered as joining the majority opinion? As we shall see, this point turned out to be a key issue rather than a technicality concerning the procedure for counting the participants' votes. Indeed, a substantial part of the antagonistic letters exchanged between Beirav and Ben-Haviv was devoted to this particular matter.

---

39. Ben-Haviv, *Responsa*, pp. 2, 13–14, 17–18, 25, 29–30, 49–50, 57.

40. *Ibid.*, pp. 12, 29.

41. *Ibid.*, pp. 18, 40, 47, 49–50.

Behind the scholarly debate, not exceptional in Jewish juridical milieu, lay three axes of principal disagreements: (i) The first axis concerned the rabbinical ethos concerning the chain of transmission of the Oral Torah. In this context, this ethos necessitated that only a bearer of *Semikhah* could confer it on his own disciple (*samukh mi-pi samukh* in rabbinical terminology), and thereafter down the succeeding generations. Once this personal chain ceased to function, sometime between the fourth and eighth centuries, was it even possible to renew it? Would not any renewed *Semikhah* be a mere shadow and fictitious imitation of the original, with only a semantic similitude?[42] As expected, Beirav was perfectly aware of this fundamental barrier, yet he offered a counter-position of daring innovativeness: in Islamic legal tradition, we could designate such a position as *Ijtihad*. (ii) The second point, touched on above, can be summarized by the more general term "legal consensus." As unanimous agreement among professional jurists is hardly expected, some kind of mechanism is required to form a consensus and reach a conclusion. This mechanism is not necessarily formal or institutional and could indicate some internal debates among the members of the legal milieu. Again, such an issue is highly pertinent to the Islamic context, under the title *Ijma'*. (iii) What would be the concrete implications, especially in legal proceedings and in rabbinic Responsa and courts of law, should the *Semikhah* be reinstated and henceforward again internalized in Jewish tradition? As presented by R. Beirav, this question concerned less the inner circle of scholars, or the master–disciple interaction, and more the new status of a religious court (*Beit Din*) comprised of members holding a formal *Semikhah*. Such a court enjoyed juridical authority in three specific domains: adjudicating cases where financial penalties (*dinei qenasot*) were imposed on the convicted person; the activation of corporeal sanctions (*'onshei guf*) as part of penalization and mainly as a mode of penance; and finally setting the Jewish calendar.[43]

A rabbinical discussion where the two disputants disagree on every issue is a rarity, but this rarity manifested itself throughout the *Semikhah* polemics. There was, however, one thing on which both Beirav and Ralbach shared a common position: the unique position of the city of Safed within the Jewish Ecumene.[44] A unique opportunity emerged as the city grew economically and demographically during the sixteenth century and attracted leading intellectuals and scholars in all domains of Jewish learning. A clear source of attraction was the vicinity to the places where R. Shimon bar-Yochai, the ascribed composer of the *Zohar* (the "Book of Splendor") lived and was buried. His grave became a popular site for pilgrimages, very much like the *Ziyarah* in Muslim traditions. The *Zohar*, printed for the first time during the sixteenth century, furnished the basis for a mystical renaissance in early modern Safed that was later disseminated across the entire Mediterranean Basin and well beyond, to Eastern and

---

42. *Ibid.*, pp. 1–2, 12, 22, 39, 43, 52, 56, 79.
43. *Ibid.*, pp. 2–13, 15–17, 19, 21–23, 25, 33–44, 46, 56, 69–74.
44. Weinstein, *Kabbalah and Jewish Modernity*, passim. See a more elaborate discussion below, on Ch. 5, esp. §5.5.

Central Europe.[45] Works composed in Safed in this period—by various writers and in diverse religious domains—or by figures affiliated with the Safed authorities deeply affected Jewish culture and religiosity for centuries to come. The leading local rabbis inspired a spirit of innovation in almost every respect, and Beirav's innovative fitted well into this atmosphere.

The declaration as drafted by the sages of Safed did not explicitly mention any messianic motivations: "This act of righteousness and peace would come, first, as a beginning for our souls' salvation."[46] The expression "our salvation" is charged with rich connotations, not necessarily referring to active Messianism. However, the reference in the concluding sentence in the declaration to this verse in Isaiah—also quoted in Maimonides' Mishnah exegesis, echoed some messianic vision, even if this was not stated openly. The explicit motivation was certainly not messianic. When the confrontation with R. Ben-Haviv began to heat up, Beirav alluded more openly to some apocalyptic expectations on his part, but the allusion was still very subtle: "This major and sanctified act [of renovating *Semikhah*], fulfilling the prophets' words and providing a channel for our salvation."[47] This evasive rhetoric fitted well the announced intention of Beirav and his colleagues to organize the legal mechanisms—in their words,

> to choose among us the leading [persons] in sagacity and age, the Supreme Sage (*ha-chakham ha-shalem*), the great Rabbi Jacob Beirav to be bestowed with a *Semikhah* and head-ship of the Yeshiva [the central religious school in Safed], and he would host [in that same Yeshiva] the more advanced scholars among us, and they would be [officially] nominated as Rabbis and carriers of *Semikhah* forever, acting truthfully and justly, implementing the Torah laws in courts.[48]

The professed masterplan, therefore, was to establish a centralized institution author-ized to handle all legal and scholarly activities through a formal college of scholars bear-ing the *Semikhah* title. This apparatus would be headed by R. Beirav, considered primus inter pares alongside his colleagues in terms of prestige and the monopoly to confer *Semikhah*. This structure clearly echoes the glorious and mythical past of the *Sanhedrin*, headed by the elevated figure of the *Nasi*. It was this very reading of Beirav's project that aroused the opposition of Jerusalem sages, following Ralbach:

> You wrote, and I quote, that there is a need for a head of the supreme court of law; and you further wrote that this person is essentially the head of the Yeshiva and *Nasi*. The person heading the Major Yeshivah is actually a *Nasi*, or would become a *Nasi* in the future once the number of Sanhedrin members [seventy sages] is accomplished [...] You

---

45. Boaz Huss, *The Zohar: Reception and Impact*, tr. by Yudit Nave, Oxford and Portland [Or.], Littman Library of Jewish Civilization, 2016, passim.
46. Ben-Haviv, *Responsa*, p. 2.
47. *Ibid.*, p. 43. See also, *ibid.*, 40.
48. *Ibid.*, p. 2.

are misguiding the gullible by saying that your *Semikhah* project is mandatory and highly beneficial in order to expedite the construction of the Holy Temple and draw nearer the coming of the Messiah [...] Praised be the Lord that enabled me to identify your intention, saying that the construction of the Holy Temple and coming of the Messiah depend on *Semikhah*, to verify the words of the Prophet "I will restore your magistrates as of old, And your counselors as of yore." You certainly intended to reestablish the institute of *Nasi* and reinstate the *Sanhedrin*.[49]

Thus it was Ralbach, rather than the Safed sages, who attributed to his Safed rival unstated messianic intentions, hidden under his ostensibly halakhic claims. Ralbach's statements were taken at face value by contemporaries, later rabbinical authorities, and modern scholars, all of whom presented the rabbinical arguments as a hidden messianic vision to construct a formal and centralized institution, a kind of Supreme Court headed by one dominant figure. Membership of this prestigious body would depend on a formal procedure of inclusion into the rabbinical guild through the granting of the *Semikhah* title.

The interpretation offered to date for the *Semikhah* affair is problematic, in particular, in that it ignores the historical circumstances in which the *Semikhah* was to take place: the position of the Jewish minority and the political and legal status of the Holy Land under the Ottoman Empire in early sixteenth century. The military thrust of the early years of the sixteenth century gave way to the consolidation of an empire during the second half of Sultan Süleiman's rule in the late sixteenth and early seventeenth century. This transformation was so profound that there is ample justification to suggest that a Second Empire replaced the patrimonial empire, the perfect form of which is intimately associated with the reign of Süleyman the Magnificent (1520–1566). It was marked administratively by an early modern state, as opposed to a medieval dynastic institution; economically by a more market-oriented economy; legally by a more unified legal system that came to exert some authority over the dynasty; monetarily by a more unified currency system; and politically, by the development of a type of limited government by the Sultan.[50]

The axial role of law and justice was presented in the introduction. In this chapter, it is pertinent to add the formation of a circle of professional jurists who played a role in running the Empire. In his important book, Guy Burak characterized the awareness of these professionals of the law as an "establishment consciousness" relying on

---

49. Citations from *ibid.*, pp. 79, 86, 56. See also *ibid.*, pp. 12, 86. A similar position is stated by R. Moses de Castro, see Dimitrovsky, "New Documents Regarding the Semichah Controversy," p. 146.

50. Baki Tezcan, *The Second Ottoman Empire: Political and Social Transformation in the Early Modern World*, Cambridge: Cambridge U.P., 2010, esp. p. 10. For an important characterization of the reign of Süleyman, see Cornell H. Fleischer, "The Lawgiver as Messiah: The Making of the Imperial Image in the Reign of Süleymân," in: Gilles Veinstein (ed.), *Soliman le Magnifique et son temps*, Paris: La Documentation Française, 1992, pp. 159–177.

the law as one of the pillars of the empire and on a distinct professional ethos.[51] The legal guild leaned on a tightly organized and state-controlled hierarchy. The study and the texts used in schools were monitored, especially in the famous and prestigious schools in the major cities. These studies paved the way for alumni to assume future posts in various places across the empire, if they were talented and connected to the right families and patrons. The cohesiveness of this group derived, to no small extent, from the adoption of the Hanafi school of law as the quasi-official state norm, at the expense of other traditions, and even of the non-Ottoman traditions within the Hanafi *Madhhab*. Judges were expected to follow the instructions and rules of this tradition, and especially those emanating through several channels from the person heading the legal hierarchy, the Şeyḫülislâm.[52] The pride and sense of distinctness were shown in the literary genre of *Tabaqat*, which detailed the various generations of legal scholars and their meticulous hierarchic grades. Each rank was limited in prestige and authority relative to the previous one. This literature explicitly provides tools for resolving internal jurisprudential disputes and determining the canonical doctrine for the members of the Ottoman learned hierarchy.[53] From the late sixteenth century and into the seventeenth, the major roles in the legal hierarchy were filled by members of a limited number of families, a kind of juridical aristocracy, or "Lords of the Law" (*Mevali*) as they were aptly dubbed by Baki Tezcan.[54] These positions imbued social and political prestige, and no less so substantial financial benefits. These *Mevali* families were hardly inclined to share their control over the legal system with other contenders within Ottoman society, and particularly with contestants from the non-Muslim minorities, including the Jewish *Dhimmi*. The legal milieu provided one pillar in constructing the Ottoman state, alongside the bureaucratic elite. As scholars of both *Kanuname* and *Shari'a*, they felt that they could transform Ottoman ideology and law from within according to their own ideals.[55]

At the final chain of command in the legal hierarchy functioned the Kadi—a judge, but also in many respects, the daily and living intersection point between the ordinary population and the Sultanic authority. It is well-known that the functions of the Kadi

---

51. Guy Burak, *The Second Formation of Islamic Law. The Hanafi School the Early Modern Ottoman Empire*, Cambridge: Cambridge U.P., 2015, p. 161.

52. See esp. *ibid.*, p. 79.

53. *Ibid.*, pp. 72–73, 76.

54. Baki Tezcan, "The Ottoman Mevali as 'Lords of the Law'", *Journal of Islamic Studies* 20:3 (2009), pp. 383–407, esp. pp. 383–384. See also idem., *The Second Ottoman Empire*, pp. 37–38. For a general discussion on Ottoman scholars of the law, see Michael Nizri, *Ottoman High Politics and the Ulema Household*, London: McMillan and Palgrave, 2014.

55. Abdurrahman Atcıl, *Scholars and Sultans in the Early Modern Ottoman Empire*, Cambridge: Cambridge U.P., 2017, esp p. 215. See also, *ibid.*, p. 131: "It is in this period, the late 1530's and 1540's, that we see an energetic compilation, codification, and modification of imperial ordinance, its regularization, universalization, and reconciliation with the dictates of the Holy Law, and also the rapid expansion and deepening of the machinery of government based on newly articulated principles of hierarchy, order, meritocracy, regularity, and replicability of basic structures based on function rather than on persons."

under the Ottoman Empire extended far beyond his formal function as judge. He was also a public administrator who played various roles, thereby symbolizing the merger of public and private law through his very office, occupied with the public and private domains.[56] The Kadi's authority embodied that of the Empire and the Sultan, and it clearly took precedence over non-Muslim legal authorities. The role of the Kadis within Muslim communities, in the heartland of the Ottoman Empire and in the Arab lands, was further enhanced due to the help Ottoman courts extended to contending parties in order to reach a compromise by an amicable settlement (*Sulh* in Arabic, and later in Turkish).[57] The Kadis' courts had the advantage of providing official certification for documents, at times serving at a kind of state archive. This institution provided a rapid service to those who turned to it. Add to this, the hierarchic nature of the legal mechanism enabled to direct submission of appeals to the Sultanic courts, in case the local legal authorities were failing to provide justice.

The incorporation of vast territories inhabited by Arab Muslims, whose traditions predated the Ottoman conquest by centuries, did not take the form of the simple and linear imposition of Ottoman patterns nor by the submission of the conquered side.[58] The military and political expansion of the Ottoman Empire was accompanied by what Timothy Fitzgerald called "Rituals of Possession" in the new territories, through which the legal and bureaucratic patterns of the Ottoman Empire were gradually imposed.[59] Ottoman officials and bureaucrats initiated land surveys for future tax impositions and introduced the Ottoman legal system. The local elites were incorporated into the legal institutions, while local traditions were certainly taken into consideration. Ottoman dominance was manifested in legislation following the conquest, in which the preambles

---

56. Tezcan, *The Second Ottoman Empire*, p. 36. Karen Barkey, "Aspects of Legal Pluralism in the Ottoman Empire," in: Lauren Benton and Richard J. Ross (eds.), *Legal Pluralism and Empires, 1500–1850*, New York and London: New York U.P., 2013, pp. 83–107, esp. p. 90, noting that the court and the magistrate became the main representatives of state hegemony at the local level. On various aspects of Kadis functioning, see also Metin M. Coşgel and Boğaç A. Ergene, "Dispute Resolution in Ottoman Courts: A Quantitative Analysis of Litigations in Eighteenth-Century Kastamonu," *Social Science History* 38, no. 1–2 (Spring/Summer 2014), pp. 183–202; Rossita Gradeva, 'A kadi Court in the Balkans: Sofia in the Seventeenth and Early Eighteenth Centuries', in: Christine Woodhead (ed.), *The Ottoman World*, Routledge: London and New York, 2012, pp. 57–71; Eyal Ginio, "The Administration of Criminal Justice in Selânik (Salonica) during the Eighteenth Century," *Turcica* 30 (1998), pp. 185–209.

57. Abdülmecid Mutaf, "Amicable Settlement in Ottoman Law: *Sulh* System," *Turcica* 36 (2004), pp. 125–140.

58. Burak, *The Second Formation of Islamic Law*, passim.

59. Timothy J. Fitzgerald, "Rituals of Possession, Methods of Control, and the Monopoly of Violence: The Ottoman Conquest of Aleppo in Comparative Perspective," in: Stephan Conermann & Gül Şen (eds.), *The Mamluk-Ottoman Transition. Continuity and Change in Egypt and Bilād al-Shām in the Sixteenth Century*, Bonn: Bonn U.P., 2017, pp. 249–273, esp. p. 265. A detailed research on the encounter between local Arab traditions and Ottoman centralistic policy in the city of Aleppo, see Idem., "Murder in Aleppo: Ottoman Conquest and the Struggle for Justice in the Early Sixteenth Century," *Journal of Islamic Studies* 27, no. 2 (2016), pp. 176–215.

to the *Kanunname* stated the centralistic policy.[60] It was further and clearly expressed in the nomination of judges from the capital and the control of local *Waqf* institutions.[61]

The Ottomans respected the legal traditions of the various non-Muslim minorities (the *Dhimmis*) but subjected them to the imperial juridical system, so that they enjoyed only a very limited autonomy until the eighteenth century. Eleni Gara viewed this policy as part of the overall control of *Dhimmi* within the early modern Ottoman Empire in regard to the Orthodox, Armenian, and Eastern Churches or the Jewish religious leaderships. They were not used as agents or intermediaries of indirect rule on behalf of the Sultan, but mainly for extracting additional taxes. Bishops were spiritual leaders but not administrative heads of their communities, and their efforts to influence communal affairs were a common cause of friction. Christian and Jewish judicial autonomy had a limited scope and was largely informal.[62] The frequent replacement of the Greek Patriarchs in Constantinople was an indication of their precarious position relative to the Ottoman authorities.[63] The Church was considered by the Ottomans as a fiscal institution. Ecclesiastical offices offered an economic benefit to their holders, as they functioned as tax farms and became an object of intense competition for members of the Greek Orthodox community, and they were increasingly occupied by wealthy lay people. Gara concludes that "This new description counters the received wisdom that the patriarch was the leader of the Greek *millet*, having both religious and civil authority over the non-Muslim Greek Orthodox Christian community."[64]

If Greek Orthodox autonomy under the Ottomans was limited, this was much clearer in the case of the Jewish communities of much weaker bargaining position, both in the core territories of Anatolia and Rumelia and in the recently conquered Arab lands. The restrictions on Jewish legal autonomy were lucidly presented by Joseph

---

60. Rifa'at Ali Abou-El-Haj, "Aspect of the Legitimation of Ottoman Rule as Reflected in the Preambles to Two Early *Liva Kanunnameler*," *Turcica* 23 (1991), pp. 371–383. A discussion on preambles to Ottoman law codes, see Snjezana Buzov, *State Law and Divine Law Under the Ottomans: Encounters Between Shari'a and the Sultan's Law*, London: I. B. Tauris, 2012, passim. See the discussion in this regard in the previous chapter.

61. Zouhair Ghazzal, "Waqfs and Urban Structures: The Case of Ottoman Damascus by Richard van Leeuwen," *International Journal of Middle East Studies* 33, no. 4 (2001), pp. 618–620.

62. Eleni Gara, "Conceptualizing Interreligious Relations in the Ottoman Empire: The Early Modern Centuries," *Acta Poloniae Historica* 116 (2017), pp. 57–92, esp. esp. p. 70. On the increasing legal autonomy during the eighteenth century, see *ibid.*, pp. 58, 71. On Ottoman "Legal Pluralism" in regard to religious minorities, see the observations of Barkey, "Aspects of Legal Pluralism in the Ottoman Empire," pp. 84, 90. See also important discussions in: Tom Papademetriou, *Render unto the Sultan. Power, Authority, and the Greek Orthodox Church in the early Ottoman Centuries*, Oxford: Oxford U.P., 2015; Hasan Çolak and Elif Bayraktar-Tellan, *The Orthodox Church as an Ottoman Institution. A Study of Early Modern Patriarchal Berats*, Istanbul: The Isis Press, 2019.

63. Papademetriou, *Render unto the Sultan*, esp. p. 214.

64. *Ibid.*, pp. 219, 215. On the position of the Armenian Patriarch, see Kevork B. Bardakjian, "The Rise of the Armenian Patriarchate of Constantinople," in: Bernard Lewis and Benjamin Braude (eds.), *Christians and Jews in the Ottoman Empire: The Functioning of a Plural Society*, New York: Holmes & Meier, 1982, pp. 89–100.

Hacker.[65] Jewish courts had no independent status and required the approval of a local Kadi to implement their decisions. This position was explicitly stated by contemporary senior rabbinical figures, such as R. Samuel de Medinah (known as *Maharashdam*) or R. Joseph Karo, testifying to the situation in Istanbul and Safed.[66] Jewish courts tended to limit their discussions to typically "religious" or ritualistic matters, avoiding discussion of financial, public, or political issues. It was common among the Jewish public to address the Kadi rather than the rabbinical courts, even in personal-religious matters such as marriage and divorce. When confronted with violent or strong-minded persons, the Jewish court was virtually ineffective and incapable of implementing its verdicts. Toward the end of the sixteenth century, Muslim officials and *Kadi*s were increasingly involved in the nomination of Jewish judges. Trusting communal solidarity, rabbinical authorities consistently insisted on maintaining the Jewish legal tradition and autonomy, while doing everything in their power to keep this below the Ottoman radar. Informing on Jewish scholars that they participated in a formal procedure of Jewish court, or even that they dissuaded others from addressing a Muslim court, gravely endangered them.[67] The lack of a "Chief Rabbi" overruling the ranks of local rabbis and Talmudic scholars, nominated by Ottomans or chosen by the local scholars—to serve as an intermediate link between the Jews and Ottoman authorities—further weakened the legal autonomy of the Jewish minority.[68]

All these circumstances could hardly encourage any design to construct a central and formal institution of judicial autonomy, entirely independent of Ottoman authorities and deriving its legitimacy from pre-Islamic era, and certainly preceding the Ottoman presence in the Near East. Any such attempt to challenge the imperial dominance in the juridical domain, as in political and military one, would have incited a ferocious reaction on the part of the Ottoman state. Furthermore, the city of Safed as part of the Galilee (the northern part of the Holy Land) was directly controlled by the Ottoman governor of Damascus, which would consider a Sanhedrin-like institution a portent of a rebellious movement. It is improbable that the *Semikhah* procedure was intended to restore complete legal autonomy—a Sanhedrin-like institution as under the Roman rule, still less to serve later as basis of a quasi-international court of law within the Jewish

65. Joseph Hacker, 'Jewish Autonomy in the Ottoman Empire: Its Scope and Limits. Jewish Courts from the Sixteenth to the Eighteenth Centuries', in: Avigdor Levy (ed.), *The Jews of the Ottoman Empire*, Princeton (N.J.): Darwin Press in cooperation with the Institute of Turkish Studies, Washington, D.C, 1994, pp. 153–202. See also, Jacob Barnai, 'The Status of the 'General Rabbinate' in Jerusalem in the Ottoman Period', *Cathedra: For the History of Eretz Israel and Its Yishuv* 13 (1979), pp. 47–69.
66. Joseph Hacker, 'The Limits of Jewish Autonomy: Internal Jewish Adjudication in the Sixteenth-Eighteenth Centuries' [Hebrew], in: Shmuel Almog et alii (eds.), *Transition and Change in Modern Jewish History: Essays Presented in Honor of Shmuel Ettinger*, Jerusalem: Zalman Shazar Center and the Israeli Historical Society, 1987, pp. 349–388, esp. pp. 368, 359, 370, 374–377.
67. Hacker, 'Jewish Autonomy in the Ottoman Empire', pp. 170–174.
68. Idem., 'The 'Chief Rabbinate' in the Ottoman Empire in the 15th and 16th Century' [Hebrew], *Zion* 49 (1984), pp. 225–263.

Ecumene.[69] All these facts were well-known to Ottoman Jews, living either in the core lands or in Arabic territories. Contemporary rabbinical and community documents testify that the Jews in the core areas of Ottoman Empire and in *Bilad a-Sham* periphery knew well the political and judicial mechanisms of the Sultanic rule. The Safed rabbis understood entirely that such an aspired project could not materialize but only jeopardize local community and others as well.

What were, then, the hidden goals that the Safed rabbis—at least those involved in the *Semikhah* project—sought to promote? The rhetoric relied on motives found in Talmudic heritage, but this was no more than a screen. The well-known rabbinical strategy of endorsing new elements in religious-political heritage under the garb of traditional rhetoric echoed a similar strategy used by other religious traditions familiar to Jewish intellectuals: Catholic Jesuits, Protestant reformers, or the *Kadizadeli* movement within the Ottoman Empire. It is no mere coincidence that the two leading contestants, R. Beirav and Ralbach, provided numerous hints that halakhic formalities and arguments were not the main issue at stake. Talmudic experts of such a stature were expected to adhere to legal post-Talmudic arguments. Yet they repeatedly "strengthened" their positions by recourse to invalid arguments. R. Beirav is constantly confronted with the problem that the *Semikhah* procedure essentially depends on a living and oral master–disciple chain of transmission; once broken, this could not be restored. His support of the Safed project resorts to imprecise phrasing:

> As the rabbi [Maimonides] wrote that if all the Holy Land sages agree, etc., and explained in his Mishnah exegesis that this agreement requires but a commitment in people's heart (*Hit'orerut be-lev ha-anashim*) to worship God, there should be no formal encounter nor negotiation [among rabbis and scholars], but merely a declaration that they consent, and it is all clear even to schoolchildren.[70]

Beirav provides a free interpretation of Maimonides' words when he presents the rabbinical consensus ("if all the Holy Land sages agree, etc.") in terms of an obscure "commitment in people's heart." Not only does such an expression not appear in Maimonides' exegesis, but it is entirely inconsistent with halakhic phrasing,[71] and actually implies that any consent will recreate *Semikhah*.

Ralbach, for his part, stated implicitly that once *Semikhah* was abrogated, it could only be renewed with the coming of the messianic era. The person in charge of this hypothetical mission is none other than the living Prophet Elijah:

> Verily, *Semikhah* during the messianic era by him [the Messiah] and by the Prophet Elijah is no religious innovation, since according to our tradition Elijah still lives, and he himself bears *Semikhah* conferred by a person with *Semikhah* (*samukh mi-pi samukh*), and the Messiah

---

69. See below, Chapter 8.
70. Ben-Haviv, *Responsa*, p. 40.
71. *Ibid.*, pp. 17, 19, 39–40, 42, 47.

himself would be conferred with *Semikhah* by the Lord our God, so formally he is permitted to confer *Semikhah*.[72]

The important yet folkloric figure of Elijah has thus become a living person in body and soul, part of the rabbinical establishment and living in the real present ("according to our tradition Elijah still lives"); moreover, he is a member of the generational chain of the *Semikhah* title.[73] Halakhically speaking, he, rather than any regular rabbi, bears the potential authority to reinstate the *Semikhah* procedure. Such a mixture between heavenly figures or revelations and halakhic legality runs counter to the entire rabbinical ethos.

The exchange of letters between Beirav and Ralbach does not rely only on juridical arguments, though again this is what would have been expected of such prominent scholars. It is saturated with expressions of personal shaming and degradation of their rivals' arguments. As the epistolary exchange advances, the weight of such expressions becomes ever more current and dominant. Both parties are aware of the unusual tone of writing yet could not resist, once the rival drags them into this antagonistic exchange. In an exceptional revelation of personal feelings—a rarity in the rabbinical literature—Ralbach mourns the shaming of R. de Castro by R. Beirav:

> What he [Beirav] composed, especially against the important *Chakham* [a Sephardi title for a rabbinical position] R. Moses de Castro, and how he dishonored his Torah unjustifiably; this shame has broken my heart and left me soulless. Only due to this situation I would forsake my straight way, he [R. Beirav] is to be blamed, since he ignited the fire of rage and wrath and enlarged the bonfire. And yet I would control my spirit and be cautious in front of old age and erudition [both of Beirav].[74]

It is a contest of honor, and as such both parties are required to expose some personal, and at times even intimate, aspects of themselves when their rivals cast doubt on their motivations and professional competencies. For his part, R. Beirav completely disregards a contemporary social and halakhic taboo that Jews forced to convert to Catholicism (*Conversos*) were not to be reminded of their past after they returned to the Jewish faith, and still he throws this allegation at Ralbach's face. Ralbach faces this challenge directly, not denying or ignoring the fact of his forced conversion but claiming his innocence and emphasizing his penitential mood ever since this misfortune fell upon him. He incites Safed rabbis to distance themselves from R. Beirav "not for my honor's sake, God forbid, but for the sake of all those who experienced these misery and great

---

72. *Ibid.*, p. 58. He reiterates this position on p. 13: "The Elijah, peace be on him [an expression referring to persons that passed away – R.W.], is about to arrive together with the Messiah and he [Elijah] still exists in body and soul [*Samukh Kayam beGuf veNefesh* in Hebrew], and he can confer *Semikhah* upon all courts of law in Israel, and upon the Messiah himself", and p. 39. See also, Dimitrovsky, 'New Documents Regarding the Semichah Controversy in Safed', p. 149.

73. Ben-Haviv, *Responsa*, pp. 3, 14–15, 29–30, 53, 56, 79–80.

74. *Ibid.*, p. 23. For more insults, see *ibid.*, pp. 22, 29–31, 38–42, 45–49, 52–53, 55–56, 59–62, 64–65, 76, 78–79.

dangers, who escaped [from Christian Europe] and saw no good until they repented. Many among them gained a place in the Divine World." He describes the tactics chosen by his rival as typical of Catholics who engaged in religious debate with Jews: when confronted with a good argument and unable to respond, they would accuse their opponent of blaspheming their religion "in order to fortify their false arguments."[75] Turning the argument around, he thus claims that his rival, rather than himself, is the one who has adopted a Catholic worldview. R. Beirav also needs to justify his special position as the first person granted *Semikhah*. Preoccupied with publicizing his project, he dispatches a letter to the Rhodes community in which he states unabashedly that

> even though it is improper to glorify oneself, yet in regard to well-established facts it is proper to glorify oneself, all the more so in relation to Torah issues. It is well-established that should there be just one person in all the kingdoms and places to which the Sephardi refugees migrated, a person capable of reading Halakhah properly and deeply, recurring to the methodology of Scholasticism (*pilpul*) and exposing all its secrets; this person is me, speaking justly. For God, blessed be his name, has conferred grace upon me.[76]

R. Beirav immodestly presents himself as the leading scholar of his contemporary generation and the most proficient in the particular Sephardi methodology of Talmudic studies. The right to initiate the *Semikhah* process is a small and inevitable step forward. The confrontation is indeed very personal and occasionally resorts to *ad hominem* arguments, as well as direct shaming. However, the honor ethos was an important part of Sephardi Diaspora culture, and of Mediterranean social life in general,[77] and the personal confrontation between Ralbach and Beirav thus formed part of a much bigger game. The documents in our possession seek to color the *Semikhah* polemic as a personal issue, where each of the two protagonists represents a clear position, while the remaining participants were relegated to the shadows. This provides us with a key to unlock this affair: Each of them incorporates one of the antagonistic opinions. The issue at stake concerns the question as to who would hold the position of "the Leader" and head the hierarchy of the rabbinical-scholastic milieu. It is a narrow perspective to consider the confrontation as merely a matter of ego and personal ambitions. The head figure— be it Beirav or Ben-Haviv—is significant as the embodiment of a broader construct, a metonym if one will. This explains why the choice of the individual who will carry the

---

75. *Ibid.*, p. 53. Further expressions about the personality of Ralbach, see *ibid.*, pp. 38–39, 47, 76–78.

76. The letter to Rhodes appears in *ibid.*, pp. 82–87. The citation appears on p. 82. Further expressions about the personality of Beirav, see *ibid.*, 2–3, 26, 30, 39, 81.

77. Yaron Ben-Naeh, 'Honor and its Meaning among Ottoman Jews', *Jewish Social Studies*, New Series, 11,2(Winter, 2005), pp. 19–50. On another Jewish Mediterranean context, see Roni Weinstein, 'L'ethos dell'onore nella vita famigliare e comunitaria della società ebraica italiana all'inizio dell'età moderna', in: Francesco Aspesi, Vermondo Brugnatelli, Anna Linda Callow, Claudia Rosenzweing (eds.), *Il mio cuore è a oriente. Studi di linguistica, filologia e cultura ebraica dedicati a Maria Modena Mayer*, Quaderni di Acme 101, Milano: Cisalpino Istituto Editoriale Universitario, 2008, pp. 771–790.

personal authority of *Semikhah*, and no less importantly will maintain the right to confer it upon others, also becomes competitive and antagonistic.

Most of the confrontation between Beirav and Ralbach is devoted to technical and formalistic halakhic argumentation, as expected in a dialogue between two experts of the law. The main thrust lies not in these parts, however, but in two recurrent themes: (i) The rabbinical consensus and (ii) The status of the Talmudic "Leader of the Generation" (*Gedol Ha-Dor*). Jewish erudition encouraged free discussion among the participants in Torah study. The rabbinical ethos draws from a founding narrative of the entire People of Israel attending the conference of oral and written Torah at Mount Sinai, whereby the entire collective enjoys the same share in its tradition.[78] Open discussions among scholars continued through the classical rabbinical period under Roman rule, despite severe political restrictions on Jewish autonomy. The enforcement of any official rabbinical opinion was impossible, and this necessitated ceaseless internal rabbinical negotiations and the securing of a *scholarly consensus* on every issue during the composition of the Mishnah and Talmud. Surprisingly enough, there are hardly any direct discussions as to how were these moments of consensus to be reached and what were the processes or mechanisms–be they formal or informal—for terminating the discussions and offering a clear-cut instruction. The *Semikhah* documents provide one of the most elaborated discussions on rabbinical consensus, uncommon elsewhere from the Talmudic period through the Middle Ages. Its formal focus revolves around Maimonides' assertion that the reinstatement of *Semikhah* requires the consent of all the Holy Land sages—in other words, a consensus in the scholarly community. But what does this precondition mean in practice? Has there ever been total unanimity in any Talmudic debate or for that matter within any scholarly community in any other historical setting? The disputants Rabbis Beirav and Ralbach elaborated and weighed the value of various positions on this matter across the spectrum: starting from literal unanimous consent and terminating with a simple counting of votes to ensure a numerical majority. These were the extreme end points, less relevant to rabbinical discourse and to the Talmudic ethos, as neither was ever adopted in practice in Jewish scholarly traditions. In between, lay the grey zone of some informal processes for imposing the position of majority on the minority. In the Muslim context, the term *Ijma'* is the title used for the periodic discussions on how to reach a legal consensus.

The vast Talmudic and post-Talmudic literature is a product of collective debates and study. Ever since the rise of the Sages (*Chakhamim*), and especially after the destruction of the Second Temple (70 AD), certain scholars acquired a unique position. Such exceptional persons among the Mishnaic and Talmud scholars, and later among the *Geonim* and Sephardi and Ashkenazi communities, were considered as a personification of the Torah, its living examples in human life. In his introduction to the first code of Talmudic law (the *Mishneh Torah*), Maimonides provides a vivid presentation of these figures within

---

78. This theme is elaborated in *Sefer HaKuzari*, a fundamental tract of Jewish medieval philosophy. See Adam Shear, *The Kuzari and the Shaping of Jewish Identity*, Cambridge: Cambridge U.P., 2008.

the rabbinical ethos. The chain of transmission of the Oral Torah (the rabbinical term for the Talmudic and post-Talmudic tradition) is continued by these exceptional figures. Maimonides also contributed to the notion that each generation has its own leading figure (*Gedol Ha-Dor*, literally "the great one of/among the generation," i.e. the major scholarly figure of his time). These major figures were not merely credited with intellectual talent and expert knowledge of the entire Talmudic lore, but their figures were hallowed with sanctity and a special linkage to past generations of scholars. They were entitled to suggest substantial innovations in the Talmudic heritage, and indeed some of them did so (such as Rashi, Rabbenu Tam, Maimonides, *Rashbah*, to briefly mention just a few of the most famous instances). None of them was ever seriously requested to justify their new positions in Halakhah nor did they ever apologize for it. It was the privilege of the very few.

The *Semikhah* initiative was presented to a large extent as a one-man show, headed primarily by R. Yaakov Beirav.[79] The self-image of R. Beirav was vividly and directly presented in his above-mentioned letter to the Rhodes community: "should there be just one person in all the kingdoms and places to which the Sephardi refugees migrated, a person capable of reading Halakhah properly and deeply [...] this person is me." Undoubtedly, he took upon himself the role of the Scholarly Leader of his generation, and hence his commitment and responsibility to initiate all the changes required under contemporary historical circumstances. It should be noted that in his *Semikhah* polemics, R. Beirav softened the tone of his personal grandeur, instead emphasizing the changes required in response to his time. His personal involvement and role in mobilizing this process was kept in the shadow. Yet his bitter rival R. Ben-Haviv constantly insisted that Beirav was acting as if he were superior to all others.[80] He was not mistaken, since Beirav indeed enjoyed an entirely exceptional status in the city of Safed.[81] His Yeshiva was considered the most prestigious in the city, and he bequeathed the famous Sephardi methodology of Talmud scholarship to an entire generation of local scholars. R. Beirav was hailed as an impressive expert in the scholastic mode of Talmudic studies. Among the Yeshiva's members were the leading scholars of the city, who potentially could already maintain schools of their own. As such, it functioned as both a scholarly hub and a kind of a supreme court of law. Its general aim was to enable advanced students to serve later as judges and Talmudic arbiters (*posqim*) across the entire Sephardi Diaspora. All these components, concentrated in the same scholarly persona, inspired Beirav and his admirers to consider this Yeshiva as an incarnation in their day of the historical

---

79. The life and prestigious rabbinic status of R. Yaakov Beirav are discussed in Haim Z. Dimitrovsky, 'Rabbi Yaakov Beirav's Academy in Safed' [Hebrew], *Sefunot: Studies and Sources on the History of the Jewish Communities in the East* 7 (1963), pp. 41–102.

80. Ralbach, *Responsa*, p. 26: "This scholar [R. Beirav] considers himself superior to all [scholars of] his generation. Not only does he regard them as worthless, but he doesn't peruse deeply the books to understand them properly, thinking that only by exfoliating them he gets their intentions fully and completely, and that there are no complications nor contradictions [in these Talmudic texts], since he has an instant and comprehensive perspective". See also *ibid.*, pp. 3, 30, 81.

81. Dimitrovsky, 'Rabbi Yaakov Beirav's Academy in Safed', passim.

Sanhedrin, with all the prestige and sanctity that this venerable institution had enjoyed. It is probable that sometime during the *Semikhah* initiation Beirav adopted the title *Nasi*, again recalling the past leaders of Holy Land communities and scholars and the person heading the Sanhedrin. This title added to those already conferred on him by his Safed contemporaries and his admirers: *HaRav, Morenu, HaRav HaGadol, Nagid* (the Rabbi, Our Master/Teacher, the Major Rabbi, Political Leader).[82] Attending his school on certain occasions, the debates acquired a public status, and the conclusions were considered as binding on the inhabitants of Safed. No wonder that his disciples considered the city as "under the Dominion of This Master" (*Atrei deMar*), echoing a similar saying in regard to Maimonides as the "Master of the Oriental Jewish Diaspora." His close disciples considered their halakhic verdicts as valid only as and when they were approved by their master. His closest and most enthusiastic supporter, R. Moses di Trani (known by the acronym *HaMabit*), a distinguished scholar in his own right, would simply describe him as "the Supreme Court of Law i.e. R. Beirav," emphasizing his status as is *Gedol Ha-Dor*, the personification of justice in practice and of generations-long scholarship. Again, the issue of certain persons of exceptional erudition encompassing all aspects of knowledge, personal sanctity, and summation of past scholarship echoes the ethos concerning the founders of the Islamic legal schools (*Madhhabs*).

R. Karo and *Semikhah*

What was the role of R. Joseph Karo in the entire chain of events during and after the lifetime of R. Beirav? We have seen that the structuring of the *Semikhah* polemics left little room for protagonists other than R. Beirav and Ben-Haviv. The one exception to this was R. Karo. One of the complaints raised by Ralbach concerned a court document addressed to him by Karo, probably after the return of the envoy from Safed to Jerusalem and the public opposition to the *Semikhah* headed by R. ben-Haviv:[83] "I indeed had a grievance against R. Joseph [Karo], who undersigned the official document issued by a court of law, since he did not address [us] respectfully, as he and other undersigned sages should have, as is perfectly clear to whoever sees it [this document]."[84] It was R. Karo, rather than any other rabbi or Talmudic scholar in Safed, who was charged with maintaining the channel of communication between the two antagonistic rabbis. But, as R. Ben-Haviv protests, he did not adopt a peaceable approach or start a negotiation but rather dispatched a court order. Such an act in itself was not exceptional in early modern Safed, when many eminent scholars were working in close vicinity to each other, and often some of them refused to accept the collective authority.[85] It was

---

82. *Ibid.*, p. 54 notes 82–83.
83. This is the suggested reconstruction of events, in Dimitrovsky, 'New Documents Regarding the Semichah Controversy in Safed', p. 129.
84. Ralbach, *Responsa*, p. 55.
85. The ceaseless disputes between R. Karo and R. Moses of Trani [known as *HaMabit*], are colorfully presented in Meir Benayahu, *Yosef Bechiri* [My Chosen One, Joseph], Jerusalem: Yad HaRav Nissim, 1991, passim.

less expected, and certainly less respectable, when addressing a scholar of renown in another city—all the more so the holy city of Jerusalem. Sending a decree issued by an official court of law turned the message into a threatening act, forcing the addressee either to surrender or to disobey and face the consequences. Moreover, it put the recalcitrant in the position of a "disobedient sage" (*zaqen mamreh* in rabbinical-Talmudic parlance). This framing sought to ensure that the Safed–Jerusalem confrontation would echo incidents retold in the Talmud about revolts or disobedience concerning the central institution of Holy Land scholars or the person heading it, the *Nasi*. The position undertaken by R. Beirav, shared completely by R. Karo as his chosen emissary, is that *Semikhah* is an institutional matter, not a personal one of R. Beirav, or for that matter later on even of R. Karo. As such, it requires disciplinary measures, even if this clashes with the rabbinical ethos of internally conducted negotiations in a restrained and well-mannered mode. The approach of R. Ben-Haviv was depicted as rebellious and met with a formalistic and juridical attitude.

Years later, in his mystical visions, R. Karo would be praised and promised with the renovation of *Semikhah*:

> I shall raise you to become master and leader over the entire Jewish diaspora in Arabistan. Since you have deeply devoted yourself to reinstating *Semikhah*, you shall be honored to be ordained by all the sages of the Holy Land, and by the sages abroad. Through you, I [the Mishnah, i.e. the mystical figure] would re-establish the glory of *Semikhah*, and I would benefit you by finishing your major corpus.[86]

The key to understanding R. Karo's motive for keeping alive the *Semikhah* vision in later generations was his position relative to R. Beirav (d. 1541). R. Karo could not ignore the Beirav's talent and dominant position, and on several occasions calls him "My Master" (*Mori*), as a disciple does when referring to his Talmud teacher. Yet he also used the same title in regard to second-grade scholars from his own close family.[87] Unlike other devoted students of the towering figure of R. Beirav, especially R. Moses di Trani, Karo's praises were always restrained. With the exception of the *Semikhah* affair, he never waged any public legal-Talmudic battles in defense of R. Beirav.[88] It is very likely that at some point they even had a harsh confrontation, causing a crisis and a temporary distancing.[89]

R. Beirav cast a heavy shadow over all the early modern Safed scholars, R. Karo included, and for good reason. Anyone aspiring—like R. Karo—to play a role in Jewish culture or to leave his imprint on public domain was inspired by Beirav.[90] After his death, the dominancy of Maran increasingly became clear. This was facilitated by the fact that he enjoyed several advantages over R. Beirav. To start with, he combined an

---

86. See supra footnote 4.
87. Dimitrovsky, 'Rabbi Yaakov Beirav's Academy in Safed', p. 60 note 124.
88. *Ibid.*, p. 65 note 155.
89. *Ibid.*, p. 63.
90. *Ibid.*, p. 77 note 228.

exceptional halakhic talent with an intense mystical life. These inseparable aspects of his life (see Chapter Six) charged his life with a sense of destiny and personal mission. While R. Beirav left behind written works of relatively restricted extent and importance, Karo's literary production was impressive, especially his fundamental codes of law. No scholar could ignore their contribution once they had appeared in print. Karo also attempted to expand his imprint on the Jewish Ecumene by establishing a kind of international court of law (see Chapter Five); he managed to establish several Yeshivas, attended by an impressive number of advanced students, unmatched by any other local Talmudic school.[91] He also managed to plant his students in important positions in Safed, thereby arousing the indignation of senior scholars.[92]

R. Beirav was nominated by the leading Safed scholars to be the first person entitled to *Semikhah* (1532), with the additional authority to confer this title upon others by his personal decision. Opposed by local scholars wishing to have their own vote in the coming round of *Semikhah*, he refrained from continuing. Yet constrained to leave the city of Safed—probably due to personal reasons rather than to halakhic issue[93]—he hastily conferred the *Semikhah* on four more scholars, R. Karo among them.[94] The third and final phase took place years later, after R. Beirav's death. Karo, then, stands in between the first, personal-oriented phase of *Semikhah* and the following ones in much later years, as he conferred the title upon scholars affiliated to him.[95] His vision behind the *Semikah* procedure was wider than anything R. Beirav could have imagined, as testified in the opening words of this chapter. It would contribute to new patterns of authority, especially within the rabbinical guild, establish mutual interaction between center and periphery, renovate religious life, and redefine the balance between rabbis and community members.

Semikhah Polemics: A Second-Turn Reading

The words of Maimonides were composed centuries before they were activated as a platform for the early modern *Semikhah* initiative by R. Beirav. Was it mere coincidence that all this took place in the mid-sixteenth century, in Safed, within a Sephardi milieu (both R. Beirav and Ralbach came from Sephardi families), and, moreover, within a Muslim (Sunni) and Ottoman setting? Maimonides' suggestions, especially in his Mishnah commentary, had been well-known to scholars for centuries, but had hitherto remained dormant without any practical impact. Now his words were suddenly used as an anchor for a project that made sense in a particular context. I would suggest a second-turn reading that considers the historical settings behind an ostensibly halakhic confrontation.

---

91. See below Chapter 5.
92. See previous note.
93. See the sarcastic comment in Ralbach, *Responsa*, p. 55: "for some reason better left unsaid" [*mi-sibah sh-hashtikah yafa lah* in Hebrew].
94. Ben-Naeh claims that R. Karo was the first one to be ordained, yet does not provide any documents supporting such a claim. See idem., 'Rabbi Joseph Karo and His Time', p. 107.
95. Benayahu, 'The Renovation of Rabbinic Semichah in Safed', pp. 256–257.

In general terms, reference to Muslim tradition is essential for understanding some of the major themes in Jewish tradition ever since the rise of Islam, but this broader theme requires a separate discussion. This connection is also relevant to the *Semikhah* affair, in the sense that beyond the discussions of legal technicalities regarding the effect of the reinstatement of *Semikhah* renovation, two themes accompany the exchange of letters between the main chief protagonists: Rabbinical consensus and the figure of the Leader of this Generation. Both these themes reverberate in Islamic tradition, particularly following the emergence of the distinct schools of law (*Madhhabs*). Synthesizing the latest research insights on this theme, Guy Burak presented their main elements regarding their rise, evolvement, the formation of internal consensus, the balance between innovation and conservatism or stability, codification and summation books, the adherence to the eponymous founders' authority, confronting internal juridical disagreements, and the independence of the *'Ulama* relative to "lay" political authorities. The composition of codes of law provided an important focus of consensus. It comprised a backbone of authoritative opinions and served as a repository of these opinions as expressed by the founders of the schools, their immediate students, or eminent authorities of later centuries. Of particular significance is the emergence of the *compendium* (or *mukhtaṣar*) in all four schools during the ninth and tenth centuries. In addition to the compendium, each school canonized legal works that were considered particularly authoritative.[96] By the sixteenth century, in R. Karo's time, it became more common to promote legal fusions of various schools of law, despite the opposition of Arab jurists, such as 'Abd al-Ghanī al-Nābulsī and others, who sought to preserve the boundaries between the schools. This practice of combination (known as *talfīq*) was particularly prevalent across the Ottoman Empire's Arab provinces, although in later centuries it spread to other parts of the Islamic world.[97] As underlined by Burak, an issue that preoccupied all four main *Madhhabs* was the process or challenge of reaching an internal consensus. This was resolved by several channels, such as the aggrandizement of the founding father's figure as the supposed fountain of all the school's legal achievements. Another mechanism is the expanding role of tradition and "imitation" at the expense of "innovation." In the inter-*Madhhab* context, the question was even more urgent, due to the impressive legal pluralism of various schools, local traditions, and state control of justice mechanisms. Seen in this light, the issue of consensus was all the more crucial.

These twin themes of scholastic consensus and the Leading Figures of legal tradition came to forestage in the Safed polemics for good reason: they carried deep sense in the Muslim–Ottoman environment rather than in any other Jewish Diaspora. The legal pluralism in Islam and the secondary role of political authorities in managing the mechanisms of "making justice" enhanced the autonomy of the *'Ulama*, and simultaneously necessitated the formation of channels or mechanisms to reach some form

---

96. See Guy Buak, 'Madhhab', in: *The [Oxford] Encyclopedia of Islam and Law*, Oxford Islamic Studies Online, http://www.oxfordislamicstudies.com/article/opr/t349/e0094 (accessed 1.11.2017). See also the rich bibliographical list appended there.

97. *Ibid.*

of consensus among legal experts. One such mechanism was the conference of certificate—the *Ijaza*—testifying that its holder has attained mastery in certain religious studies.[98] This was not an institutional document conferred on a student by an institution such as *Madrasah*—expanding ever since the Seljuk period—but rather a personal confirmation from a master to his personal disciple. It concerned the mastery of specific texts or religious domains, particularly law (*Fiqh*). The *Semikhah* polemics reflects the Muslim *Ijaza*—not that of the Classical period of Islam, but more precisely the Ottoman of the early modern period following the consolidation of an empire.

The Ottoman *Ijaza*s were still bestowed by masters on worthy students, but they were now integrated with a well-organized and hierarchical schooling system under the direct management and control of the state.[99] Accordingly, they acquired the character of an official state confirmation that a young scholar was performing well in a state-governed school and was about to find his place either in the state bureaucracy or legal system. In this respect, it was no longer under the sole control of the scholarly circle (the *'Ulama*) but was now embedded in the much wider setting of empire management. This imperial polity was served by judges, scholars, study curriculum, legal guild, a leading/dominant figure among the legal experts, and a *cursus honorum* of expected jobs.

The *Semikhah* as presented by R. Beirav and his rabbinical colleagues and direct disciples sought to install a Jewish parallel to the Ottoman *Ijaza* with the same characteristics. It relied on a formal procedure of nomination—the gathering of prestigious Safed sages nominating R. Beirav in the first round, and later a second formal round of *Semikhah* by R. Beirav and his milieu; it emphasized the role of R. Beirav as *Gedol Ha-Dor* and hence as a dominant figure in the entire affair; ordination became an official act of superiority within rabbinic milieu; it was applicable in all domains of Halakhah; the center at Safed considered itself the leader of the entire Jewish Ecumene; and finally, *Semikhah* supposedly provided a kind of virtual autonomy, interacting directly with the past ethos of Jewish legal autonomy.

These parallels may explain the uncharacteristic ignoring by the participants in the *Semikhah* polemics of concrete patterns of *Semikhah* during late antiquity and the Middle Ages, whether in Gaonic Babylonian tradition, Mediterranean Jewish communities in Italy and Spain, or further north in Ashkenaz. These past precedents and their related halakhic discussions were well-known to both Ben-Haviv and Beirav and their omission was certainly no coincidence. It indicated that both of them did not consider the Safed project as an extension of past patterns, in a "more of the same" way but rather a break with the past and the definition of a new balance within the rabbinical milieu and its modes of "producing justice." The new game was to fuse the rabbinical traditions originating from the entire Jewish Ecumene in one center, one dominant figure, and one institution.

---

98. Wael B. Hallaq, *The Origins and Evolution of Islamic Law*, Cambridge, and New York: Cambridge U.P., 2004; idem., *Shari'a: Theory, Practice, Transformations*, Cambridge: Cambridge University Press, 2009; George Makdisi, *The Rise of Colleges: Institutions of Learning in Islam and the West*, Edinburgh: Edinburgh U.P., 1981.

99. See the Introductory chapter.

Inserting (or, alternatively, resisting) a new turn in Jewish rabbinic tradition— such as the renovation of *Semikhah*—required strong, new argumentations, but presented under old garb. In our case, the argument was anchored in the classical halakhic heritage, but the classical arguments were manipulated by new and even invalid twists. Both contenders used typically non-halakhic arguments, quite surprising for persons of their stature.[100] Not only was the Prophet Elijah resurrected and presented as a contemporary member of the rabbinical milieu; Ralbach further presented the "failure" of the *Semikhah* project as a heavenly sign that from the start it had lacked any halakhic basis.[101] The manifest level of the *Semikhah* debate, and the one most easily related to detailed arguments of Talmudic scholarship, referred repeatedly to the Maimonides' assertions in his Mishnah exegesis and in the *Mishneh Torah*. Surely, he was practically the sole Talmudic scholar openly discussing the option of the future reinstatement of *Semikhah*. Yet his words were far from clear, contained repeated expressions of self-doubt and were not devoid of inconsistencies. Constructing anew such a fundamental institution as *Semikhah* on the basis of sole rabbinic authority (while he himself relies on a prophetic verse, rather than on any Talmudic debate or other rabbinical precedent) was highly problematic. But Maimonides was an excellent agent for anchoring this new project: He composed the first Jewish code of law, which remained unique for many years. In its legal, philosophical, and ethical aspects, his *Mishneh Torah* was more than a technical legal summary or a post-Talmudic tract. Furthermore, his entire halakhic worldview and extensive writings reflected a deep dialogue with Islamicate culture,[102] which suited the needs of Safed inhabitants and scholars, under Ottoman-Sunni rule ever since 1516, the annexation date of Arab territories to the Ottoman Empire.

Another important theme that needs reinterpretation is the supposed Messianic motivations of the advocates of reinstated *Semikhah*. R. Beirav consistently avoided mentioning explicitly any messianic or apocalyptic motivations behind his project. It was rather his rival Ralbach who constantly attempted to depict him as a would-be messianic figure claiming the right to impose a careless and unfounded shift in Halakhic domain. The political and down-to-earth nature of Beirav's approach is consistent with his actions prior to arriving in Safed, a city charged with its mystical and messianic currents. When

---

100. See above, section "Medieval Discussions of *Semikhah*".
101. Ben-Haviv, *Responsa*, pp. 30, 56.
102. Gideon Libson, 'Parallels between Maimonides and Islamic Law', in: Ira Robinson, Lawrence Kaplan, Julien Bauer (eds.), *The Thought of Moses Maimonides. Philosophical and Legal Studies*, Lewiston/Queenston/Lampeter, The Edwin Mellen Press, 1990, pp. 209–248; Idem., 'The Linkage of Maimonides to the Shari'a in the Context of His Period', in: Ravitzky (ed.), *Maimonides: Conservatism, Originality, Revolution*, pp. 247–294. See further in this regard Mark R. Cohen, *Maimonides and the Merchants: Jewish Law and Society in the Medieval Islamic World*, University of Pennsylvania Press, 2017; Marc C. Cohen, *Systermatizing Gods' Law: Rabbanite Jurisprudence in the Islamic World from the Tenth to the Thirteenth Centuries*, Ph.D. submitted at Pennsylvania Univesity, 2016. Regarding the deep imprint of Islamic on Jewish law in the various and important works of Gideon Libson. Also see Uriel Simonsohn, *A Common Justice: The Legal Allegiances of Christian and Jews under Early Islam*, Philalphia: University of Pennsylvania Press, 2011.

holding a rabbinical post in Egypt, he attempted to persuade his Egyptian rabbinical colleagues to reinstate the *Semikhah* mechanism.[103] Egypt was one of the major Arabic territories annexed to the central rule of Istanbul through "rituals of possession and methods of control," implemented by sending major bureaucratic experts, imposing new laws of the *Kanunname*, and drastically changing the local traditions concerning the appointment of Kadis.[104] The policy of gaining control was publicly stated in a detailed preamble, addressing the local population in Arabic, in contrast to the remainder of the text, which was written in Turkish. As a prominent scholar and judge, he could well understand the change undergoing the Arab-Sunni civilization—both in Egypt and in *Bilad a-Sham*—under the control of a centralizing regime.[105]

In the declaratory letter of the Safed sages, as a collective, and not as individual followers or disciples of R. Beirav, they explicitly stated the aim of nominating worthy judges as the legitimating motive behind the *Semikhah* project

> (There is no prophet, i.e. a master of justice [*moreh tzedeq*, meaning judge – R.W.], there is none among us [capable of] ruling on cases that require the imposition of fines, nor anyone castigating the evildoers [...] He [R. Beirav] would nominate the sagacious among us, [to serve] next to him, they would be called Rabbis and endowed with *Semikhah* for eternity, carrying the Torah law with truth and justice, in order to judge the powerful [...] to smiten him according to the Torah [Laws].[106]

Practically, the proposal advocated a formal mode of nomination based on a hierarchic structure of several grades of legal experts and embodying a distinction between persons included in or excluded from the rabbinic guild. It is important to note that the intended *Semikhah* concerned only the nomination process, and not the procedures of Jewish courts of law, which enjoyed a limited legal autonomy in Safed as in the Ottoman heartlands. It certainly had nothing to do with the content of the halakhic law. The urgent issue at stake was to define the marking lines between the professionals of first grade and others. A formal procedure, emanating from the Safed center and headed by a single, dominant scholar of the Talmudic law, would convey this difference. It is interesting that the persons entitled to *Semikhah*—R. Beirav and later generations—never used this title to reinforce their judicial authority when issuing or attempting to enforce court verdicts.[107] Nor did they ever endeavor to implement the classical privileges of

---

103. Katz, 'The Controversy on the Semichah', p. 30.

104. Cornell H. Fleischer, *Bureaucrat and Intellectual in the Ottoman Empire. The Historian Mustafa Ali (1541-1600)*, Princeton: Princeton U.P. 1986; Fitzgerald, 'Rituals of Possession, Methods of Control'.

105. Reem Meshal, 'Antagonistic Shari'as and the Construction of Orthodoxy in Sixteenth Century Ottoman Cairo', *Journal of Islamic Studies*, 21, no. 2 (May 2010), pp. 183–212, esp. pp. 194–195.

106. Ralbach, *Responsa*, p. 2.

107. Katz, 'The Controversy on the Semichah', p. 36; Benayahu, 'The Renovation of Rabbinic Semichah in Safed', pp. 258–259.

Semikhah in the three fronts of confrontation: imposing corporal punishment, extracting financial fines, and setting the Jewish calendar.

The opposition to the Safed *Semikhah* emerged primarily in Jerusalem, but R. Beirav also faced strong opposition on his home ground. Some scholars "from the Yeshiva"– whose number and names remained anonymous—refused to accept his dominant position and insisted on having a shared part in the second round of *Semikhah* so that further scholars would be nominated by R. Beirav and themselves. This divergence integrated well with a simultaneous confrontation between the ruling center in Istanbul and their nominated officials, on the one hand, and the local Arabic scholars and population in the periphery, on the other, as the latter persistently sought to resist the Ottoman centralistic encroachment over their ancient traditions. The discussions on reaching rabbinical consensus and the special position of *Gedol Ha-Dor* are legalistic themes, part and parcel of the rabbinical milieu's quest to define its modus operandi.[108] The two contending figures impersonated two conflicting positions, which served only to exacerbate the personal and acrimonious debate. The *ad hominem* arguments certainly rely on the strong personalities of both Rabbis Beirav and Ben-Haviv, fueled by the honor ethos of Spanish Jews, and especially the Castilians. This particular trait of Mediterranean rabbinical discourse was noticed by the contemporary observer R. Messer Leon

("I conducted myself with love and sympathy towards them [the Portuguese Jews], as I am accustomed to respect the Portuguese rather than the Sephardi. Because though they are quick to rage, they incline to follow the instructions of Sages/Rabbis, they are truthful and generous, and not covert and secretive and proud as the Castilians [Jews from former Castile—R.W.].")[109]

But the driving force behind the personal issue was the two conflicting modes they represented: a centralist, institutional, and strict ethos versus a collective, dialogical, and community-oriented one. This was also a clash between an innovative person impatient to implement what had laid dormant in halakhic discourse for centuries and another more cautious following the trodden road. The imposing figure and arguments of R. Beirav were not a personal whim, or at least not only so, but were also inspired by the important figure of Şeyḫülislâm, demanding obedience due to his institutional role no less than to his erudition in *Fiqh*. The collision between the innovative aspect and the cautious and conservative was interestingly shown in relation to Ralbach, whose self-designation as "A Man from Jerusalem" (*Ish Yerushalayim*) evoked a sharply sarcastic response from R. Beirav.[110] This squabble reflects the symbolic battle as to which city in the Holy Land would gain priority and prominence: would it be the traditional and sanctified city of Jerusalem, the focus of Jewish longing and memory

---

108. See the illuminating discussion in Hagai Pely, 'Studies in the Adjudication Project of Rabbi Joseph Karo' [Hebrew], in: *Rabbi Joseph Karo. History, Halakhah, Kabbalah*, Jerusalem: Zalman Shazar Center, 2021, pp. 172–184.
109. Messer Leon, *Kevod Chakhamim*, pp. 5–6. See also ibid., pp. 9–10, 13, 16.
110. On this issue, see Ralbach, *Responsa*, pp. 39–40, 47–48, 50, 53, 81.

for centuries, or the young and vigorous city of Safed? Again, it is impossible to ignore a similar symbolic rivalry between the classical cities of Islamic history (the two holy cities [*Haramayn*], Cairo, Damascus, and Kufa versus Istanbul), the "new fountain of wisdom and piety."

The third round of *Semikhah* took place after both R. Beirav and Ben-Haviv were no longer alive.[111] It apparently included 10 more sages, adding to the four ordained by R. Karo and his contemporaneous colleagues, who in their turn received *Semikhah* from R. Beirav. Those 10 figures of the seventeenth century were the last ones, and so the Jewish *Ijaza* seemed to evaporate in the air. The authority of Safed was not dominant enough to impose its nomination patterns. Again, this resonated with changes in the Ottoman Empire, as the direct rule of the Ottoman center over the Arab periphery declined and local elites in *Bilad a-Sham* become more dominant, in the legal domain as in others. It also reflected the resistance of the rabbinical milieu to adopt hierarchical patterns and forsake their autonomous position. Fragmentation among the Sephardi communities along the Eastern Mediterranean—in large communities such as Istanbul and Salonica, as well as in Safed—became a common phenomenon, rendering the universalist perspective and vision of a central judicial authority for the entire Jewish Ecumene less viable and less desirable.

The voice of R. Karo is not particularly prominent in the *Semikhah* documents, which as we have seen centered on the two main protagonists. When heard, it is a voice of an establishment person: once again, in his rabbinical career in Safed, he decides to stop rabbinical arguments not by counter-arguments or internal dialogue but by implementing a command issued by a formal rabbinical court. In this sense, he is harsher than Beirav, adopting a demanding tone and imposing his will on his adversary. After the death of he "Master of Safed" R. Beirav, Karo's turn came and he positioned the *Semikhah* procedure within a much broader arena. In his mystical vision, Karo presented himself as one who had been promised the role of the political and religious-halakhic leader of the entire Eastern Jewish Diaspora, aided by the composition of a comprehensive magnum opus of a Jewish code of law. The angelic voice of his vision crowned R. Karo as a Jewish Şeyḫülislâm. To implement his authority, he would need, like his Ottoman corollary, the tool or mechanism of Jewish *Ijaza* ("Since you have deeply devoted yourself to reinstate the *Semikhah*, you shall be honored to *be ordained* by all the sages of the Holy Land."). Unlike R. Beirav, who insisted on the monopoly of Holy Land sages in reactivating *Semikhah*, following the Talmudic formalities, R. Karo pushes his vision far beyond, insisting that his personality and *Semikhah* authority be recognized by the entire community of Jewish scholars ("You shall be honored to be ordained by all the sages of the Holy Land, and by the sages abroad.") The local Safedian context was expanded—much like the expansion of the Ottoman Empire—to universalistic dimensions.

---

111. Benayahu, 'The Renovation of Rabbinic Semichah in Safed', pp. 257–261.

Chapter Five

R. KARO IN SAFED: ESTABLISHING
A DOMINANT STATUS

R. Karo spent most of his adult life in the city of Safed. We know very little about the first part of his life and virtually nothing about the public impact of his early writings, for instance, as a composer of Responsa nor about his community activity, rabbinic authority, public preaching, or his Talmudic master(s). His significant imprint, whether through his writings or his communal activities, relates predominantly to the Safed years. Here he waged the chief battles discussed in this chapter: establishing his dominant position as a rabbinic persona whose instructions are heard and followed; founding and managing several yeshivas; participating in the procedures of the leading court of law (*Beit-Din Ha-Gadol*); and establishing and supporting a large network of loyal and advanced disciples.

The Unique Position of Safed

The general exile of Iberian Jews in late fifteenth century was followed by waves of immigrations across the globe, weaving international networks of political, economy, family, and religious ties.[1] This process eventually led to the establishment of two main Diasporas.[2] The "Western Sephardi" Diaspora in Western and Northern Europe was influenced by Christian traditions under centralizing states and maritime empires. A parallel network, the "Eastern Sephardi" Diaspora, was deeply immersed in Ottoman–Muslim civilization and the Arab lands. The differences between the two traditions related to their use of languages, religious changes, economic activities, and political affiliations—Christian Europe or Ottoman Islamicate traditions. This chapter relates mainly to the story of the eastern Sephardi Diaspora. This extended along vast zones, but its main actors lived and prospered in several important cities in the Ottoman Empire—such as Istanbul, Salonica, Edirne, and later Izmir—and in the classical Arab lands occupied by the Ottomans in the early sixteenth century, including the cities of Damascus, Cairo, Jerusalem, and Safed.

---

1. See Roni Weinstein, *Kabbalah and Jewish Modernity*, Littman Library of Jewish Culture, London, 2016, Ch. 7 – 'Catholic Traditions in Safed Kabbalah. Sephardim and Conversos', pp. 142–165.
2. Jonathan Rey, *After Expulsion 1492 and the Making of Sephardic Jewry*, London and New York: New York U.P., 2013.

During the first half of the sixteenth century, Safed became a vibrant hub of Jewish life due to its economic prosperity. This enabled the city to attract several waves of Jewish immigration from across the Mediterranean basin. The city still comprising a relatively small Jewish population, however, and in most respects could not compete with the large and established communities of major Ottoman cities, such as Istanbul or Salonica. Yet there was one aspect in which Safed enjoyed a significant edge over these cities: Torah and Talmud scholarship, in particular, and erudition, in general. Several foci of Talmudic scholarship were founded during the sixteenth century along the Mediterranean, sparking a veritable renaissance in Talmudic and juridical studies in the eastern Sephardi Diaspora. This expansion was noticed by contemporary observers and was reflected in an impressive volume of responsa literature, increasing numbers of scholars dedicated to studying the Talmudic and post-Talmudic heritage, and also the expanding activities of religious courts. The important Yeshivas (*Beit-Midrashim*, in Sephardi parlance) were headed by impressive scholars whose writings and juridical concepts inform Yeshiva studies to the present day. The importance of Safed lay in the fact that it hosted some of the leading scholars of the sixteenth and seventeenth centuries, R. Karo included.

The city of Safed had another and more significant advantage over other major communities in the Ottoman Empire: it was located in the Holy Land, the object of longing of the entire Jewish Ecumene and the fountain of its heritage. It thus served as a kind of "capital city" of Jewish religiosity and as a destination for Jewish pilgrimage, as did Rome in the Catholic world and Mecca and Medina in Islam. No less significant was the proximity—very sensual and geographical – of Safed to the area where the mythical stories of the Book of Splendor (*Sefer Ha-Zohar*) took place—the mystical corpus that provided the basis and inspiration for the pietistic and mystical renaissance of Jewish tradition in the early modern period. This was the first time in Jewish religious history that secretive traditions crossed the boundaries of esoteric circles and reached somewhat larger parts of the Jewish population. In this specific aspect, no other Jewish community in the Ottoman Empire, and certainly not in Europe, could compete with Safed.

The Jewish elites in Safed—Kabbalistic, Talmudic, pietistic, and liturgical—were the first to promote and proclaim the sacred stereotype of their city.[3] The proximity to the concrete arena where the divine secrets were revealed to the Zoharic mystical confraternity was not coincidental. The place was deemed fit for Torah study and for vicinity to God: "Safed is propitious to achieve the depth of Torah and its secrets, for there is no fresh air in the entire Holy Land such as in Safed," as an adherent of Safedian Kabbalah proclaimed in the seventeenth century.[4] The printing of the section "New Zohar" in Salonica in 1597 included the heading "There is no Torah as the one in

---

3. Eyal Davidson, *Safed's Sages between 1540–1615, Their Religious and Social Status* [Hebrew], Ph.D. submitted at the Hebrew University, 2009, passim. On Safed community 'between Reality and Myth', see Yaron Ben-Naeh, 'Rabbi Joseph Karo and His Time' [Hebrew], in: *Rabbi Joseph Karo. History, Halakhah, Kabbalah*, Jerusalem: Zalman Shazar Center, 2021, pp. 61–67.

4. *Idem.*, p. 47.

The Holy Land, it became famous in all places, i.e. Safed may it be erected and glorified, Amen."[5] The glory of the Sanhedrin as a leading scholarly center and juridical instance—a kind of pristine Supreme Court of Law—had now as if shifted to Safed.[6] The sanctity of the city and the high prestige of its sages were reflected by the almost folkloristic habit of Sephardi merchants around the Mediterranean of reinforcing their statements by swearing on the name of Safed sages.

Safed was presented as a sanctified enclosure, a place in need of solid economic or financial basis for its subsistence, since its main essence lay in Torah study. The presence of so many impressive scholars provided some factual support for this stereotype of a holy city. It encouraged the construction of an international network of charity and support for the local scholars. Eyal Davidson collected several comments reflecting this status. In one of them, a person inheriting some property claims: "The subsistence of the Yeshivah is the reason for living in the Holy Land [more specifically in Safed], since this place is not intended for business and worldly activities."[7] Local scholars and visitors from abroad idealized the city as a place replete with Torah wisdom, not only among the "professional" scholars but also among the Jewish population in general.[8] Safed is a fountain of wisdom for the entire Jewish Ecumene, providing further motivation for supporting the city by charity. The construction of this image of Safed could certainly rely on concrete facts, since famous rabbis encountered the public at large in local synagogues, where they would preach and teach Halakhah.[9]

No wonder that local rabbis and leading Talmudic scholars attempted to turn Safed into a focus of Jewish legal authority. They were increasingly involved in the legal disputes and complicated juridical issues raised in other communities around the Mediterranean Basin, going as far as Italy and Provence.[10] They did not hesitate to use threats against rebellious persons opposing their authority, or alternatively to plead for cooperation by those faraway communities, lest the honor of the Safed rabbis be tarnished.[11] A letter sent in 1560 from Avignon begged the Safed rabbis to act harshly against a person intending to proceed with a levirate marriage:

The clarion call horn issued from your court [in Safed] would make the doorsteps tremble [...] Thus you, angels of God, sitting on a high chair, authorized as the Sanhedrin in

---

5. *Idem.*, p. 1.
6. On the role of the *Sanhedrin* and its 'virtual' extension in the Safedian context, see esp. Ch. 4, as well as Ch. 7.
7. Davidson, *Safed's Sages between 1540–1615, Their Religious and Social Status*, p. 166.
8. *Ibid.*, pp. 230, 238–240.
9. Haim Z. Dimitrovsky, 'Rabbi Yaakov Beirav's Academy in Safed' [Hebrew], *Sefunot: Studies and Sources on the History of the Jewish Communities in the East* 7 (1963), pp. 41–102, esp. 50; In *ibid.*, footnote 58 he refers to further research of Meir Benayahu.
10. See the discussion on Ch. 8 – R. Karo's attempt to construct 'A Jewish International Court of Law'.
11. Meir Benayahu, 'The Renovation of Rabbinic Semichah in Safed' [Hebrew], in: S.W. Baron, B. Dinur, S. Ettinger, I. Halpern (eds.), *Yitzhak F. Baer Jubilee Volume. On the Occasion of his Seventieth Birthday*, Jerusalem: The Historical Society of Israel, 1960, pp. 248–269.

the holy precinct of the Temple, do not spare them [all the persons involved], and curse and excommunicate them in all the synagogues and Talmudic schools [again, in Safed] [...] and order all communities not to join them in ritual acts, and allow all Jews to harm them physically, or to hand them over to non-Jewish courts, so as to harm their bodies and property.[12]

Over the course of the sixteenth century, the dominant status of Safed was manifested in another area, as its scholars and leaders assumed responsibility for collecting charity for the poor and needy population of the entire Holy Land.[13] In 1600, R. 'Amram "the Ascetic" (*Ha-Nazir*) was sent on behalf "of the Sages and leaders of Safed" to collect all the entire charitable donations from Europe, passing via Venice, to the Holy Land. The money would arrive as a lump sum to Safed, and the local scholars would take care to divide it among all the Holy Land communities.[14]

Karo shared and propagated the very same exalted image of Safed. In the opening words of his responsum *Avqat Rochel*, the city was lauded as "the best in the entire Holy Land" (*zvi hi le-khol ha-aratzot*).[15] Furthermore, it was a place saturated with religious devotion. In a paean on the glories of the city—clearly echoing a well-known literary genre in Ottoman Empire on the marvels of important cities—Karo considers Safed "a place from where Torah and light would disseminate to the entire Jewish Ecumene."[16] In such an atmosphere, the lay leadership was constrained—pace R. Karo—to accept the authority and guidance of the religious-rabbinical elite: "Its heads and leaders behaved properly in fulfilling their responsibility towards the poor and Torah-scholars [...] and the honor of Torah and its fear fell upon the heads and leaders of the above mentioned city [Safed] [...] They would do nothing before consulting with the old Scholars and Rabbis. Everything would follow their words."[17]

Safed versus Jerusalem?

Historically, Jerusalem stood at the core of Jewish tradition. It was here that the pact between God and His chosen people materialized in the most visible and concrete way. The two historical Temples and their material remains made Jerusalem the undisputed center of Jewish life and the focus of longing in the collective memory for centuries. But beyond these valid and grand assertions, was the city of Jerusalem truly invincible?

When R. Karo asserted that Safed was "the best city in the entire Holy Land"—a claim echoed by other Safedian scholars—he was actually challenging the supremacy of the historical role of Jerusalem as the beating heart of Jewish tradition. Not for a moment did he intend to replace one for the other. It was rather an intricate saying

---

12. *Ibid.*, p. 253.
13. Davidson, *Safed's Sages between 1540–1615, Their Religious and Social Status*, pp. 203–208.
14. *Ibid.*, p. 207.
15. *Ibid.*, pp. 241–242, the discussion of this citation.
16. Joseph Karo, *Responsa Avkat Rochel*, Salonica: 1791, §1.
17. Davidson, *Safed's Sages between 1540–1615, Their Religious and Social Status*, pp. 241–242.

regarding the balance between the old and the new, especially under concrete historical circumstances in the early modern period, such as extensive Jewish immigrations,
construction of a new Sephardi Diaspora, the rise of modern centralistic states, and
certainly Jewish life under the expanding and prosperous Ottoman Empire and the rule
of Sultan Süleyman. Again, what he never have asserted explicitly in regular rabbinical
rhetoric would be stated implicitly in his mystical diary *Magid Meisharim*: "In times of
[this] exile, the earthly Jerusalem is destroyed and empty of [Jewish] population."[18] The
assertion is double edged: Jerusalem is devastated, while Safed prospers.

The concrete implication of such an assertion was that R. Karo— alongside others—needed to attend to the needs of Jerusalem inhabitants. He did so by acting as a
kind of patron for the other city. In 1575, he sent a letter on their behalf beseeching the
Mediterranean communities to provide charity for the city's poor.[19] The fact that Safed
sages and leaders took upon themselves the task of organizing collectively the charity
for the entire Holy Land only underlined their supremacy, relative to the Jerusalem
sages. Inevitably this advantage did not remain in the administrative or economic
level, but also extended to the cultural domain. In the polemic that stirred local rabbis
regarding the issue of *Semikhah*, the Safed rabbis had no hesitations in underscoring
their superiority over Jerusalem scholars.[20] R. Karo was one of the heroes of this vocif-
erous affair, as he played a dominant role in imposing the authority of Safed on other
communities in the Mediterranean and the Holy Land, Jerusalem included. Further,
Jerusalem rabbis occasionally addressed Safed for legal consultation; we are not familiar with an opposite case.[21]

The Battle over Leadership in Safed

When R. Karo arrived in Safed, he was already an established scholar and a figure
of renown among the Rumelian communities, where he lived previously. In Safed, he
encountered a rabbi of unsurpassed position: R. Jacob/Yaakov Beirav (1474–1546).[22]
Safed was considered a place under the Halakhic control and authority of R. Beirav
(*Atrei de-mar*, in Aramaic). As the leading scholar in the city—full of other prestigious
and talented ones—his halakhic rulings were regarded as binding and were widely publicized. The halakhic decisions of other eminent rabbis were sometimes considered con-
ditional and dependent on his approval. R. Beirav headed the major Yeshiva in Safed,
whose attendants included scholars of renown capable of maintaining their own schools.
He assiduously acted to evolve, teach, and disseminate the Sephardi methodology of

---

18. See the citation and its discussion in *ibid.*, p. 64.
19. Abraham David, 'New Data on the Biography of R. Joseph Karo' [Hebrew], *Proceedings of the World Congress of Jewish Studies* C, 1 (1989), pp. 201–207, esp. p. 206.
20. This issue is discussed extensively on Ch. 4.
21. Benayahu, 'The Renovation of Rabbinic Semichah in Safed', pp. 251–252.
22. For a more elaborate presentation of R. Beirav, see Ch. 4. See especially Dimitrovsky, 'Rabbi Yaakov Beirav's Academy in Safed', passim.

Talmudic studies.[23] Alongside his scholarly activities, he presided over the major courts of law, including the legal institution assembling the sages and judges of various ethnic groups in the city. This court was presented by R. Beirav as a historical extension of the Sanhedrin and entitled to similar privileges. Thenceforth, it was a small step toward the vision of turning this general or Supreme Court (*Beit Din Ha-Gadol*) into a formal institution and reviving rabbinical ordination. As in the case of other Talmudic schools in the core lands of the Ottoman Empire, the size of the Yeshiva and the number of attending scholars testified to its importance and the prestige of its head.[24] As we shall see below, the institution functioned as an agent for the dissemination of the halakhic positions of the grand Talmudic master. R. Beirav had talented disciples, devoted to him while living, and continuing his heritage after his death; the most prominent among them was R. Moses di Trani (1500–1580; known as *Ha-Mabit*).

The death of R. Beirav left a considerable vacuum in the city, especially among the rabbinical milieu. This situation could evolve in several directions: (A) The city would dwindle progressively and cease to function as a Talmudic and religious center. This possibility indeed materialized in the seventeenth century following the death of major local rabbis, the crisis in the textile industry—providing livelihood to many city dwellers, and a serious earthquake in the city. The harsh policy of local Ottoman officials and those from the center in Damascus exacerbated this decline; (B) One of Beirav's eminent scholars and disciples would take his place in legal and public functions; (C) In search of internal rabbinical consensus, a collective or cooperative mode of action would inherit the dominant role of one person; (D) A scholar beyond the circle of R. Beirav's disciples might attempt to assume his dominant position. R. Karo did everything in his power to become precisely this scholarly leader of Safed, the city of Torah scholarship. Indeed all the three options (B, C, and D) occurred simultaneously during the second half of the sixteenth century, and this inevitably resulted in endless clashes over dominance and control.

The leadership battle in Safed (I): Karo versus Ha-Mabit

The late Meir Benayahu, in his vast study devoted to R. Karo, could not ignore the fact that a substantial part of his time was devoted to ceaseless disputes with R. Moses di Trani.[25] These disputes extended over several decades of their shared life in Safed. Its roots return to their shared affiliation to the grand master of the previous generation, R. Jacob Beirav. The differences between them were well noticed by Dimitrovsky. Di Trani's admiration

23. Yoel Marciano, *Sages of Spain in the Eye of the Storm - Jewish Scholars of Late Medieval Spain* [Hebrew], Jerusalem: Bialik Institute, 2019, pp. 140–214; Davidson, *Safed's Sages between 1540–1615, Their Religious and Social Status*, pp. 142–146.

24. *Ibid.*, pp. 145–146.

25. Meir Benayahu, *Yosef Bechiri* ['Joseph, My Chosen One' – in Hebrew], Jerusalem: Yad HaRav Nissim, 1991, esp. pp. 9–98. See also Haim Z. Dimitrovsky, 'A Dispute between Rabbi J. Caro and Rabbi M. Trani' [Hebrew], *Sefunot. Studies and Sources on the History of the Jewish Communities in the East* 6 (1962), pp. 71–123.

for his master knows no bounds, and he never allows others to cast any doubt on his sayings. In all his numerous books and responsa, *Ha-Mabit* did not even once show any doubt regarding his master's opinions, and certainly never disagreed with him. By contrast, Maran's approach was more critical.[26] On occasions, he cites Beirav and then raises alternative opinions; sometimes, he even records Beirav's position anonymously before stating his objections, and in some instances, he ignored his positions altogether. "While the sentiments of Maran towards R. Beirav are somewhat hidden and restrained, *Ha-Mabit* expresses them publicly and out loud."[27] Di Trani justifiably considered himself the most senior of R. Beirav's disciples, and hence entitled to inherit his status and his domineering leadership in Safed.

The question as to who was closer to R. Beirav and more worthy to inherit his position in Safed created the battleground for both R. Karo and *Ha-Mabit*. The battle itself concerned the domination and control of the rabbinical milieu in Safed, and later on Safed's growing role in other Torah centers of the Sephardi Diaspora around the Mediterranean Basin. The confrontation between these two dominating and highly erudite scholars was almost inevitable. They participated in the same legal discussions that preoccupied Safed's inhabitants, and their voices were heard at the central legal institution of the city.[28] It comes as no surprise that the number of legal cases in which they disagreed increased over the years. These included mundane issues of community life and commercial activities, such as the ambiguous status of women whose husband's death could not be confirmed,[29] legal documents and their value,[30] the right to slaughter and consume possibly sick beasts,[31] widows' dowries,[32] inheritance confrontation,[33] preparing cheese and its Kosher status,[34] a will made on the deathbed,[35] doubtful betrothal,[36] commercial pacts between merchants,[37] and finally the ritual issue of tithes.[38]

These were routine confrontations to be expected in juridical work, but they served to maintain alive the tension between the two figures, to a lesser or greater degree, over the years. The major conflicts were of a different nature and erupted mainly around the issues of constructing local courts, their authority, and the status of the leading scholar

---

26. Ben-Naeh claims that R. Beirav and R. Karo maintained close relationship, yet rabbinic testimonies do not confirm this claim. See idem., 'Rabbi Joseph Karo and His Time', esp. pp. 84–87.

27. Dimitrovsky, 'Rabbi Yaakov Beirav's Academy in Safed', pp. 64–65.

28. See section "The leadership battle in Safed (II): General court of law—Beit Ha-Va'ad".

29. Dimitrovsky, 'A Dispute between Rabbi J. Caro and Rabbi M. Trani', p. 95. See also *ibid*., p. 90 – the Taranto versus Gabison case.

30. Benayahu, *Joseph My Chosen One*, pp. 17–18.

31. *Ibid.*, p. 19. See also *ibid.*, p. 86.

32. *Ibid.*, p. 29.

33. *Ibid.*, p. 30.

34. *Ibid.*, pp. 42–43.

35. *Ibid.*, p. 56.

36. *Ibid.*, p. 64.

37. *Ibid.*, pp. 84–85, 86.

38. *Ibid.*, p. 88.

(*Gedol Ha-Dor*).[39] All these elements later coalesced into the major polemic between Safed and Jerusalem scholars around the issue of *Semikhah* and the intention of Safed rabbis to take the lead role on this issue.[40]

But there were other occasions that raised to the surface the competitive relationship between these two dominating figures. A delicate halakhic issue concerns the status of betrothal (*qiddushin*) as a preparatory phase before full marriage.[41] In case of doubts regarding its legal validity, or the wish of one (or both) of the parties involved to retract their commitment, a full divorce procedure is often necessary. Disobeying such a course might affect the status of the woman marrying another man, including the risk that any future children would be considered bastards under religious law. This is the main reason for the extreme cautiousness of rabbis in cases of "doubtful betrothal" (*qiddushei safeq*) and their efforts to reach a consensus in such cases. One case of "doubtful betrothal" occurred in mid-sixteenth century Safed.[42] In order to maintain the autonomy of the separate Jewish ethnic groups in the city, it was agreed by the scholars that none of them would intervene in the affairs of another subcommunity. This time the situation followed the worst-case scenario, since the woman without divorcing the first betrothed man married another one. R. Karo alleged that *Ha-Mabit* had infringed the internal consensus by granting a verdict in this case:

> How strong is his domineering power, to overstep his boundaries and enter the territories of others. For these man and woman do not belong to his community. By violence he intends to contradict the decisions of other courts and to ruin what they built. Instead, he should have retract from his own position and abide by the opinion of other scholars, even if these man and woman would have appertained to his own community [...] It is all due to his arrogance. Not only that, he put things in writing and provide them to the person betrothing [the first betrothal], to show to all people. It shows that he clings to discordance at all price, with heart and spirit. And not only that, but he invents things from his heart with no real [Halakhic] validity.[43]

Once the case became a general issue, beyond its original arena of subcommunity boundaries, it required discussion by all the major scholars of the city. *Ha-Mabit*, once again according to a polemic letter composed by R. Karo, avoided turning the case over to this general juridical institution as local custom required, thereby undermining the authority and halakhic rulings of other sages. He infringed another—implicit yet highly important— element of rabbinical etiquette, namely, ensuring that internal disagreements remain hidden from the public at large: "He assembled various public groups (*hiqhil qehilot*), informing them that R. Karo and others were mistaken."[44]

---

39. See section "The leadership battle in Safed (III): R. Karo's strategy".
40. See above, Ch. 4.
41. See Roni Weinstein, *Marriage Rituals Italian Style: A Historical Anthropological Perspective on Early Modern Italian Jews*, Leiden: E.J. Brill, 2003, pp. 154–212.
42. Benayahu, *Joseph My Chosen One*, pp. 34–37.
43. *Idem.*, p. 34.
44. *Idem.*, p. 37.

The motivation for his comportment was stated explicitly, in relation to another case of "doubtful betrothal" some years later: "He [Ha-Mabit] nominates himself [as a formal authority] over Safed inhabitants without their consent."[45] Other allegations were made over the years, and in each case they were raised by R. Karo rather than by any of the other scholars in Safed: Ha-Mabit disobeys the decisions of his colleagues; he incites participants in court procedures to disobey the verdicts; he does not even refrain from referring some cases to Muslim/Ottoman courts; he pursues a double standard of inciting litigants in courts of other scholars to ask the reasons for verdicts, while prohibiting this conduct in his own court; and finally he disregards Sephardi legal traditions and customs when this suits him. Another allegation expressed by R. Karo, especially interesting in this context, is the preference for compromise over regular court procedures, according to juridical-formal rules. Such an approach certainly reflects the tendency of Muslim and later Ottoman courts to encourage procedures of arbitration and mutual agreement among the contesting parties through the informal procedure of *Sulh*.[46] Karo, however, argues that this recourse to compromise enfeebles the Jewish legal tradition and the search for justice on earth, as it prevents the offended party from securing full compensation according to the Talmudic instructions (granted by God).[47]

One should not take all Karo's allegations literally, as they were often expressed in polemic letters and public exchanges. Nevertheless, they raise the very same features that Ha-Mabit could have certainly inherit from his master R. Beirav: a claim for dominant status as *primus inter pares* among Safed scholarly community; abrogating the rules and halakhic decisions of others; intervening in procedures of other subcommunities and other courts of law; and even turning to the Ottoman authorities. Yet unlike his master, who did not encounter any open opposition during his lifetime, Ha-Mabit faced a determined rival in the battle for primacy and authority.

The leadership battle in Safed (II): General court of law—Beit Ha-Va'ad

Consensus was an important mechanism in classical Jewish tradition from the Talmudic period, if not earlier, and certainly during the Middle Ages. One channel for reaching consensus is manifested in a recurrent expression in Talmudic and rabbinical tradition:

---

45. *Idem.*, p. 64.
46. Abdülmecid Mutaf, 'Amicable Settlement in Ottoman Law: *Sulh* System', *Turcica* 36 (2004), pp. 125–140.
47. R. Karo is cited in Dimitrovsky, 'A Dispute between Rabbi J. Caro and Rabbi M. Trani', p. 88, footnote 63: "When you realized that you lost the legal case, you sent useless notes of no value ... Regarding what you wrote that [the litigating parties] should reach a compromise [*Pesharah* in the original – R.W.], it is indeed your customary attitude ... you acquit the guilty party by saying such things [using persuasion or force to reach a compromise – R.W.], and then you use the legal act of *Kinyan* [transferring some symbolic property to demonstrate an adherence to legal commitment – R.W.] from both litigating parties to reach a compromise, as YOU saw fit".

"The number of attending scholars was counted in order to consent on a Talmudic rule" (*nimnu ve-gamru*). This mechanism of counting votes functioned alongside others, such as recognizing the special position of the "Leader of his Generation" (*Gedol Ha-Dor* in Hebrew],[48] or the leadership of certain Jewish centers over others. Reaching a rabbinical consensus was almost unavoidable in a city such as Safed, where important ethnic traditions from the entire Jewish Ecumene encountered one another in a relatively small city, and particularly since these distinct heritages were defended by important and erudite rabbis and scholars.

In such a unique cultural context, the Sephardi immigrants in Safed sought to impose their particular cultural patterns, as they did across the rest of the Mediterranean Basin in the sixteenth century. Here, in particular, they had to reckon with the local population and the adherence of other immigrants to their customs. As in other major cities of the Ottoman Empire–especially in the core lands of Anatolia and Rumelia[49]—general institutions were established in Safed to represent the interests and traditions of the various Jewish ethnic communities (*'edot*).[50] Their corollary in the legal domain was *Beit Ha-Va'ad* (House of Convening) that functioned in Safed along the sixteenth and seventeenth centuries. The functions and history of this institution were meticulously shown in the works of Meir Benayahu, and especially Eyal Davidson.[51]

Beit Ha-Va'ad was comprised of the leading scholars, halakhic arbiters (*posqim*), and religious judges (*dayanim*) of early modern Safed. It addressed issues concerning the entire Jewish population of the city, as well as particularly complicated matters requiring special expertise in Jewish law. Its decisions and rulings were considered binding on the entire local Jewish population. Benayahu claimed that, similarly to Jewish court procedures, the decisions of *Beit Ha-Va'ad* were ultimately reached by counting votes. To demonstrate the internal rabbinical consensus, the signatures of important figures who were not members of this institution were added by way of further consent.[52] To enhance the appearance of cohesiveness and unanimity—presenting its decisions as "the Voice of Torah"[53] or "the Voice of the Talmud/Oral Torah"—members of rabbinic milieu sought to conceal internal disagreements from public knowledge. Exposing moments of strife and disagreements was regarded as a grave breach of rabbinical ethos and even as a sin.[54]

---

48. See above Ch. 4.

49. Joseph R. Hacker, 'Communal Organization among the Jewish Communities of the Ottoman Empire (1453-1676)' [Hebrew], in: Avraham Grossman and Yosef Kaplan (eds.), *Kehal Yisrael – Jewish Self-Rule through the Ages*, Vol. 2 – 'The Middle Ages and Early Modern Period', (Jerusalem: Shazar Center for Jewish History, 2004), pp. 287–309.

50. Davidson, *Safed's Sages between 1540–1615, Their Religious and Social Status*, passim.

51. *Ibid.*, pp. 261–263; Benayahu, *Joseph My Chosen One*, pp. 5, 12–14, 16, 35–37, 63; Idem., 'The Renovation of Rabbinic Semichah in Safed'; Dimitrovsky, 'Rabbi Yaakov Beirav's Academy in Safed'.

52. Benayahu, *Joseph My Chosen One*, p. 35.

53. *Torah* as a metonym for the entire Jewish heritage.

54. Benayahu, *Joseph My Chosen One*, pp. 37, 98.

Was *Beit Ha-Va'ad* in a position to enforce its rules and verdicts or strong enough to overcome the rampant strife between scholars? Certainly, the decades-long disputes between R. Karo and *Ha-Mabit* were not the only ones among Safed scholars, as was convincingly shown by Davidson. It convened for the first time in 1530, grouping "Safed's sages, counselors, and leaders" (*chakhmei Zefat, yo'atzeha ve-manhigeha*).[55] The new mechanism was to serve as the local supreme court of law and was defined as "a place convening the Sages" (*meqom qibbutz chakhamim*). This expression was far from neutral, recalling the past rabbinical traditions of a "Supreme Court" enjoying extensive legal rights. This prestigious mechanism extended its authority not only to the inhabitants of Safed but also actively sought to enforce its decisions on communities outside the Holy Land. Safed sages demanded that other scholars and communities accept their authority and did not refrain from using threats and excommunications to this end.[56]

Beit Ha-Va'ad never became a regulated and steady institution, in the Weberian sense. Once it ceased convening, its role was assumed by a more formal court of law, the "High Court of Law" (*Beit Din Ha-Gadol*). This secondary phase was neither more regulated nor steady and functioned mostly ad hoc. In 1569, *Beit Ha-Va'ad* convened once more, composed of three senior judges of the city and demanding full obedience from the various ethnic groups: "And we took upon ourselves, each and every one [of the various sub-communities] to follow the orders in our communities, as a binding custom."[57] The internal strife and disagreements among scholars and the mutual accusations enfeebled the functioning of *Beit Ha-Va'ad*. It even gave leeway to important halakhic arbiters not to accept or implement its decisions. In 1573, R. Moses Galante attempted once more to reestablish some kind of central organ of a legal nature, but without success.[58] This failure was probably related to the passing away of the major Talmudic and Kabbalistic figures of the previous generation and the sense of inferiority of the remaining scholars relative to the previous generation. In the early seventeenth century, *Beit Ha-Va'ad* is once again mentioned, possibly merely in the sense of an important court of law.[59]

The leadership battle in Safed (III): R. Karo's strategy

The death of R. Beirav provided the opportunity for R. Karo to wage his own battle and become the *primus inter pares* of the Safed scholars. He was unique in his strategy of combining several simultaneous and interconnected channels of action. This was no mere chance but a well-planned vision, fortunately exposed in explicit assertions in his mystical diary *Magid Meisharim*. These assertions included:

---

55. Davidson, *Safed's Sages between 1540–1615, Their Religious and Social Status*, pp. 261–263.
56. This provides further settings for the attempt of R. Karo to establish an International Court of Law. See Ch. 8.
57. Davidson, *Safed's Sages between 1540–1615, Their Religious and Social Status*, p. 272.
58. *Ibid.*, p. 273.
59. *Ibid.*, p. 274.

A. The attempt to establish a court of law of international horizons.[60]

B. The codification project, in its double short and long version, to which R. Karo dedicated almost 35 years of his life.[61]

C. If there were moments in which the long-years confrontations between R. Karo and *Ha-Mabit* were sure to reach boiling moments, it related to issues regarding the legal procedures and functioning of local courts.[62] In these disputes, the parties often abandoned the "professional" and juridical arguments required in dialogue between Talmudic scholars and embarked on courses of personal animosity with highly charged emotional tones. It seemed at times that R. Karo and Di Trani were more interested in settling scores, and this particular issue of court procedures provided the most fitting arena. At one moment, R. Karo rebuked his opponent by claiming that Safed scholars were planning to revoke his right to judge in local courts.[63] Di Trani's defiant attitude, in regard to the consensus achieved by other scholars and their common rules, aroused this supposed harsh response.

These clashes were so important that they crossed beyond the (generally) restricted milieu of rabbinical discussions and involved the lay leaders of Safed. Both Karo and *Ha-Mabit* addressed these leaders in the hope of gaining their trust and mobilizing their support for their respective suggestions for reform in the legal system. Concretely, this concerned two issues. The first was limiting the independence of judges younger than 40 years. According to *Ha-Mabit*, they would only be allowed to sit on the bench while supervised by two elderly judges.[64] The second: the plaintiff of a legal case has the right to demand that his case be heard in a Supreme Court (*Beit Din Ha-Gadol*) attended by the towering scholars rather than in his local/ethnic court of law. Ostensibly, these might seem to be two procedural issues of no great impact, but they actually embodied a battle for control of the legal mechanism in Safed, and more so for restructuring modern legality, as both parties knew and showed in their polemical tone. Further, these suggestions for reform resonated beyond the limits of the Holy Land and involved distinguished Sephardi scholars such as R. David ben Zimra (*Ha-Radbaz*) in Egypt and R. Samuel di Medina (*Ha-Maharashdam*) in Istanbul.[65] Limiting the independent status of "young" judges and scholars would allow the older scholars, and especially *Ha-Mabit* himself, to enjoy a de-facto monopoly over legal procedures in Safed. His rulings and Talmudic heritage would prevail over the scholarship and writings of others. The price was to be paid not by R. Karo—since his status as a halakhic scholar and arbiter was well established—but by his young disciples. They would be forced to accept the authority of an elderly and prestigious scholar rather than that of their own master. The second

---

60. See Ch. 8.
61. See above, Ch. 1.
62. Dimitrovsky, 'A Dispute between Rabbi J. Caro and Rabbi M. Trani', passim.
63. *Ibid.*, p. 80.
64. *Ibid.*
65. *Ibid.*, p. 83.

item on the list indicated the intention to subdue all local and ethnic courts to Di Trani's direct authority.

R. Karo, in his infuriated responses, showed that he well understood the implications. As Dimitrovsky clearly explained:

> Maran did not only intend to oppose the suggestion of Di Trani, but more so the unique status of the court that Di Trani wished to establish. Therefore he blamed him for undermining the value of city sages, refusing to abide by their general consent, and aspiring to overpower them.[66]

The overall direction of *Ha-Mabit* was that a handful of elderly scholars would hold all the power in their hands, in one centralistic institution, at the expense of the young generation, particularly the talented disciples of R. Karo. I will offer another perspective on this issue below.

D. The Yeshiva of R. Karo continued to a very large extent the Talmudic scholarly tradition of the Sephardi style.[67] This tradition had its main proponents in the famous Yeshivas in the Ottoman lands, mainly in Salonica and Istanbul, where the famous rabbis managed to establish large institutions and enjoy the support of rich Maecenas. They generated a close network around the Mediterranean of communication between scholars and communities, exchanging requests for Talmudic councils and legal opinions, sending their discussions to other scholars for comments, and attempting to reach legal consensus in complicated and controversial legal cases. Most of these erudition centers followed the Talmudic study methodology of *'Iyyun* evolved prior to the expulsion from Spain by R. Isaac Canpanton (1360–1463). All the major scholars of the succeeding generations considered themselves, in one way or another, disciples and successors of this great master. Even R. Beirav, the dominant figure in Safed until his death, was a devotee of this "methodology of tight reading" (*shitat ha-'iyyun*) and was responsible for its dissemination in Safed.[68]

---

66. *Ibid.*, p. 80.
67. See especially, Marciano, *Sages of Spain in the Eye of the Storm - Jewish Scholars of Late Medieval Spain*, pp. 140–216. See also Dimitrovsky, 'Rabbi Yaakov Beirav's Academy in Safed', passim; Davidson, *Safed's Sages between 1540–1615, Their Religious and Social Status*, pp. 125–127, 143–145; Benayahu, *Joseph My Chosen One*, p. 155. The impact of this methodology on R. Karo's work, Hagai Pely, 'Studies in the Adjudication Project of Rabbi Joseph Karo' [Hebrew], in: *Rabbi Joseph Karo. History, Halakhah, Kabbalah*, Jerusalem: Zalman Shazar Center, 2021, pp. 142, 149.
68. See Khaled El-Rouayeb, *The Rise of "Deep Reading" in Early Modern Ottoman Scholarly Culture*, Cambridge (Mass.) and London, Harvard U.P., 2015, passim. This is a further indication, requiring an extensive elaboration beyond the scope of this book, of the deep and significant cultural dialogue between Muslim-Ottoman and Jewish religious traditions.

The Yeshiva of R. Karo prospered and became well-known in the above-mentioned Sephardi network following the death of R. Beirav. Similar principles guided its management, such as encouraging independent minds toward renewing the Halakhah; an internal hierarchy within the Yeshiva distinguishing advanced scholars (*chaverim* or *me'aynim*) from young ones (*talmidim*); the practically oriented course of study training the talented students to function as judges and halakhic arbiters; and finally the study methodology of *'Iyyun*.

The Sephardi Talmudic schools were largely identified with the person heading them, so the Yeshiva was actually Karo's Yeshiva. The exceptional prestige of R. Karo, as the scholar of his generation and composer of the leading halakhic compendium, endowed his Yeshiva with an additional stratum of importance and sanctity. Contemporaries, either important local scholars or Jewish travellers in Safed, spoke with superlatives regarding the atmosphere of study and its importance as a Talmudic authority, defending it against all detractors.[69] As we shall see in the next section [E.], his disciples held some major positions of power in Safed. Even the *Magid* assured R. Karo that his disciples would eventually be considered more significant than those of R. Beirav, the previous generation's master.[70] Moreover, they would be more numerous and lead the entire Jewish Ecumene.

What distinguished R. Karo from other scholars in the Sephardi Mediterranean network and from R. Beirav was the fact that he not only conducted his own school but actually founded or patronized another four Yeshivas. In a letter addressed to scholars in Mantova (Italy), he beseeches them to send their financial support to his five schools. R. Karo in this sense was a one-man empire in Talmudic schooling, in charge of an unprecedented number of disciples. Like other heads of Talmudic advanced schools, he was in charge of furnishing their economic basis, as testified in the letter just mentioned. In one of the moments of distress, his Magid again assures him that God has not abandoned him and that financial sustenance would soon arrive.

E.   A rabbi that patronized five Yeshivas evidently had numerous students and disciples. One testimony speaks of two hundred; another exaggeratedly raises the figure to seven hundred. Even if the lower number was correct, R. Karo was undoubtedly in charge of an unprecedented number of disciples. The interaction, dependence, and support between the master and his advanced disciples were strong and much felt in the city of Safed. The observant, if critical, witness of their presence was unsurprisingly *Ha-Mabit*, who encountered Maran and his disciples many times over the course of their decades-long clashes. As mentioned previously, R. Karo's Yeshiva encouraged and appreciated free discussion, creating what one casual visitor as a war-like and antagonistic atmosphere, up to the conclusion of the debate. The visitor's concluding remarks were reserved for the head, R. Karo. On certain occasions, he would attend the Yeshiva and the students would encircle him, a

---

69. Benayahu, *Joseph My Chosen One*, p. 163.
70. Karo, *Magid Meisharim*, p. 3a-b.

practice reminiscent of Muslim Madrasas where the students would form a circle around the scholar. As the Yeshiva and the study curriculum was oriented more to religious practice than to theoretical debates with no concrete effects, Karo took care to install his advanced and talented students in key positions in Safed, as rabbis (*marbitz Torah* is the parallel terminology in Sephardi communities) and judges (*dayanim*). He thus created a dense network of clientele: a great scholar of the religious law and his young protégés. This pattern was common and effective among Ottoman '*Ulama* in the early modern period.

The disciples, for their part, showed loyalty and support to their great master. Indeed, according to *Ha-Mabit*, this obeisance went even further:

> I was shown a halakhic ruling of R. Joseph Karo acquitting [a certain] person, for no good reason. Nor did he mention the local custom, as is generally done. And the Sages, some of his disciples, cling to his words in respect and awe, without any basis. They tie themselves to a tall tree [a Talmudic expression signifying that they rely on a prominent authority in order to justify an invalid position], yet they have no reason to do so, neither according to formal Halakhah nor according to custom, as I wrote.[71]

Loyalty, then, was the main motivation. No wonder that during the common internal conflicts among Safed scholars, especially between the two old rivals, R. Karo's disciples supported his positions and rallied to the group cause, whenever a rabbinical consensus was needed.[72] *Ha-Mabit*, as claimed previously, clearly represented the world view of an old generation refusing to surrender to the changes of time and unable to recognize the need to integrate the young generation alongside the eminent scholars of his own. His testimony should not be dismissed, however. It was not only the lack of experience that failed R. Karo's disciples, pace Di Trani, but their intention to please the ethnic community that hired them, or even powerful and rich individuals. Moreover, they pressured other judges sitting on the bench with them to comply with their positions.[73] Karo, for his part, not only avoided rebuking them, but supported them, adding his own oral approval for one such verdict. They seemed to have the impression that their clientele network protected their positions and resolutions, regardless of their validity and halakhic veracity. Moreover, in one of their exchanges of letters, *Ha-Mabit* rebukes R. Karo, suggesting that his young disciples "stir his heart" (*meni'im et libo*), the implication being that he is motivated by group solidarity rather than the search for truth.[74] Despite of Di Trani's claim that his students were no less talented or numerous,[75]

---

71. Benayahu, *Joseph My Chosen One*, p. 75–76. See also Pely, 'Studies in the Adjudication Project of Rabbi Joseph Karo', pp. 76, 112, 117–118.

72. Dimitrovsky, 'A Dispute between Rabbi J. Caro and Rabbi M. Trani', p. 100.

73. See the interesting remarks of Benayahu, *Joseph My Chosen One*, p. 43.

74. Dimitrovsky discusses this expression in his 'A Dispute between Rabbi J. Caro and Rabbi M. Trani', pp. 77–78.

75. *Ibid.*, p. 75.

it is perfectly clear that he had no legions or clientele of students to support his cause. He could only rely on his personal prestige and erudition and on the solidarity of his generation.

F. The elevating titles used by R. Karo's disciples did not express solely their admiration to his undoubtedly exceptional erudition as Talmudic scholar. The revelations of the *Magid* were not kept as a secret within closed doors of his house. They were loud enough to be heard in the close vicinity of his house. The dense housing conditions of Safed, and the tradition of constructing several houses around a closed courtyard,[76] enabled the dissemination of information regarding what happened behind closed doors. R. Karo was regarded in Safed as a sanctified Talmudic scholar.[77] It seems that one of his Yeshivas was constructed as a sacred "enclosure" (*hesger*). Like similar institutions in Safed and throughout the Ottoman Empire, it combined a regular curriculum of Talmudic studies with a devotional and pietistic atmosphere. The studies were intended to continue ceaselessly and maintain a sequence of sanctified activity, as had been customary in the Holy Temple.[78] R. Karo participated in the overall innovative current of Safed Kabbalists to expand the mystical lore beyond the confines of esoteric circles. A contemporary sage testified that he supported the new ritual practice of the "New Month Eve" as a suitable occasion for collective and private repentance under the guidance of Kabbalistic rituality.[79] More conspicuous was his role in enforcing social discipline and controlling public morality on occasions where popular religiosity and pietism were manifested. The massive public participation in pilgrimages to saints' graves increased during the sixteenth century. Direct contact with saints acquired increasing importance, either alive or by visiting their graves. Rabbinical authorities looked critically on these occasions, with their crowds of men and women mixed together and their carnivalesque free spirit. R. Karo decisively ruled in the *Shulchan 'Arukh* that such occasions must be monitored. The motivation was clearly of a new spirit: the aspiration to achieve sanctity:

> The court must assign policemen during three festivities of pilgrimage, to roam around and examine the orchards and gardens and rivers, so that women and men would not assemble to eat and drink together. They should also warn all people regarding this issue, to prevent men and women mixing at home during festivities, and not to engage in drinking wine, less they be tempted to sin, for *they must all be saints.*[80]

---

76. Carsten Wilke, 'Kabbalistic Fraternities of Ottoman Galilee and their Central European Members, Funders, and Successors', in: Tijana Krstić and Derin Terzioğlu (eds.), *Entangled Confessionalizations? Dialogic Perspectives on the Politics of Piety and Community Building in the Ottoman Empire*, 15th – 18th Centuries, Piscataway (NJ): Gorgias Press, 2022, pp. 255-283.
77. On the importance of the intertwined aspects of Scholar-cum-Kabbalist, see Ch. 6.
78. Wilke, 'Kabbalistic Fraternities of Ottoman Galilee'; Ronit Meroz, 'The Circle of R. Moses ben Makhir and Its Regulations' [Hebrew], *Pe'amim*, 31 (1987), pp. 40–61.
79. Davidson, *Safed's Sages between 1540–1615, Their Religious and Social Status*, p. 247.
80. *Ibid.*, 239.

Sanctity, a term with vague limits, started to enter the formal domain of juridical debates.

G. When necessary, R. Karo had no hesitations in confronting the lay political leaders of Safed. The initiative to impose part of the burden of collective tax payment on Torah scholars encountered a fierce reaction by the rabbinical milieu, and Karo was a leading proponent in this context.[81]

The Battle over the Cultural Capital City: Summary

The battles waged by R. Karo in Safed within the Jewish domain in Safed focused on a concrete and achievable goal: to gain prominence and leadership after the death of R. Beirav. This goal was different from the plans and visions described in other chapters of this book, which had little chance of being materialized in his own time: to position himself as the Jewish Şeyḫülislâm, to form an international court of law, to charge Jewish law with mystic and pietistic dimensions, and, above all, to compose codes of law applicable to entire Jewish Ecumene.

The special status of early modern Safed in the eyes of some of its inhabitants—leading figures of the Talmudic heritage and Kabbalah in the Jewish Diaspora around the Mediterranean—enabled the city to compete with other important Torah centers in such Ottoman cities as Istanbul and Salonica, but not less so with the city of Jerusalem. This dynamic resembles the way Istanbul competed with the sacred cities of Islam—particularly the Two Holy Cities (*Haramayn*)—over the role of leading the Muslim world and as fountains of Muslim religious learning. The battle over scholarly leadership in Safed became an acute matter due to its reverberations in the entire Jewish world of the Mediterranean Basin, under the Ottomans, in Italy, in Northern Africa, and even among Conversos in the Iberian Peninsula who pursued a secret Jewish life.

The central role of Safed was tightly linked to the figure of R. Beirav, a charismatic person and impressive scholar, contributing to the spread of Sephardi Talmudic scholarship to this place. Having maintained a dominant position during his lifetime, his death created a substantial vacuum. It was followed by a decades-long confrontation between his senior disciple and favorite, R. Moses di Trani, and R. Karo. Certainly these confrontations were not devoid of personal motivations, and they reflected similar clashes between Sephardi rabbis to impose their methods and resolutions. All this was natural and inevitable in the rabbinical milieu and its juridical ethos. Both were strongly minded persons, well-connected in their professional networks, and considered by their peers as impressive scholars of the Talmudic and post-Talmudic traditions. In this instance, however—at least from R. Karo's perspective—the dispute was not intended to remain on the local level.

In order to win the battle and enjoy supremacy in the city, R. Karo mobilized all means at his disposal. He headed his own Yeshiva and formed a relatively wide nucleus of supportive and loyal disciples, who followed him in his battles, backed his

---

81. *Ibid.*, pp. 271–277.

positions, and disseminated his halakhic rulings and court verdicts in all the subcommunities of the city. After his death, they would function as dissemination agents for his
double magnum opus, the *Beit Yosef* and *Shulchan 'Arukh*. The diversity of Safed's inhabitants heightened the need to reach rabbinical consensus, so as to overcome the various
traditions and fuse them, as much as possible, into a unified amalgam. This resulted in
the creation of general institutions for the entire Jewish population in Safed, such as a
Supreme Court of Law, charity on a supra-local basis, schools for children of several
ethnic origins, and emissaries on behalf of the entire city. Reaching halakhic consensus
was part of this general effort and provided a fundamental basis for R. Karo's vision in
regard to his codes of law.[82]

Karo mobilized his energies and time to establish a clientele of disciples and former
disciples and install them in key positions in various subcommunities in Safed. Around
their master, they formed a strong power base in Safed and acted collectively. They
contributed to forming a consensus in support of their master, in his legal confrontations, especially with Di Trani. When functioning as judges in semi-formal courts,
they put pressure on their colleagues to accept their rulings or verdicts. R. Karo was
accused by *Ha-Mabit* of actively supporting these actions. This was a sign of the passage of generations and the entrance of new cadre of halakhic sages, marginalizing
the authority of previous generation. In a society such as Safed, and particularly its
rabbinical milieu, that venerated the old, this change was presented as an inversion of
the natural order:

> A topsy-turvy world I [Di Trani] saw: the lower ones wish to rise to the grade unworthy of
> them, and the upper ones restrain themselves from rebuking them. The lower ones over-
> come the upper ones, each of them [the lower ones] claims 'I would rule,' knowing not his
> place, allocating the ignorant a legitimate role, so that a young boy scolds his elder, and the
> despicable [scolds] the dignified. They degrade the honor of Torah and its scholars, and the
> adjudicators of its rules [...] There is none to rebuke them, yet if there is not justice below
> [on earth—R.W.], there is justice above.[83]

The institutions mentioned thus far—even *Beit Ha-Va'ad* or *Beit Din Ha-Gadol*—should
not be measured with the modern Weberian perspective as patterned by regularity
and strict rules of functioning. Due to the persons activating them and their modes of
work, they always depended on changing circumstances and especially on personal
interactions. It comes as no surprise that the rhetoric of many of these confrontations
that R. Karo and his former disciples waged along the second half of the sixteenth century were argumentative and polemical, at the expense of regular halakhic reasoning.
In their fervor to win the argument, both *Ha-Mabit* and R. Karo were not always consistent, sometimes retracting their former positions or raising unjustified arguments or
accusations. For instance, *Ha-Mabit* exerted his efforts to strengthen his court of law as

---

82. See above, Ch. 2.
83. A citation and discussion of this document, see Dimitrovsky, 'A Dispute between Rabbi J.
Caro and Rabbi M. Trani', pp. 85–86.

a general institution in Safed, yet at the same time encouraged arbitration procedures rather than formal court legality. Both sides sought as far as possible not to impair rabbinical solidarity and its internal etiquette. Accordingly, they strove to keep their quarrels hidden from the public and the lay leadership. The longstanding policy of endogamous marriages between sages' families contributed further to this professional solidarity. The son of R. Di Trani went to study at one of R. Karo's schools, regardless of their long-years rivalry. These connections maintained the cohesion of the rabbinical network on both the social and professional levels.

Within this dense circle of Talmud scholars, R. Karo appears to have adopted the most calculated and long-term strategy, on several parallel fronts. His codes of law certainly gave him a significant edge over the others and established his position as an eminent scholar in the entire Mediterranean Basin and beyond, even as far as eastern Europe. If one adds to this his contacts with R. Beirav, the incessant confrontations with *Ha-Mabit*, his mobilization of his students' clientele, the efforts to establish an international court of law, the formation of several religious schools, and his role as a saintly scholar—then it seems clear that he became a dominant person in Safed. His aim was much grander, however: to turn the city under his command—as repeatedly promised by the *Magid*—into a virtual capital city of Jewish culture radiating to the entire Jewish Ecumene. Capital cities evolved in the early modern time—such as Madrid, London, papal Rome, Amsterdam, Istanbul, and cities in Persia and Mughal India—where the management of large states, empires, and colonial regimes were centralized and intricate mechanisms of domination activated. The battle over Safed was a battle for the religious and cultural control of the entire Jewish Ecumene. R. Karo encountered a fierce rival in his attempt to construct his virtual capital city in Safed; The Jewish community in Salonica enjoyed ingrained advantages, positioned in the core lands of the Ottoman Empire, it was much wealthier, and well-connected politically and financially, not to mention its demographic size. Its rabbis did not have any intention to obey the instructions of a peripheral city in the Arab lands. R. Joseph Taitatzak—heading the leading Yeshiva in the city—was considered by others as "Head of the Entire Diaspora," a claim that unavoidably clashed with a parallel one, suggested by R. Karo.[84]

---

84. Meir Benayahu, 'R. Joseph Taitatzak from Salonica, Head of Sephardi Diaspora' [Hebrew], in: Zvi Ankori (ed.), *Then and Now. Annual Lectures on the Jews of Greece (1977–1983)*, Tel-Aviv: The School of Jewish Studies, Tel-Aviv University, 1984, pp. 21–34.

Chapter Six

LAW AND MYSTICISM: AN ENVITABLE ENCOUNTER

R. Joseph Karo was not the first Jewish rabbi to act in the interface between halakhic expertise and immersion in mystical life.[1] But he was certainly the most prominent and effective example of this phenomenon. His deep commitment to a mystical *vita activa* was documented in his mystical diary *Magid Meisharim*, a remarkable and exceptional document in Kabbalistic and rabbinical tradition until the sixteenth century. The interface between a highly professional occupation with law and mystical activity is a rarity in Western or European tradition, yet it is a common and native occurrence in Islamicate tradition. In this sense, the life course of R. Karo integrates smoothly with the Muslim tradition of his surroundings. Further, it corresponds with the Ottoman culture of the time, within which he prospered, and which was well-known to him and his generation. Law and mysticism are not two distinct hats worn by the same person, but two complementary occupations. Law and legal traditions were key aspects in the political ethos of Ottoman and Eurasian rulers in the early modern period, as fundamental legitimizing factors. These rulers were also often regarded as providers of law and justice and as people of saintly and mystical character.

The Mystical Course of R. Karo

By the time R. Karo arrived in Safed, he was already an adult and an established halakhic scholar. Over the coming years, he would gradually reinforce his position and come to be recognized as a major figure in early modern Jewish culture.[2] The publication of his double codes of law—*Beit Yosef* and *Shulchan 'Arukh*—during his lifetime, and while he was living in Safed, placed him at the top of this dense scholarly environment. No less noteworthy is that R. Karo was involved in deep mystical experiences that intensely affected his concrete activities and life course. It is impossible to reconstruct exactly when and under what circumstances R. Karo embarked on his Kabbalistic path, but it is apparent that one of the constitutive moments along his mystical course

---

1. On Ashkenazi precedents, see Ephraim Kanarfogel, *"Peering Through the Lattices". Mystical, Magical, and Pietistic Dimensions in the Tosafist Period*, Detroit: Wayne State University Press, 2000.
2. See above Ch. 5.

occurred during the Pentecost festivities in Salonica in 1533.[3] Pentecost (*Shavu'ot*) is celebrated as the moment of the Granting of the Torah at Mount Sinai. Kabbalistically viewed, it is perceived not as a one-time historical event, but a recurring mythical symbol of the unique and continuous pact between God and His people through the Torah; a pact that is renewed in every act of Torah study.

R. Salomon Alkabetz (1500–1576), an inspiring and charismatic Kabbalistic figure, and R. Karo jointly headed a mystical fraternity in Salonica.[4] It is highly plausible that some of the fraternity members were Talmudic scholars and disciples in the prestigious Yeshiva headed by R. Joseph Taitatzak (1465–1546), who himself experienced angelic revelations alongside his important halakhic scholarship.[5] Toward midnight on the festival, they convened and began to read texts from the Jewish canon or more precisely to chant them with a certain intonation. Divine inspiration descended on R. Karo, and he spoke on behalf of the *Shekhinah*, the revelatory and feminine aspect of divinity according to the Book of Splendor (*Sefer Ha-Zohar*). Disappointingly, not all the members of this secretive fraternity were present during this night, which caused the divine voice to rebuke those absent. On the following night, the number of participants increased and the same ritual cycle was followed, again opening the door to further and even deeper revelations by R. Karo.

The testimony of this event was left by Alkabetz, who obeyed the instruction of the *Shekhinah* and migrated to the Holy Land, later followed by R. Karo himself. The letter documenting this event is not a direct and unbiased testimony but saturated with rabbinical and literary rhetoric. The divine voice is described as using a literary and flowery language, echoing the classical poetry of Sephardi tradition. The allusions to the rabbinical heritage place the event in a triple context: First, as the reconstruction of Mount Sinai revelation—the formative moment in the construction of the historical link between God and his people; second, as the encounter of scholars of Yavneh after the destruction of the Second Temple, a constitutive moment in rabbinical tradition; third, the fraternity members attending the sacred moments bore the same titles as the mystical fraternity of the Zohar, implying that they existed in historical time, carrying on their mystical secrets in the settings of the early modern world.

The deep attachment to *Sefer Ha-Zohar* during the two-night Pentecost event would continue throughout the early modern period. This work would eventually become the mystical canon of Jewish culture, relegating to the margins other and previous mystical

---

3. Mor Altshuler, *The Life of Rabbi Yoseph Karo* [Hebrew], Tel-Aviv: Tel-Aviv U.P., 2016, Ch. 8 – 'Tikkun Leil Shavuot', pp. 139–159. See also Meir Bar-Ilan, 'Tikkun Leil Shavuot: Its Formation and Precedents' [Hebrew], *Mechkari Hag* 8 (1997), pp. 28–48; Y.D. Wilhelm, 'Sidrei Tikunim' [Protocols of Kabbalistic Emendations – in Hebrew], in: *'Alei 'Ayin. Homage to Shlomo Zalman Schocken for his Seventieth Birthday*, Jerusalem: n.p., 1948–1952, pp. 125–146.

4. Altshuler, *The Life of Rabbi Yoseph Karo*, p. 159.

5. Gershom Scholem, 'The Magid of R. Yosef Taitazak and the Revelations Attributed to Him' [Hebrew], *Sefunot: Studies and Sources on the History of the Jewish Communities in the East* 11 (1969), pp. 69–112.

traditions of the Middles Ages.[6] The event also explains the mystical commitment of R. Karo to these Zoharic traditions as a fundamental point of reference in his future years. The suggestions offered by the Zohar, or in the writings of its principal composer R. Moses di Leon, to project mystical aspects of divinity into parallel ritual activity were transformed into concrete reality in the mystical fraternity of Alkabetz and Karo. This is the first testified occasion on which such a ritual event of convening and reading sacred texts, inspired by Kabbalistic motivations, had taken place on the night of *Shavu'ot*. The entire happening was documented so that it would reach further circles, and indeed during the sixteenth century what took place in Salonica inspired other people as well, and became a ritual practice celebrated to the present day. The ceremony is known as *Tiqqun Leil Shavu't*, literally "the Emendation of Divinity during Pentecost's Eve".

The event directed and confirmed Karo's mystical itinerary for future years. He would be deeply involved in mystical, scholarly, juridical, and leadership roles, all of which were regarded as inseparable. The revelations he experienced in Salonica were public, in the sense that the messages were heard by other persons as well and were not confined to some inner or mental process. They were instantly accepted as legitimate and sacred, and not challenged as false or demonic. What is even more important is that the pattern of revelation established in Salonica would continue for the rest of his life: the revealing figure is predominantly feminine, mostly under the guise of the *Shekhinah*. Additionally, the technique for reaching these mystical moments was related to some form of musicality and the recitation of a sacred text. The term used by Alkabetz in this regard, borrowed from the Song of Songs—*Qol Dodi dofeq*—would become a common refrain in Karo's mystical diary.

It was not mere coincidence that neither R. Karo's revelations at Pentecost nor his broad mystical enterprise were challenged as false or inadmissible. Again, Karo was responding to a changing religious atmosphere in early modern Jewish Diaspora around the Mediterranean Basin whereby revelations of various kinds were increasingly regarded as legitimate. In the late fifteenth century, prior to the general expulsion of the Iberian communities from Spain (1492) and Portugal (1497), the "Book of Splendor" circulated in relatively esoteric and restricted channels and had not yet achieved the status of a canonical book. This changed dramatically in the mid-sixteenth century, due to the rise of Safed as a leading Kabbalistic center and following the double printing of *Sefer Ha-Zohar* in Italy, the center of Jewish printing in this period. The change in religious atmosphere was inspired by yet another set of writings, known as the "Book of the Respondent" (*Sefer Ha-Meshiv*).[7] This is a fiery discourse on revelations and the capability to establish a bridge between an inspired Kabbalist and the divine sphere, intermediated by a *Magid*, some kind of angelic figure. Karo adopted

---

6. Boaz Huss, *The Zohar. Reception and Impact*, tr. by Yudith Naveh, Oxford and Portland [Or.]: The Littman Library of Jewish Civilization, 2016, passim.

7. See mainly Moshe Idel, 'Inquiries into the Doctrine of "Sefer ha-Meshiv" ' [Hebrew], *Sefunot: Studies and Sources on the History of the Jewish Communities in the East* 2 (1943), pp. 185–266. See also Scholem, 'The Magid of R. Yosef Taitazak'.

this term, which later formed part of the title for his mystical diary *Magid Meisharim*. The time, according to the anonymous Sephardi composers of *Sefer Ha-Meshiv*, was suitable for unprecedented revelations of hidden Torah secrets, as the messianic era was imminent. As Idel and Scholem noted, the Magid was a new actor in Jewish mystical tradition specific to the sixteenth-century context.[8] Though not derived from any direct Talmudic sources, and certainly not suitable to legalistic mindset of the rabbinical ethos, it was not rejected by the rabbinical authorities. R. Joseph Taitatzak, the leading Talmudic scholar of Salonica, one of the main centers of Sephardi erudition in early modern period, was known "to have a Magid." The question whether these revelatory figures affected the Talmudic and juridical work of either R. Taitatzak or R. Karo will be examined in this chapter.

Sixteenth-century religious life in the Jewish communities of the Mediterranean Basin was suffused with similar types of revelation. The rising Kabbalistic domain provided various channels for bridging the gulf between humans and the ineffable God.[9] The binary distinction between God and man, good and bad, and sanctified and polluted was filled with intermediary entities that could help the believer to approach God more intimately or conversely impose obstacles: the tree of souls, reincarnations, impregnation, treasure of souls, and demonic torture instruments related to the human body, birth, and death. Mental life became a complex balance of reward and punishment reverberating between the poles of sanctity and pollution, Shekhinah and the demonic, angels and demons, the eternal life world and the world of the dead. Kabbalistic creativity permitted passage between the material world and the hidden world, mutually intertwined by reincarnation and possession, spirits, demons, Magidim, and angels. The evolvement of print technology, especially the printing of *Sefer Ha-Zohar* and other Kabbalistic literature over the course of the sixteenth century, made it possible to share this dichotomous Kabbalistic attitude among broad lay circles.[10] An entire spectrum of agents and techniques and ritual practices played on this stage: Magidim, dreams, prophecies, trance states, reincarnations (*gilgulim*), impregnation (*'ibbur*), demons, and black magic, angelic figures, dreams,[11] Elijah "the Prophet" as a source of mystical secrets, attachment to masters and to a Righteous Person (*tzaddiq*), and finally pilgrimages to sacred graves. Even the body was not immune to infiltration by supra-human elements, as testified by the dramatic increase of possession cases and their public and theatrical shows of healing. It was a suitable arena to present the dividing lines between the forbidden and normative and to enhance social control.[12]

---

8. Scholem, 'The Magid of R. Yosef Taitazak', pp. 70–72, on the new phenomenon of revelatory voices in the sixteenth century, including the *Magid* of R. Joseph Karo, next to Possession cases.

9. Rachel Elior, "Possession' in the Early Modern Period: Speaking Voices, Silent Worlds and Silenced Voices' [Hebrew], *Jerusalem Studies in Jewish Thought* 18–19 (2005), pp. 499–536.

10. Elior, 'Possession' in the Early Modern Period', see esp. pp. 500–501.

11. Idel, 'Inquiries into the Doctrine of "Sefer ha-Meshiv"', pp. 201–215.

12. Elior, 'Possession' in the Early Modern Period', pp. 522–524.

The Book *Magid Meisharim*

Was the *Shavu't* dramatic event a leap forward in R. Karo's mystic course or did it continue a preexisting chain of less intense revelations? No documents have remained that can answer this question, but we have more information regarding what happened later. Karo embarked on an active and intensive mystical road, which he documented meticulously in what was termed by later generations *Sefer Ha-Magid*, the "Book of the Divine Figure."[13] The great Jewish bibliographer of the eighteenth centuries, R. Hayim Yosef David Azulai (1724–1806, known by his acronym *HaChidah*)[14] claimed that the original version of the manuscript—or even a series of manuscripts—was twenty times bigger than the printed text. *HaChidah* was a meticulous and avid observer of the books and manuscripts he encountered during his long years of wandering years through various Mediterranean Jewish communities. There is no particular cause to doubt his testimony. But even if the original version of Karo's mystical diary was somewhat smaller than R. Azulai's estimation, it is still an exceptionally long diary. The material at hand—both a printed book and several manuscripts[15]—includes hundreds of pages of dense handwriting. It reflects an ongoing experience across several decades of life, during which the contact between R. Karo and the divine revelatory entities continued on an almost daily basis.

The revealing figure is clearly feminine and presents itself under various names: *Shekhinah* (the feminine aspect of God), *Matronita* (grand lady), *Neshamah* (soul), *Ha-Em Ha-Meyaseret* (the chastising mother), and finally *Ha-Mishnah* (the Mishnah). The last of these names is especially important for several reasons. The Mishnah as an independent textual unit was neglected during the Middle Ages and was regarded as part of the Talmudic conglomerate. As such it was not printed separately until very late and rarely served as a basis for commentaries. The Safed Kabbalists changed its status and prestige, presenting the Mishnah not only as the epitome of the Oral Torah but even more significantly as the last of the divine Spheres. This perspective inspired the study by heart of the Mishnah text, and later the establishment of confraternities dedicated entirely to its study.[16] *Mishnah* and *Neshamah* are considered as close words in Kabbalistic traditions, since they share the same three root letters, albeit arranged differently. Thus, the *Mishnah* addressing R. Karo symbolizes a direct link to his higher spiritual aspect,

---

13. R.J. Zvi Werblowski, *Karo: Lawyer and Mystic*, Philadelphia: Jewish Publication Society of America, 1977, passim. See also, Altshuler, *The Life of Rabbi Yoseph Karo*, passim. An important oral lecture of Moshe Idel would be mentioned later on. A recent important discussion, see in Moshe Idel, 'Rabbi Joseph Karo as Kabbalist' [Hebrew], in: *Rabbi Joseph Karo. History, Halakhah, Kabbalah*, Jerusalem: Zalman Shazar Center, 2021, pp. 337–400.

14. On *HaChidah*, see Meir Benayahu, *R. Hayim Yosef David Azulai* [Hebrew], 2 Vols., Jerusalem: Yad Ben-Zvi and Mosad HaRav Kuk, 1959; Avital Sharon, *Hidas' Kaballah in his Hallakhic Writings* [Hebrew], Ph.D. submitted at the Hebrew University, 2014.

15. Photocopies of these manuscripts can be found at the National Library of Israel (Jerusalem), The Department of Jewish Manuscripts.

16. Aharon Ahrend, 'Mishnah Study and Mishnah Confraternities in the Early Modern Period' [Hebrew], *JSIG* 3 (2004), pp. 19–53.

the *Neshamah* or soul. It also echoes additional Kabbalistic positions, since the Mishnah is the impersonation of the Oral Torah or the *Shekhinah*—one of the aspects of divinity within the system of Kabbalistic Spheres. In the case of R. Karo, the Mishnah provided a channel of communication, offering a concrete mystical technique to initiate a dialogue with the above. As we noted above, this process began with the dramatic *Shavu't* revelation, but it continued for decades until Karo's death. Karo would use a form of musicality or intonation to recite the Mishnah text and then divine messages would begin to pour down. The expression from Song of Songs could be taken literally: *Qol Dodi dofeq* could be translated "the voice of my Beloved is beating (or: knocking at my doorstep)." These three words embody the main elements of Karo's mystical states. The voice was verbal and accessible to outside persons close enough to Karo to hear the words. The concept of the Beloved relates to a deep intimacy with divinity,[17] a theme that will be discussed later. Lastly, beatings (or knocking) could signal the uniqueness of the situation, derived not from regular states of mind or from Talmudic erudition but related to divine powers. Another manifestation of this different state again relates to music: "While doing this I fell asleep, and slept over an hour, and then woke up and read [parts of] the Mishnah until dawn for half an hour. Then I sat on a bench, still reciting Mishnah, and lo the voice of my Beloved is beating in my mouth (*qol Dodi dofeq be-fi*) and a violin playing by itself, saying [...]"[18] The sublime mixes with the daily and the mundane. The revelation, followed by unwished sleep, and again followed by another encounter with the Mishnah, is aided by textual recitation, the internal beats, and a musicality of an automatic and uncontrollable character ("a violin playing by itself and saying [...]").[19] The speaker and his body, the divine partner, and the message have almost converged into a single entity. Put differently, the body turns into musical instrument, played by the above.

Magid Meisharim is unique and unprecedented in rabbinical tradition and ethos, where personal and intimate aspects are extremely rare in the vast literature at our disposal.[20] The text contains the secrets of the Torah and of Jewish traditions,[21] yet mundane aspects of R. Karo's life are not lacking. His bodily needs and habits are discussed again and again, with no apologetic tone:

> I am in charge of castigating men at night, as said in the holy Zohar. Thus I came now to castigate you lest you drink wine during the day, and incite you to asceticism. During the night you should drink no more than one glass, as you [usually] do. Should you want to drink a little, do that, and do not fear of sickness. Only do not exceed, for it harms the body, and medicine/health is an important prologue to the worship of God; if you act so, your

---

17. The term *Dodi* was commonly translated as 'My Beloved'.
18. Joseph Karo, *Magid Meisharim*, Wilnius: Judah Leib Lipman Metz Print, 1875, p. 17b.
19. This expressions echoes the Midrash on King David's Violin, played by the wind, as if by itself. See for instance TB Berakhot 3b and Sanhedrin 16a.
20. On the autobiographical aspect of Karo's writing, see §6.5.
21. See for instance Karo, *Magid Meisharim*, pp. 4b, 5a, 6a, 7a, 9a, 10b, 13a, 15a, 17a, 17b, 25a, 27b, 28b, 52b.

heart and thought will always be a nest and domicile for Torah and not separated from her [from the Torah] for one moment.[22]

Even Karo's family and private life are discussed by the divine figure, including moments of intimacy between the great rabbi and mystic and his wife:

> I would now reveal the mystical secret of your third wife. You should know that this woman in a previous time [incarnation] was a righteous Talmudic scholar, yet stingy with his money and reluctant to give charity. He was also miserly in sharing his wisdom [Talmudic erudition] and refused to behave in a manly manner [generously]. For this reason, she does not give birth while living with you. But I would act so that feminine sparks would shine in her. And this is the mystical meaning of the verse in the Book of Ruth.[23]

R. Karo married several women during his lifetime. One of them is described as a masculine woman, due to her previous incarnation as an ungenerous masculine Talmudic scholar. This not only explains her current sterility, to be changed by divine grace but also the sexual incompatibility between them. Further, when having sexual intimacy with her, R. Karo is instructed to avoid any joy and only care for the fulfillment of the biblical command to multiply.[24] In one of the dramatic moments documented in *Magid Meisharim*, R. Karo is notified that he has been sentenced to death due to his sins. A grave battle was waged in heavenly spheres to spare him, and it was a last minute change that kept him alive.[25]

---

22. *Idid.*, p. 49a. See also, ibid., p. 19a: "You should adhere only to me and to my Torah, your bodily members would turn into arena for the *Shechinah*, and your internal organs would be constantly aiming at my worship. And all your occupations would be aiming at my name. Do you find it worthy, the fact that along this night you drank too much water? And the previous night you ate until you reached satiation, and the regular quantity of wine did not suffice, and you asked to bring more. On the first time [the previous night – R.W.] we are displeased, and you have added further sin ...". Further references to bodily functions and their discipline, see *ibid.*, pp. 3a, 3b, 5b, 6a, 6b, 19b, 28b, 39b, 44b, 49a, 52a. On the centrality of body images in the Kabbalistic tradition at Safed, see Assaf M. Tamari, *The Body Discourse of Lurianic Kabbalah* [Hebrew], Ph.D. Thesis submitted at Ben-Gurion University (Israel), 2016.
23. *Ibid.*, p. 11b. For further references about private and daily life, see *ibid.*, pp. 3a, 6b, 7a, 11b, 12a, 17a, 25b, 26a, 28a, 51a.
24. *Ibid.*, p. 19a: "And the pleasure that one had in these matters [sexual acts – R.W.], should be considered as if one is constrained to copulate and this is the secretive sense about what the wife of R. Eliezer said that her husband copulated as if constrained by a demon. Meaning that his entire intention was to fulfill the commandment to be fruitful and multiply to the fulfill the sexual obligation of a husband towards his wife, and not to draw any enjoyment at all, but to copulate as if constrained by the demon, so that he enjoys not". See also *ibid.*, pp. 5a, 6b, 11b. An extensive discussion on Kabbalistic sexual morality, see Roni Weinstein, *Juvenile Sexuality, Kabbalah, and Catholic Religiosity among Jewish Italian Communities. "Glory of Youth" by Pinhas Baruch b. Pelatya Monselice (Ferrara, XVII Century)*, Boston and Leiden: E. J. Brill, 2008.
25. Karo, *Magid Meisharim*, pp. 26b, 50a, 52a.

The diary, even in its shortened and heavily edited version, accompanies R. Karo's life over many years, reflecting his increasing self-awareness of his major mystical position and his role in leading the entire Jewish Ecumene. These sensations are often sustained along his heavenly journeys. In these glorious moments, he is welcomed in heaven as a king, surrounded by a regal cortege of scholars of the heavenly Yeshiva, a choir of angels, and the entourage of the *Shekhinah*, who is the Mishnah speaking to and through him. This image is reminiscent of the processions when kings and conquerors entered major cities, an important political and theatrical show of power in both Europe and the Ottoman Empire in the early modern period. To increase the public dimension, this event is announced by a heavenly herald:

> I am the mother castigating her children. Beware to adhere to me, for I and all my entourage surround you, and you are as a king in his regiment. Had it been permitted to see, you would have seen all over that you are circled by heavenly figures created by the breath of your mouth when you occupy yourself with the Mishnah, and they are all stationed around you, and you are circled by my entourage, and as a king in his regiment. They all declare, show honor to the vision of the holy king [R. Karo] for he is our *Tanna* and our *Sevara* [scholars involved in the creation and study of the Mishnah and Talmud, respectively].[26]

The reasons behind R. Karo's esteem in heaven were provided on several occasions. His words, writings, and contributions affect the heavenly spheres and win him the affection of God Himself:

> [The heavenly herald] declares: this is the man cherished by the King of Kings [God] and by the precious heavenly escort, since he is the Tanna of the Holy Land, Head of Yeshiva of the Holy Land, Head of all Diasporas, our Talmudic Arbiter, our Scholar, our Book Composer. When you cease from concentrating on holy issues and turn to worldly matters, this herald dwindles, and all the worlds shake, asking: "Why did the heavenly herald cease announcing?" So hold yourself steady and do not detach your thoughts from me even for one instant.[27]

His status is equated with the itinerant tabernacle that accompanied the Israelites on their journey from Egypt to the Holy Land:

> As you learned five and half sections of the Mishnah [out of six sections] you are absorbed in the Clouds of Honor ['Ananei Kavod, encircling the itinerant tabernacle along the way

---

26. *Ibid.*, p. 18b. See also *ibid.*, p. 4a: "All the [heavenly] entourage escorts you and heralds your coming, saying show honor to the vision of the holy king and make way to the vision/image of the holy king ... so many regiments and soldiers and worlds shake when hearing this heraldry. They all ask what is this voice, and respond, saying this is a person [R. Karo – R.W.] by whom God is glorified every day. And so every time you finish studying with your companions a voice is heralding in this way to publicize your spiritual grade/status, and they fear the might of your master [God – R.W.]."

27. *Ibid.*, p. 21a.

from slavery in Egypt to Canaan], as your erudition accompanies you, and they [these majestic clouds] will not leave you, but I [the Mishnah] will always bring them back.[28]

The Torah, this heavily charged word in Jewish tradition, is bestowed upon him, taken out of the secretive treasury of God himself:

> I bestowed upon you a free gift, since a wonderful gift and a precious gem was in my treasure house, and I took it out and gave it to you gratis, as it is said: "To my mother's house and to the chamber of the one who gave birth to me." "To my mother's house" means Matronita, and "the chamber of the one who gave birth to me" alludes to the divine Sphere Shekhinah. A wonderful gift I took out of my treasure house and gave to you, so my son be very cautious. It is I, I the Mishnah, speaking to you.[29]

The terms chosen for this vision allude to midrashic tradition that refers to the Torah— again a metonymy of the entire Jewish heritage—as coexisting eternally next to God, even prior to the creation of the world. Was this an implicit allusion to the eternity of Karo's soul next to almighty God? And if so, what was the sense of this presumptuous claim? Further, it echoes the famous debate in Islamic tradition regarding the created or eternal character of the Koran.[30]

Many descriptions present R. Karo as immersed in the heavenly abodes during his encounters with the *Shekhinah*. In an impressive moment of elation, Karo shares a mutual status with the feminine figure of the *Shekhinah*:

> I am the Mishnah speaking in your mouth. I kiss you kisses of love, and embrace you. I place your head in the shadow of [God's] wings, my glory is upon you, and your glory upon me, my radiation upon you and your radiation upon me, I would not forget you and you would not forget me, not in this [earthly] world and not in the coming world. You would rise to the upper divine worlds, and glorify, and be crowned, and amuse yourself with the righteous ones in paradise, saying precious and sublime words, and you would adhere to the righteous ones by secretive secrets of God.[31]

Moshe Idel considered this description, along with others in *Magid Meisharim*, as indicating the partial deification of R. Karo.[32] During such mystical moments he becomes part of God, especially through his intimate contact with the *Shekhinah*. His body, voice, and personality do not merely serve as instruments for conveying the message; he merges momentarily with God, and what he and the *Shekhinah* say is the same thing. This is the fundamental reason, following Idel again, that Karo allocates a very marginal place to

---

28. *Ibid.*, p. 8b.
29. *Ibid.*, p. 19b. See also *ibid.*, p. 26b.
30. *Ibid.*, p. 50a – the promise to Karo, while still alive, that he has an assured place in Heaven after his death.
31. *Ibid.*, p.47a.
32. See the link to his oral lecture available on YouTube: https://www.youtube.com/watch?v=MApzihqtE-Y&t=3351s.

angelic revelations, even though these were so customary in his Sephardi mystical traditions. Such a channel of contact is of much lower grade than the direct dialogue and merging with divinity. The interaction with the feminine divine is suffused with sexual and intimate allusions, reflecting some kind of direct contact and union.[33]

R. Karo as a Kabbalist: Talmudic Scholar

The concomitant activity of R. Karo as a leading jurist and halakhic expert, the composer of the double codes of law, and an active and passionate mystic aroused deep discomfort among scholars of the previous generation. In his seminal and inspiring work on R. Karo as "Lawyer and Mystic," Zvi Werblowsky regards the two spheres as essentially parallel and distinct.[34] He dedicated an entire chapter to the Halakhic traces of the revelatory moments, as documented in *Magid Meisharim*, but did not consider them an inseparably interwoven aspect.[35] The scholars of Jewish history, culture, and religion who founded the Hebrew University of Jerusalem originated mostly from areas dominated by Protestantism. In general, law was perceived as a relatively lower manifestation of religious life and experiences, in respect to inner "spiritual" space. They regarded the Halakhah as "legalism" largely devoid of any mystic or transcendental significance. The following generation of scholars followed suit and rarely attempted to discuss the interface of law and Kabbalah in R. Karo's works.

They could certainly support their position on several grounds. The *Shavu't* event, of major importance in the life of R. Karo, R. Alkabetz, and their companions in the mystical fraternity, inspired the "invention" of the Shavu't Vigil (*Tiqqun Leil Shavu't*) in later generations and become particularly popular in Israel in recent years. Yet this event left no trace in R. Karo's halakhic works, even though the new ritual was considered as sanctified.[36] In general, R. Karo was highly cautious in publicizing his visions, and certainly in projecting their potential halakhic implications. To do so would have run the risk that an inexperienced reader of his diary might deduce that he based some of the halakhic rulings—those found in his writings or offered in his court of law—on his visions or on Kabbalistic reasoning as a legitimate basis for halakhic ruling. This would be liable to jeopardize the content or method of halakhic ruling (*pesiqah*).[37] Another consideration can be offered for Karo's reticence

---

33. Karo, *Magid Meisharim*, pp. 26b, 35a. Further moments of Karo's glorification in the divine world, see *ibid.*, pp. 3a, 3b, 4a, 5b, 10a, 13b, 14a, 16a, 16b, 18b, 19b, 21a, 23b, 24b, 25a, 26b, 29a, 29b, 35a, 35b, 37a, 41b, 47a, 49a-b, 50a.

34. R.J. Zvi Werblowsky, *Joseph Karo Lawyer and Mystic*, Philadelphia: The Jewish Publication Soceity of America, 1977.

35. *Ibid.*, Ch. 8 – 'The Halakhah of the Maggid', pp. 169–188.

36. Bar-Ilan, 'Tikkun Leil Shavuot'.

37. Hagai Pely, 'Halakhah, Pietism, Kabbalah and Revelation in Sixteenth Century Safed: A Study in R. Yosef Karo's Works' [Hebrew], *Jerusalem Studies in Jewish Thought* 24 (2015), pp. 201–234. See also idem., 'Kabbalah in R. Karo's Halakhic Decisions: A Chapter in the Genealogy of Castilian Halakhic-Ruling until the Sixteenth Century' [Hebrew], *Kabbalah:*

to combine these two domains. When he—along with others in the strong halakhic establishment in Safed—encountered attempts by individual pietists (*Chasidim*) to change local customs on the basis of mystical rather than formal halakhic motivations, he vehemently opposed such efforts.[38] Indeed, he did not even deign such attempts worthy of a halakhic battle, as did others among the same juridical milieu; rather he castigated his anonymous rival or rivals as marginal and outsiders to the rabbinical-Talmudic arena.

The interactions between Halakhah and mysticism as two major building blocks of Jewish traditions in the early modern period have been exposed in some fascinating recent works.[39] Important roots for the interface between these two domains are found in the Sephardi tradition, particularly the Castilian. Following the expulsion from the Iberian Peninsula and the mystical renaissance in Safed, this combination later expanded to the entire Jewish Ecumene. Hagai Pely's works offer an illuminating presentation of this process. Pely noted that the first signs of the halakhic use of authoritative Kabbalistic sources appeared in the late thirteenth century, for instance, in the writings of R. Shem-Tov ibn Gaon. However, the systematic infiltrations of Kabbalah into the domain of Halakhah occurred only around the turn of the fourteenth and fifteenth centuries. After the Zoharic corpus established its authority in Safed, this phenomenon accelerated. It is no mere coincidence that the arena for these changes was typically Sephardic. The most dramatic change took place in the *Beit Midrash* (the Sephardi parallel of the *Yeshiva*—R.W.) of R. Isaac Canpanton. This tradition was later absorbed by some major halakhic figures of the sixteenth century, including prominent scholars in Safed. R. Karo embedded this encounter between the Halakhah and mysticism in his codes of law to a greater extent than any previous halakhic figures.[40] The study of Kabbalah progressively infiltrated the writings of some of the leading Sephardi Talmudic schools. The welcoming attitude to Kabbalistic traditions adopted by R. Isaac Canpanton,[41] the most prestigious Talmudic scholar in the years immediately prior to the general expulsion, legitimized the infiltration of Kabbalistic elements into Talmudic discourse. R. Canpanton, it is important to recall, was hailed as the inventor of the new study methodology of the Talmud—the *Pilpul* or *'Iyyun*, later disseminated in the major scholastic centers and Sephardi communities around the

---

Journal for the Study of Jewish Mystical Texts 26 (2012), pp. 243–272. See further idem., 'Studies in the Adjudication Project of Rabbi Joseph Karo', pp. 131–333.

38. Pely, 'Halakhah, Pietism, Kabbalah and Revelation in Sixteenth Century Safed'; Idem., *The Lurianic Kabbalah: Halakhic and Meta-Halakhic Aspects*, Ph.D. submitted at Ben-Gurion University (Beer-Shevah), 2014, esp. pp. 14–15, where he asserts that change of Halakhic rules due to purely theosophical-mystical motivations prevailed mainly among the 'secondary elite' of pietists, excluded from the rabbinic 'primary elite'.

39. See the research of Hagai Pely and Mor Altshuler mentioned previously, and the ones of Maoz Kahana to be mentioned below.

40. Pely., *The Lurianic Kabbalah: Halakhic and Meta-Halakhic Aspects*, esp. pp. i, 1.

41. On Rabbi Isaac Canpanton, see Yoel Marciano, *Sages of Spain in the Eye of the Storm - Jewish Scholars of Late Medieval Spain* [Hebrew], Jerusalem: Bialik Institute, 2019, passim.

Mediterranean Basin. R. Karo was one of the distinguished scholars who inherited and benefitted from this methodology.

Two options or channels of interaction between Halakhah and Jewish legality had been present since the thirteenth century but reached a high point of intensity during the sixteenth and seventeenth centuries.[42] The more radical channel sought to employ theosophical and mystical knowledge about divinity or divine domains in shaping halakhic norms. The other, more closely aligned to mainstream halakhic patterns, regarded the authoritative and reliable Kabbalistic books, especially *Sefer Ha-Zohar*, as legitimate sources in Talmudic discourse, albeit only under strict restrictions. In the same Sephardi Yeshivas where mysticism was welcomed as a legitimate though partial partner, and especially in the milieu around R. Canpanton, a firm rule was adopted. Even the most established and reliable of the mystical compositions could serve as a Talmudic source only if they did not stand in contradiction to an explicit Talmudic ruling.[43] When the Talmudic discussion was relatively vague, or did not reach a conclusive point, mysticism might step in and become a partner in ruling Halakhah (*pesiqah*). It thus becomes less surprising that some of the leading figures in Safed engaged both in halakhic and Kabbalistic studies.[44]

Karo was one of the inheritors of the Castilian heritage, in this respect as in others. This approach created room for halakhic norms derived from authoritative Kabbalistic sources, but denied the validity of any halakhic argument based on an abstract theosophical foundation unrelated to any authoritative text—not for filling some halakhic void, and certainly not as an element of some halakhic sophistry.[45] Karo's main contribution to the mystical-legal fabric of the sixteenth century and beyond was the inclusion of many Zoharic references in his double codes of law. He legitimized the Zohar, considered among his peers as typically related to the Sephardi heritage, and transformed it into a legitimate partner in Talmudic and legalistic discourse. The borders between these two domains, maintained even by R. Karo himself, become more porous and less certain. The main reason for this change was that each ritual activity reflected some secretive parallel in the divine. This position at times overcame even the sobriety of jurists involved in Talmudic discussions. It would lead R. Karo, in one instance, to rely in his code of law on a thirteenth-century Jewish-Italian Kabbalist, inserting directly in his text a dream that person had regarding a Tabernacle ritual, which had to be done in a way that would reflect and contribute to harmony in the Sephirotic world.[46]

What could only be implicitly hinted at when using rabbinical and Talmudic language would be openly and explicitly stated in R. Karo's mystical diary. The exposure of the secretive-mystical reading of Jewish tradition by the divine *Magid* offers an alternative perspective for apprehending this unique document. The ritual acts and commandments (*mitzvot*), the Talmudic discussions, and the entire Jewish sacred canon are read

---

42. Pely., *The Lurianic Kabbalah: Halakhic and Meta-Halakhic Aspects*, passim.
43. Pely, 'Kabbalah in R. Karo's Halakhic Decisions'.
44. Idem., *The Lurianic Kabbalah: Halakhic and Meta-Halakhic Aspects*, pp. 75–77.
45. *Ibid.*, p. 77.
46. *Ibid.*, p. 23.

through a mystical lens (*raza de* ... is the Aramaic expression often used by R. Karo).[47] It relates to the highly textual character of rabbinic tradition and the fundamental role of Torah study [*Talmud Torah* in Hebrew] in the Jewish ethos. Any hermeneutic innovation must eventually be anchored in a textual basis. R. Karo is promised that he will enjoy this privilege after reaching the Holy Land: "I will reward you to migrate to the Land of Israel, and unite with Salomon my friend [Shlomo Alkabetz] and with the fraternity members, and study Torah."[48]

The interaction between R. Karo and the *Magid* figure is not a one-way experience in which the *Magid* utters his words and Karo serves as a passive receptacle. As noted above, the encounter leads to a progressive sense of empowerment, a growing immersion in the divine world, and even the divinization of Karo's personality. The study of Torah acquires in this context an entire novel character of a heavenly journey. When ascending to divine domains, the figure of R. Karo is heralded not as a Kabbalist or a grand magician, but as a leading scholar. There he meets the important scholars of all previous generations, assembled in the divine Yeshiva. His entrance is described as a regal procession, hailed by all those in attendance. This is no mere symbolic description but a highly tangible one. The contact with these towering figures of Jewish past scholarship is personal and emotional:

and what you said, regarding the assertions of the God-fearing Jacob [the composer of the code of law *Ha-Turim*] and his father R. Asher, he did not make the right legal distinction. You have aimed well. You should know that generally the sayings of Maimonides are correct, since he adheres to ancient versions, such as the ones of R. Hananel and our Rabbi Hai, whose versions are clear, while at times the *Tosafot* scholars engaged in legal casuistry (*pilpula*) in opposing these versions, which is an error. And the interpretation provided by Maimonides is generally valid. Regarding the issue you interpreted, suggesting two modes, God smiled satisfactorily enjoying your casuistry, but the second [Talmudic] interpretation [you suggested] is clearer. Yet do not disregard the first one, which is sharp.[49]

The ultimate confirmation for this mutual interaction is provided in a dramatic moment when R. Karo is doomed to die due to his sins, but the leading scholars of rabbinical and Talmudic tradition intervened on his behalf and actually saved his life:

I am the Mishnah speaking well of you. Like Jacob my chosen one, Moses my elected one [Maimonides], Rashi [R. Salomon Itzhaki], the *Tosafot* scholars, and all the *Amoraim* [the scholars of Talmudic times.] and *Tanaim* [scholars of the Mishnah era] with whose sayings you occupy yourself. They have saved you from death, due to all malicious matters, and offered other precious persons [...] as ransom [in the sense of substitute].[50]

---

47. Besides the references mentioned previously, see also Karo, *Magid Meisharim*, pp. 10b, 16b, 18b, 25a, 25b, 29b, 30a, 34a, 52a.

48. *Ibid.*, p. 3a.

49. *Ibid.*, p. 27a.

50. *Ibid.*, p. 28b.

The study of Talmud becomes a sanctified activity, so much so that studying the section *Qodashim* of the Talmud— dealing with the ritual cycle in the Jerusalem Temple—is equated with service in the Holy of Holies (*Qodesh ha-Qodashim*) in the sacred Temple in Jerusalem, prior to its destruction.[51] The study even of Talmud, if attached to its mystical dimensions, was elevated to a sanctified performance beyond its intellectualistic parameters and regarded as an enterprise that could influence the divine domains.

The diary is suffused with Talmudic terminology to such an extent that one has the impression of attending a Yeshiva study hall.[52] The sublime and revelatory dimension blends with the technical and academic mode of studying Talmudic and legalistic literature. The mystical and the juridical have to a large extent become one. In spite of R. Karo's efforts to distance the inspirational and juridical domains, a policy underlined even further by the later editor of this text, the voices from above instruct him in very concrete cases he examines in his capacity as a Jewish scholar and judge. In the case of a woman wishing to convert to Jewish religion in order to marry a Jewish man, Karo is strongly advised not to accept her into the Jewish fold, a position that was reflected later in his rabbinical responsum in this regard. This also affected the status of the son born to this couple:

> This soul should better remain gentile, and better stay thus, for she [and her daughter from previous marriage—R.W.] is a polluted soul, and they would never be rooted in the Jewish people. And their born son is a polluted soul. Had I not known that he is about to turn defective [sinful], I would not have prevented you from circumcising him. So regarding the man and woman about to approach you regarding their divorce, deal diligently with their case, because their match could never end well.[53]

Time and again Karo is reassured that his halakhic rulings and readings of Talmudic and post-Talmudic discussions are correct, in contrast to the erroneous paths of other leading scholars.

Law Mysticism in Islam and in the Ottoman Context

What are the origins of the deep interaction of law and mysticism so common in the pages of *Magid Meisharim*? Some precedents, especially in the Sephardic context, can be found during the Middle Ages, such as Nachmanides and the Rashba. Both were great scholars of Halakhah, community leaders, and committed to Kabbalistic tradition. Yet

---

51. *Ibid.*, p. 49a. See also *ibid.*, pp. 25b, 32b.
52. See for instance, *ibid.*, pp. 6a, 8b, 9a, 12a, 13a, 16b, 17a, 40a, 42a, 45a, 46b, 49a, 52a.
53. *Ibid.*, p. 50b. See also *ibid.*, p. 27a: "He [the *Magid*] kept on saying that you ruled well not to practice asceticism during the day of Sabbath, except for those three cases. And you ruled well not to practice asceticism following a dream that a Torah scroll fell of man's hands, he should not practice asceticism, except on those cases, even though there is not Halakhic consensus regarding this … and you would later know the secretive meaning of this".

none of them, nor other figures, contributed so profoundly to the bilateral dialogue between Halakhah and Kabbalah as Karo. His mystical path was documented meticulously on a daily basis, and Kabbalistic assertions were inserted officially and openly into halakhic discourse in his codification opus. The European juridical heritage can hardly offer a model for such a fusion. Law in Medieval Europe was taught in Church schools or at law faculties in the universities. None of the most prominent figures in the fields of Canon Law, Civil Law, and later *Ius comune* was a both a legal expert and an active mystic.[54] In the Islamic tradition, however, this interface was common from the early history of the faith. As Ahmed Shahab pointed out, there was a potential antagonism between the Sufi tradition and religious law:

> The Sufi lays claim to an *epistemological and hermeneutic authority that is superior to that of the jurists* of whom Muḥyi al-Din Ibn ʿArabī once said: "The jurists [*al-fuqahā'*] in every age have been, and still are, in relation to those who have realized Truth [*al-muḥaqqiqūn*] at the station of pharaohs in relation to prophets." The Sufi and philosophical claim to a Real-Truth (*ḥaqīqah*) that lay above and beyond the truth of the Revealed law (*sharī'a*) was not a bit of intellectual or esoteric social *marginalia*, but was effectively the manifesto of a wide-ranging social and cultural phenomenon that Fazlur Rahman has called "a religion not only within religion but above religion." We might profitably characterize this "religion not only within religion but above religion" as the *Sufi-philosophical (or philosophical-Sufi) amalgam*.[55]

The potential tension between law and mysticism was just one aspect of their interaction. As Shahab's fascinating book shows, mysticism pervaded various aspects of Muslim civilization and religious life. It was not uncommon to find distinguished mystics who were experts of the law, or even officiating judges in courts, such as Al-Ghazali.[56]

Important Sufi masters who were at the same time immersed in and deeply knowledgeable of the Islamic legal tradition flourished close to Karo. A case in point was the famous seventeenth-century Damascene ʿAbd al-Ghanī al-Nābulusī.[57] Originating from a family of religious scholars, he studied law from infancy. His father was about to be appointed to two of the most senior posts in the religious hierarchy: chief judge (*qadi al-qudat*) and head of the Sufi brotherhoods (*shaykh al-shuyukh*). He was distinguished as a Shafiʿi jurist, became the Shafiʿi *mufti* of the city, and taught *fiqh*, both at the Umayyad Mosque and at four different madrasas. As for the son, throughout his life Nabulusi experienced a tension between his role as a religious scholar—excelling in his studies

54. Antonio Padoa-Schioppa, *A History of Law in Europe. From the Early Middle Ages to the Twentieth Century*, Cambridge: Cambridge U.P., 2918; Paolo Prodi, *Una storia della giustizia. Dal pluralismo dei fori al moderno dualismo tra conscienza e diritto*, Bologna: Il Mulino, 2015; Diego Quaglioni, *La giustizia nel Medioevo e nella prima età moderna*, Bologna: Il Mulino, 2004.

55. Ahmed Shahab, *What is Islam. The Importance of Being Islamic*, Princeton and Oxford: Princeton U.P., 2016, pp. 22, 25, 31.

56. Erik S. Ohlander, *Sufism in an Age of Transition. ʿUmar el-Suhrawardi and the Rise of the Mystical Brotherhoods*, Leiden and Boston: Brill, 2008, p. 34.

57. Elizabeth Sirriyeh, *Sufi Visionary of Ottoman Damascus. ʿAbd al-Ghani al-Nabulusi 1641–1731*, London and New York: Routledge Curzon, 2005.

on law and serving as a traditionalist expert of *Hadith*—and his life as an illuminated mystic and popular saint.[58] It never occurred to him or to his admiring disciples and followers that the *Shari'a* posed any obstacle to his mystic role. Nabulusi was hailed as a Sufi master inspired by Ibn 'Arabi. His admiring contemporaries spoke of him as the *qutb*, the spiritual "pole" or "axis" of his time at the head of the saintly hierarchy on which the order of the universe depended. His grandson and biographer affirmed that Ibn 'Arabi had been the Seal of Muhammadan Sainthood in his own age, but added that there were other seals later in time, of whom Nabulusi was one.[59] Damascus was the political and administrative center of the *Bilad a-Sham* area, to which the small city of Safed belonged. The Sufi lodges in Safed[60] provided the bridge for information, stories, and Sufi traditions elaborated in Damascus and elsewhere. At some point of his life, R. Karo was allured by the music and mystic atmosphere of the Sufi encounters and entered their meeting place, which he refers to as *Tekke*, following the Turkish terminology.[61] He and his contemporaries were exposed to fundamental elements of Sufi traditions, such as popular hagiographic tales about Nabulusi and others, contact with Sufi masters of past generations, spiritual journeys among the living and the dead, religious and legal advice presented through dreams, visions of reforming religion and purifying its current corrupt state, and finally their glorifying self-esteem.[62] Elizabeth Sirriyeh noted that

> In addition to communication with the spirits of the saintly dead, Nabulusi believed that he was guided by the Prophet in dreams and visions, and was also directly instructed by God. The closest model for him in this respect among Naqshabandis near to his time is the famous Indian *mujaddid*, renewer of his age, Shaykh Ahmad Sirhindi (d. 1624). Sirhindi also believed that he came to be divinely guided after a period of training under a Naqshabandi master. The implication is that both men understand their experience as being brought near to God so as to share in the Prophet's experience as His disciples, but that they also remain in a servant–master relationship to the Prophet.[63]

58. Sirriyeh, *Sufi Visionary of Ottoman Damascus*, pp. x, 3–6.

59. *Ibid.*, p. ix.

60. See Yosef Stepansky, 'Archeological News regarding the Eastern Galilee' [Hebrew], *Nikrot Zurim* 17 (1991), pp. 21–34; Paul B. Fenton, 'Solitary Meditation in Jewish and Islamic Mysticism in the Light of a Recent Archeological Discovery', *Medieval Encounters* 1, no. 2 (1995), pp. 271–296. Regarding the contact between Jewish mysticism and Sufi traditions, see idem., 'Influences soufies sur le développment de la Qabbale à Safed : le cas de la visitation des tombes', in : Paul B. Fenton, Roland Goetschel (eds.), *Expérience et écriture mystiques dans les religions du livre*, Leiden : Brill, 2000, pp. 163–190; idem., 'Devotional Rites in a Sufi Mode', in: Lawrence Fine (ed.), *Judaism in Practice. From the Middle Ages through the Early Modern Period*, Princeton and Oxford: Princeton University Press, 2001, pp. 364–374.

61. See the discussion in Altshuler, *The Life of Rabbi Yoseph Karo*, pp. 175–186.

62. On common religious traditions of various communities of believers along the early modern Mediterranean basin, see Josef M. Meri, *The Cult of Saints among Muslims and Jews in Medieval Syria*, Oxford: Oxford U.P., 2002.

63. Sirriyeh, *Sufi Visionary of Ottoman Damascus*, p. 44.

The interface between law and mysticism was certainly not confined to the Arab world but was shared to an even deeper extent among Mamlukes, and later among the early modern Ottomans. Rulers usually regarded Sufism as legitimate, and even as a complement to Muslim scholarly knowledge (*'ilm*) and experience. It was far from exceptional that Ottoman *'Ulama*, employed as qadis, *madrasa* professors or administrators in religious institutions, decided at some point to forsake their careers and join the Sufis, sometimes even choosing the unruly dervish groups. This also happened in the Arab lands, but to a lesser degree.[64]

This interaction could reach imminent persons in the religious and political echelons within ruling elite. An Ottoman legal expert who showed deep sympathy for the Sufi tradition is the towering Şeyḫülislâm Ebu's Suud (1490–1574). As in the case of Nabulusi, the family background foretells the future story of his life and professional course. Ebu's Su'ud's father was a man of orthodox learning and skilled in the law, but he combined this expertise in the *Shari'a* with the mystic path. As a dervish sheikh, he acquired a reputation for miracle working sanctity, which attracted the attention of the pious Sultan Bayezid. His political acumen and practical mind stood next to belief in the immanence of the divine and of God's intimate presence in the life of every individual. He believed in the magical effects of vows made in God's name, and in the efficacy of the saints, and that God speaks directly to man through dreams.[65]

Biographies and Mystical Autobiographies

Biographies, and certainly autobiographies, were not part of the rabbinical and Jewish heritage or its literary repertory. The genre of the mystical autobiography emerged in sixteenth-century Safed, with works by R. Joseph Karo, R. Elazar Azikri, and R. Hayyim Vital, though autobiographical fragments had been written previously by Kabbalists such as R. Abraham Abulafia, R. Isaac of Acre, and others.[66] The very few and cursory Medieval ego documents in which Jews describe their personal life only serve to prove this assertion.[67] The rise of Jewish autobiographies is intimately related to the flowering of mysticism in early modern Safed. Moshe Idel has argued that their emergence provided one of several indicators of the new "subjective" turn in the Kabbalah of the mid-sixteenth century. Some of the daring theological constructs of leading Safed Kabbalists actually reflected their inner life and personality. This

---

64. Michael Winter, 'Egyptian and Syrian Sufis Viewing Ottoman Turkish Sufism: Similarities, Differences, and Interactions', in: Eyal Ginio and Elie Podeh (eds.), *The Ottoman Middle East. Studies in Honor of Amnon Cohen*, Leiden and Boston: Brill, 2014, pp. 93–111. The citations from *ibid.*, pp. 94–95.
65. Colin Imber, *Ebu's-su'ud. The Islamic Legal Tradition*, Edinburgh: Edinburgh U.P., 1997, pp. 9, 269.
66. Joseph H. Chajes, 'Accounting for the Self: Preliminary Generic-Historical Reflections on Early Modern Jewish Egodocuments', *Jewish Quarterly Review* 95, no. 1 (2005), pp. 1–15, esp. p. 3.
67. See *ibid.*, p. 3, footnote 12.

development enhanced the importance of the individual Kabbalist, with his personal soul history, his unique path and mission, his charisma and revelations, in a more pronounced manner than ever before in the history of the Kabbalah.[68] It is no coincidence that the major Safedean Kabbalists led this new trend, documenting in writing their personal experiences; others were the subjects of new (and again unprecedented) hagiographic literature.

The book *Magid Meisharim* is a pioneering model of personal writing, not by a secondary personality but by a leading rabbinical figure himself and not as a secondary activity or under the guise of some apologetic reasoning. The text accompanies the life, thoughts, and activities of R. Joseph Karo, and his self-construction as a mystic. No aspect of his life was excluded from this highly personal and intimate writing. Karo describes directly and lucidly his family life and intimate relationship with his wives, or his future son:

> He [the *Magid*] further said: "You did well marrying a righteous woman, daughter of a Talmud scholar. You should know that you are about to have a blind son, and he will be extremely poor. Yet his heart will be open to Torah study. So he will not be completely blind as he would study Torah. His heart would be opened to the wisdom of Kabbalah, more than Salomon my friend [R. Salomon Alkabetz]."[69]

Karo often refers to his body and his physical needs and habits:

> Be cautious to eat and drink for the sake of pleasure and delight, even during the days of Sabbath and Festivities. Your thought should adhere to my Torah even when you speak to people or when you eat and drink. Thus your soul will rise to a heavenly Yeshiva while you sleep.[70]

The work also refers to the important stations along the course of Karo's life. He is reassured about the composition of his future works—both the *Beit Yosef* and *Shulchan 'Arukh*—and their enthusiastic acceptance, as well as regarding the position of his Yeshiva in Safed and the status of his personal position by comparison to other contemporary rabbis within the Sephardi Mediterranean-Ottoman domain: "He [the *Magid*] told me that he would help me to finish my magnum opus, devoid of any faults or defects, and that I would name it *Beit Yosef* [Joseph's Home], for it is worthy of that name, since it is indeed my home in this world and the world to come."[71]

Yet the leading thread of this immense mystical diary is the mystical empowerment of R. Karo along his long life, especially after the *Shavu'ot* event described above. His

---

68. *Ibid.*, p 3. See further discussion in Roni Weinstein, *Kabbalah and Jewish Modernity*, Littman Library of Jewish Culture, London, 2016, Ch. 2 – ' "Like Giants sitting on the Shoulders of Dwarfs". The Rise of the Jewish Saint', pp. 44–66.
69. Karo, *Magid Meisharim*, p. 25b.
70. *Ibid.*, p. 28b.
71. *Ibid.* p. 28b. Regarding the promise to compose his second magnum opus – the *Shulchan 'Arukh* – see ibid., p. 30a.

need for self-assurance is repeatedly supported by the divine *Magid*, during the glorification moments when his entrance to the Divine Yeshiva is pronounced by a herald in front of a large choir of angels and members of the heavenly Yeshiva, and certainly during some precious moments of his divinization and complete adherence or immersion (*devequt* is the current Kabbalistic term) to the *Shekhinah*:

> Thus you shall be elevated if your mind adheres to me [the figure of *Mishnah* or *Shekhinah*] as you should, if indeed you wish to see your spiritual figure as a king in his regiment. For so many soldiers surround him from all sides. Thus I, the Mishnah and all my soldiers often surround you, as you would be the major figure in the Holy Land. So you should imagine yourself as being often surrounded by me and my soldiers. You are as a king among us, surrounded by soldiers. You should not separate your thoughts from me or from my soldiers. Fare well.[72]

Centuries of Jewish life in Medieval Europe and its Catholic heritage have not aroused any significant Jewish response to the impressive body of autobiographical writing, dating back to early Christianity. The *Confessiones* of St. Augustine provided a paradigmatic model. There is evidence that Jews were well aware of the biographical genre, yet they reacted with an almost deliberate indifference. The nourishing ground for the dramatic rise of autobiographical rise in early modern Safed lay elsewhere: the Islamic biographical tradition.[73]

From the early days of Islam, the life of the Prophet Mohammed provided a model of religious devotion and communal adherence. Eventually, this encouraged the biographical writings on his life, the early adherents, his family, and later of eminent persons in Islam. Judith Tucker observed how these early writings continued and expanded in later generations.[74]

Tucker presented four major parameters of Arab biographies over the centuries, which mainly underscore the social and historical circumstances in which the "hero" acts, at the expense of his mental and personal aspects: (i) his social and cultural accomplishment, showing "his worthiness of a life in the context of the age"; (ii) the absence of overt descriptions of individual character, and its presentation through anecdotes about his behavior and deeds in concrete situations: "There is no direct analysis of the self"; (iii) location of the individual in a lineage of blood or scholarship in continuity with his family/profession/tradition predecessors. In scholarly context of *'Ulama*, this genre underlined the relationship between teachers and their disciples. In general, it aimed to group individuals in professional, confessional, or community clusters, highlighting

---

72. *Ibid.*, p. 10a.
73. Steve Tamari, 'Biography. Autobiography. and Identity in Early Modern Damascus', in: Mary Ann Fay (ed.), *Auto/Biography and the Construction of Identity and Community in the Middle East*, New York: Palgrave, 2001, pp. 37–49, esp. p. 37, on the rich and varied autobiographical documents among Damascene historians during the four centuries of Ottoman rule.
74. Judith E. Tucker, 'Biography as History: The Exemplary Life of Khayr al-Din al-Ramli', in: Fay (ed.), *Auto/Biography and the Construction of Identity and Community in the Middle East*, pp. 9–17. Citations from *ibid.*, pp. 9–10.

human contexts and interconnections; and (iv) the individual lives serve as a metonym to illuminate an entire generation, either as office holders or in terms of the roles played in important events. The activities of these heroes provide meaning to political and social currents of their time.[75]

Much of the Ottoman biographical and autobiographical writing was very similar to what Tucker presented. In early modern Ottoman autobiographies, the individuals are barely distinguishable from each other except in their social functions. Like figures in an Ottoman shadows theater (*Karagöz*), they appear only as a şeyhzade, a cloth-merchant, a çavuş, a Mevlevi or a representative of some other profession, rank, descent, career, or order. As much as it represents a fresh break from traditional genres, the Ottoman *Sohbetname* sits squarely within the world of classical Ottoman arts and letters, which did not care to develop perspective paintings, novels, or stage performances.[76]

In her seminal article on biographical literature in the Ottoman civilization, Derin Terzioğlu drew attention to the evolution of the profound Sufi imprint on this genre. Sufi writers left a rich corpus of personal literature in Arabic dating back to the ninth century and in Turkish from the sixteenth century:

> Moreover, in both languages, Sufi writers played a leading role as *self-narrators, leaving highly personalized records* of their experiences both as part of larger works and as texts in their own right. It is true that these writers were not guided by anything like the modern notion of individualism, but neither were the Catholic and Protestant pious who authored a large chunk of the first-person literature in medieval and early modern Europe [...] It is no accident that a *large majority of the people who authored first-person writings in the Ottoman Empire in the sixteenth and seventeenth centuries were practitioners of Sufism.* There were many factors that made Sufi practitioners more likely to pen self-narratives than others. First and foremost would be their access to the written word [...] As writers of self-narratives, Ottoman Sufis also had an advantage over the rest of the literate minority in that *Sufism provided them with a set of highly sophisticated concepts and vocabulary with which to write about themselves* as well as with a reason to do so. Central to the Sufi quest for God was the view that *one can only know God if one knows oneself.* This was in fact an ancient idea that went back to the Delphic oracle "Know yourself," and had been reworked into the Islamic tradition in the form of the hadith, "One who knows oneself knows one's Lord" (*Man 'arafa nafsahu, 'arafa rabbahu*). The self that was the object of this knowledge was a self in the making, in a continuous process of transformation (emphasis mine—R.W.).[77]

---

75. Ibid., p. 11.
76. Cemal Kafadar, 'Self and Others: The Diary of a Dervish in Seventeenth Century Istanbul and First-Person Narratives in Ottoman Literature', *Studia Islamica*, 69 (1989), pp. 121–150.
77. Derin Terzioğlu, 'Man in the Image of God in the Image of the Times: Sufi Self-Narratives and the Diary of Niyāzī-i Mışrī (1618-94)', *Studia Islamica*, 94 (2002), pp. 139–165. Citations from *ibid.*, pp. 139–143. Further important research on Ottoman biographical and autobiographical writing, see Olcay Akyildiz, Halim Kara, Börte Sagaster (eds.), *Autobiogrpahical Themes in Turkish Literature: Theoretical and Comparative Perspectives*, Würzburg: Ergon Verlag, 2007 (especially the article of Derin Terzioğlu); Aslı Niazioğlu, *Dreams and Lives in Ottoman Istanbul. A Seventeenth Century Biographers' Perspective*, London and New York: Routledge, 2016; Idem., 'Dreams, Ottoman Biography Writing, and the *Halveti-Sünbüli Şeyh*s of 16th

This kind of writing interacted well with the expansion of the Sufi Tariqas and their increasing role within the Ottoman Empire. The process of incorporation continued under state supervision, although the Ottoman state never co-opted the Sufi orders to the same extent that it did the 'Ulama.[78]

The close interaction between this tradition and the autobiographical writings of R. Karo—and some of his Kabbalistic contemporaries in Safed—can be assessed if *Magid Meisharim* is placed next to the mystical diary of Mehmed el-Niyazi el-Misri (1618–1694), as analyzed by Terzioğlu.[79] In the following summary of similarities, references to R. Karo are followed by their parallel in Niyazi and others:

- *Magid Meisharim* follows the mystical course of R. Karo and its heightened moments through his *via mystica*.

  "Other extant Ottoman first-person accounts written in the mode of self-examination were written by Sufi writers still in the process of completing *suluk* [mystical course towards God—R.W.] [...] In addition to these ideas about and techniques of self-transformation, Ottoman practitioners of Sufism also inherited from earlier generations a whole lore of life stories, the life stories of their masters, masters of their masters and other great Sufis of the past [...] Some Ottoman dervishes, like their South Asian counterparts, wrote a great deal about themselves in the compilations they made of the oral teachings of their masters (*malfuzat, makalat*). Others, one might speculate left autobiographical accounts at least partly in the hope of exercising some control over the biographies their disciples might later write about them, not an uncommon motivation among autobiographers in general."[80]

- The final version of the diary is an edited product that only partially reflects the original version.

  "A comparison of the original diary with the later editions, nevertheless, reveals that the copyists edited the text considerably, leaving a much thinner stratum of personal material."[81]

Century Istanbul', in: Ralf Elger and Yavuz Köse (eds.), *Many Ways of Speaking about the Self. Middle Eastern Ego-Documents in Arabic, Persian and Turkish (14th-20th Century)*, Wiesbabden: Harrassowitz Verlag, 2010, pp. 171–183; Gülru Necipoğlu, Howard Crane, and Esra Akin, *Sinan's Autobiographies. Fife Sixteenth-Century Texts*, Leiden and Boston: Brill, 2006; John Renard, *Friends of God Islamic Images of Piety, Commitment, and Servanthood*, Berkeley Los-Angeles London: University of California Press, 2008. For earlier precedents of Sufi autobiographical writing, see Arin Salamah-Qudsi, 'The Will to be Unveiled: Sufi Autobiographies in Classical Sufism', *Al-Masaq. Journal of the Medieval Mediterranean* 24 (2012), pp. 199–207.

78. Terzioğlu, 'Man in the Image of God in the Image of the Times', p. 149.
79. *Ibid.*, p. 142, notices the novel features in this mystical diary.
80. *Ibid.*, pp. 143–145.
81. *Ibid.*, p. 144.

- The diary was composed with the intention of influencing others.[82] The teachings revealed by the *Magid* later served Karo in his public sermons and classes.[83]

  "The famous Celveti master Mahmud Hüda'i (d. 1623), for instance, authorized his disciples to make copies of both the diary he kept as a Sufi adept and the visionary account he wrote as a 'perfected' master."[84]

- Karo's diary is replete with moments of self-examination, remorse, and a commitment to act differently in order to remain close to the Mishnah and the *Shekhinah*: "Those who think of food and drink adhere to the demonic powers in charge of food and drink. Those who ponder on fornication adhere to those powers in charge of fornication. And those who ponder on dominion and honor would adhere on those powers in charge of these. The result is that they [the demonic powers] tie him to a hellish torture instrument, because he is ruled by these demonic powers it is as if he were tied to these torture instruments in hell, due to the fact that the man was thinking of a certain pleasure and they start to dominate him [...] so, my son, devote all your thoughts to my worship and remain God-fearing."[85]

  "All the *elements of self-scrutiny* also appear but in a decidedly retrospective fashion in spiritual autobiographies or 'conversion' accounts written by Sufi masters after the completion of their *suluk* [...] That Hüda'i's case was not an anomaly is clear from the fact that virtually all the other extant Ottoman first-person accounts written in the mode of self-examination were written by Sufi writers still in the process of completing *suluk*. This is not to say, however, that this was the only factor that shaped their accounts."[86]

- Karo is aware that his mystical vision turns him into a unique person, entirely different from his rabbinic colleagues.

  "It has been argued that this divergent, more internalized approach to piety, particularly well represented among the Sufis of Anatolia and the Balkans, lent itself to a 'deviant individualism.'"[87]

- The diary accompanies Karo toward the height of his mystical career and even intensifies during his sojourn in Safed as an established persona.

  "The visionary autobiographies were typically written by Sufi masters at the height of their careers. In these texts, Sufi writers related the visions and other extraordinary experiences that signaled their election to the highest spiritual distinctions in

---

82. See below section "Governance, Law, and Mysticism".
83. Karo, *Magid Meisharim*, pp. 37a, 52a.
84. Terzioğlu, 'Man in the Image of God', p. 144.
85. Karo, *Magid Meisharim*, p. 19b. See also *ibid.*, pp. 3a, 3b, 4a, 4b, 5a, 6b, 8a, 13a, 16a, 19a, 13b, 22a, 26a, 28b, 37a, 43a, 52a.
86. Terzioğlu, 'Man in the Image of God', pp. 145–146.
87. *Ibid.*, p. 146.

the bold and often deliberately transgressive idiom of shath or 'ecstatic speech.' As Sufi apologists explained, this was an idiom that mystics had devised to describe realities that they knew only from experience and which were paradoxically understood to be indescribable."[88]

- The teachings rely on utterly personal experiences and do not derive their immediacy from written traditions or an encounter with some human master. They confer upon Karo the status of a leading mystic, since these secrets were revealed only to him: "On this issue all in the Divine Yeshiva agreed, as well as God. The members of the Divine Yeshiva sent me to instruct you innovative teachings, unheard of until now. When contemporary sages would hear them from your mouth they would accept them and praise you [...] Since you learned the entire six parts of the Mishnah you elevated yourself, and I am about to discover to you these secrets, until today not revealed, which you will not find in any book nor discovered by any contemporary sage."[89]

"More likely, like the Tibetan Buddhist monks who were also prolific writers of visionary autobiographies, the Sufi authors were concerned to highlight the fact that their teachings about the divine or invisible realms were grounded in their personal experiences, experiences they had in a particular place at a particular time. As in the case of the Tibetan texts, the Sufi visionary autobiographies might have also served to establish the authority of their author/subjects as the preeminent masters of the time."[90]

- Karo is intimately linked to the chain of past scholars, along the various phases of Jewish scholarship. His eminent position is measured in relation to the chain of transmission present in the Divine Yeshiva.

"These autobiographies inserted their author/subjects in a continuous chain of spiritual authority, going all the way back to the prophet Muhammad. In this regard, it would be difficult to overemphasize the intertextuality of these narratives, woven with references to the ascension of Muhammad as well as of earlier Sufis."[91]

- The diary exposes moments in Karo's daily life and habits: "Sabbath night, twenty third of [the month of] Tevet. I ate a lot, and drank wine, and then drank too much water, and I couldn't recite the Mishnah chapters early at night. After sleeping a little I woke up and drank more water, and recited the Mishnah chapters. I felt a heaviness in my head as if I had not slept at all, and returned to sleep. I woke up in daylight, and thought to myself that I had forgotten to 'deposit' [say the benediction

---

88. *Ibid.*, p. 147.
89. Karo, *Magid Meisharim*, pp. 26b, 35a.
90. Terzioğlu, 'Man in the Image of God', p. 147.
91. *Ibid.*, p. 148.

of depositing one's soul with God before falling asleep—R.W.]; and as the daylight rose a voice started saying 'God is with you'…"[92]

"In terms of its contents, Misri's writing represents an interesting amalgam of a secular diary and a visionary account. It is very much as a secular diarist that Misri described in each entry how he spent the day, not sparing us details about how he slept, what he ate and his state of health as well as the people who visited him and who brought him news. While we would look in vain for this kind of mundane information in medieval Sufi self-narratives, we can find plenty of parallels in Ottoman Sufi literature. In fact, some of Misri's fellow Halvetis like Seyyid Hasan recorded in their diaries nothing but such mundane occurrences […] Regardless of the genre in which they wrote, whether they wrote during or after their *suluk*, they often gave glimpses (and sometimes more) into their everyday lives. They mentioned their friends and foes by name, reported conversations that had no obvious religious or mystical content, and even gave information about their intimate family lives. Parallel to the increased visibility of the mundane, dates, the markers of worldly time are also much more prominent in the life writings of Ottoman Sufis."[93]

- Karo's diary reached other hands shortly after his death, but during his life his experiences remained private and unexposed. People in Safed witnessed his different states of consciousness, and at times even entered his house and interrupted these moments: "[…] then people came in and interrupted the [*Magid's*] speech."[94]

  "Particularly telling in this regard are Misri's instructions for his real and imaginary readers about how to read his text, explaining his system of dating, and accounting for certain contradictions he detected in earlier entries […] In a number of places, the Sufi diarist [Niyazi–R.W.] writes explicitly of having lent the 'history' of this or that day to a disciple or a fellow Sufi or of having allowed a disciple to read a certain entry."[95]

- Karo is ordered to document in writing the Magid's secrets and instructions and rebuked for occasionally failing to do so. Writing is even regarded as an exercise of his special spiritual abilities: "He rebuked me for not writing the revealed secrets, for had I written them I would have heard marvelous secrets […] and he rebuked me for not writing the innovative teachings […] he strongly insisted that I write everything said to me, and that I study twice and three times a week the wisdom of Kabbalah, and the wide gates [of this wisdom] would open to me."[96]

  "In yet another passage, nevertheless, he also writes that God gave him permission to write but not to have copies made of his writing. This suggests that while the Sufi

---

92. Karo, *Magid Meisharim*, p. 6b. See also, *ibid.*, pp. 3a,, 7a, 11b, 12a, 17a, 25b, 26a, 28a, 51b.
93. Terzioğlu, 'Man in the Image of God', pp. 148, 153.
94. Karo, *Magid Meishrim*, p. 40a.
95. Terzioğlu, 'Man in the Image of God', p. 152.
96. Karo, *Magid Meisharim*, pp. 6a, 22b, 42b.

writer did not keep his diary as a strictly private document, neither did he intend to circulate it widely."[97]

- Expressing emotions in writing is a rarity in rabbinical tradition. Yet Karo occasionally expresses his apprehensions and dislikes, alongside records of moments of joy.

"Misri's diary also gives us considerable insight into his emotional state at the time. The most commonly represented emotions in the diary are all of a negative nature—fear, distrust, anxiety and anger—and refer the reader back to the central theme of the diary: persecution."[98]

- Karo's desire to become a martyr is a very prominent theme in his diary. His martyrdom is assured by the *Magid*, as a sign of his personal greatness and commitment: "On Thursday, the eighth of [the month of] Tishrei, after midnight [the *Magid* said], since you finished studying all six parts of Mishnah my cloud is upon you, the entire seven divine clouds unite and escort you daily. So be strengthened in God-fearing and in my Torah, do not separate yourself from them even for one moment. Thanks to these six [Mishnah] sections that you studied, I will benefit you with migrating to the Holy Land, studying and teaching, and having sons and grandsons, and you will burn for my Name's sanctity, and your ashes will lay in front of me [God]. Therefore be strong in God-fearing and in my Torah."[99] R. Karo waited his entire life for this instant of martyrdom, inspired by the real martyrdom of Shlomo Molho, but it never materialized.

"While these speculations can be attributed to a mental state of extreme fear and even paranoia, fear was also mixed with desire for Misri. Throughout his diary, the Sufi sheikh expresses desire for martyrdom, giving voice to a sentiment well known from the life stories and writings of such early Sufis as Mansur al-Hallaj. The problem in Misri's case, however, was that the awaited moment of martyrdom failed to come, keeping him waiting in trepidation and prompting him to chide (in the seeming privacy of his diary) Sultan Mehmed IV for not being sultan enough to punish him as he deserved to be punished."[100]

- Issues of family life, finding a life partner, and the suitability of his wives are exposed in the diary. Even sexual intimacy is included in the Magid's instructions: "You despaired of marrying that woman. Until this very moment you did not have the right to marry her, so it was necessary to show you that the right moment was

---

97. Terzioğlu, 'Man in the Image of God', p. 152.
98. *Ibid.*, p. 153.
99. Karo, *Magid Meisharim*, p. 27a. See also *ibid.*, pp. 3a, 5b, 6b, 8b, 13b, 14a, 21a, 26a, 29a, 33a, 47a, 49a, 51a.
100. Terzioğlu, 'Man in the Image of God', p. 153.

delayed, and now you are entitled to marry her." He further said: "What I [the *Magid*] asserted regarding your wife's pregnancy is utterly true."[101]

"Misri's grievances against the Ottoman authorities also had an intriguing sexual subtext, and were related at least in part to his marital problems. While the Sufi sheikh had enjoyed an apparently peaceful marriage with his first wife for nineteen years, the same could not be said of the three marriages he made after her death. He had made all three marriages shortly before or after his first banishment, and his prolonged absence from home had probably soured his relations with his wives and in-laws."[102]

- The figure of the *Magid*, as a revelatory agent of secrets, is affiliated to the very same source of the Holy Scriptures and Torah.

"He [Niyazi] identified the bearer of the revelations as the archangel Gabriel, who had brought Muhammad the Qur'an. The revelations themselves were all purely aural with the exception of one accompanied by a vision. Speaking 'in the Turkish tongue' (*bi-lisan-i Türki*), Gabriel would give instructions about the cifr applications, or explain, sometimes directly to Misri and sometimes to 'the people of the Book' (presumably Jews and Christians as well as Muslims) about the high spiritual rank that had been hoisted upon the Sufi."[103]

- In spite of the unambiguous rabbinical distinction between prophecy and Talmudic methodology, Karo presents himself as virtually a prophet: "It is I, I who speak [directly] to your Soul [*neshamah*], not to your Mind [*nefesh*], nor to your Spirit [*ruach*], but to your soul herself, for even if Prophecy has ceased among Jewish people it has not ceased in your case. Every time I arrive to guide you regarding the way to follow."[104]

"The assumption of prophetic role in Islam is all problematic since the claim of Muhammad as 'Seal of Prophecy' is fundamental to right belief and orthodoxy. Still, 'The prophetic-eschatological passages in Misri's diary, if read literally, can be construed as going against the Islamic dogma that Muhammad was 'the seal of the prophets' (*hatm al-anbiya*) and the last messenger of God. This is not, however, how Misri and most of his readers understood these revelations. They did not because they made sense of the revelations in the context of a centuries-long tradition of Sufi thought that accepted the finality of Muhammad's prophetic mission but also postulated the continuity of a form of prophecy in the person of the saints (*awliya ullah*, literally, friends of God). It is true that conventionally the divine disclosures received by the saints were called *ilhamat* or 'divine inspiration' to distinguish them from *wahy* or prophetic revelations proper."[105]

---

101. Karo, *Magid Meisharim*, p. 7a
102. Terzioğlu, 'Man in the Image of God', p. 154.
103. *Ibid.*, p. 157.
104. Karo, *Magid Meisharim*, p. 47b.
105. Terzioğlu, 'Man in the Image of God', pp. 157–158.

• The most inspiring figure in Karo's mind was the mythical hero of *Sefer Ha-Zohar*, living in the period of classical rabbinical times during the composition of the Mishnah. His diary is a linguistic imitation of the invented Aramaic of the Zohar and is replete with dozens of Hebrew words and expressions, transformed into aramaicized linguistic patterns.[106] In this sense, the diary is constructed as a continuous flow of inspiration from the founding figures of the past mystical tradition.

"Over and above all, however, the one Sufi thinker to whose writings Misri made constant reference both in his diary and elsewhere was Ibn 'Arabi, or as he was better known among the Ottoman Sufis, the Sheikh Akbar, the Greatest Master. Ibn 'Arabi combined in his voluminous writings at once a deeply personal narrative of illumination and one of the most systematic expositions of Sufi metaphysics. His visionary writings had such an appeal for later Sufis that it has even been argued that they led to a certain closure, or homogenization in later Sufi literature. A close analysis of the way Misri made use of Ibn 'Arabi's writings, however, indicates that while the Ottoman writer drew on the Sheikh Akbar's hagiological script, he also personalized this script and adapted it to his own particular circumstances."[107]

• R. Karo aspired throughout his adult life to achieve personal sanctity (*Qedushah*), as a precondition for both prophecy and for sealing the law and legal tradition (*Halakhah*)—as he did in his double codes of law.

"Particularly important in the context of Misri's diary were Ibn 'Arabi's teachings about the relations between the saints and the prophets. Ibn 'Arabi had argued that just as the saints inherited their spirituality from the prophets, particular saints inherited their spirituality from particular prophets [...] The highest rank of all, however, belonged to the Muhammadan saints, who inherited their spirituality directly from Muhammad. Finally, Ibn 'Arabi postulated that just as legislative prophethood (*nubuwwa al-tashri'*) had been sealed by Muhammad, so would sainthood be sealed by the 'seal of the saints' (*hatm alawliya*) [...] The elliptical way in which Ibn 'Arabi wrote about the seal also enabled later Sufis to lay claim to the title, and redefine it in the process. Misri was in good company, therefore, when he acknowledged the identity of the Sheikh Akbar as the 'seal of the saints,' but also considered that seal to be a spiritual rank that was held by different Sufis in different periods. Hence he wrote: 'there is one seal of the saints at all times and in this time, God [...] made Misri the seal of the saints.' Since the seal of the saints was supposed to have inherited the spiritual stations of all the prophets, it also allowed Misri to represent himself in terms of a rich prophetic typology."[108]

---

106. Karo, *Magid Meisharim*, pp. 6a, 6b, 7a, 8a, 9a, 10b, 12b, 13b, 14a, 15a, 17b, 21b, 22b, 27b, 34a, 38b, 44a, 44b, 52b.
107. Terzioğlu, 'Man in the Image of God', p. 158.
108. *Ibid.*, pp. 158–159.

- Karo linked his elevated status in the heavenly domain to his being an offshoot of the First Adam (*Adam ha-Rishon*): "The rights you acquired in previous days when you repented, and those dark days of sins were illuminated by sequential fast—day and night. You have fasted in the same manner as your father, i.e. the First Adam, did when he sinned."109

"On the one hand, the Sufi sheikh identified with Adam the prophet to whom God had revealed the divine names, and found therein a significant parallel to his own preoccupation with esoteric exegesis and Kabbalistic prognostications. On the other hand, the very human dimension of Adam enabled Misri to answer a number of difficult questions about his own claim to prophethood [...] Iconographically, this image of Misri as Adam, with its strong symbolism of left and right, can be traced to a Christic vision of Adam described by Ibn 'Arabi. In the most general sense, both images provided a commentary on the relationship of God to humanity as well as the relationship of the Perfect Man to God and humanity."110

The rise of autobiographical writing in Jewish tradition has hardly any precedents prior to the sixteenth century and is intimately affiliated to the mystical renaissance in Safed. The source of inspiration for this innovation was close at hand: the rise of personal, individualistic, and at times intimate writing within Sufi circles in the Ottoman Empire. *Magid Meisharim* by R. Karo joined that shared Jewish-Muslim mode of writing, as shown above regarding the numerous parallel elements. It shed light on his life project, motivated by nonlegalistic aspirations and vision.

Governance, Law, and Mysticism

The establishment of Sufi orders (*Tariqat*) during the eleventh to thirteenth centuries was marked by their parallel insertion into community life. Slowly but surely Sufism blended into mainstream religiosity. The coalescence of Sufism with Sunni communalism was not the work of Sufi propagandists alone but came about as the result of an implicit alliance between Sufi masters and their followers and the state. Sufis recognized the need to smooth the rough edges of their erstwhile individualistic piety, a task which they took very seriously, to judge by the number and prominence of communalistic Sufi manuals produced during the tenth and eleventh centuries. This was a sign of the increasingly communal nature of Sufism. The Sufi masters now stepped out of their restricted social enclaves to embrace the Muslim community at large. Their spiritual and physical presence became evident in the form of great numbers of tomb complexes that dotted the landscape of Islamdom.111 The establishment of the Ottoman Empire from the late

---

109. Karo, *Magid Meisharim*, p. 8b. See the elaborate discussion in Altshuler, *The Life of Rabbi Yoseph Karo*, pp. 200–206.
110. Terzioğlu, 'Man in the Image of God', pp. 161–162.
111. Ahmet T. Karamustafa, *God's Unruly Friends. Dervish Groups In The Islamic Later Middle Period 1200–1550*, Salt Lake City: University of Utah Press, 1994, esp. pp. 30, 88.

fifteenth century onward, and its territorial expansions and conquests throughout the sixteenth century, provided an even more important arena for Sufi movements:

> It was only during the next four centuries, a period which began with the resurgence of nomadic tribalism under the Seljuks and ended with the formation of more durable empires by the Ottomans, Safavids, and Mughals – that Sufism became truly popularized. The organizational features of Sufi communities were also transformed during this period.[112]

The Sufi role in Ottoman culture and religious life was characterized by Andrews and Kalpaklı in even more dramatic terms:

> By the Age of the Beloved [early modern period] Sufism had acquired a popularity that dramatically altered both its character and its social role [...] popular Islamic mysticism step aside from Arabic and its scholastic tradition and re-inscribe the emotional inspiration of Islam in Persian and Turkish and Urdu. Mysticism became a spiritual springboard from it the Turkic peoples of Central Asia entered the mainstream of Islam [...] Arabic remained the language of ritual, of theology and canon law, but, by the mid-fifteenth century, *it seemed that almost everyone in Ottoman lands was a mystic of one sort or another*; these mystics' texts were poetry and hagiographies, their languages Persian and Ottoman Turkish [...] Sufism, as it existed in the Ottoman Empire from the sixteenth century on, did not represent a reformation. It broke the hegemony of the privileged language and diffused religious literacy (including oral literacy) across class and education barriers. It weakened the grip of the traditional religious authorities and multiplied the rituals and metaphors of religion.[113]

The varied Sufi and Dervish movements were strong and popular enough that the Ottomans could not simply turn them into a state agent. Instead, the relationship developed into one of mutual interaction and an ongoing search for equilibrium and cooperation. Eventually, the Ottoman state became dominant and could patronize the important Sufi orders.[114] Fundamental in this interaction was the role of the grand master Ibn-'Arabi and his vast heritage, pursued and cherished by the Ottomans more than by the Arabs. His extensive corpus of writings provided an endless repository of

---

112. Derin Terzioğlu, 'Sufis in the age of state-building and confessionalization', in Christine Woodhead (ed.), The Ottoman World, London and New York: Routeldge, 2012, pp. 86–99, esp. p. 86.
113. Walter G. Andrews and Mehmet Kalpaki, *The Age of the Beloved. Love and the Beloved in Early-Modern Ottoman and European Culture and Society*, Durham and London: Duke U.P., 2005, esp. pp. 334–335.
114. Nabil Al-Tikriti, 'Ibn-i Kemal's Confessionalism and the Construction of an Ottoman Islam', in: Christine Isom-Verhaaren and Kent F. Schull (eds.), *Living in the Ottoman Realm. Empire and Identity, 13th to 20th Centuries*, Bloomington and Indianapolis: Indiana U.P., 2016, pp. 95–107, esp. p. 96. See also Derin Terzioğlu, 'Sunna-minded Sufi Preachers in Service of the Ottoman State: the Naṣīḥatnāme of Hasan addressed to Murad IV', *Archivum Ottomanicum* 27 (2010), pp. 241–312; Winter, 'Egyptian and Syrian Sufis Viewing Ottoman Turkish Sufism'.

possibilities for alternative interpretations, and he quickly rose to the status of a patron saint for the Ottoman establishment. Patronizing the heritage of Ibn 'Arabi, or the Greatest Sheikh, as he was now commonly called, provided the Ottomans with a Sufi forefront for an intensive ideological warfare against the Safavids.[115]

The insertion of Sufi individuals, institutions, and religious heritage into the Ottoman state benefitted both parties. Again, it was not confined to the Ottoman context but characterized their political rivals in the Safavid and Mughal areas, as well as the rising empires in Europe. The important works of Hüseyin Yılmaz, Kaya Şahin, Christopher Markiewicz, and others illuminated the role of leadership in fusing aspirations for universality, a messianic role, and personal sanctity. The Ottomans envisioned the caliphate as a comprehensive cosmological position that encompasses both temporal and spiritual realms. This perspective was embroidered in discursive narratives constructed by dynastic apologists and enigmatic writers, as well as by mainstream scholars through literary articulation, artistic representation, and occultist revelations. The caliphate myth was part of the imperial ideology, claiming that the House of Osman had been commissioned to rule as the "Great Caliphate" of the end of times foretold in the Qur'an, prophesied by Prophet Mohammed, envisioned by saints, and proven by discernible manifestations of divine providence. This political myth was closely tied to an eschatology drawn from indigenous traditions and Abrahamic teachings conveyed via Islamic sources. It encompassed a syncretic amalgamation of popular imageries and formal teachings of Islamic disciplines.[116] Major rulers in Europe shared an analogous political vision during the early modern period.[117]

It is important to note that this eschatological vision of rule was not confined in the Ottoman case to the ruling elite but was mediated by political, literary, and visual means to wider circles of the population. In the age of Süleyman, writing on rulership and government became part of a public discourse where ordinary scribes, obscure

---

115. Hüseyin Yılmaz, *The Mystical Turn in the Ottoman Political Thought*, Princeton: Princeton U.P., 2018, pp. esp. 18. See also Winter, 'Egyptian and Syrian Sufis Viewing Ottoman Turkish Sufism', esp. pp. 98–99, the important Sufi masters in the Ottoman Empire pursuing ibn 'Arabi's legacy, next to Arabic opposition to his bold positions. See also the discussions in Chrisotrpher Markiewicz, *The Crisis of Kingship in Late Medieval Islam. Persian Emigres and the Making of Ottoman Sovereignty*, Cambridge: Cambridge U.P., 2019; Kaya Şahin, *Empire and Power in the Reign of Süleyman. Narrating the Sixteenth-Century Ottoman World*, Cambridge: Cambridge U.P., 2013; Al-Tikriti, 'Ibn-i Kemal's Confessionalism and the Construction of an Ottoman Islam'.

116. Yılmaz, *The Mystical Turn in the Ottoman Political Thought*, esp. p. 5. See also Şahin, *Empire and Power in the Reign of Süleyman*, esp. pp. 27–28. On the wider Eurasian context, see Markiewicz, *The Crisis of Kingship in Late Medieval Islam*, p. 18, regarding the Ottoman sultan, the Safavid shah, and the Mughal padishah. See also A. Azfar Moin, *The Millenial Sovereign. Sacred Kingship and Sainthood in Islam*, New York: Columbia U.P., 2012.

117. John M. Headley, 'The Habsburg World Empire and the Revival of Ghibellinism', in: David Armitage (ed.), *Theories of Empire, 1450–1800*, London and New York: Routledge, 2016, pp. 45–79. In the same volume, see Franz Bosbach, 'The European Debate and the Revival of Ghibellinism', pp. 81–98.

mystics, low-ranking provincial commanders, and poets with no training in statecraft could write on political matters.[118]

There was a further channel for disseminating the ideal of sacred ruler. The fusion of religious and political elements such as personal sanctity, charismatic authority, and visions of earthly political rulership motivated several Sufi leaders of popular movements to aspire for leadership, and even to rebel against the Sultanic authority. A conspicuous person in this regard is Ibrahim Gülşenī (1423–1540) presented in detail by Side Emre. Side Emre situates Gülşenī among several *kutb/mehdī*s who survived trial and persecution by the central Ottoman government in Istanbul. While Gülşenī does not claim, in his surviving poetry, to be the *mehdī*, at least one of his better-known deputies did, and suffered the consequences. Kāşifī, a deputy to Gülşenī, claimed to be the messiah of his age during the first decades of Süleymān's rule, and despite his reputation as a mentally instable man was executed as a result of these claims. Aspirants such as Kāşifī harbored political missions, with the apocalyptical atmosphere surrounding them.[119] These ideas echoed widely and reached wide places in the Muslim Mediterranean, as far west as Morocco, spurring Messianic-Mahadist hopes and activities.[120]

The long rule of Sultan Süleyman witnessed changes in the political ethos and his role as messianic leader. Cornell Fleischer, and later Kaya Şahin, noted that while the first half of his rule was characterized by military expansions and universal aspirations, during the second part—when the military achievements came to a halt—his main efforts were devoted to stabilizing the immense empire:

> Under Süleyman, however, the portrayal of the Ottoman sultan entered a new stage. In tune with the struggles of the period, universalist political theologies portrayed the Ottoman sultan on a world-historical scale, battling the forces of evil and claiming supremacy over both Muslims and Christians. After the messianic fervor of the earlier decades abated, the emphasis changed from *apocalyptic warfare* to a more docile, culturally and religiously conservative discourse on *justice and order*. Süleyman's reign symbolizes, among other things, the construction and promotion of Istanbul as the imperial and dynastic center par excellence. The Süleymaniye complex [one of his largest construction projects—R.W.] meets different needs: the ideal of a Sunni Muslim empire, the claim of civilizational superiority over the Safavids and the European Christians, and the urge *to leave a cultural legacy* that represents the whole imperial edifice (emphasis mine—R.W.).[121]

---

118. Yılmaz, *The Mystical Turn in the Ottoman Political Thought*, p. 12. See also Şahin, *Empire and Power in the Reign of Süleyman*, p. 72.

119. Side Emre, 'Crafting Piety for Success: Gülşeniye Literature and Culture in the Sixteenth Century', *Journal of Sufi Studies* 1 (2012), pp. 31–75, esp. pp. 62–63. See also the works of Markiewicz, Terzioğlu, Yılmaz and Şahin mentioned above.

120. Mercedes Garcia-Arenal, *Messianism and Puritanical Reform. Mahdis of the Muslim West*, Leiden and Boston: Brill, 2006, passim.

121. Şahin, *Empire and Power in the Reign of Süleyman*, pp. 142, 187, following Cornell H. Fleischer, 'The Lawgiver as Messiah: The Making of the Imperial Image in the Reign of Süleymân', in: Gilles Veinstein (edited by), *Soliman le Magnifique et son temps*, Paris: La Documentation Française, 1992, pp. 159–177.

The legitimacy of the Ottoman Empire was corroborated by its leading Islamic role, a process impressively analyzed by Derin Terzioğlu and Tijana Krstić (and others inspired by their work), and termed the "confessionalization" of Ottoman society, or as its peculiar course within the Islamicate context was coined "Sunnitization." This marked a shift in Ottoman religious politics in the early sixteenth century from a comfortable acceptance of "confessional ambiguity" to an increasing concern with defining and enforcing a particular understanding of "correct" belief and practice. Scholars still discuss the roots and purposes of this change, but it certainly related to Ottoman state-building, particularly urbanization, monetization of the economy, institutionalization, and bureaucratization launched in the 1450s that were conductive to the rise of an increasingly self-confident class of Ottoman scholars. This professional group—which was also deeply involved in the codification projects of the Ottoman state—sought to assert its vision of what Islam was and where boundaries of belief began and ended.[122] Similar processes of confessionalization took place in the Ottoman Empire and Christian Europe; in both cases, they were closely connected to the ethos of a dominant political leadership aspiring to fulfill a universal messianic role.[123]

The borders separating the Orthodox and permitted, on the one side, and the heretical and dangerous, on the other, became sharper than ever before in Islamic tradition. A simple profession of faith (*shahāda*) was no longer sufficient to be considered as a Muslim, now that a more thorough knowledge of the tenets of faith (*ʿaqīda*) was expected of each believer.[124] Guidance books containing the correct religious positions and religious teachings addressed the public at large and were hence composed in Turkish.[125] It became more important and urgent to distinguish the pious from the heretics and sinners. Even those who followed the religious way of life in a scrupulous way were not

---

122. Tijana Krstić, 'State and Religion, "Sunnitization" and "Confessionalism" in Süleyman's Time', in: Pál Fodor (ed.), *The Battle for Central Europe. The Siege of Szigetvár and the Death of Süleyman the Magnificent and Nicholas Zrinyi (1566)*, Leiden and Boston: Brill, 2019, pp. 65–91. Citation from *ibid.*, p. 66. See also Derin Terzioğlu, 'How to Conceptualize Ottoman Sunnitization: A Historiographical Discussion', *Turcica* 44 (2012–2013), pp. 301–338, esp. pp. 305, 313, 321. See also Nir Shafir, *The Road from Damascus: Circulation and the Redefinition of Islam in the Ottoman Empire, 1620–1720*, Ph.D. thesis submitted at the University of California, 2016; Reem Meshal, 'Aantagonistic Shari'as and the Construction of Orthodoxy in Sixteenth Century Ottoman Cairo', *Journal of Islamic Studies* 21, no. 2 (2010), pp. 183–212.

123. Headley, 'The Habsburg World Empire and the Revival of Ghibellinism'.

124. Tijana Krstić, 'From Shahada to ʿAqida: Conversion to Islam, Catechisation and Sunnitization in Sixteenth Century Ottoman Rumeli', in: A.C.S. Peacock (ed.), *Islamisation: Comparative Perspectives from History*, Edinburgh: Edinburgh U.P., 2017, pp. 296–314, esp. p. 297. For early modern Islamic discussions regarding meticulous distinctions between various kinds of heretical traditions, see Al-Tikriti, 'Ibn-i Kemal's Confessionalism and the Construction of an Ottoman Islam', p. 105, regarding the increasing sensitivity to heretic positions and sects.

125. See Derin Terzioğlu, 'Where ʿIlm-i Hal Meets Catechism: Islamic Manuals of Religious Instruction in the Ottoman Empire in the Age if Confessionalization', *Past and Present* 220 (2013), pp. 79–114, next to the work of Krstić, mentioned in the previous footnote.

exempt from suspicion if their religious opinion did not conform to the expected Sunni creed.[126]

Yılmaz presented three main channels of constructing the political ethos of Ottoman rule during the early modern period:

> The *administrative language* of the bureaucrats was empirically drawn from the very Ottoman experience in statecraft and therefore exclusively belonged to its specific context. The *juristic language* was part of the standard Islamic law and enabled one to speak for and engage with the universal legal imperative of the broader 'ulama network. The *esoteric and symbolic language of Sufism* was an encrypted medium of communication and always purported to have contained hidden messages intelligible only to the properly trained.[127]

Law was a central axis in this wide political vision. *Shari'a* and Muslim legality were considered as compatible with Sufi mystic heritage at this period; Law was increasingly playing a key role in the salvation of a good Muslim believer and subject of the Sultan. The composition of the guidance books [*'ilm-i hal*s in Turkish] indicated a new "turn to piety." This was *a piety grounded in adherence to the shari'a*, which had become the norm among the Ottoman ruling elites as well as segments of the urban populace in the latter half of the sixteenth century and still more pronounced in the following century. The project of Sunnitization went hand in hand with the suppression and marginalization of the non-Sunni elements among the empire's Muslim subjects, as well as the enactment of more proactive measures to establish Sunni orthopraxy in the Ottoman domains.[128] The law further added as a factor of increasing orthodoxy, beyond the classical role of guiding the believer's life: "In the late 16th and early 17th centuries shariah-abiding 'sunnitizing' Sufi from such orders as the Halvetiyye and Celvetiyye played an even more active role than the top ranking ulema in propagating in what might be best called state Sunnism."[129] The spread of Sufi orders, their insertion in state mechanisms, the political ethos of the saintly ruler, the apocalyptic expectations and renewal of religion, the tight linkage between mysticism and law, the composition of guidance tracts aiming at the public at large, and the sharper borders between correct belief and heresy—all created the foundation for the life projects of R. Karo.

The visionary moments of R. Karo were not necessarily private or secretive —at least not all of them. On some occasions, people entered his home and by their mere presence interrupted the fluency of the *Magid*'s voice.[130] The interstice between the withdrawn and secretive—the interaction between R. Karo and the divine agents—and

---

126. Terzioğlu, 'Where 'Ilm-i Hal Meets Catechism', p. 92.
127. Yılmaz, *The Mystical Turn in the Ottoman Political Thought*, p. 15.
128. Terzioğlu, 'Where 'Ilm-i Hal Meets Catechism', p. 85.
129. Idem., 'How to Conceptualize Ottoman Sunnitization', p. 319. See also idem., 'Sunna-minded Sufi Preachers in Service of the Ottoman State', p. 277; Krstić, 'From Shahada to 'Aqida'; Shafir, *Circulation and the Redefinition of Islam in the Ottoman Empire*; Yılmaz, *The Mystical Turn in the Ottoman Political Thought*, p. 14; Şahin, *Empire and Power in the Reign of Süleyman*, pp. 190–191, 193.
130. Karo, *Magid Meisharim*, p. 40a.

the community-oriented aspects had to be established anew in every phase of his life. The revelations needed to be put into writing, so Karo was instructed, and this in itself established a channel of communication with his surroundings.

The printed diary begins not with one of the early revelations during the encounter between Karo and his Magid but with a type of guidance booklet containing a list of ethical, pietistic, and practical instructions, under the editorial title "Warnings and Emendations and Strictures" (*Azharot ve-Tiqqunim ve-Seyagim*). Perusing the entire diary, it becomes clear that the various items on this list provide an extract or résumé of the practical or concrete aspects of the revelations. It is beyond our reach here to determine whether this list was composed by Karo himself or later by R. Jacob Zemach, one of the first editors of *Magid Meisharim*.

In any case, it represented one of the important channels for the spread of Safed Kabbalah in the Jewish world: customs that were either completely invented by the local Kabbalists, or, alternatively, traditional rites charged with new mystical vigor, yet practiced only by pietistic persons in private, or willingly adopted by mystical confraternities, later flowed to wider circles in the city. They were later still carried into faraway Diasporas, where they were absorbed as sanctified and legitimate, as if like old times.[131] Seen from this perspective, the diary is a laboratory and workshop for ritual, moral, and even theological innovations. This is testified by R. Karo himself, when he recounts that the teaching he acquired via the Magid served him quickly in his public preaching to the community:

> Later he [the Magid] expounded the first chapter of Mishnah, tractate *Avot*, saying that he need not provide a secretive-mystical reading followed by the literal sense, so that ordinary people could understand. He related to some objections raised by previous commentators [on tractate *Avot*], and still more, and resolved them all [...] and thus I interpreted the entire chapter and presented it in my public preaching, and I was lauded for what I said [in public].[132]

Of greater importance than concrete instructions or the invention of ritual acts was the general pietistic mood radiating from Safed to the Jewish Ecumene. The Catholic background is intensely present regarding the proximity of sin in every moment of life.[133] The diary repeatedly gives vent to endless voices of rebuke and scolding of R. Karo by the divine Magid, with intermitting moments for secretive reading of the Jewish heritage and instructions for Karo's life course. There is hardly any aspect in his life devoid of some blame or fault: "I am in charge of castigating men during night hours,

---

131. This mechanism is discussed in Weinstein, *Kabbalah and Jewish Modernity*, pp. 44–66.
132. Karo, *Magid Meisharim*, p. 35a. See also *ibid.*, pp. 35b, 37a, 52a.
133. *Ibid.*, 13b: "... for one must distinguish between cautiousness and agility [*Zehirut* versus *Zerizut* in Hebrew]. Cautiousness is when a person tackles a sinful situation and he keeps away. Agility is before tackling a sinful situation, when a person keeps the sin at distance". On the dramatically increasing occupation with sin in Safed, see Weinstein, *Kabbalah and Jewish Modernity*, Ch. 6 – 'Sin and Repentance. Jewish Confession', pp. 123–141.

as mentioned in the sacred Zohar, and so I came to castigate you so that you would completely avoid drinking wine during the day, and practice some ascetics, and during night hours you would not drink but one glass."[134] One has the impression that despite his prestigious position as a leader and scholar in Safed, Karo himself believed that he could never achieve a state of innocence beyond sin. It is reflected in his problematic vision, if compared to previous Jewish discussion in this regard, that only in the apocalyptic period of the Resurrection of the Dead, following the messianic era, would the human "Evil Inclination" (*Yetzer ha-Ra'*) be calmed and cease to bother human beings: "During the resurrection of the dead, which is the era following the messianic days, the world will be cleansed of passions and longings for worldly matters. In this time the Evil Inclination will cancel itself, and the commandments ordering active practices will be abolished, as will some of the commandments prohibiting certain practices."[135] It is mostly his bodily basic needs such as food—drinking wine or even water[136] and eating too much—that constantly preoccupy the rebuking voice. It certainly concerns the sexual domain, even regarding the intimacy with his legitimate spouse:

I would bestow upon you a righteous and modest spouse[...] and beware to retract from worldly pleasures, as I instructed you, and sanctify yourself during the coitus [...] A man must not enjoy this world at all, even when obliged to eat and drink and do 'other things' [a euphemism for sexual relations]. One should participate in these activities only to sustain his body and for the sake of later worshiping God, and not for his own pleasure. Had it been possible to do all things necessary to sustain his body [food and sexuality] without any pleasure involved, it would have been better.[137]

Karo was one of the pioneers in turning sexuality into a charged and problematic issue in the Jewish context.[138] The instruction regarding the taboo of sexual enjoyment is once again reminiscent of the Counter-Reformation instructions in Catholic Europe. Since the body reflects the Godhead, but also conditions human life, it is the most fitting arena for the battle between good and bad: "Your body members would become a residence for the *Shekhinah*, to worship and fear me [...] understand the [mystical] meaning of the verse 'from my own flesh I would view God'" (the text continues with allusions to the Kabbalistic Spheres).[139] The preoccupation with halakhic legality and with norms regarding rituals and communal life, mysticism, and heavenly revelations through the Magid formed a single cultural and religious continuum in the diary. Yet

---

134. Karo, *Magid Meisharim*, p. 49a.

135. *Ibid.*, p. 26a. See also *ibid.*, p. 43a, representing 'evil inclination' as an enchanting young woman.

136. *Ibid.*, p. 19a.

137. *Ibid.*, pp. 3a, 19a.

138. The sexual morality became an obsessive issue in Kabbalistic writings, especially the ethically-oriented. An extensive discussion, see Roni Weinstein, *Juvenile Sexuality, Kabbalah, and Catholic Religiosity among Jewish Italian Communities. "Glory of Youth" by Pinhas Baruch b. Pelatya Monselice (Ferrara, XVII Century)*, Boston and Leiden: E. J. Brill, 2008.

139. Karo, *Magid Meisharim*, pp. 3b, 5b.

this continuum is not to be considered as particularly Jewish, since it interacted and resonated with parallel processes—of much greater extent and importance—in Ottoman
culture whereby law and mysticism were inseparably weaved together. This was apparent in its political ethos along several channels mentioned previously: the leader as a
universalistic and sanctified figure in the Sufi tradition; the process of Sunnitization;
and the conception of law as a prime lever in religious reform.

Karo: Mystical-Lawyer and Juridical-Mystic

R. Karo was first and foremost an impressive Talmudic scholar, unique even among the
impressive group of rabbis and halakhic arbiters of Safed and the Sephardic Diaspora
in the Eastern Mediterranean.[140] His codes of law contributed to the halakhic renaissance of Sephardi scholarship in the sixteenth and (partially) seventeenth centuries.
But he was not a regular scholar, as he combined an active and intense visionary and
ecstatic life with his arduous and unceasing study of the immense "ocean" of Talmudic
and post-Talmudic literature (*Yam ha-Talmud*).

There were certainly precedents for scholars combining sober Talmudic dialectics
with enthusiastic mystical life and experiences, especially in the Sephardi tradition
prior to the general expulsion. Yet none of them weaved these two domains—which
nowadays seem so estranged to us "moderns"—so deeply one with the other, inserted
typically Kabbalistic sources into the literature of Talmudic rulings (*Sifrut Pesiqah*), and
enabled each domain to nourish the other, as did R. Karo. He could not have borrowed such a model from the place of origin where his family and forefathers lived
for centuries—Catholic Spain, or Christian Europe in general. No significant model
for the fusion of juridical and mystical activities in the same person can be found in
Church institutions (Canon Law), nor somewhat later in university law faculties (*Ius
civile*), let alone any individual with as impressive a stature as R. Karo. Not surprisingly,
looking at his neighbors next door in the Ottoman Empire, during his early life in
Rumelia, and later as a scholar in Safed within the *Bilad a-Sham* area, he could certainly
observe impressive scholars of the Muslim *Shari'a* who were at the same time important
and venerable Sufi masters.

Yet Karo's response to the Islamicate and Ottoman space where he lived his entire
life (excepting his years as a small child just before the expulsion) went much deeper.
The vision that he had of himself, his life course, and the codification project resonated
with what he saw around him. Like other important Sufis of the early modern period
in the Ottoman Empire—either in the core lands or in the Arabic territories—he composed a mystical diary of immense measures, the *Magid Meisharim*. This was all unheard
of in the Jewish context—both the autobiographical writing and the exposure of inner
life as an important component of the *via mystica*. Although the *Magid Meisharim* at our

---

140. On Talmudic studies as Karo's main occupation, see Pely, 'Studies in the Adjudication
Project of Rabbi Joseph Karo', p. 131.

disposal is much shorter and intensely edited, it is a completely unique artifact of its kind in Jewish tradition as a whole, and certainly in the rabbinical milieu.

The work follows R. Karo in his daily life, his relationship with his family, intimate moments with his wives, corporeal habits, sleep and waking, or personal and "professional" aspirations. His emotions and moods of self-criticism are a recurring theme throughout the diary. Yet the text is far from being a documentation of a personal life for its own sake. It revolves around meetings with a divine agent, named the *Magid*, *Shekhinah*, *Mother* (or better *Rebuking Mother*), *Matronita*, or *Mishnah*.[141] The interaction is often stern and demanding on the part of the Magid, yet there are soft moments of proximity and even an erotic flavor of hugging and kissing. In some exceptional moments, Karo is elevated to high spheres in the divine world. The various entries in the diary present a journey not only of revelation of Torah secrets and various aspects of Jewish heritage and life but no less so an intensifying glorification of R. Karo himself. Pace Moshe Idel, in certain moments he is even absorbed in God and becomes completely immersed in the *Shekhinah*.

An alternative mode of reading *Magid Meisharim*, and a constant theme in this diary, is the fundamental contact between R. Karo and imminent past scholars, the fountains of Talmudic scholarship. Karo is elevated to the Divine Yeshiva, where all the great names of Talmudic erudition of past generations face one another in regular and continuous study, as conducted in his contemporary world. There he was hailed and heralded by an angelic voice, and his exceptional erudition and talent were recognized by past scholars, from the Mishnah through the seventeenth-century sages. Past and present blend into one continuum of Jewish erudition, and all the scholars are searching for Talmudic truth and rabbinical consensus. The intimate interface between arduous Talmudic labor and grand mystical vision was masterfully described by Maoz Kahana:

> The highlight of amassing and organizing [Talmudic] knowledge is, in fact, a moment of unification of God, the exhilarating moment in which the internal harmony between various halakhic traditions of the legal culture is revealed to the industrious composer. This exhilarating moment—constructing the Holy Temple by letters of the law—is identical and concludes the utopian methodology for exhausting the legal books, as expressed by R. Joseph Karo in his preface to *Beit Yosef* [...] In his world, of a librarian, bibliographer and omniscient Halakhist, a cosmic unification of God is possible by means of a methodology of utopian-sober and daily writing, to which he aspired and materialized by writing *Beit Yosef* along dozens of years, by the unique ruling method that he set for it. In this sense, no less significant than inserting the Zohar to *Beit Yosef*, one should consider the *Beit Yosef* and *Shulchan 'Arukh* as the utopian-legalistic materialization of total-knowledge methodology that the Zoharic-cosmogonic perspective furnished one of its bases, and actively participated in its self-construction [of total knowledge]. The diligent halakhic sage seen in the prism is a kind of creative and active Kabbalist. The law canon would be completed only after years of arduous work, yet the godly unification—this momentary tabernacle—is

---

141. On thes various channels and figures of revelation, see Idel, 'Rabbi Joseph Karo as Kabbalist', pp. 347–357, 367, 389.

the daily highlight of writing each and every item of the law, when all the various sources integrate into an effective synthesis, explaining and illuminating one another. The Holy Temple is constructed by letters and words, words-courses of the Divine-total law, joining one harmony and construct an entire universe. *A universe saturated with Law.*[142]

As much as R. Karo was no ordinary Talmudic scholar, so were his double codes of law no regular halakhic corpus. In at least two encounters with the Magid, Karo receives a promise that he will live to complete his codes, and is even provided with their exact titles: *Beit Yosef* and *Shulchan 'Arukh*. The plan behind this immense corpus was vividly exposed in his important preface to *Beit Yosef*, and to a lesser extent to *Shulchan 'Arukh*.[143] Its goal was to foster unity and harmony in the Jewish tradition and to be implemented in concrete Jewish life and rituals. The gap between heaven and earth was to be bridged by his halakhic work. Time and again, the diary documents how specific Talmudic discussions and their ramifications that preoccupied Karo due to his responsibilities as rabbi, judge, community leader, or public preacher were discussed in the Divine Yeshiva. At times he was provided with an assurance that his mode of reading or interpreting certain Talmudic discussion (*sugiya*) was correct, and it even filled the almighty God with satisfaction and aroused a smile. Beside the political-institutional aspects of his codification project, discussed in other chapters, the law had turned into axis of salvation. But some caution is needed here: salvation does not necessarily imply active or urgent apocalyptic stands or some form of collective Jewish messianism. It defines law and normative instructions as a prologue to the reformation of Jewish life and tradition.[144]

The multiple points of similarity between the diary of R. Karo and his somewhat later Sufi master Niyazi el-Misri reveal how deeply they both share the same cultural platform of Islamicate and Ottoman civilization. The Sunnitization process of the Ottoman Empire during the life span of R. Karo, masterfully analyzed by Derin Terzioğlu and Tijana Krstić, became significant as a state project. In constructing an empire of unprecedented geographical extent and ethno-religious diversity, the Ottoman elite mobilized both people of the law—the 'Ulama and the Madrasa heritage—and impressive masters of various Sufi orders. It was not uncommon that religious scholars would embody both these domains in their studies and public activities. The political paradigm of the Ottoman sultan and state blended together aspirations for military campaigns, religious innovation, messianic hopes, and Sufi traditions—all under the umbrella of law and justice. The period of Süleyman *Kanuni* has been shown to have comprised two major phases, from expansion and visions of immanent salvation and universal rule to the stabilization of an empire. Common to both of them was

---

142. Maoz Kahana, 'A Universe Made of Words. The Self-Image of R. Joseph Karo as Composer of Halakhah' [Hebrew], *Hebrew Law Annual* [*Shnaton Ha-Mishpat Ha-'Ivri* in Hebrew] 30 (2019–2020), pp. 79–127. See *ibid.*, p. 121–122.

143. See above, Ch. 2.

144. Kahana, 'A Universe Made of Words'. I concur with this perspective and disagree with the 'Messianic' reading of Mor Altshuler

the element of providing justice, laws, and security as a constitutive part of the Sultan's political role. The Jewish minority was less inspired by the first factor— universal rule, since it lacked any substantial political leverage. It certainly internalized important aspects of the second phase, regarding the dominant role of law, codification, and just rule as the foundation of collective life. For R. Karo, it further offered a vision for religious renovation and reform in which the law enjoyed universal horizons of applicability throughout the Jewish Ecumene. Such a vision fell on a fertile ground of a Jewish heritage of universal justice dating back to the biblical prophets.

Karo did not have access to any political tools or instruments of coercion. But his vision directly projected into the Jewish environment the same vision of law as a channel to salvation. He would study Talmudic lore as a regular scholar, yet in tandem he related his Talmudic devotion to mystic terminology and presented it as a continuous encounter with the Divine Yeshiva and its past scholars; suggested pietistic model of devotion and adherence to God (*devequt*), and ultimately dreamed of becoming the leader of the Jewish Ecumene: "It is I, the *Mishnah*, speaking through [or: in] your mouth, the mother castigating her sons [or children], the one embracing you. And you shall often adhere to me, I shall return to you and you shall return to me. I shall raise you to become master and leader (*sar ve-nagid*) over the entire Jewish Diaspora in *Arabistan*."

Chapter Seven

"PROVIDE ME WITH THE REASONING FOR YOUR VERDICT": THE PRESTIGE AND STATUS OF JEWISH COURTS

Modern Western thinking considers it almost unthinkable to issue a court verdict without providing the reasoning behind it. Justice and legal reasoning should be transparent and subject to potential counterarguments. Legal reasoning is regarded not only as part and parcel of the defendant's rights but also as a mechanism for exposing juridical thinking and allowing its discussion in further instances so as to achieve optimal justice. This rule, however, is far from being universal.

Even in Jewish tradition, where legality holds a prominent place in the collective ethos, this obligation was far from certain. It had its own history in various periods and cultural contexts and was occasionally discussed by prominent rabbinical scholars throughout the Middle Ages. R. Karo added a significant contribution to this discussion in two long responsa, alongside his codification works. He related the matter to his grand plan to construct courts of differing role and prestige. The functioning of the contemporary Ottoman legal system stands behind the discussion of the formal halakhic rule "provide me with the reasoning for your verdict" as discussed below.

The Talmudic Tradition regarding Legal Reasoning

Rabbinical tradition offered two formal options for the administration of justice: courts of law and the responsa literature (respectively *Beit Din* and *She'elot u-Tshuvot* in Hebrew). As mentioned in the Introduction, there were also nonformal means for securing justice. Rabbinical responsa began to evolve and play an increasing role from the Gaonic period, though there are some testimonies for its earlier functioning in late antiquity among Talmud scholars (*Amora'im*).[1] Most of the responsa were composed by way of a reply to concrete persons—dispatched either by regular people or "professional" jurists—addressing rabbis of prestige for legal counsel; only a minor portion were composed as an academic drill for schooling purposes. The rabbinical responsa constitute the Jewish corollary of a jurisprudential genre customary in Roman law, later in European writing (the *Consilium*), and in the Muslim legal tradition (the *Fatwa*). I shall

---

1. Menachem Elon, *Jewish Law: History, Sources, Principles*, tr. by Bernard Auerbach and Melvin J. Sykes, Philadelphia and Jerusalem: JPS, 1994, Vols. I-IV; Haym Soloveichik, *Responsa as Historical Source* [Hebrew], Jerusalem: Shazar Center, 1990.

seek in particular to draw attention to the deep similarity in its mode of use among Muslim and Jewish legal scholars.

The Jewish courts of law that operated under the constraints of majority society, be it Sassanian, Roman, Islamic, or European Catholic were the more accessible of the two frameworks. The extent of legal autonomy changed during the Middle Ages and early modern period, depending on the broader position of Jews and other minorities within the majority society. Both frameworks express the profound desire of the Jewish population to conduct its collective life according to its particular religious tradition and customs. Yet there are several differences between these legal tools. One difference relates to the need to elaborate on the reasoning behind the legal conclusion (in the case of a responsum) or to abstain from so doing (in the case of a court verdict). In his detailed article on the subject, Eliav Shochetman noted that the importance of this aspect far exceeds the narrow discussion of legal procedures and is distinct from the question of the legal formality of court procedures. Discharging the judge from the obligation to provide reasoning for his verdict could imply that he was awarded a large degree of freedom and was not entirely bound by the written law. Obliging him to state his reasons, on the other hand, might designate a contradictory orientation, narrowing his capacity to deviate from the written law.[2] These aspects of court proceedings were less applicable to rabbinical responsa. In their immediate impact, responsa were secondary to formal court procedures, as they entailed a longer period of addressing a rabbi and waiting for his response; moreover, the enforcement of these halakhic instructions was not obligatory. In order to substantiate their assertions, the composers of responsa, therefore, needed to elaborate on their legal motives.[3] Furthermore, it was far from rare that litigants addressed their queries to several respondents simultaneously, in spite of recurring objections of rabbis to this habit, so that they were able to choose the most suitable response for their own needs. This pattern also obliged the composers of responsa—well aware that their opinion would be tested by others—to accompany their legal statements with persuasive arguments.[4]

Talmudic scholars in the Holy Land, and in the dominant Babylonian Diaspora under Sassanian rule and early Islam, discussed another related element, which is the internal hierarchy of prestige and erudition. A derivative of this principal discussion concerned the hierarchy of various courts of law presided by scholars of differing positions within the rabbinical hierarchy: starting from small and local courts regulated by nonprofessional personnel up to the Sanhedrin, the leading and centralistic court of law in the capital and holy city of Jerusalem and in vicinity to the Holy Temple or its equivalents in the leading yeshivas of Babylonia, in Sura or Pumbedita. A parallel source of legitimacy for Jewish legality and autonomy relied on "lay" leadership. During the Gaonic period, in the early centuries of Islam, this political leadership represented

---

2. See Eliav Shochetman, 'The Obligation to State Reasons for Legal Decisions in Jewish Law' [Hebrew], *Shenaton ha-Mishpat ha-'Ivri: Annual of the Institute for Research in Jewish Law* 6–7 (1980–1981), pp. 319–397, esp. p. 321.
3. *Ibid.*, esp. pp. 339–340.
4. *Ibid.*, p. 340.

a very substantial Jewish minority and maintained direct connections with the non-Jewish political authorities, either in the Holy Land under its leading *Nasi* or in Babylon under the "Head of Exile" (*Reish Galuta* or *Reish Galut*). Centralistic and authoritative courts related to such important figures were not expected to provide legal reasoning for their verdicts to the same extent as smaller and less prestigious local courts of law, an exemption that marked their superior status.

Lengthy Talmudic discussions had established precedents regarding the issue of providing reasonings for court verdicts or legal decisions in general. This subject was discussed in tractate *Sanhedrin*, dedicated mostly to legal procedures:

> Rav Safra says that Rabbi Yoḥanan says: With regard to two who were struggling in judgment, one of whom says: Let us go to court here, and one of whom says: Let us go to the place of the Assembly, the latter litigant is compelled to appear and be judged in a court that presides in his own city. And if the local court needs to ask a higher court about a certain matter, the judges will write to the Assembly, and the higher court sends its response. And if one of the litigants says to a court: Write me for what reason you judged me in this manner and give it to me, as I do not trust your decision without explanation, the judges write it and give it to him. And with regard to a woman whose husband had a brother, and he died childless [*vehayevama*], she follows her brother-in-law [*hayavam*] for him to free her of the levirate bond through *ḥalitza*. The *yavam* does not have to go to her. How far does she have to go? Rabbi Ami says: Even from Tiberias to Sippori. This is the *halakha* even though the court in Tiberias is more prestigious than the one in Sippori.[5]

The Talmudic discussion concerns a situation in which the litigating parties disagree which court should adjudicate their case: the local one or a more prestigious court in a more distant location. The latter option is naturally less accessible and requires further financial expenses. In such a situation, a wealthier litigant would be tempted to use his economic advantage as a lever in managing the court proceedings. The Talmud provides a concrete example of a woman wishing to discharge herself from a levirate marriage who was forced to debate her case in a distant (in relative terms, of course) court of law—in the city of Sippori—rather than her hometown of Tiberias. By way of compensation, the party constrained to prosecute in a place he did not chose is entitled to ask the judges for their reasoning. The Talmudic expression *mi-eizeh ta'am dantuni* ("What was the reason for your judgement of me?") became less common in the Middle Ages and was partially substituted by *horuni mi-heikhan dantuni* ("Provide me the legal/written basis for your judgment of me").

Several issues were left unresolved in this Talmudic *sugiyah* (discursive unit), as in many others: Is the disagreement regarding the location the only grounds for providing legal reasoning or are there other circumstances? What happens when one of the litigating parties suspects that the judge or judges are biased or bluntly unjust? Does this entitle him automatically to demand the legal reasoning? When the Talmudic *sugiyah* alludes

---

5. BT [Babylonian Talmud], p. 31b. I used the translation of William Davidson, found at www .sefaria.org internet site.

to the provision of information ("the judges write it and give it to him"), how detailed and elaborate should the court document be? Should it contain all the testimonies, the verdict, and its detailed clarification, or does it only contain a very general description of the case and nothing beyond? Furthermore, how does the Jewish justice mechanism confront the inevitable policy of some litigants to protract legal procedures in order to exhaust their rivals? The demand for legal reasoning could potentially serve as a tool for protracting or delaying justice (*'inuy Ha-din*). With this in mind, should this right be restricted by the rabbinical legal authorities? When the Talmudic discussion refers to *meqom ha-va'ad* ("the place of the assembly"), what is the exact semantic and juridical sense of this term? These issues were discussed throughout the Middle Ages without reaching any clear consensus. A further term was added in this context—the "Supreme Court of Law" (*Beit-Din Gadol* or *Beit-Din ha-Gadol*), the highest Talmudic authority in post. How does one determine that a certain person, institution, or school represents this highest authority? What is the concrete legal sense of "forcing" a litigant to participate in court proceedings in a determined place ("the latter litigant is compelled to appear and be judged in a court that presides in his own city") and what is considered a free choice of court? Finally, what are the financial or economic constraints: To what extent is it legitimate to "drag" one of the litigating parties away from home, and what is the legitimate limit of expenses for this purpose?

These issues were discussed by rabbis, halakhic arbiters, and Talmudic scholars throughout the Middle Ages. The obligation to provide the reasoning for a halakhic decision or verdict was not absolute. Shochetman observed two currents in the rabbinical literature in this respect. The "liberal" approach tends to reduce the obligation to provide reasoning and to limit the circumstances entitling the litigant to raise this claim. The second current tends to enlarge the extent of this duty, including even cases where such a demand was not raised by the litigants. Halakhic arbiters supporting the former position seemed to consider the request as injurious to the court's status. Motivated by the intention to protect the prestige of legal system, they reduced the litigants' right to this instrument. Shochetman noted that many halakhic arbiters in the late Middle Ages and early modern period sensed that they lacked the vast authority of the "Early Generations" (mainly those during the Middle Ages), and consequently did not consider this request as implying any disrespect for the court's status.[6]

The evolving discussion about the rule *Horuni mi-heikhan dantuni* is an interesting indication of the growing professionalization of the rabbinical milieu during the Middle Ages and its increasing sense of its own distinct status. The rabbinical consensus around this issue in the Sephardi domain was broadly reflected in the famous codes of law: *Mishneh Torah* by Maimonides, *Ha-Turim* by R. Jacob ben Ha-Rosh, and finally in the double codes of R. Karo, who followed suit his predecessors.

Maimonides reiterated the literal sense of the Talmudic *Sugiyah* regarding the need to provide legal reasoning in a case when a litigant was forced to pursue their case in a

---

6. *Ibid.*, 332, 335.

court they did not freely chose. The term *Beit Ha-Va'ad*, this higher juridical instance, acquired a very specific meaning:

> If the local judges feels the need to ask for clarification from the Supreme Court in Jerusalem regarding a certain matter, they should write down their question and send it. After their inquiry, the judgment should be rendered in the local court on the basis of the answer written to them by the Supreme Court.[7]

This particular Talmudic context provides Maimonides with an opportunity to project his general attitude that the Halakhah should be one and the same for all the Jewish people; this suits its optimal functioning. In order to achieve this goal, centralistic institutions and unified law are required. This is basically the great vision behind the composition of the *Mishneh Torah*. In discussing the particular issue of legal reasoning, the supreme legal instance is none other than the Supreme Court of Law (*Beit-Din Ha-Gadol*). It is interesting to note that the concrete issue—regarding a request for a legal reasoning—is not discussed here at all. Whoever wishes to transfer his case to a nonlocal court is required to come to this court in Jerusalem. His main innovative words appear later, when he relates to what could best promote his grand vision under the given reality of exile and restricted legal autonomy:

> Similar concepts apply to the present, when there is no Supreme Court, but there are places where there are great sages whose expertise is well known and there are other places where there are scholars who are not on that level. If the lender says: "Let us go to this-and-this place in this-and-this land to have the case adjudicated by so-and-so, the great sage," we compel the borrower to go with him. This was the current practice in Spain.[8]

Rabbinical erudition, schools of law, and Jewish courts provide a temporary substitute for the sacred institutions in Jerusalem by the Holy Temple. Not every diaspora reaches this elevated position, however, but only those specific places "where there are great sages whose expertise is well known."[9] These unique places are symbolic extensions of those historical institutions maintained virtually alive in the collective memory. Not by coincidence, the Spanish Diaspora is regarded as unique in its leading role among the Jewish Ecumene ("this was continually the practice in Spain"). To sum up Maimonides' positions, he does not provide any conclusive statement about Horuni, yet relates the entire issue to the status of courts, especially the central one in Jerusalem. The discussion of *sugiyat Horuni* essentially becomes a pretext for discussing another theme, which is the supremacy of a centralistic court in comparison to local ones, and the way this radiates a past ethos. Karo will take this position one step further and add the personalistic

---

7. Maimonides, *Mishnah Torah*, Section 'Sefer Shoftim', subsection 'Hilkhot Sanhedrin' 6,6. I used the translation provided at www.chabad.org internet site.

8. *Ibid.*, 6,9.

9. *Ibid.*

aspect of the internal hierarchy among scholars and the one person heading the schol-arly pyramid.

The halakhic decisions of the *Arba'ah Turim*, followed by R. Karo in both his codes, continue to a large extent what was already stated in *Mishneh Torah* by Maimonides. Unlike R. Yaakov ben Ha-Rosh in his *Turim*, R. Karo takes care to emphasize, as Maimonides previously did, the issue of supreme juridical authority as part of the Talmudic *sugiyah*:

> It seems that the "Supreme Court" and "Place of Assembly" are two distinct institutions. The Place of Assembly is where the Sages gather, as understood in this Talmudic discus-sion according to R. Tam's exegesis, and the "Supreme Court" is the *Nasi* in the Holy Land [...] Even the defendant [in court] may request to be prosecuted in the Supreme Court. Nowadays it seems that the leading figure of each generation [*he-chashuv she-ba-dor*] is called a Supreme Court. Thus, said R. Tam that it was customary to nominate this person as *Nasi*.[10]

The discussion of the term *Beit ha-Va'ad* (literally "Place of Assembling") takes a new twist, referring here not to an institution or proceeding, but to a specific living person, that is the leading scholar of each generation. For R. Karo, an assembly of excellent scholars of Talmudic erudition was not sufficient to grant the right to serve as a court of appeal or supreme legal instance. Such an institution needed to be headed by a specific person. Accordingly, he distinguishes between major scholars, as alluded to by Maimonides in the citation above, and one unique person, heading this assemblage of scholars as a sort of *primus inter pares*. ("It seems that the Supreme Court and Place of Assembly are two distinct institutions.") The functioning of this internal hierarchy naturally requires their acceptance of his superior position and their collective coop-eration. In the late sixteenth century, this person, as shown in other chapters,[11] is none other than R. Karo himself. He is the early modern and concrete incorporation of the Supreme Court heading the *Beit Ha-Va'ad*, like the *Nasi* who headed the Sanhedrin of the classical rabbinical era. The historical *Nasi* of late antiquity functioned both as head of the appeal instance and as the political head of Jewish population in the Holy Land under Roman rule. He benefitted from wealth, political connections, and excel-lence in Talmudic erudition. This position is still relevant in present times: "*Nowadays it seems that the leading figure of each generation is called Supreme Court. Thus said R. Tam [...]*"

This issue of providing legal reasoning was debated throughout the Middle Ages and the early modern period among rabbis and Talmudic scholars without reaching a conclusive point. What is common to these debates, though, is their proximity to other components of Jewish life and its social mechanisms, such as community organization, authority within the rabbinical circle, and their authority as an erudite elite vis-à-vis the general public. The last theme demonstrates that rabbis and Talmudic scholars

---

10. Joseph Karo, *Beit Yosef*, section 'Choshen Mishpat' 14,1.
11. See above Chs. 4, 6.

were well aware of the importance of non-halakhic components in their work in general, and in this specific matter of *Horuni*. The party objecting to provide legal reasoning underscored the importance of court prestige and authority. Don Isaac Abrabanel (d. 1508), one of the esteemed Bible commentators of the Sephardi tradition, stated in his long discussion of Moses' promotion of justice and law mechanisms (Exodus Ch. 18): "And people would always cast doubts and qualms regarding their verdicts, saying *Horuni mi-heikhan dantuni* due to animosities and hatred, or due to other reasons so as to oppose their opponents in court. If they address other judges, since the opinions and views of people vary, this one [judge] would convict while the other [judge] would acquit, the rules [*ha-torot*] would increase as much as the disputes, and they would end up by addressing Moses [...] [Jethro] advised him [Moses] to nominate judges as was customary in Median, and is still customary in Muslim states [the Ottoman Empire], God-fearing people, [provided with] truthful, non-greedy [judges]".[12] Abrabanel furnishes an interesting perspective of a Jewish thinker affiliated deeply to European and Christian heritage—in both Spain and Italy—regarding the hierarchical and centralistic character of the Ottoman justice mechanism. The need for efficiency in responding to litigants' demands prevents the court from providing reasonings for its verdicts. The same line of argument was presented by the Sephardi R. Joseph ben Habibah in the late fifteenth century.[13] Other thinkers, conversely, supported the demand to provide legal reasoning on the grounds that one of the prime tasks of justice mechanism is to appease the litigants and restore social peace. Such a position was adopted by R. Yosef Elashkar (1470–1540, North Africa) in his Mishnah Commentary *Merkevet ha-Mishnah*:

Be gracious to every person [...] thus you will do away with enmity and robbery, and everyone would love you [as a judge]. Or according to the second reading, if you have ruled [as judge in court] by yourself, after cross-examination, the litigants will not bear hatred towards you. And even when the culpable party would ask you *Horuni mi-heikhan dantuni*, show him the verdict clear and shining as the sun. Then both parties would acquiesce, the culpable as well as the innocent [...] You [again addressing the judge] should know that it is unnecessary to delve deeply into legal details, but judge according to your legal common sense, as you reckon the matter.[14]

---

12. See the commentary of Isaac Abravanel on Exodus 18, 13.
13. See R. Joseph Habibah, commentary on the Talmud [*Nimukei Yosef* in Hebrew], on tractate Bava Metziah 40b.
14. Joseph ElAshkar, *Merkevet ha-Mishnah* [his commentary on the Mishnah], ed. Yaakov Shmuel Spiegel, Lod: Orot Yahadut Ha-Maghreb, 2007, commentary on tractate Avot, ch. 1. See also Ephrayim Lunchich, *Kli Yakar* [his Torah commentary], Jerusalem; Machon Pe'er Ha-Torah, 2012, commentary on Exodus 18,15; Abraham Saba', *Zror HaMor* [his Torah commentary], ed. Zebulun Buaron, Jerusalem: Ben-Zvi Institute, 2015, commentary on Exodus, Pericope 'Jethro'; Isaiah Horowitz, *Vavei Ha'Amudim* [ethical tract], Haifa: Makhon Yad Ramah, 1994, section 'Amud Ha-Din 18,5.

The willingness to provide legal reasoning is not limited to the conditions mentioned previously by the eminent halakhic arbiters in the codes of law. According to Alashkar, it should be provided as a routine matter in court proceedings. Furthermore, the motivation is not juridical in any sense but focuses clearly on the desire to pacify both litigating parties and increase their trust in Jewish courts of law.

Further indication that the issue was not resolved is provided by rabbinical responsa dealing with concrete legal cases and often referring to court procedures. R. Samuel de Medina[15] (known under the acronym *Ha-Maharashdam*), one of the leading rabbis in sixteenth-century Salonica, shows profound ambivalence on this issue:

> And so he [a litigant] returned to me one day, wishing to oppose the verdict by claiming *Horuni mi-heikhan dantuni*. My complaint does not concern him, for he is a foolish young man, but [concerns] his vicious advisor, advising him to rob the rental payment [the issue discussed in court]. He and his mother instructed him about this trickery, in order to do away with the complaint [against him]. And even though I should have disregarded [his request], for I have not summoned him, yet I saw the sense in providing him with reasoning for the obligation to pay the rent.[16]

The request to provide legal reasoning is presented by de Medina, who functions in this case in the double role of respondent and judge, as a legal trickery intended to protract the achievement of justice, and hence should have evoked an irritated rejection. And yet de Medina was ambivalent ("even though I should have disregard [his request] [...] yet I saw the sense ...") and decided to inform him of the reasons for his ruling. Other responsa testify that the persons addressing the courts insisted on receiving the reasoning as a condition for abiding by the court's verdict.[17] An eminent Sephardi rabbi and arbiter, R. Levi ben-Haviv (1480–1540),[18] regarded this clearly as an integral part of current court proceedings and as a basic obligation of judges toward their "clients": "It seems unreasonable that the court would not provide the plaintiff with his verdict, and only mention what the court said to the witnesses [...] it is a new and strange matter, unheard of [...]".[19] It is no wonder that rabbis held opposing views in this regard and stated them plainly in their own responsa. Such was the case of an important rabbi we met above, R. Moses di Trani (1500–1580),[20] a contemporary of R. Karo in Safed. He could state in one case that

---

15. Morris S. Goodblatt, *Jewish life in Turkey in the XVIth Century: As Reflected in the Legal Writings of Samuel de Medina*, New York: JTS, 1952.

16. Samuel de Medina, *Responsa*, New York: 1959, Section 'Even Ha'Ezer', §184, and Section 'Choshen Mishpat', 45, 279.

17. R. David ben Zimrah [The Radbaz], *Responsa*, Jerusalem 1972, Part III, §578.

18. R. Levi ben-Haviv played an important role in the Semichah polemic, see abov Ch. 4.

19. R. Levi ben-Haviv [The *Ralbach*], *Responsa*, Jerusalem: Keren Re'em Institute, 2018, §109. See also Binyamin ben Matitya of Arta, *Responsa Binyamin Zeev*, Jerusalem: 1959, §249.

20. On R. Moses di Trani (1505–1585), see Ilan Vaya, *Moral and Social Aspects in the Doctrine of Rabbi Moses Trani* [Hebrew], M.A. Thesis submitted at Bar-Ilan University, 2015; Isaac Pesach Zinger, *The Life and Compositions of HaMabit* [Hebrew], Jerusalem: 2007.

in this particular case the judge was nominated by the community, and he enjoyed the status of *Beit Ha-Va'ad* [hence discharged from the obligation to provide legal reasonings].[21] For long years he adjudicated and discharged the accused [from paying], who never asked *Horuni mi-heikhan dantuni*, only now that he found a solicitor for his claim.[22]

Yet in a second case, his evaluation of the poor standard of contemporary judges was presented as justification of his decision to take the opposite approach:

> and even though it is said in the Talmud that one is not concerned whether the court is mistaken, and one court does not control the work of another court, yet in our time we are concerned. R. Yerucham citing the Rashbah wrote in a Responsum that nowadays [judges] are not very proficient in legal details, so we control court decisions [by examining their detailed verdicts, accompanied by legal reasonings]. If that was true in the time of Rashbah, it is all the more so valid in the present time.[23]

When taking into consideration all the arguments regarding the issue *Horuni mi-heikhan dantuni*, it is apparent that there was no clear-cut position. The issue was only touched upon incidentally, while discussing other themes of legal procedure, and rarely as an issue in its own right. Even though Jewish scholars did not reach a consensus in this regard, it became increasingly common in Jewish courts of law to provide verdicts without elaborating on their reasoning. Shochetman noticed this tendency in rabbinical literature.[24] Where important religious schools prospered— such as in Spain—and certain rabbis acquired a prominent position and prestige among local communities, the request for legal reasoning was increasingly considered as illegitimate and verging on the impudent.

Two Responsa of R. Karo on *Horuni mi-Heikhan Dantuni*

R. Karo was the first scholar to dedicate an elaborate discussion to the issue of providing legal reasoning for court verdicts.[25] His responsa *Avqat Rokhel* included a first responsum (§17) relatively short, a counter-responsum by an anonymous scholar from Safed (§18),[26] and a second responsum (§19) providing his own response to the position of his unnamed opponent. All three items, as we shall shortly see, are not responsa

---

21. Meaning that he is accepted willingly as judge by both litigating parties, and hence none can ask for legal reasoning following his verdict.

22. R. Moses di Trani, *Responsa*, Jerusalem: 1974, Part II, §173.

23. *Idem.*

24. Shochetman, 'The Obligation to State Reasons for Legal Decisions', pp. 345–349, 394–395.

25. Joseph Karo, *Responsa Avkat Rochel*, Salonika: 1791, §17–19.

26. Benayahu thinks that the anonymous person was R. Avraham Shalom, yet provides no reasons to substantiate his assertion, while Davidson maintains his anonymity. I incline to accept Davidson's position, since Karo would hardly leave his adversary unnamed, as seen in the rest of this respona, where he proposes his counter-positions to suggestions of other rabbis, all mentioned by their names.

per se but rather part of a public debate, cast into the responsa pattern so that it could be included in his book. This fits well with the general nature of the *Avqat Rokhel* responsa in printed form.

The first responsum is prefaced by the editor's remark that it is entirely dedicated to the issue of *Horuni mi-heikhan dantuni* and alludes to an imaginary perfect situation in the past: "In earlier days, better than our own, we have not encountered a person demanding from the court *Horuni mi-heikhan dantuni*. If, by chance, such a person was found, he was rebuked. And now an event happened, that a litigant was taught to present this demand to an important court, accepted by the communities and nominated to adjudicate the city—a big city by God's grace— insisting to have the legal reasoning, and he had someone backing his request. This necessitated the composition of a response on this matter."[27] These "early days, better than our own," completely unspecified in time and place, were typified by rare requests for legal reasoning, due to general trust in the Jewish courts. In rare exceptions, a rebuke was enough, necessitating no harsher reaction. More important is the fact that R. Karo does not specify what the circumstances for such a request were, or indeed under what conditions this was permissible. In this mythical and imaginary past, this appeal was generally neither necessary nor legitimate. In a quick shift to the present, such a request does appear but is presented as no more than legalistic trickery. The demand is rejected out of hand due to the position and prestige of the chief court of law in place, entitled to the same rights as the Supreme Court of law of the classical rabbinical-Talmudic period. The current situation is again presented as unrelated to any specific circumstances. The narrative of events lacks any historical settings that initiated the request for legal reasoning or the composition of R. Karo's responsum dedicated entirely to this issue. A request *Horuni mi-heikhan dantuni* is considered by R. Karo an insult to the status of the Jewish court of law. No less so it is an affront to Talmudic scholars and the Torah, in the sense of the entire Jewish religious heritage. The Aramaic term used is *Hefqeruta*—"unruliness" or "contempt."

What was left as a general saying at first is stated explicitly further on: the Supreme Court discussed here refers specifically to the city of Safed:

> In the present time, the court of this city [where Karo currently resides, i.e. Safed] is accepted by the entire community; it comprises important and elderly sages, better than [the courts in] all [other] places. Its reputation has spread, and from four ends of the world questions are dispatched, and people would not deviate from their rules as it is a Supreme Court of Law [*Beit-Din Ha-Gadol*].[28]

The Safedian court reverberates the functioning modes of the Sanhedrin, a Supreme Court entitled to adjudicate the entire Jewish people. As the highest legal instance,

---

27. Karo, *Responsa Avkat Rochel*, §17, p. 12b.
28. *Ibid.*, p. 13b. See also *ibid.*: "We heard of a case addressed to our grand Rabbi Jacob Beirav, may his name be commemorated in the afterworld, that someone asked him *Horuni miHeichan Dantuni* and he excommunicated him".

it is not required to present its juridical motivations, since there is no higher appeal court above it. Further, the concrete situation of this Safedian court substantiates Karo's claim to supremacy by the double fact that it relies on the oldest and most professional Talmudic scholars ("comprising important and elderly sages") and that it attracts requests for legal counseling from the entire Jewish Ecumene ("from four ends of the world questions are dispatched"). In this sense, it is not only the leading legal instance but also an international institution in its authority, validity, and prestige.[29] In attributing an international and global character to the court, as one addressed by all Jewish communities, R. Karo relies on Maimonides and other halakhic arbiters, as mentioned previously.

R. Karo reminds his readers that even when the reasoning for a ruling is indeed provided, this should include only the documents involved, the main arguments of the witnesses, and the precise verdict: nothing beyond, and certainly not the legal arguments leading to a specific verdict. In general, §17 is not really a responsum but more of a statement of positions. It is clear, direct, and unequivocal and only briefly refers to the circumstances that necessitated its composition.[30]

It ends with a detail that might have been an anti-climax to the entire affair:

> After all the toil and effort, arbiters entered among them [the litigating parties], and achieved some kind of compromise. Yet we [R. Karo referring to himself] deemed it right to put things in writing, words of truth and sentences of justice, and God may benefit us to obey him.[31]

As in many cases in premodern societies, the legal formality of courts served as a channel leading to out-of-court negotiations, compromise, and appeasement (*pesharah* in Hebrew, *sulh* in Arabic and Turkish).[32] But this fact did not discourage R. Karo, and rightly so. The concrete case was less important in itself, since it served as a springboard to publicize his principled position regarding the status of law courts. Further, as we shall see in the next section ("Past Confrontations regarding Courts' Status"), this specific affair—despite its vague presentation under general phrases— was but a chain in a long sequence of events in Safed. Even after the concrete case ended beyond court procedures, and thus seemed to undermine the value of the entire responsum, the general issue at stake still remained.

The anonymous counter-responsum (ibid., §18) refutes Karo's key assertions. It opens with an overt denial of the special status of the court at Safed:

> Regarding what the distinguished rabbi [R. Karo] composed, that the Safed court of law is to be considered as an unrivaled supreme court of law, and hence not required to respond

---

29. See also below Ch. 9.
30. Shochetman, 'The Obligation to State Reasons for Legal Decisions', pp. 338–352.
31. Karo, *Responsa Avkat Rochel*, §17, p. 13b.
32. See above Introductory chapter, regarding my discussion on 'Anthropology of the Law'.

to the demand *Horuni mi-heikhan dantuni* [...] I am doomed, whether I speak or keep silent, as this concerns the desecration of God's name."[33]

With fear and trembling he approaches the issue of the Safedian Supreme Court, due to his intention to deny its special status. The fear of "desecrating God's name" refers to his claim that uncontrolled procedures would lead to judicial malfunctioning, unnecessary excommunications, and unchecked arrogance of judges.[34] This is not a theoretical or a speculative notion, but one firmly rooted in the functioning of courts at the time: "All the more so nowadays that we need to be concerned about malfunctioning courts of law, regarding various issues, as several later generations of halakhic arbiters have commented [...] [there are] corrupt judges, the ordained among them are many yet the knowledgeable are certainly few."[35] Absolving courts under such conditions from supplying the reasoning for their decisions is clearly unwise. Instead, the anonymous respondent proposes that if one of the litigating parties asks in a humble manner (*be-'anavah*) to receive the legal reasoning, then there is no obstacle to doing so.[36] The writer mentions a divorce case—a highly sensitive issue in the Halakhah—in which a grave mistake was prevented precisely due to the fact that the court supplied its reasoning and left the door open for the potential rediscussion of the case.[37] He even takes a step further and claims that a minor court is entitled to challenge a more superior one, if it provides valid arguments: "Hence [following a Talmudic argumentation] one can infer that a lesser court of law may challenge a supreme court as mistaken, on condition that it does not conduct itself arrogantly."[38] To substantiate his claims, he provides a no less

---

33. Karo, *Responsa Avkat Rochel*, §18, p. 14a. To intensify his challenge even further, he later claims that should there be a Supreme Court of Law at present time it would not reside in Safed but incorporated in the figure of R. Joseph Peso of Salonica. See *ibid.*, p. 14b: "... yet the court of the comprehensive Sage rabbi Yossef Peso and his encounter/place of old scholars function as Supreme Court. Since the time that devoted scholars are not to be found he handles his authority as a king in his regiment, with love and solidarity [with his colleagues], no harm should touch him, and he strictly commands his disciples ...".

34. *Ibid.*, §18 p. 14a: "What His Honor the Rabbi [R. Karo – R.W.] wrote that the Safed court functions as the Supreme Court, to be equaled with none other, and should NOT comply with the demand *Horuni miHeichan Dantuni* ... this causes the desecration of God's name. It is well-known that arrogant [judges] are very common, and each considers himself as second to none, claiming that they should not respond to the claim *Horuni miHeichan Dantuni*. It corrupts the courts, and causes them to issue unjust verdicts, and excommunicate the blameless".

35. *Ibid.*, §18, p. 13b.

36. *Ibid.*, p. 14a: "There is no Supreme Court.. for there are various opinions and Responsa are endless in their number. More, according to Rabbenu Tam, following the position of Maimonides, that if he [the litigant] asks humbly, saying you might have been mistaken, then it is customary to write him the courts' reasoning. Yet if he suspects [the court's integrity] there is no such need, it is permissible to mislead him".

37. *Ibid.*

38. *Ibid.*

impressive list than that provided by R. Karo of "big names" among past Talmudic scholars and arbiters who supported his position.

Karo's counter-responsum (*Ibid.*, §19) is longer and contains more juridical-halakhic discussions to validate his position. At the same time, it is also more polemical in tone and contains many disrespectful and blunt expressions aimed at his rival. Once more he insists on the special and unrivalled role of the supreme court in Safed:

> And so it is customary in the present time in a court accepted by the communities, such as the one in this place [Safed], as is well known to all, and its prestige spreads to all lands. It is considered as a supreme court of law, as presented in the writings of Maimonides [...] and so it is the rule nowadays, that there is no Supreme Court of Law, yet in certain places there are distinguished scholars, recognized by the communities, and [in the sense of "unlike"] other places with disciples, unlike them [in their Talmudic expertise].[39]

Here it is stated directly, paraphrasing Maimonides' code of law, that even though there is no "real" supreme court of law, courts comprising leading scholars and considered by local community as "Experts of the Law" (*mumchim la-rabbim*) serve as a substitute for, or as a continuing link to, the historical court in Jerusalem. Once again, R. Karo asserts as a matter of fact that the situation in Safed fulfills precisely these preconditions, and that this requires no verification. As we saw in §18, one of the leading Safed scholars challenged exactly this assertion.

Karo reiterates all the prohibiting conditions for demanding *Horuni mi-heikhan dan-tuni*, as mentioned in the Talmudic and post-Talmudic literature. But he then suddenly radicalizes his position by stating:

> It seems clear that even when a litigant is forced to come to a small [secondary juridical instance], the Talmudic rule is to provide him with reasoning, yet if he demands such, certainly he is NOT provided with it, but is placed under excommunication. He is considered as disparaging the court.[40]

Even the minimal condition for demanding legal reasoning—being forced by a local (and not a supreme) court to litigate there—is denied as a legitimate channel. The ensuing result, *pace* R. Karo, is that any demand and under any circumstance to ask *Horuni mi-heikhan dantuni* is illegitimate, considered an affront to the court and the rabbinical authorities, and merits excommunication. Again, this assertion is not to be taken literally as a halakhic-juridical rule and was not included in Karo's codes of law. It is rather part of a public campaign and a rhetorical slip of tongue in the overall effort to state a position: The Safed Supreme Court of Law is beyond appeal, as it serves as a substitute for the historical Sanhedrin of the golden days of old.

---

39. *Ibid.*, §19, p. 15b.
40. *Ibid.*

The second part of Responsum §19 states explicitly what was only hinted at in §17. The double responsa were composed in relation to a concrete case, putting a grave challenge on R. Karo's vision of the Jewish courts of law, especially the one in Safed:

> And the third [reasoning] is that this is a Supreme Court, accepted by the communities, as in this city [Safed], well-known and famous in the entire world, the litigant is not provided with legal reasoning, as I showed above. *This is true even if one of the judges helps him* [encourages him to do so]. The fourth [reasoning is that], even if the court was not considered as Supreme Court, the verdict is decided according to majority [among the judges]. Once it [the verdict] was issued and the litigant asked *Horuni mi-heikhan dantuni* in writing, he would be denied. I have already written above, that nowadays the Safed Supreme Court, accepted by many, has the authority of a Supreme Court of Law.[41]

After listing all the regular arguments, R. Karo approaches the core issue behind all the debate and the polemical rhetoric: The challenge to the rabbinical courts is presented not by some outside factor—either Jewish laypersons or Ottoman or Muslim authorities—but from within, by Jewish scholars, refusing to cooperate with the rules of the game. It seems that this affair was only but one incident in a long sequence of clashes. Yet it provided a suitable occasion to examine the differences between R. Karo and other colleagues in Safed, in regard to the changes of professional ethos in the rabbinical guild.

Past Confrontations regarding Courts' Status

As the polemics advances, R. Karo sharpens his tone:

> I consider it an utter waste of time to follow the paths you chose, since it is nothing but juvenile mischiefs and time wasting to argue with a person denying things as clear as daylight [...] you are accustomed from old time to act as you please against Jewish scholars, unjustly and contrary to the law; this is no new matter for you, and [you have done so] not once. From the day I met you, you have never retracted this comportment.[42]

The core issue that stirs Karo's ire is disobedience. Judges are not expected to agree on all matters in the case at hand, yet once a majority among them have reached a decision regarding the verdict, the minority is bound to accept it. If they are not willing to sign the verdict, they should at least abstain from publicizing their objections. Such an act could incite the offended party to continue the legal confrontation by other means or channels. Disobedience in the rabbinic milieu has a long history and attracted the attention of Talmudic scholars. A particular term was even adopted to refer to disobedient scholars: *zaqen mamreh* (insubordinate old man). Those so defined faced a sanction of exclusion from the rabbinical milieu, either temporarily or permanently. The anonymous rival—probably affiliated to R. Moses di Trani, against whom R. Karo directs his ire—is accustomed to act as he pleases and rejects rabbinical authority.

---

41. *Ibid.*, p. 16a.
42. *Ibid.*, p. 15b.

On a certain occasion, this anonymous scholar and judge actively supported one of the litigating parties and even encouraged it to oppose the court's decision. The legal trickery was the claim *Horuni mi-heikhan dantuni* reinforced by the fact that the defendant was informed that the judges were not unanimous regarding the verdict:

> Your position in this case is unthinkable, as you stirred the defendant against us, to unjusti-fiably rebel against us, and to reject the verdict unless he sees your signature. You are bound to sign, to silence him, and to prevent him from informing us [to the local Qadi or Ottoman authorities] [...] Your claims run counter to the Talmudic provisions, since as a rule courts are to be trusted in their decisions, and one court does not overrule the verdicts of a previ-ous one, nor can one of the presiding judges on the bench claim "I cannot rule in this case and refuse to join their words" [verdict]. More so, these words of yours contradict what you told the Sages that you are bound to sign [the verdict], and so you will. Later on you fooled them [...] Regarding what you said that they [the two contending parties in court] should reach a compromise. Your habits are known even among babies in their cradle, that when you wish to acquit someone you claim such things [that you cannot reach a verdict like the other judges], so that both parties will reach a compromise as you seem right, and this act is an outright injustice, as is well known.[43]

According to Karo, informing the defendant of the discord among the judges incited him to rebel against the Supreme Court of Safed. Moreover, anyone reading the ver-dict would notice the absent signature of this anonymous judge. His act is rebuked as lacking any Talmudic basis, since the court is generally not mistaken in his judgment; moreover, this anonymous judge had his opportunity to persuade others that his posi-tion was more valid and failed to do so. This scholar judge is not neutral in his position, stating his hypothetical indecisiveness ("you do not claim 'I cannot rule in this case'") but actively oppose the majority position and seeks to annul the verdict from outside the courtroom by inciting the defendant to claim *Horuni mi-heikhan dantuni*, thereby enabling him to transfer the case to another court (Salonica or Istanbul, perhaps). A more plau-sible option is to remove the case from the formal juridical channel according to the Halakhah and refer it for arbitration (*pesharah*). For Karo, this effort denied the other party his right for justice ("this act is an outright injustice, as is well known").

Karo was right in his lament that such confrontations were not a rarity in Safed ("you are accustomed from old time to act as you please against Jewish scholars ... Your habits are known even among babies in their cradle"). In his extensive and impor-tant work, Meir Benayahu examined a sequence of similar clashes over a period of almost 40 years, especially between R. Karo and his rabbinical "rival" R. Moses di Trani.[44] He detected a recurrent pattern in most cases: R. di Trani—an opinionated

43. *Ibid.*, p. 16a.
44. Meir Benayahu, 'The Schools of R. Moses di Trani and R. Joseph Karo and their Confontation' [Hebrew], in: idem., *Joseph My Chosen One* [Hebrew], Jerusalem: Yad HaRav Nissim, 1991, pp. 9–98. Haim Z. Dimitrovsky, 'A Dispute between Rabbi J. Caro and Rabbi M. Trani' [Hebrew], *Sefunot. Studies and Sources on the History of the Jewish Communities in the East* 6(1962), pp. 71–123.

personality[45]—resisted the position of others when sitting on the bench with other judges in court or when asked to provide a legal ruling in a responsum or add his confirming signature to responsa composed by other arbiters. Many of the testimonies were provided by Karo himself, and as such are obviously biased. But for our discussion, this is actually an advantage, as it offers fulsome insight into Karo's positions and vision over such protracted confrontations. Often he blamed di Trani for shifting the legal discussions out of court space to the public area, which he regarded not only as displaying a lack of solidarity with other local rabbis, but more importantly as undermining the authority of the leading court of law in Safed. It is not superfluous to add that these cases represent only a small minority among the hundreds discussed in the Supreme Court in Safed during the life of R. Beirav and after his death under the three leading scholars and arbiters: R. Karo, R. Moses di Trani, and R. Israel Di Curiel. But their importance lies in the way they mark the borders between accepted norms of justice and court procedures and those regarded as breaking the rules. The disobedience of R. di Trani, or what was presented as such, caused important scholars in Safed to consider the option of putting him under ban, until he receded and accepted the consensual position of his colleagues. The sequence of such cases indicated that Jewish courts in Safed were undergoing a profound change toward increasing formality and institutional regulation.

The Ottoman Settings

The hierarchical and centralistic character of the legal system in the Ottoman Empire during the early modern period has already been presented.[46] The period of Sultan Süleyman witnessed the increasing power of the head of this intricate machinery. The man most identified with this change was Ebu Su'ud, serving for long years as Şeyḫülislâm under Süleyman.[47] Ebu Su'ud managed to re-establish this post as the leading juridical person in the entire empire. His position enabled him to nominate the local judges in the core lands of the Ottoman Empire and after the extensive conquests during the sixteenth century in the Arab lands as well. The role of Ottoman judges made them one of the important points of encounter between the local population and the Ottoman ruling polity and elite. His authority and functioning represented the Ottoman authority; the commitment to procure justice for all population living under this rule was considered as one of the pillars of legitimacy of sultanic rulership. Next to them functioned the muftis whose legal opinions and rules, as expressed in *fatwa* in response to concrete cases, carried much weight in court proceedings.

Ottoman legal (and political) authorities responded harshly when the rulings of judges or muftis were disregarded. Ottoman muftis ruled in the early sixteenth century

---

45. Idem., 'Rabbi Moses ben Yosef di Trani' [Hebrew], in: *Joseph My Chosen One*, pp. 101–151.
46. See the introductory chapter.
47. On his position and role during the era of Süleyman, see Colin Imber, *Ebu's-su'ud. The Islamic Legal Tradition*, Edinburgh: Edinburgh U.P., 1997.

that scornful treatment of a legal ruling issued by an officially appointed mufti was blasphemy. The famous sixteenth-century Şeyḫülislâm Kemâlpaşazâde stated that a person who disparaged a ruling by questioning its relevance to an unspecified case should renew his faith and be severely punished (ta'zîr balîġ).[48] Such a ruling had a precedent in Hanafi schools, but now it was enforced as state policy.

The strict observance of rulings issued by muftis and judges nominated by Ottoman authorities was all the more valid in regard to the Şeyḫülislâm. As Ömer Lütfi Barkan pointed out, questioning the validity of the chief muftīs ruling was considered "a major transgression against the religious and social order." Chief muftīs increasingly underscored the binding and enforceable nature of their legal opinions, insisting that all members of the Ottoman learned hierarchy, muftīs and judges alike, were to follow their rulings. When Şeyḫülislâm Sun'ullah Efendi (d. 1612) was asked about a judge who was not "following the şerî'at, the imperial edicts, and the şer'î fatwa" in his rulings, Sun'ullah Efendi replied that this judge should be removed from office, punished, and denounced as a heretic (kâfir olur) for abasing the sacred law. It is clear that the ruling in question was issued by an official jurisconsult, perhaps even by the chief mufti himself.[49] The opinions of the Şeyḫülislâm had an effect on legal procedures in court and affected quite often by the verdicts, either in courts within Ottoman core land in Anatolia and Rumelia[50] as well as in Arab lands. Judith Tucker has drawn attention to the congruence between the muftis' rulings and the judges' resolutions. Cases from sixteenth- and seventeenth-century Jerusalem, for example, suggest that litigants sought to obtain a fatwa from the chief mufti or from the officially appointed provincial mufti in Jerusalem, since their opinions carried particular weight in court.[51]

Within the machinery of state justice, there were important distinctions in the legal functioning of state-nominated judges and muftis, and certainly in regard to the person heading the legal machinery, the Şeyḫülislâm. One of the distinguishing marks of his superiority was that he was not obliged to cite the legal sources used in his legal opinions and decisions. Hezârfen Hüseyin Efendi, a seventeenth-century historian and encyclopedist, analyzed the differences between different ranks of Muftis:

> He merely explains that their rank is lower than the chief muftīs. Their lower rank is reflected in the requirement that they mention the authoritative text (nukûl) they consulted for their ruling, whereas the chief muftī was not expected to do so.[52]

It marked the different grades within the juridical hierarchy and legal guild, and also could further serve the capital city in controlling the judges elsewhere. The obligation

---

48. Guy Burak, *The Second Formation of Islamic Law. The Hanafi School the Early Modern Ottoman Empire*, Cambridge: Cambridge U.P., 2015, p. 60.

49. *Ibid.*, p. 60–61.

50. *Ibid.*, esp. p. 61.

51. *Ibid.*, pp. 61–62.

52. *Ibid.*, pp. 40, 58.

to cite the books of law ensured that judges followed the right books. The legal standardization was based on a list of books approved by the Şeyḫülislâm that state-nominated personnel in the justice machinery were expected to follow. In the words of Guy
Burak:

> The emergence of a corpus of "books of high repute" or "reliable texts" was accompa-
> nied by surveillance mechanisms that were meant to ensure that members of the imperial
> learned hierarchy consulted only these texts in their rulings and writings. It is in this con-
> text that we might recall Hezârfen Hüseyin Efendi's comment, that one of the main differ-
> ences between the chief muftī (the *şeyḫülislâm*) and the provincial muftīs (*kenâr müftîleri*) is
> that the latter are required to cite the texts they consulted for their ruling (*nükûl*). Another
> example is Murâd III's (r. 1574–95) 1594 imperial edict to the judge and the local appointed
> muftī of the Anatolian town of Balıkesir, perhaps in response to a petition submitted by
> the judge himself, demanding the proper citation of the jurisprudential works on which he
> relied (*nakl yazmak*). According to the submitted complaint, the muftī of Balıkesir used to
> reply by merely stating "yes" or "no" without referring to any legal authority. By explicitly
> mentioning the texts, the appointed muftīs demonstrated their adherence to the imperial
> jurisprudential canon of "texts of high repute." What is more, they enabled their superiors,
> and also those who solicited their opinions, to inspect their use of the texts.[53]

Another element distinguishing the Şeyḫülislâm from other legal experts and scholars
concerned the production and phrasing of *fatwa*. Again, it was the same Ebu Su'ud
who created a professional and highly efficient mechanism to provide an impressive
number of legal rulings for people addressing him in capital city of Istanbul from across
the Empire. The system which Ebu Su'ud had instituted became sophisticated and
the questions reaching the Şeyḫülislâm were already framed and edited by his professional staff, so that he was required to add no more than a simple "yes" or "no" answer
and his signature. After his time, it was the highly trained and permanent staff that
effectively did most of the work, ensuring continuity and maintaining legal standards
in *fatawa*.[54] It was the privilege of the man heading the legal system to provide short
answers, without adding the legal reference, and adjoining no reasoning for his precise
decision. It was a sign of authority and control, reserved for one person. Opposing his
positions, in court procedures or as stated in a *fatwa*, was considered as impudent and
at times dangerous.

Summary: The Ottoman Settings of the *Horuni mi-heikhan dantuni* Controversy

The discussion over the *Horuni mi-heikhan dantuni* rule seems to be a technical discussion,
hundreds of which preoccupied Jewish scholars in the early modern Mediterranean
Basin. It is indeed so, as it resonates a long chain of post-Talmudic discussions regarding

---

53. Ibid., pp. 152–153.
54. Imber, *Ebu's-su'ud. The Islamic Legal Tradition*, p. 14.

halakhic procedures. As such, it attracted very little interest from Jewish historians and historians of Jewish law during the early modern period in particular. It is very tempting to fall into this trap and consider the entire debate taking place in mid-sixteenth century and beyond in Safed as formalistic and trivial. The entire discussion is conducted in halakhic legalese, referring effusively to discussions in the Talmud, Gaonic literature, and medieval Responsa and Talmudic commentaries, and paying little, if any, attention to the world beyond the Talmudic schools. Yet as much as this discussion has the appearance of an academic debate among Jewish scholars, it has a history of its own. *Horuni mi-heikhan dantuni* was constantly discussed, but always in regard to other issues, such as the authority of the local court of a relatively small community in comparison to prestigious courts of big communities, in relation to various aspects of court procedures, or in the context of commentaries on Talmudic discussions. It was Karo who, for the first time, turned it into an issue *sui generis*. Indeed, it became a pivotal theme around which to weave other elements in Jewish legality and the "production of justice."

The Talmudic and post-Talmudic discussions in this regard were relatively simple: if a litigant was forced to be adjudicated in a local court, he was entitled to ask for the legal reasoning. This meant, in general, a summary of the documents and testimonies and the final verdict rather than an elaborate exposition of the legal rationale behind the final verdict. Further, the litigant could address a higher legal instance whenever he suspected some kind of court malfunction in his case. The various discussions regarding the rights of litigants vis-à-vis the courts did not reach a consensus, and many Jewish scholars were inclined to enlarge the permission or even obligation to provide legal reasoning.

What characterized Jewish legal tradition and its mechanisms was the manifest gap between the elaborate and sophisticated juridical tradition and halakhic scholarship, on the one hand, and the very limited capability to enforce halakhic decisions, on the other. After the Gaonic period, Jewish legal autonomy was exceedingly restricted, certainly in medieval Europe and around the Mediterranean Basin. Its power depended on the voluntary cooperation of Jewish "clients" and solidarity with the Jewish Diaspora. This could certainly lead to fragmentation and centrifugal tendencies, which could only be avoided through a profound commitment to a centralistic ethos woven over many centuries by scholars and rabbis. Addressing Jewish courts of law—rather than "Gentile" ones (*'Arka'ot shel goyim* is the Talmudic term)—furnished a further element of internal solidarity. The Jewish elite associate these juridical institutions with collective past memories, including a link to the city of Jerusalem, the Holy Temple, and the Sanhedrin when it still played a leading role. The Sages presented themselves as the bearers of the unique heritage, including in the legal-normative domain. The fragmentation, caused by the lack of a political center, and its consequent limited legal autonomy, posed a serious challenge to their functioning as religious elite. These weaknesses could be remedied, at least temporarily, by means of two factors intended to encourage consensus among scholars: (i) the figure of a leading scholar (*Gedol Ha-Dor*) serving a focal and ultimate address for legal counseling and halakhic rulings; (ii) An internal hierarchy among Jewish courts, in which the "lesser" ones, functioning predominantly in small communities, were subjected to the authority of leading and centralistic courts or even to a single court regarded as a supreme court of law (*Beit-Din Ha-Gadol*).[55]

The Talmudic and post-Talmudic discussions regarding the theme *Horuni mi-heikhan dantuni*, and their continuation later through the Middle Ages and well into the early modern period, are not only important in relation to technicalities and formal procedures of Jewish courts. Above all, they mirror wider and more fundamental issues: how were justice, social order, authority, and law conceptualized and practiced in various periods and historical circumstances? What were the interactions between uniquely Jewish traditions and the broader non-Jewish legal traditions? Were global changes in legal history during the early modern period in the Eurasian context mirrored among the Jewish minority? These questions bear a direct relevancy to the debate on the relatively restricted and technical issue of furnishing a litigant with legal reasoning.

R. Karo was an innovator in this respect, too. He turned *Horuni mi-heikhan dantuni* into a theme of its own rather than a secondary issue attached to other Talmudic discussions.[56] In two relatively elaborate responsa, he presented this demand as impudent and illegitimate. Since it harms the prestige of court, of judges, and of Jewish heritage in general, he argued that such a request merited the harsh reaction of excommunication. These responsa were more polemical than halakhic in their general nature, particularly the second one addressed to an anonymous rival. The issue at stake was not the status of Jewish courts, in general, but that of a very specific court: the central one in the city of Safed, headed by R. Jacob Beirav and following his death by three leading scholars: R. Karo, R. Moses di Trani, and R. Israel Di Curiel. This court of law functioned, according to Karo, not as a standard city court in a city where each ethnic Jewish group maintained its own court of law but as a supra-ethnic and centralized institution. The presence of prestigious scholars, such as himself and his erudite colleagues, endowed the court with special status: it functioned as a supreme court of law echoing past glories of the Holy Land and the Sanhedrin. Its authority was to spread not only over the city of Safed, but over the entire Jewish Ecumene. Indeed it was in practice addressed by communities and individuals beyond the urban context of Safed. This claim was not necessarily a Talmudic or scholarly one, but an assertion of a political tone. It sought to establish a new focal point of power and authority by presenting the Safedian central court as a link and continuation of authoritative courts of the Jewish past, especially the historical and prestigious one in Jerusalem. As a political statement, it was flatly denied by the anonymous rival of R. Karo, one of his eminent colleagues in Safed.

---

55. These double mechanisms are discussed from another perspective on Ch. 4, in relation to rabbinic *Semichah*.

56. See another Responsum of a sixteenth-century Polish rabbi, of clear academic and scholastic character, where there is hardly any reference to concrete circumstances behind its composition: R. Joel b. Samuel Sirkish [known as *HaBach*], *Responsa (The Old Ones)* [*Shut HaBach Ha-Yeshanot* in Hebrew], New York: 1966, §22.

Sephardi rabbis constantly lamented their precarious position in communities under the Ottoman Empire throughout the sixteenth century.[57] Their freedom of action was limited by the Ottoman authorities, and their prestige and verdicts were often challenged by members of the Sephardi communities. Still, the real impediment, according to R. Karo, to the formation of an institution of prestige and authority, recognized as dominant and commanding in the entire Jewish Ecumene, were the scholars of Talmudic erudition and officiating rabbis. The concluding part of his second responsum (§19) is a sharp polemic against a specific scholar, but still more so against others who concur with him. No wonder, since his vision of such a centralistic court of law, headed by a joint collective but later to be headed by him alone,[58] was a true innovation in Jewish legal tradition. It could not but limit the traditional liberty of other Jewish scholars, and hence invite such a polemical response by the anonymous scholar.

The opposition by this unknown scholar touches on the hard core of R. Karo's vision for a universal and centralistic court. The joint work and solidarity among judges of such a court is injured by the incitement of a litigant to request *Horuni mi-heikhan dantuni*— a relatively simple challenge, and one that is partially legitimized in the Halakhah. Precisely this act is considered as opposing and challenging its position as an ultimate legal instance. The recurring allusion of R. Karo to the Supreme Court in Jerusalem, the Sanhedrin, appears to constitute an attempt to substantiate his claim on a legal-formalistic basis, but no less importantly to provide legitimacy for his vision in light of recurring cases of opposition among Safed scholars.

His colleague and rival of almost four decades, R. Moses di Trani, headed this opposition. These two dominant and talented persons cooperated closely at the central court of law in Safed. Oftentimes, one of these scholars would compose the verdict and the other joins him by signing on this document as token of approval. Still on several occasions they disagreed, and R. di Trani challenged the court and R. Karo personally by inciting the litigant—offended by the verdict—to ask the court to state its reasoning. Such acts were not only offensive to R. Karo, his colleagues, and their honor;[59] disregarding the officiating judges impaired the status of such a court and its stability. A position such as di Trani's ran counter to the classical rabbinic rules of court procedures in general, and turned the functioning of the court of law into an *ad hominem* confrontation between two individuals. The claim of R. Karo had a wider horizon, seeking to reinstate the institutional status of *Beit-Din Ha-Gadol* like the one in previous times. The institution comes first, before the persons officiating. He *Horuni* request challenges the

---

57. Joseph Hacker, 'Jewish Autonomy in the Ottoman Empire: Its Scope and Limits. Jewish Courts from the Sixteenth to the Eighteenth Centuries', in: Avigdor Levy (ed.), *The Jews of the Ottoman Empire*, Princeton, NJ: Darwin Press in cooperation with the Institute of Turkish Studies, Washington, D.C, 1994, pp. 153–202.

58. See Ch. 8, on the construction of 'International Court of Law', headed by R. Karo.

59. Karo, *Responsa Avkat Rochel*, §19, p. 16a: "God knows and testifies that we are ashamed and embarrassed, since he who erodes the Honor of one of the colleagues [*Chaverim* in Hebrew, in the sense of 'Rabbis' – R.W.] in this matter, erodes the Honor of us all". See Ch. 4, on the issue of Honor ethos among Sephardi communities and rabbis.

court's status, and more so the position of its heading person—R. Karo, and the principle of hierarchy among scholars.

The vision of a universalistic court of law (authoritative in the entire Jewish Ecumene), residing in the new center in the Holy Land (the city of Safed),[60] the final legal instance, and headed by a leading scholar of present generation (naturally R. Karo himself),[61] and finally the composition of comprehensive double codes of law, all responded to the Ottoman settings. The establishment of the widest Empire in Islamic history relied on the construction of a centralistic and hierarchical mechanism. The management of this wide machinery was conducted from the capital city, by imposing the nomination of Ottoman judges rather than local persons, their training in prestigious schooling system in the main Turkish cities, and the requirement that they follow a list of "trusted books" and *fatawa* composed by Ottoman Hanafi scholars. At the head stood the Şeyḫülislâm, a state-nominated official whose rules and decisions carried the weight of the Sultan's delegated authority. His status as head of the legal guild was manifested by the fact that, unlike local or regional judges and muftis, nominated by him or his predecessors, he was not constrained to state the reasons for his legal rulings or his *fatawa*. His decisions were beyond appeal, the last word of legal authority. The highly efficient mechanism established by Ebu Su'ud, a contemporary of R. Karo, enabled him to provide a quick response to legal queries dispatched from the entire Ottoman Empire. The questions rephrased by the professional clerks working under him enabled the provision of a short yes-or-no answer. No legal reasoning was attached to such answers. It was the privilege of one person, a sign of his authority, and of the authority of the state.

---

60. On the competitive tension between Jerusalem and Safed, see Ch. 8, esp. §8.2.
61. See Chs. 6, 8.

Chapter Eight

ESTABLISHING AN INTERNATIONAL COURT OF LAW

Jewish communities during the Middle Ages adhered to their local.[1] This was also apparent in their legal institutions, so that internal juridical and ritual matters were commonly discussed by local rabbinical authorities or lay leaders. More controversial and complicated issues were addressed to Talmudic scholars of the same district or Diaspora (Sephardi, Ashkenazi, Italian, North African, etc.). It would have been almost unthinkable, and was indeed rare to dispatch a halakhic query from Spain to Ashkenaz and vice versa. This fragmentation was not due only to communication barriers, but mainly because they were considered as distinct halakhic heritages. The fragmentary character continued to a large extent in early modern period, though there was a slow but steady shift toward supra-local institutions. R. Karo's attempt to found a new type of court that was intended to extend its authority beyond the Muslim lands, which relates precisely to this course of change. Like other elements in his grand program, it was not a completely new pattern, but neither was it a mere continuation. The innovative dimension was the aspiration to serve the entire Jewish Ecumene; in other words, Karo sought to establish an international court of law—the first in Jewish tradition since the Gaonic period of late antiquity. An international legal pattern of this kind evolved in the European context, and following the colonial expansion in the New World, inspired by legal-theological discussions of the "Second Scholasticism." No less significant in this context are the changes in the Ottoman Empire at the time, following its impressive expansion into new territories, and accompanied by the imposition of the same state law in all the territories under Ottoman rule. State law was international in its special extent, and the Ottoman courts adjusted to the same legal traditions across the empire.

International Law in European and Ottoman Empires

The rise of international law, as practiced today by the United Nations, the International Court of Justice, and similar institutions, is described in most current research as a derivative of political and ideological changes in early modern European history. Scholars of international law, in its various domains, are predominantly interested

---

1. Avraham Grossman and Yosef Kaplan (eds.), *Kehal Yisrael – Jewish Self-Rule through the Ages*, Vol. 2 – 'The Middle Ages and Early Modern Period', Jerusalem: Shazar Center for Jewish History, 2004.

in the rise of modern centralist states and the unprecedented colonial expansion of some European grand states—such as Spain and England—into the New World.[2] State-oriented scholars consider the Westphalia Peace (1648) between Catholic and Protestant political rulers in Europe as a paradigmatic moment in establishing a political pact based on inter-state juridical balance. In other words, law became a regulator of interaction between states, beyond its classical function within states or communities. The Tordesillas Pact (1494), which arranged the division of the Americas between the two Iberian maritime powers, attracts the attention of empire-oriented scholars. These political agreements had extensive repercussions in later European political and military history, and no less so in future political theories. They were based on Roman law, which enjoyed a renaissance in early modern era, though it was now applied entirely in new circumstances. The encounter with significant non-Christian populations and the fundamental importance of oceans in the establishment of the colonial empires charged the old juridical concepts of "Roman" law with new vigor when applied to territories and maritime spaces beyond the European pale and civilization, characterized as no man's land (the legal term was *terra nullius*).[3] Spain was certainly one of the leading imperial powers and more specifically the Castilian court heading the recently united Spain. It also set the scene for innovative discussions in the theological context, leaving an important imprint on the political domain. The theology faculty at the University of Salamanca housed some of the innovative discussions regarding the privileges of various states in the new domains, their rights in relation to conquered native populations, and the importance of neutral space at sea. The discussions of Francisco de Vitoria and his successors in Salamanca, and others contributing to the "Second Scholastics" in Europe, informed both his contemporaries and later jurists of international law, such as Hugo Grotius, Samuel Pufendorf, Christian Wolf, and Emer de Vattel.[4]

The state-centered perspective of law historians has recently been recognized as a European perspective, projecting backward the rise of modern state and its radiating affect over the entire globe. Historians of early modern Europe have acknowledged that theological and juridical discussions on "international law" were merely a front for other factors, such as messianic aspirations and the political clash between Christian Europe and the expanding Ottoman Empire, with the fears this aroused. In short, constructing worldwide empires played a fundamental role in the rise of international law. It was empires, and not proto-national states, that provided the background for

---

2. The secondary literature on this subject is immense; see for instance John H. Elliot, *Empires of the Atlantic. Britain and Spain in America 1492–1830*, Yale: Yale U.P., 2006.

3. Martti Koskenniemi, 'Introduction: International Law and Empire—Aspects and Approaches', in: Idem., Walter Rech, Manuel Jiménez Fonseca (eds.), *International Law and Empire Historical Explorations*, Oxford: Oxford U.P., 2016, pp. 1–18; José María Beneyto and Justo Corti Varela (eds.), *At the Origins of Modernity. Francisco de Vitoria and the Discovery of International Law*, Cham, Switzerland: Springer, 2017.

4. Anthony Pagden, 'Introduction: Francisco de Vitoria and the Origins of the Modern Global Order', in: Beneyto and Corti Varela (eds.), *At the Origins of Modernity*, pp. 1–17.

the rise of international law, in both its juridical theory and politico-legal practice.[5] The works of John Headley offer a seminal contribution regarding the political vision of Mercurino Arborio de Gattinara, the secretary and secretive councilor behind the empire of Charles V. The territories of his kingdom encompassed wide parts of Europe, allowing him to be cast as a leader of a miraculous time, participating in a prophetic scheme of history. The early modern vision was inspired by medieval religious and political prophecy and received its ultimate stamp under the influence of the twelfth-century Calabrian abbot, Joachim of Fiore, particularly concerning the idea of the progressive and triple-phase elaboration of world history, culminating in the Age of the Spirit and politico-religious renewal. The Joachimite pattern aspired to witness a time of an outstanding ruler, a monarch of the whole world, a second Charlemagne, repeatedly identified either with a current French *Rex Christianissimus* or with a German *Rex Romanorum* who would renew the church, chastise its ministers, conquer the Turk, and—like David—gather all sheep into one fold. Some expositors of the Joachimite tradition believed that an angelic pope, a *pastor angelicus*, shunning temporal goods and collaborating with the savior-emperor, would rule the Holy See.[6] Biblical motives and medieval apocalyptic visions were among the factors that spawned a broad political vision of unified Europe and a renewed religious and community life. The present time was regarded as a continuation of the times of both King David and Charlemagne, incorporated in one person: Charles V.

Justice and law played a fundamental role in this international vision of Gattinara, and Charles V. Gattinara charged the emperor with the task

> to declare, interpret, correct, emend, and renew the imperial laws by which to order the entire world, it is most reasonable that in following up the suggestions [*vestiges*] of the good emperor Justinian, your Caesaric Majesty should early select the most outstanding jurists that one may find to undertake the reformation of the imperial laws and to advise on all possible means for the abbreviation of trials and for presenting such clear laws that the entire world may be inclined to make use of them and that one may say in effect that there is but a single emperor and a single universal law.[7]

He placed Justinian as a model for the emperor and cited Celsus, a famous jurist of late antiquity, that the emperor is the Vicar of God in his empire in order to accomplish justice in the temporal sphere. He is the prince of justice. The plan was inspired by the Dantean vision of a jurist emperor, the guardian and expositor of Roman law who as *dominus mundi* (the world's ruler) champions justice and the law through a preeminent moral and juridical authority rather than imposing them by force. Dante's political writings had enjoyed support during the fourteenth century in the teaching of the famous

---

5. John M. Headley, 'The Habsburg World Empire and the Revival of Ghibellinism', in: David Armitage (ed.), *Theories of Empire, 1450–1800*, London & New York: Routledge, 2016, pp. 45–79. Citation from *ibid.*, p. 65.

6. *Ibid.*, p. 46. See also *ibid.*, pp. 50, 56, 66.

7. *Ibid.*, p. 51.

Italian jurist Bartolus, and the medieval vision was now resurrected.[8] Like Justinian, Charles V was expected to become a legislator for an entire empire, legitimizing his universal rule by *justitia et pax* (justice and peace), the two great correlates of Augustine.

Among the various people comprising his wide empire, the Spanish—or more precisely the Castilians—were depicted as the "Chosen People" charged with pursuing this grand mission within the confines of Europe, and certainly in the New World. The Spanish humanist Alfonso de Valdés[9] identified the Spaniards as the elected people of God and presented the imperial victory and unification of Spain as preceding an ambitious political plan to attack the Turks and the Moors, recover the empire of Constantinople, and retake the Holy Sepulcher in Jerusalem. This would fulfill the words of the Redeemer, "Fiet unum ovile et unus pastor" ("Let there be one flock and one shepherd").[10] Catholic-Castilian superiority is pertinent to the Jewish context, since the Castilian Jews were the dominant collective among the Jewish-Iberian Diaspora, established after the expulsion. Their political, religious, linguistic, and legal concepts prevailed over the other Jewish-Iberian traditions.[11]

The rise and urgency of establishing a European empire was not isolated from its immediate environment and was certainly linked to the non-European context, especially challenged by the rise of the Ottoman Empire and its rapid expansion into European territories. The siege of Vienna marked the culmination of this threat and unleashed deep fears all over Europe. The advance of the Ottoman troops was read as a universal cataclysm; it sent tremors throughout Europe and aroused terror even among the humanist community. Erasmus composed one of the most bellicose tracts that flooded the press: *Consolation concerning the Turkish War together with an Exposition of Psalm 28*. This was the last work ever to be read by Gattinara before his death. Even Juan Luis Vivés, an outstanding proponent of peace and concord among Christian princes, now rejected any accommodation and urged common action against the Turks.[12]

On the other side of the power equation stood Süleyman "the Law Giver," a grand ruler and military leader with a political vision no less broad and universal than that proposed to Charles V by Gattinara. Kaya Şahin presented its various aspects. His advisors—very much like Gattinara—portrayed the Ottoman sultan on a global and historical scale as a figure battling the forces of evil and claiming supremacy over both Muslims and Christians. The belligerent and apocalyptic phase of the first half of his sultanate gave way to a more docile and culturally and religiously conservative discourse on justice and order. Again, this echoed past traditions, such as references to ancient Iranian kings and Alexander the Great. The early modern monarch became

---

8. *Ibid.*, pp. 50–51. See also *ibid.*, p. 53.
9. *Ibid.*, p. 56: "Alfonso de Valdés, who had been a permanent scribe in the imperial chancellery since 1521 and became one of its Latin secretaries in 1526".
10. *Ibid.*, pp. 51, 56.
11. See the discussion on Ch. 2.
12. Headley, 'The Habsburg World Empire and the Revival of Ghibellinism', esp. pp. 66–67. See also Alan Mikhail, *God's Shadow. Sultan Selim, His Ottoman Empire, and the Making of Modern World*, New York: Liveright, 2020, passim.

the figure around whom revolved the new ideas of universal monarchy, the ideals of religious rectitude and salvation, and the search for justice. The title of caliph, accorded to Süleyman as early as 1524, implied a unification of spiritual and temporal authority or a mixture of divine sanction and personal accomplishment. Süleyman was also called *sahib-kıran*, the conqueror born under an auspicious astrological conjunction, and thus destined to rule over the whole world.[13]

Lauren Benton noted the challenge that faces empires when they expand and construct bureaucratic institutions, confronting legal diversity and local traditions regarding law and justice.[14] Efficient administration and control of wide territories and various ethnic groups required some kind of equilibrium between the domineering pressure from the capital city or the center and the local foci of juridical autonomy. Toward the late sixteenth century, this power equation tended to favor state domination. The Ottoman authorities increased their efforts to bend the conquered populations of the Arab territories to their patterns of law and justice. As a predominantly agrarian society and economy, the Ottoman legal hegemony revolved around the administration of the land under the *timar* system, and its regulation demonstrated predominantly by formal state legislation, the *Kanuname*. Local institutions in a conquered region had to be somewhat "Ottomanized" in order for the *timar* system to be established, after a careful survey of population, lands, and resources in the area. Each official land registry, or *deftar*, included a listing of Kanun laws to be applied in the province. Halil Inalcik noted the continuity of these *Kanuname*s and the way they fused Ottoman laws with pre-conquest practices, so long as the latter did not clash with imposed law.[15]

Safed as a Jewish Metropolis

Jewish history and internal life was characterized by two opposing and competing predispositions: the *centrifugal* predisposition toward locality, zealous maintenance of communal independence, and resistance to centralistic authorities, alongside the *centripetal* predisposition toward the cultivation of a pan-Jewish network and solidarity. This second predisposition was manifested by shared activity to free ransomed Jewish captives, a collective heritage of liturgy, rituals, calendar, and sacred canon, shared messianic visions, and the centrality of the Holy Land.[16] During the early modern period, Jewish community life and cultural religious traditions slowly tipped toward the centripetal direction, searching for new and more dominant foci of leadership

13. Kaya Şahin, *Empire and Power in the Reign of Süleyman. Narrating the Sixteenth-Century Ottoman World*, Cambridge: Cambridge U.P., 2013, pp. 187–189.
14. Lauren Benton, *Law and Colonial Cultures. Legal Regimes in World History, 1400–1900*, Cambridge: Cambridge U.P., 2004, passim.
15. *Ibid.*, pp. 109–110.
16. See the wide-perspective discussion in Ben-Zion Dinur, *People of Israel in Exile [Israel baGolah in Hebbrew]*, Tel-Aviv: Dvir Publishing House, 1959, Vol. I/1, pp. V-L.

and authority[17]—regarding the political–institutional aspects—and accompanied by a search for clearer boundaries between the Jewish culture and religious heritage and non-Jewish traditions. The codification project of R. Karo certainly constituted a further and significant contribution to the centripetal predisposition. The shift toward centralization was clearly related to increasing, and at times massive, Jewish immigrations and expulsions, especially across the Mediterranean Basin. In another geographical, cultural, and political setting—the formation of a new center of Jewish life in Central and Eastern Europe (especially in Poland, Bohemia, and the Ukraine)—similar processes of centralization took place.

Some cities became dominant in their political or cultural roles and left their mark on others, inspiring the periphery to follow their patterns. The city of Safed became a microcosm of the Jewish Ecumene, reflecting the deep changes undergone by Jewish culture through the early modern period. To start with, the Jewish presence in the city emblematized a "return to the East," to the original cradle of Jewish culture within the confines of the Holy Land. As in the classical Gaonic period, during which the entire Jewish Diaspora could find a prosperous and well-established center under Gaonic leadership, the Safed Jews were part of a large and prosperous Ottoman Empire at its height during the sultanate of Selim I and Süleyman *Kanuni*, the conquerors and founders of Ottoman rule over Arabic territories. As for administrative and direct political rule, the city belonged to the area of *Bilad a-Sham* (Great Syria), managed from its center in Damascus. In the early sixteenth century, the city of Safed enjoyed economic prosperity, enabling a striking increase in the Jewish population.[18] It owed much to the dominance of Jewish communities in textile production and trade within the Ottoman Empire and the formation of a quasi-monopoly on supplying uniforms to the army, especially the *Yeniçeris*. From a marginal city in the Holy Land, Safed became the leading city, home to the largest Jewish community.

Safed attracted Jewish immigration from the entire Jewish Diaspora, and each distinct Jewish tradition could find its representatives in that city. In this sense too, it functioned as a Jewish microcosm and a sort of laboratory of modernity. Its inhabitants had the sense of a big place and a kind of "capital city" of the Jewish Ecumene. This was explicitly stated by R. Karo in the opening words of his responsa collection *Avqat Rokhel*: "Safed is the best place[19] in the entire world" (*"Tzefat hi tzvi le-chol ha-aratzot"*).[20] It ranked alongside the other big cities in the Ottoman Empire, where Jewish life and culture also prospered and witnessed a religious renaissance, such as Istanbul and Salonica and later Izmir. Safed was unique in hosting the most significant concentration of various Jewish traditions: from the Maghreb (Morocco) and North-Africa, Italy, Iberia—Portuguese and Sephardi, Ashkenazi, Provençale, local-*Musta'arbi*, former Byzantine—*Romanioti*,

---

17. Elisheva Carlebach, *The Pursuit of Heresy. Rabbi Moses Hagiz and the Sabbatian Controversies*, New York: Columbia U.P., 1990, esp. p. 2, discusses the early modern Jewish 'quest for center'.
18. See Lawrence Fine, *Physician of the Soul, Healer of the Cosmos. Isaac Luria and His Kabbalistic Fellowship*, Stanford, CA: Stanford U.P., 2003.
19. Alternatively translated as 'praiseworthy' or 'leading'.
20. Joseph Karo, *Responsa Avqat Rokhel*, Salonica: n.p., 1791, §1, p. 1a. The expression is a pun on the classical epithet of the Holy Land *Eretz HaZvi* (see Daniel, Ch. 11).

and casual visitors from Poland and Yemen. It was indeed an international, almost global, city in its cultural horizon.

The city attracted distinguished Jewish scholars and intellectuals and was considered by many as the epitome of Jewish heritage, not only in the sense of traditionalism and continuity, but particularly as an arena for innovators of Jewish classical tradition. The impact of Safed at its height on Jewish culture remains indelible to the present day. For the first time in Jewish history, mysticism (the Kabbalah) stepped beyond its secretive circles and addressed the public at large. The mystical, pietistic, and ritualistic innovations of Safed Kabbalists reshaped Jewish culture by infusing the religious experience of many believers with mystical elements.[21]

The leading Safed Talmudic scholars and eminent Kabbalists—often the very same persons[22]—considered the city uniquely sacred. It was located in proximity to the grave of R. Shimon bar-Yochai, the assumed author of the "Book of Splendor" (*Sefer Ha-Zohar*), the core magnum opus of Jewish mysticism in the early modern period. Looking at the world through their mythical and poetical glasses, Safed mystics re-enacted the life and events of the Zoharic heroes by their mystical creativity and inspiration.[23]

The aggrandizement of Safed by its leading rabbinical scholars and local mystics reached such a point that they considered their local space as competing even with the sanctity and historical role of Jerusalem. The sharp polemics over rabbinical ordination (*Semikhah*) in this period could partially be presented as a rivalry between the authorities of these two cities.[24] This shift could certainly suit the Sephardi knowledge and their intimate acquaintance of Spanish counter-reformation. The Spanish Catholics considered themselves the vanguard of the rejuvenation of Catholic religious life and carriers of the Catholic message to the entire Christian world. In their apocalyptic visions, the city of Toledo would replace the city of Rome—the seat of the Pope and emblem of Catholicism since early Christianity.[25] This myth of transferring the old center of religion to a new, vigorous center also had clear echoes in Ottoman civilization as well during the early modern period. The wide conquest of Arab territories, including the Two Holy Cities, positioned the Sultans as defenders of Islam, and the capital city of Istanbul as the new fountain of wisdom and orthodoxy for the entire Sunni Islam world.[26]

---

21. Roni Weinstein, *Kabbalah and Jewish Modernity*, London: Littman Library of Jewish Culture, 2016.
22. On the importance of this phenomenon, see Ch. 6.
23. Elchanan Reiner, 'From Joshua to Jesus: Three Chapters of the Galilean Jewish Foundational Myth', Taubman Lectures, Berkeley University, April 2015.
24. See above Ch. 4.
25. Stefania Pastore, *Un'eresia spagnola. Spiritualità conversa, alumbradismo e inquisizione (1449–1559)*, Firenze: Leo S. Olschki Editore, 2004, pp. 80–82, 89. On the fervent messianic atmosphere in early modern Spain, see Alain Milhou, *Colón y su mentalidad mesiánica en el ambiente francicanista español*, Valladolid: Casa-Museo de Colón: Seminario Americanista de la Universidad de Valladolid, 1983.
26. Şahin, *Empire and Power in the Reign of Süleyman*, pp. 51–52, 142–143, 195, 212; Guy Burak, *The Second Formation of Islamic Law. The Hanafi School the Early Modern Ottoman Empire*, Cambridge: Cambridge U.P., 2015, passim.

The responsum in which R. Karo characterized Safed as the best of all places in the Jewish Ecumene was composed in relation to the battle by Karo and other scholars against a Jewish local leader intending to impose on Talmudic Scholars in Safed the payment of taxes. This issue of tax exemption had been debated previously, but Karo's fierce and threatening tone was new. It related to his idealistic vision of the city as a haven and exceptional place of Talmudic scholarship and religious devotion that could inspire the entire Jewish people. The city, pace Karo, should be considered a sacred space where lay leaders obey the sacred rabbinical figures and endow them with economic advantages to enable their economic security and devotion to learning. In his responsum, he joined the assertion of other leading rabbis that considered the historical circumstances of contemporary Safed as an opportunity to revitalize the institution of the *Sanhedrin*,[27] the Supreme Court of Justice, divinely inspired and authorized to guide the entire Jewish population in the Holy Land and beyond.

Certainly, its scholars and inhabitants were devoted to the traditional guarding of Jewish ethnical traditions, the legacy of centuries-old automatism, as customary in many communities. Safed was unique in its innovative aspects, so that several institutions underscored the shared supra-ethnic character of the city. These institutions were meant to serve the entire Jewish population and endow the multiethnic city with an international and universalistic outlook. They extended from political management, charity to schooling:

[1] Charity collection and its distribution were regularly conducted on an ethnic basis, but Safed inhabitants established a "General Coffer" (*Quppah Rashit*). The donors of these funds knew in advance that their charity would not be directed to any specific ethnic group (mostly their own), but would serve the needs of all people, regardless of their origins.[28]

[2] The local schools for young children and for adolescents—initiating them to more advance Talmudic scholarship—served the entire population. The community even subsidized the needs of poor families—again, regardless of their ethnic affiliation.[29]

[3] The Safed leadership addressed issues concerning the entire Jewish population through an institution called the "Delegates of Various Communities" (*Memunei Ha-Qehilot*). As its name suggests, this body comprised leaders of the various groups within the city.[30] Joseph Hacker noted that Ottoman communities followed two alternative political patterns in conducting their public life.[31] The Istanbul pattern

---

27. See, supra footnote 17.
28. Eyal Davidson, *Safed's Sages between 1540–1615, Their Religious and Social Status* [Hebrew], Ph.D. submitted at the Hebrew University, 2009, pp. 204–209.
29. *Ibid.*, 204–205.
30. *Ibid.*, 291–292.
31. Joseph R. Hacker, 'Communal Organization among the Jewish Communities of the Ottoman Empire (1453–1676)' [Hebrew], in: Grossman Kaplan (eds.), *Kehal Yisrael – Jewish Self-Rule through the Ages*, Vol. 2, pp. 287–309.

implied the erection of centralist mechanism to deal with common issues, on a basis of regular convening. This pattern was customary in the capital and among Jewish communities in the Arab lands. The Salonica pattern, on the other hand, underscored the fragmentary character of multiethnic Jewish community and favored internal independence. It was prevalent among Jewish communities in the Balkans. The Safed inhabitants, then, adopted the Istanbul-Arabic pattern, but intensified it to a greater degree.

[4] During time of economic duress, messengers (*Shadarim*, an Aramaic-Hebrew term for rabbinical messengers) were dispatched from the Holy Land in order to collect charity for the poor in both Jerusalem and Safed.[32] Their tours passed through the entire Mediterranean Basin, and often Western Europe as well. They formed an international network of scholars, and eventually functioned as disseminating agents for the halakhic, pietistic, and mystical innovations of the Holy Land, and especially of Safed.

[5] The sages in Safed established a semi-formal institution for convening the major scholars (*Beit Ha-Va'ad*) for discussion and adjudication of intricate legal issues. The vicissitudes of this mechanism during the sixteenth and seventeenth centuries were meticulously discussed by Davidson.[33] Casual references in rabbinical responsa from Safed suggest that this was not a formal and steady institution but rather an ad hoc gathering of scholars lacking any fixed and firm working procedures.

[6] The leading Talmudic scholars in Safed established a kind of supreme court of law (*Beit-Din Ha-Gadol*) attended by them. The prestige of this court was so great that its members transgressed the rabbinical ethos not to cancel any decisions of other courts of law (unless the resolutions were overtly mistaken). Legal charts of minor courts were annulled for the sole reason that they were prepared by less prestigious rabbis or by ethnic courts in Safed.[34]

Some of these mechanisms and institutions functioned in other Sephardi communities under the Ottoman Empire, especially Istanbul, Salonica, or Damascus. Yet Safed was unique in hosting them all at the same time, so that a centralistic institution in one domain could inspire the formation of a parallel one in a different domain, or affect its functioning. For instance, charity was partially dispensed to schools serving the entire population, and the positions of *Beit Ha-Va'ad* were heard by lay leaders. Of all the Jewish communities thriving under Ottoman rule, the city of Safed was the most ecumenical and internationally oriented.

As noted, *Beit Ha-Va'ad* was not a formal institution and was certainly not recognized officially by the Ottoman authorities and the local Qadi. As an informal institution, it left enough space to competing elements in the city. Within the hub of Safed leading

---

32. Yaron Ben-Naeh, 'The Jewish Community of Istanbul and Eretz Israel Jewry in the Seventeenth Century' [Hebrew], *Cathedra: For the History of Eretz Israel and Its Yishuv* 92 (1999), pp. 65–106, esp. pp. 94–95.

33. Davidson, *Safed's Sages between 1540–1615*, pp. 260–266. His research takes into considerations the works conducted previously by Benayahu and Dimitrovsky. See above, Ch. 5.

34. *Ibid.*, p. 267.

scholars, R. Jacob Beirav[35] was certainly the most distinguished. It comes as no surprise that he established a judicial mechanism of his own, competing with *Beit Ha-Va'ad*. His prestige and dominance were unparalleled in the city. Local sages considered him the leading contemporary rabbi and accepted him as head judge. The city of Safed and its environs were considered to stand "under his dominance" (*Atrei de-Mar*, signifying that his rules were binding). His opinions, customs, and rulings were accepted as decisive in the case of divergences among local scholars. His halakhic rulings were not confined to the scholarly domain but were published and hence binding.[36] His own Yeshiva was considered the leading one in the city—no trivial matter in a city replete with eminent Talmudic scholars in the sixteenth century.

R. Karo could hardly ignore Beirav's dominance and his precedents. As a prestigious scholar valued by his eminent colleagues in Safed, Karo founded his own court of law. Once again, he not only continued a precedent set by Beirav but shifted it to a new horizon and charged it with new import, as cogently analyzed by Davidson. In 1554, R. Joseph Karo stated openly that he considered his own court of law as a "Supreme Court" (*Beit-Din Ha-Gadol*), purposely using this highly charged term, which carried much deeper halakhic implications than the other term current in Safed, *Beit Ha-Va'ad*. The term evoked memories of another supreme court, the ancient *Sanhedrin*. It stood in perfect syntony with the epitaph he conferred on the city of Safed as "the Place of Justice" (*meqom ha-mishpat*), a biblical term implying a supreme and authoritative court of law. Davidson rightly asserts that these terminologies, standing behind Karo's plans, are not disjoint from his comprehensive halakhic magnum opus *Beit Yosef*, which by this time, between the years 1550 and 1559, was being printed and distributed in order to address the entire Jewish Ecumene. The predominant disciples in his Yeshiva probably attended his supreme court of law, should we take literally the expression "His Yeshiva, substituting for us the Itinerant Temple." The central court headed by R. Joseph Karo and two eminent figures— "The two grand rabbis [...] and some other rabbis"—is mentioned for the first time in 1548 and again in 1551. It was an authoritative gathering and might have aimed to substitute the role of *Beit Ha-Va'ad*.[37] Turning a private court of law into a general one —as R. Karo did—was not a simple move of extending its authority or enforcement capacity. Nor was it justified by any formal juridical-halakhic argument, as might have been expected of a leading Talmudic scholar such as R. Karo. It relied on his prestige and special position in the city and related to his grand vision about this court.

Foundation of an International Court of Law

The eastern Mediterranean Basin was home to numerous Jewish communities under Ottoman direct rule. These communities weaved a dense network of political,

---

35. On his dominant position in Safed, see Ch. 4.
36. Haim Z. Dimitrovsky, 'Rabbi Yaakov Beirav's Academy in Safed' [Hebrew], *Sefunot: Studies and Sources on the History of the Jewish Communities in the East* 7 (1963), pp. 71–123, esp. p. 44.
37. *Ibid.*, pp. 262–263.

economic, family, and cultural exchanges.[38] The character of this communication and exchange mechanism has yet to be analyzed in regard to the rabbinical network, concerning connections and commitment between individual rabbis and major scholarship centers such as Jerusalem, Safed, Istanbul, Salonica, and Venice. Yet even a brief perusal of the responsa books composed by some of the major early modern Sephardi rabbis—R. Karo himself, R. Moses di Trani, R. Samuel di Medina (*Maharashdam*), and R. Joseph ibn Lev (*Maharival*)—reveals the broad geographical horizons of communication between private people, business partners, and communities addressing rabbinical authorities. In some cases, the legal debates would roll on for a long period, as the Talmudic discussion would turn into a broad rabbinical polemic or even a scandal. This could be settled once the rabbinical authorities reached some kind of consensus, a process that obviously entailed not only legalistic reasoning and discourse but also the activation of sociological aspects, such as control and authority, honor, and the mobilization of supporters. Rabbis of various communities and ethnic origins were recruited to these disputes, some of which certainly had an international or even global extent.

The responsa of R. Karo, *Avqat Rokhel*, is impressive in the broad profile of those addressing him, either litigants or rabbis.[39] Indeed, the book, posthumously edited, actually reflects his personal archives, storing the major responsa, court verdicts, and polemics, in which he was involved during his long years in Safed. It is similar to the archives of officiating Muslim Qadis under the Ottoman Empire, storing not only legal cases but also other types of documents. In its extent, Karo's book truly demonstrates an international perspective. It was not exceptional in the scholastic ambient at Safed, where scholars were customarily approached by persons and communities from across extensive geographical territories. Davidson provided a long list of such places: Istanbul, Edirne, Bursa, Magnesia, Karahisar (Anatolia), Patras, Pleven (Bulgaria),

---

38. See for instance Francesca Trivellato, *The Familiarity of Strangers: The Sephardic Diaspora, Livorno, and Cross-Cultural Trade in the Early Modern Period*, Yale: Yale U.P., 2009; Matthias B. Lehmann, *Emissaries from the Holy Land. The Sephardic Diaspora and the Practice of Pan-Judaism in the Eighteenth Century*, Stanford: Stanford U.P., 2014.

39. This Responsa book contains unusually large material that was either not composed by R. Karo himself, or responded to ongoing debates and in reaction to other rabbis' rulings and Responsa. For Responsa composed by others, see Karo, *Responsa Avqat Rokhel*, pp. 5b, 8b–9b, 17a-b, 20a, 21b, 24a, 27b, 33a, 34a, 37b, 39b–40a, 45b, 48a, 54b, 57a-b, 65b, 67a, 69a, 70a, 73b, 84a, 85b, 88b, 89b, 95a, 101b, 104a, 112a, 120a, 128b. For Responsa composed by R. Karo in reaction to his colleagues, see *ibid.*, pp. 9a, 10b, 14b, 19a, 21b, 24b, 28a, 52a, 54b, 57b, 61a, 65b, 70a, 76a, 84a, 92a, 95a, 99b, 104a, 112a. Some of the Responsa documented several rounds of Responsa and counter-Responsa, see *ibid.*, pp. 9b, 10b, 14b, 20a, 21a, 35a-b, 43a, 48b, 57b, 58b, 49b, 66b, 74a, 75a-b, 79a, 96b, 99b, 111a, 120a, 122b–123a, 125a. At times, major communities and centers of Torah and Talmud studies in Anatolia addressed Safed scholars to settle a compromise among them. A case involving Edirne and Istanbul communities, see Meir Benayahu, 'The Renovation of Rabbinic Semichah in Safed' [Hebrew], in: S.W. Baron, B. Dinur, S. Ettinger, I. Halpern (eds.), *Yitzhak F. Baer Jubilee Volume. On the Occasion of his Seventieth Birthday*, Jerusalem: The Historical Society of Israel, 1960, p. 252. See also Davidson, *Safed's Sages between 1540–1615*, pp. 270–271.

Arta, Rhodes, Tokat, Amasya, Egypt, North Africa, Italy, Jordan, Galilee Villages, Tiberias, Jerusalem, Gaza, Italy, Crete, Ashkenaz, Hormuz, and South-Asian communities under Portuguese rule.[40]

Again, R. Karo used a well-known pattern among contemporary persons committed to innovation and practiced by members of all three religions: he adopted a customary and legitimate mechanism (in this case, the supra-ethnic court) and transposed it to a new context. The traditional and known would be charged with an entirely different meaning under the cloak of continuity and tradition. The acceptance of the dominant role of Safed and its scholars set the ground for the establishment of an international court of law, reminiscent of the *Sanhedrin* of the past and headed by a dominant figure— the "Leading Figure of His Generation" (*Gedol Ha-Dor*), in other words Karo himself. A formal and explicit claim for such by R. Karo would have aroused immediate opposition, as it runs counter to Jewish ethos and traditional concepts of communal legal autonomy and to traditionalism in general. However, Karo's rabbinical contemporaries recognized his implicit claim, and this indeed provoked intensive opposition. A leading contemporary scholar, R. Yom-Tov Zahalon (*Maharitatz*), discussed a case involving the cancellation of an intended marriage, due to a sexual sin on the part of the future bride and her unexpected pregnancy (obviously not by her future spouse).[41] By their nature, such cases stir boiling emotions, and the two sides could not even agree on a simple formal issue: which court of law they should address. The benefit of such responsa for the legal historian is that they cast light on the theme of the authority of Jewish courts. The juridical-Talmudic discussions in this responsum reiterate the assertion concerning the authority of contemporary courts and reject any challenge on the false grounds that in present day no court was sufficiently skilled to compete with past legal authorities. The concluding section takes into consideration the special circumstances of two hostile parties and recommends a form of arbitration:

> Regarding this [legal] question, where the two litigating parties sue each other, so than each of them is entitled to request a discussion in a major court of law [*Beit-Din Ha-Gadol*]. If they wish to avoid nuisances and financial expenses, let them write their claims and present them to a professional court, whose verdict will be considered binding on both parties. Thus I heard that Our Master Rabbi Joseph Karo was accustomed to act, so as to avoid unnecessary nuisances and financial expenses. He would address them and order them to send their allegations to a place [i.e. a court of law] of major scholars of this generation. And so it should be conducted for generations to come, and so we should all act.[42]

This is a precious testimony, given off-hand without any intention of providing a "historical" testimony on Jewish legal procedures in late sixteenth and early seventeenth centuries. The formal theme that informed the composition of this responsum was the

---

40. Davidson, *Safed's Sages between 1540–1615*, pp. 305–306, esp. footnote 12.
41. Yom-Tov Zahalon, *New Responsa* [*Shut Maharitatz HaChadashot* in Hebrew], Jerusalem: Machon Yerushalayim, 1980–81.
42. *Ibid.*, §9.

authority and tangible power of a Jewish court to enforce a discussion in local courts rather than addressing distant ones or even turning to a Muslim Qadi. R. Karo suggested a new option, legitimized by R. Zahalon ("And so it should be conducted for generations to come, and so we all should act"): he would actively address the contending parties and encourage them to refer their case not to the original and local ambient but rather to a distant and unfamiliar one. The place and the judge are clearly Safed ("a place/court of major scholars of this generation,") with Karo himself heading this international and universal court.

This leap in juridical proceedings is innovative in a further sense—the manner in which it shifts the point of gravity of Jewish court proceedings from the oral to the written level ("He would address them and order them to send their allegations" — obviously in writing). Both directions of communication—R. Karo to the contending parties and their expected allegations as sent to his court—were managed in writing rather than through an oral and personal encounter. This marks a clear moment where R. Karo challenged the established rules of court proceedings. Classical rabbinical tradition insisted on a personal encounter between the judge and the contending parties (including witnesses) and prohibited the presentation of testimonies when one of the parties was absent.[43] This legal taboo was still in force in the early modern period, to the extent that composers of responsa felt obliged to apologize for responding to queries when both parties were not present, and only one side could present his case, contrary to the formal requirement of the Talmud and Jewish legal tradition.[44] This unprecedented reliance on written documents, certainly to the extent proposed by R. Karo to remote communities, responds to changes in the Ottoman bureaucratic and legal systems, referred to by Guy Burak as "archival consciousness."[45] The increasing trust in state archives was shared by imperial administrators, the judicial elite, and ordinary Ottoman subjects. It encouraged litigants to rely on written documents, alongside the traditional pattern of oral testimonies. An explicit testimony that Jews were fully aware of this change was provided in a responsum composed by an Egyptian rabbi, R. David ben Zimrah (*Radbaz*), a contemporary of Karo.[46] Arab jurists did not reach agreement regarding the legitimacy and extent of the use of written documents held in state archives. Jurists, especially those who were officially appointed by the Ottoman dynasty, argued that the Ottoman archival practices were sufficient to guarantee their authenticity and reliability.

---

43. Eliav Shochetman, 'The Obligation to State Reasons for Legal Decisions in Jewish Law' [Hebrew], *Shenaton ha-Mishpat ha-Ivri: Annual of the Institute for Research in Jewish Law* 6–7 (1979–1980), pp. 319–379, esp. pp. 339–340.

44. *Ibid.*, p. 341.

45. Guy Burak, '"In Compliance with the Old Register". On Ottoman Documentary Depositories and Archival Consdiousness', *JESHO* 62 (2019), pp. 799–823.

46. Cited in *Ibid.*, p. 808: "I have no doubt that this was not the custom of the gentiles at the time of the deceased Rabbi, [unlike] what is done in our time that all that happened is written in the *sicil*, and is kept for many days".

The standpoint of R. Karo in regard to interference in legal cases in distant areas far beyond the authority and validity of Safed's court of law was generally shared by his local colleagues. One such collective act occurred in 1567, when the leading Safed scholars dispatched a letter to Italian-Jewish communities concerning the question of wine forbidden for use due to non-Jewish involvement in its production (*Stam Yeinam*).[47] The letter was not worded as a collegial piece of advice but as an order leaving no room for further discussion. Jewish diasporas differed in regard to how strictly they observed the rules concerning such wine, and Italian Jews were considered dangerously lenient in this respect. R. Karo and his Safed colleagues did not take into consideration the varieties of Jewish customs in this case, presenting an unequivocal position.[48] Hence, the authority of Safed court extended as far as Catholic Italy, far beyond the borders of the Ottoman Empire.[49]

Karo intervened personally in such distant communities, though the testimonies in this respect are scarce. In one case, Karo waged a determined battle against a book and its composer—"Light for the Eyes" (*Meor 'Eynayim*) by Azaria de Rossi, which he believed endangered belief in some basic elements of Jewish heritage.[50] Following massive pressure from Karo and the impact of his international prominence, the book and its author did not gain any popularity in Jewish culture for many centuries.

In another case, again in the Italian-Jewish context, R. Karo had his direct disciples act as proxies for his positions. The Tamari-Ventorozo affair preoccupied all the prominent Italian rabbis for several years. It concerned a delicate issue of betrothal (*Qiddushin*), a stage preceding full marriage. In cases of doubt regarding betrothal (*Qiddushei Safeq*), rabbinical authorities tended to adopt a strict ruling and demand a full divorce procedure if one of the sides retracted their intention to proceed.[51] Since the betrothal act can be conducted by the very simple act of transferring some property from the man to the women, as a token for their consent, the whole scene became delicate and provided leverage for young men to extort money from young unmarried women and their families. To counter this phenomenon, some rabbis assiduously attempted to declare these doubtful betrothals as invalid, but the stricter position always won the day, constraining both

---

47. Davidson, *Safed's Sages between 1540–1615*, p. 269.

48. Meir Benayahu, 'Communication of Rabbis of Egypt to Radbaz', *Sefunot: Studies and Sources on the History of the Jewish Communities in the East* 6 (1962), pp. 125–134; Davidson, *Safed's Sages between 1540–1615*, pp. 270–271.

49. Further cases of intervention in faraway communities are mentioned and discussed in Yaron Ben-Naeh, 'Rabbi Joseph Karo and His Time' [Hebrew], in: *Rabbi Joseph Karo. History, Halakhah, Kabbalah*, Jerusalem: Zalman Shazar Center, 2021, pp. 91–92, 99–100. A furious response by a leading rabbi from Salonica, reacting to R. Karo's attempt to intervene there, see Hagai Pely, 'Studies in the Adjudication Project of Rabbi Joseph Karo' [Hebrew], in: *Rabbi Joseph Karo. History, Halakhah, Kabbalah*, Jerusalem: Zalman Shazar Center, 2021, p. 190.

50. Reuven Bonfil, *Selected Chapters from Sefer Me'or 'Einayim and Matsref la-Kessef* [Hebrew], Jerusalem: Bialik Institute, 1991.

51. Roni Weinstein, *Marriage Rituals Italian Style: A Historical Anthropological Perspective on Early Modern Italian Jews*, Leiden: E.J. Brill, 2003, pp. 154–212.

parties to undergo divorce proceedings. In this particular case, the affair transcended the boundaries of internal polemic among local Italian rabbis and acquired pan-Mediterranean dimensions. R. Karo was obviously addressed, being one of the distinguished authorities of sixteenth century, yet his personal voice was not heard. Instead the rules in the affair were stated by his direct disciples (and other scholars in Safed). Davidson, following Ephraim Kupfer, rightly asserts that it is hardly plausible that they would not have consulted with their master and secured his tacit consent regarding such a delicate and notorious affair.[52]

The fame of R. Karo was acknowledged by both scholars and laypersons. As the seventeenth century progressed, Karo was increasingly referred to by the epitaph *Maran*, which was uniquely his.[53] The popular, almost folkloristic, etymological root of this title, as discussed above, implied that Karo's unique position within halakhic history was acknowledged by "two hundred rabbis" (*matayim rabanim nismakh*—in Hebrew the words form the acronym Maran) from across the Jewish Ecumene. An early hint of his international fame and status appeared when Karo was addressed by an Italian Rabbi Isaac b. Immanuel Lattes, writing to Safed from Avignon in 1560. Again the case involved the delicate issue of family law, and in this instance levirate marriage. In the face of opposition to R. Lattes' stand that levirate marriage was not the right course, he implored R. Karo:

> The voice of horn issued from your court would make the walls tremble [...] So you, Angels of God [the writer politely addresses Karo in the plural], sitting on high and elevated chair, authorized by the power of *Sanhedrin* in the Holy Temple, do not acquit them [those supporting levirate marriage], but curse and excommunicate them in all synagogues and religious schools [...] and order all communities not to adjoin them in any sacred activity, and let any Jew persecute them by force and by addressing non-Jewish courts regarding their persons [i.e. physical arrest] and their monetary affairs.[54]

In this high florid rhetorical battle, any weapon is allowed: excommunication, violence, and recurring to "gentile courts"— all for the sake of imposing communal and halakhic resolutions. The ultimate weapon is the use of the international legal authority headed by R. Karo and the imposition of its verdict on the local authorities and the parties involved. This prestige was not limited to the milieu of professional jurists; it was also considered binding and awe-inspiring by regular lay people. Another testimony mentions the custom of Sephardi merchants in the Mediterranean Diaspora of taking an oath, when needed, on the name of God, the sacred phylacteries on their hands, and the names of the three leading Talmudic scholars active at that time in Safed, R. Karo among them, of course.[55]

---

52. Davidson, *Safed's Sages between 1540–1615*, pp. 267–268.
53. See the discussion above, on Ch. 3, dedicated to the source and significance of this title.
54. Benayahu, 'The Renovation of Rabbinic Semichah in Safed', p. 253.
55. Davidson, *Safed's Sages between 1540–1615*, p. 266.

The Grand Vision

Rabbinical writings are sparing regarding the emotions and biographical aspects of their composers. Autobiography was virtually unknown in Jewish tradition until the Safed Renaissance of the sixteenth century.[56] It is no wonder that R. Karo hardly ever mentioned his intentions explicitly in his writings as a composer of halakhic literature and legal rulings. Instead, he conveyed his message by using certain code words from the rabbinic repertory that could convey a clear message. Alternatively, he efforted to dominate the supra-ethnic court in Safed (such as *Beit Ha-Va'ad*) and turn them into institutions controlled by his loyal disciples in his yeshivas. His double magna opera provided the textual background for the functioning of this Supreme Court (*Beit-Din Ha-Gadol*). As noted, he coined the city of Safed a "Place of Justice" (*Meqom ha-mish-pat*), a place worthy to host a supreme and authoritative court of law of international dimensions.[57]

The intention only implicitly alluded in the halakhic writings by keywords drawn from the rabbinical repertory was fully exposed in his mystical diary *Megid Meisharim*:

> It is I, the *Mishnah*, speaking through [or: in] your mouth, the mother castigating her sons [or: children], the one embracing you. And you shall often adhere to me, I shall return to you and you shall return to me. I shall raise you to become master and leader [*Sar ve-Nagid*] over the entire Jewish diaspora in *Arabistan*. Since you have profoundly devoted yourself to reinstate the *Semikhah* [...] and I would benefit you by finishing your major corpus [both Codification Books: *Beit Yosef* and *Shulchan 'Arukh*].[58]

This glorifying grand revelation was discussed in connection to R. Karo's involvement in re-establishing rabbinical *Semikhah*.[59] In this context, it is important to emphasize the wide geographical territories of his future halakhic and juridical authority, extending far east ("over the entire Jewish diaspora in *Arabistan*").

The term *Arabistan* was not Arabic, and certainly had no precedents in Hebrew or in rabbinical usage. Its Persian origins enabled it to shift later to the Ottoman context, but here it did not determine a geographical space but rather the extent of Ottoman author-ity after the expansion in early sixteenth century to Arab lands: "Ottomans saw this territory as beginning somewhere south of the Taurus Mountains and including much of what is today Syria in addition to the Arabian peninsula. The 17th-century Ottoman traveler Evliya Çelebi called the town Gaziantep in present-day Turkey "the bride of Arabistan," implying that the territories to the south of that city comprised Arabistan. The Ottomans never included the territory that is Iraq today as Arabistan, although Persian language sources, such as the chronicles of Shah Abbas I (r. 1587–1629), did so.

---

56. Weinstein, *Kabbalah and Jewish Modernity*, Ch. 2, pp. 44–66. See Ch. 5 in this book for full discussion.
57. Davidson, *Safed's Sages between 1540–1615*, p. 265.
58. Joseph Karo, *Magid Meisharim*, Wilnius: Judah Leib Lipman Metz Print, 1875, p. 29a.
59. See above, Ch. 4.

So there was not a clear connection between the geographical appellation and those who spoke Arabic. In Arabic, there was no equivalent geographical expression to correspond to the Ottoman Arabistan."[60]

The terminology infiltrated from the Ottoman administrative context to halakhic and rabbinical discussions. The wide territories of Arabic-speaking people were less relevant to the Jewish use of the term, since these did not host Jewish communities of significance. More relevant to Jewish perspective was essentially the area of "Great Syria" (*Bilad a-Sham*).[61] R. Moses Galante, one of R. Karo's disciples, was asked about a husband wishing to force his wife to join him in his new place. The halakhic rule in this regard permits the husband to order his wife to join him if a geographical shift takes place within the same area, but not to force a passage to a distinct geographical cultural context. The discussion, then, would focus on the borders within the Arab lands under Ottoman rule. R. Galante proclaims that:

> The sense of [the Talmudic expression] "the same area" is that he [the husband] could transfer her [his wife] from one city to the other in the same area, i.e. within entire Turkey or in the Arabistan area or the area of Egypt [...] But [the region] from Aleppo to Tripoli [in modern Lebanon—R.W.] is defined under the status of "from one city to another within the same area," since the entire zone of Arabistan is called one area, that is *Comarca*[62] [...] so he could force her, since both are designated as *Suriya* in the Talmud[...] and in the non-Hebrew language Arabistan.[63]

Arabistan is thus depicted in this description as the Arabic-speaking area in the Syrian region. Another rabbi, the eminent Samuel de Medina of Salonica, presents a somewhat different perspective, related to the centralistic reflection of the capital city of the Ottoman Empire, while he extends the geographical term to the entire Arab-speaking lands:

> Even though the Ottoman kingdom is one, still it is internally divided to several sections: Rumelia, Anatolia, Arab lands [Arabistan], and Morea [Greek-speaking area]. Although they are controlled by his Majesty the King, still each of them is a distinct kingdom [in the sense of an administrative unit] of its own. So a man cannot force his wife to immigrate from Morea to Rumelia, etc. But within Morea he could move her from one city to another.[64]

---

60. Bruce Masters, s.v. 'Arabistan', in: Gábor Ágoston and Bruce Masters (eds.), *Encyclopedia of the Ottoman Empire*, n.p.: Fact on Line, 2009, p. 45.
61. See the informative and pointed discussion in Uri Safrai, 'The Figure and Status of R. Karo in Lurian Circle' [Hebrew], *Sefunot: Studies and Sources on the History of the Jewish Communities in the East* [forthcoming].
62. *Comarca* is an Iberian terminology for 'Region'.
63. Safrai, 'The Figure and Status of R. Karo in Lurian Circle'.
64. *Ibid.*

De Medina is sensitive to the differences of various part of the empire, primarily between the core lands ("Rumelia, Anatolia, and Morea") and the periphery, designated as Arabistan.

The expression "the entire Jewish diaspora in *Arabistan*" in R. Karo's mystical diary is enigmatic enough to leave space for interpretation: was it meant to imply the entire Arabic-speaking space or more specifically the area of *Bilad a-Sham*. In any case, the term emphasized that R. Karo was envisioning a central authority for the Jewish communities in the Arab-speaking area, all submitting to the authority of one person, one code of law, and one court. The classical Talmudic terminologies in use (Supreme Court, Leader of His Generation, *Sanhedrin*) could serve as a front for this grand vision. This approach was strong enough to stir rabbinical authorities in the next generation, even after R. Karo's death. R. Jacob Beirav (the second), and other Safed scholars convened around the year 1595 to authorize R. David Thabet to "ordinate and castigate and adjudicate all those regions, the entirety of communities east of Aleppo, and further communities in Persia and surroundings, and the communities of Kurdistan and of Zagam[65] and those dependent upon them."[66] His authority was thus to be extended even further, beyond the borders of Arabistan. It is interesting to notice how, in the minds of Safed scholars—the direct disciples or colleagues of R. Karo—a hierarchical network of rabbinical control is constructed. It is headed from the new center of Jewish Diaspora, the city of Safed, as a virtual capital city of the Jewish Ecumene. This focal place delegates it authority to a single person with the goal of controlling all the eastern communities. These are divided between several regions, where the leading communities subjugate the smaller ones ("Persia and surroundings, and the communities of Kurdistan and of Zagam and those dependent upon them").

Yet the Jewish communities living in Arabic-speaking territories were not neutral or a no-man's land. The dominant halakhic authority who established himself in this domain over the centuries was none other than Maimonides, the composer of the first Jewish code of law, the *Mishneh Torah*. This was acknowledged and implicitly stated by R. Karo himself in his halakhic writings:

> The late Maimonides, who is the greatest among the halakhic arbiters, and all the communities of the Holy Land, Arabistan, and the West [Maghreb communities] followed his authority and accepted him as their rabbi. Whoever follows his instructions should not be forced to abandon it, all the more so given that their forefathers acted thus, and their sons should not deviate from Maimonides' rulings, even if the majority in a certain community follow the rulings of *HaRosh* [the acronym of R. Asher] or others. The majority could not constrain the minority who follows Maimonides to adopt their rules.[67]

65. Either referring to Georgia or to Azerbaijan.
66. Cited in Benayahu, 'The Renovation of Rabbinic Semichah in Safed', p. 251.
67. Citation and its discussion within a larger Halakhic context, see Yaron Durani, *Three Pillars of Instruction in the Rulings of R. Joseph Karo* [Hebrew], M.A. Thesis submitted at Bar-Ilan University, 2006, pp. 51–54. See also Davidson, *Safed's Sages between 1540–1615*, pp. 83, 90.

Similar assertions were made by other important rabbis. On a declaratory level, Maimonides' position was accepted by Jews living in the Mediterranean area, subduing any other major authority.

But the strong rhetoric in support of Maimonides' authority acknowledged that it was currently being contested ("Whoever follows his instructions should not be forced to abandon it [...] The majority could not constrain the minority, who follows Maimonides"). The identity of the person challenging the authority of Maimonides, the master of previous generations, was clear enough even without it being stated explicitly. The carriers of the rulings of *HaRosh*—another rabbi who immigrated in late thirteenth century from Ashkenaz to Spain and was soon after acclaimed as the leading rabbinic scholar—were Sephardim, among whom his authority became increasingly evident prior to the general expulsion from the Iberian area in the late fifteenth century. It seems that the great vision of R. Karo himself presented an even greater challenge to the heritage of Maimonides. It was translated into the concrete act of establishing a court of law extending across the Ottoman-Jewish communities, and further west into the Italian and Provençal Diasporas in Christian Europe, beyond the territories under supposed Maimonidean control in the east. In composing his codes of law, constructed as a meta-commentary on a code of R. Yaakov ben *HaRosh* rather than on Maimonides, Karo actually sought to replace the dominance of Maimonides with his own.[68]

Summary: The Settings for Karo's International Court

R. Karo was not an innovator in the sense of offering entirely new concepts or establishing new institutions. He was, however, an important innovator in the way he charged pre-existing traditions with new meanings, to such a degree that in practical terms they became new and unprecedented provisions. His ambition to establish a new focus or power center had precedents in the early sixteenth century. This was evident in the emergence of new models of leadership of a more authoritative nature. In halakhic terminology, this was reflected in the status of "Great Persons," discussing the role of the "Greatest of his Generations" or, in a different and competing channel, in the new figure of the "Jewish Saint" in Safed Kabbalah.[69] Elisheva Carlebach summarized this drive as the "quest for center," pursued simultaneously in Western European communities, in tandem with those under direct Ottoman rule, and in the new space of Jewish life in East and Central Europe over the sixteenth century.[70] This went hand-in-hand with the formation of new and larger collective identities, such as Ashkenazi or Sephardi, beyond

---

68. This reading of Karo's vision was proposed by Safrai, 'The Figure and Status of R. Karo in Lurian Circle'. He is further corroborating Isral Dienstag's suggestion on this issue.

69. On the new figure of 'The Jewish Saint', see Weinstein, *Kabbalah and Jewish Modernity*, Ch. 2, pp. 44–66.

70. Elchanan Reiner, 'The Rise of "The Big Community": The Roots of Urban Jewish Community in Early Modern Poland' (in Hebrew), *Galed. History of Polish Jews* 20 (2006), pp. 13–37.

the "parochial" community collective.[71] The indications for such supra-local identities relate to cultural aspects, such as the unification of liturgy, community patterns, the print revolution, the solidification of theological stands, and an extensive ethical or guidance literature addressing large audiences of readers. The change in legal domain and court procedures was another component in the broad thrust toward unification.

The immediate impetus for Karo's vision can be found in Safed. The city hosted several institutions that transcended the deep and centuries-old mentality of fragmentation and locality, a heritage of the Middle Ages. The city leadership, courts attended by prominent scholars, pedagogic institutions, charitable collection and its distribution, and the dispatching of envoys from the Holy Land were all leading to a new mentality that considered universalization as an urgent task, in concordance with global changes. R. Jacob Beirav incorporated all these currents in his dominant and erudite personality. He initiated a local court that would discuss important issues beyond ethnic and fragmentary boundaries. As one of the leading scholars of his generation, his court attracted queries and legal questions from distant places across the Mediterranean Basin. He established a formal hierarchy within the juridical guild through the renovation of rabbinical ordination. Inevitably, his figure served R. Karo as a model to follow and to channel toward further new destinations.

Karo attempted to take these patterns one step forward. In his vision, he was to become the leading figure for all the Jewish communities in the Holy Land and Arabistan—a term that he and other rabbis borrowed from the Ottoman political vocabulary. But he went much further. Unofficially, and without stating it explicitly, he established an international court of law. To have declared this publicly would have been highly dangerous in the Ottoman context and unacceptable in rabbinical traditionalism. But in practice this institution was involved in legal cases and religious issues from communities not only within the immediate domain of *Bilad a-Sham* but also in the major Sephardi communities of Istanbul in the core land of the Ottoman Empire, and even beyond the boundaries of Islam, in European communities under Catholicism. According to contemporary rabbinical testimony, he actively encouraged distant communities to dispatch legal cases to his court rather instruct the litigants to turn to their local courts. This was no simple move in Jewish juridical tradition, which as noted above favored the oral discussions and testimonies in the presence of all parties rather than the use of written documents.

The centralization of judicial mechanisms was one of the important innovations of the Ottoman era, and it intensified during the sixteenth century. R. Karo, living his entire adult life under the Ottoman civilization—either in Rumelia (and for a very short period in Istanbul), or later in the Holy Land—was exposed to what he saw around him. The similar elements are unmistakable: the establishment of a central city—in the case of Safed one that even aspired to succeed Jerusalem, in part; a unique person heading the legal tradition; a unified code of law producing a unified text and legal

---

71. Jonathan Rey, *After Expulsion. 1492 and the Making of Sephardic Jewry*, London and New York: New York U.P., 2013.

language;[72] legal experts sharing a collective ethos and collectively affiliated to a major authority; and finally the establishment of a concrete mechanism—the court of law—whose authority is assumed to reign across the entire Jewish Ecumene. The echoes of the Ottoman legal system could clearly be heard in rabbinical writings in the very close vicinity of R. Karo:

> Among all religions in the world, when one of them overpowers the earth or part of it, the ruler places judges in cities under his rulership, and nominates one single judge to adjudicate every conflict and struggle. And they would have one law for all the nations under his rule [...] Still, in spite the fact that Jews have divergent laws, when addressing the court, they would practice one single law.[73]

> In all the Ottoman rule, may it be glorified, from Avalona[74] until the Holy Land, and from other places in Rumelia and Anatolia until the Holy Land, everything is one kingdom [in the sense of rulership]. Commonly, along all the routes from there [the core land of the Ottomans] until the Holy Land caravans are frequent [...] In these times that the Ottoman and European rules rose to power, and they control most of the population, and most time are peaceful among them, danger is not so rampant. There are times/occasions that people could come from faraway to the Holy Land from Christian lands, from Italy, from Ashkenaz, from France to the Ottoman area, and vice versa.. and though there are bandits on the roads, and those who captivate, in most times it is safe [to travel].[75]

The close acquaintance with the Ottoman legal system is clear in the first testimony of the Safedian rabbi Samuel Ozeida, a contemporary of R. Karo. It is stated as a generality regarding all religions, but its Ottoman coloring is beyond doubt. Unity and universality of the law are depicted as the great advantage of the Ottoman legal system. The Hebrew phrasing is flexible enough to imply that every city under Ottoman rule has only one nominated judge, and simultaneously that the entire system is regulated by a single person. This is a hierarchical system controlled by its top figure, the Sultanic ruler. The benefit for the local subjects is the relative peaceful life and safe roads, as stated in the second testimony. Again, it reflects the expansion of the early modern political ethos of the *Pax Ottomanica*.

The capacity to materialize such an ambitious project—as a universal pan-Jewish court of law—was very limited. To start with, it would inevitably arouse the indignation of the Ottomans, who considered legal sovereignty as one of the pillars of state ethos. The intended project or vision had to remain very limited from the start and to function below the radar of "foreign" eyes. A no less significant source of opposition was the rabbinical milieu, whose traditional freedom would be curtailed by such an international court. R. Karo did not possess any material or political sources that he could

---

72. See above Ch. 2.
73. Davidson, *Safed's Sages between 1540–1615*, p. 298. See also the testimony in *ibid.*, p. 299 footnote 452.
74. Valona in current Albania
75. Cited and discussed in Davidson, *Safed's Sages between 1540–1615*, p. 25, footnote 8.

mobilize to further his project and had to rely solely on his personal prestige and his unique status in Safed.[76] Even in this city, there were those who criticized the intention "to overrule others" and suggested that their own court of law should play the leading role in the Diaspora rather than that of Karo.[77] As much as Safed intellectuals considered their city the "best of all Jewish places," it was a relatively small city and merely one of a series of relevant cities within the Mediterranean Sephardi network, such as Salonica,[78] Istanbul, Edirne, Izmir, Cairo, Damascus, and Jerusalem. For its sustenance and maintaining its position, it needed the financial and political support of larger cities, provided willingly by the Jewish intermediaries in the capital city or the activation of an international network of charity transference from either Venice or Istanbul.[79] The ability to mobilize such an ambitious project from a small and peripheral city, such as Safed, was very limited.

Karo's death put a definitive end to his vision, centered on one special figure. Yet it left an indelible impact as the myth around him continued to disseminate; his work and halakhic rulings were supposedly sustained by two hundred rabbis dispersed across the entire Diaspora. To be more exact, the testimonies to such recognition of his fame—the Two Hundred Rabbis myth, as well as his network of correspondence and affiliations relate predominantly to the Mediterranean context. Very few of them transcend this area, mainly to Italy—again as a consequence of its direct ties with Ottoman commerce. Basically, his vision of an international court reflected the Ottoman legal system. The local Ottoman dominance, as perceived and interpreted by R. Karo, rebounded in inter-Jewish discussion, in relation to "strangers" arriving in the Ottomanized orbit. When discussing the validity of the ancient Ashkenazi prohibition on polygamy, R. Karo, along with other rabbis, ruled that immigrants used to European traditions must adapt to local—i.e., Mediterranean and Ottoman—customs, and in exceptional cases suspend their insistence on monogamy.[80] The impact of the Ottoman model is also reflected in the patterns he adopted in his vision: the dominance of the center, one prestigious person heading the scholarly and legal network, one court assisted by one code of law, the international extent of his own court, the use of written documents. The entire project is conducted under an umbrella of sanctity.

76. Jacob Katz, 'The Controversy on the Semichah (Ordination) between Rabbi Jacob Beirav and the Ralbach', *Zion* 16, no. 3–4 (1951), p. 36.

77. Davidson, *Safed's Sages between 1540–1615*, pp. 269–270.

78. Meir Benayahu, 'R. Joseph Taitatzak from Salonica, Head of Sephardi Diaspora' [Hebrew], in: Zvi Ankori (ed.), *Then and Now. Annual Lectures on the Jews of Greece (1977–1983)*, Tel-Aviv: The School of Jewish Studies, Tel-Aviv University, 1984, pp. 21–34.

79. Ben-Naeh, 'The Jewish Community of Istanbul and Eretz Israel Jewry', passim.

80. Davidson, *Safed's Sages between 1540–1615*, pp. 89–90.

Chapter Nine

SUMMARY: SCOPE AND PERSPECTIVES

The four volumes or sections comprising *Beit Yosef*, undoubtedly one of the fundamental books in the history of the Halakhah, were printed between 1550 and 1559. Its importance was demonstrated by the enthusiastic welcome the work received shortly after its publication and by its impact in the long run.[1] For three centuries, the long code of law attracted important commentaries by the leading Talmudic scholars around the Mediterranean Basin and in Eastern and Central Europe (mainly in Poland); later, it even inspired the composition of commentaries on previous codes authored by Maimonides (*Mishneh Torah*) and R. Jacob ben Ha-Rosh (*Ha-Turim* or *Arba'a Turim*). The most impressive fact of all, however, is that along with the glosses of the contemporary Polish rabbi Moses Isserles on the short version of this magnum opus—the *Shulchan 'Arukh*—Karo's work has not to the present day been succeeded by any further code of law. The importance of both these codifications was acknowledged by their composer R. Joseph Karo in fascinating preambles, declaring that Jewish tradition is constituted through legality and halakhic instruction rather than through any other component of Jewish heritage. This was a watershed moment in the history of Jewish culture and religion, and one that prepared ground for the later crystallization of Orthodox Judaism and the contemporary ultra-Orthodox worldview and community life. Law and Halakhah were interconnected with Jewish mystic tradition—Kabbalah—and with new theological conceptions. Together these three elements provided the early modern rabbinical elite with the essential tools to reform and revitalize Jewish tradition.

What was the starting point for the composition of *Beit Yosef*, and later the *Shulchan 'Arukh*, which turned R. Karo into a Talmudic celebrity? How far back should we go in order to understand what stood behind these magna opera? The first time axis is certainly the biographical trajectory of the composer himself, and especially the scholarly path that he followed as a member of a rabbinical family and the scholarly milieu. This extremely small elite assigned the most talented among the young generation to become a Talmudic scholar (*talmid chakham*), rabbi, judge, or even a halakhic arbiter (*poseq*), at the peak of the rabbinical hierarchy. Little is known of the early phases of Karo's initiation into rabbinical scholarship, except for the fact that his uncle R. Isaac Karo was his first and probably most significant master.

---

1. On the long and successful absorption of R. Karo's codes of law in later Talmudic literature and rabbinic discussions, see Hagai Pely, 'Studies in the Adjudication Project of Rabbi Joseph Karo' [Hebrew], in: *Rabbi Joseph Karo. History, Halakhah, Kabbalah*, Jerusalem: Zalman Shazar Center, 2021, pp. 131–333, esp. pp. 234–304.

The personal life course of R. Karo cannot be disconnected from the fate of his generation or the impact of prior waves of violence toward Jewish communities—especially in 1391—culminating in the traumatic expulsion from the Iberian Peninsula in 1492 and 1497 and followed by violence, poverty, slavery, and rape. The concluding chapter of this acrimonious story was the establishment of a broad Sephardi Diaspora. In every aspect of his life and activities, Karo was a quintessential member of this cultural heritage. The codification project, extending across almost four decades of his life, continues the halakhic heritage of the Sephardi communities and their sages and responds to the two preceding codes of law. It presented itself as relying on a relatively restricted number of halakhic authorities and as applying a "mechanical" methodology for counting votes of the sages participating in the intergenerational Talmudic Study. Not all previous books carried the same weight, and some past generations of scholars had established an internal hierarchy.[2] The legal reasoning in the double codes of law was inseparable from the Sephardi Talmudic methodology of 'Iyyun, based on logic and inspired by scholasticism in Christian universities, and practiced prior to the general expulsions of Jews from Spain (1492) and Portugal (1497). This method provided a foundation for common halakhic and intellectual discourse among Talmud scholars. Another feature inherited by R. Karo from past Sephardi heritage regarding the schooling system was an internal hierarchy among masters and their disciples. Karo and other Sephardi rabbis were also motivated by a sense of Sephardi uniqueness and superiority relative to other Jewish traditions. As in the Spanish (Catholic) context, the Castilian Jews were the dominant component in the Sephardi tradition, conveying this ingrained sense of superiority. They carried it to their new destinations, and had no hesitations to impose their particular tradition on local Jews, especially when coming into contact with early modern Jewish communities around the Mediterranean Basin. All these factors will recur in the methods of operation of R. Karo. In his professional Halakhic work, he adhered predominantly to the Sephardi heritage, established along many generations. He openly declared in the preambles to his codes of law that the main authorities for his halakhic rulings were Sephardi.

A subsidiary issue related to Karo's Sephardi identity concerns his debt to one of this community's towering figures, Maimonides. Alongside the reliance of *Beit Yosef* and *Shulchan 'Arukh* on the *Mishneh Torah*, as also explicitly noted by R. Karo, and the fact that in his later years he composed a broad commentary on this work (*Kesef Mishneh*), it remains unclear why Karo did not construct his own works as a commentary on Maimonides' work but instead chose *Ha-Turim* as his point of reference. This is all the more enigmatic since the aim of both Karo and Maimonides' legal codes went beyond the composition of a Talmudic summary. Both were intended to be applied over a wide geographical domain, beyond their place of composition, relying on an exceptional

---

2. Shlomo Glicksberg and Shlomo Cassirer, 'The Halakhah and Meta-Halakhah Codification Debate: Rabbi Chaim ben Bezalel and the Maharal of Prague' [Hebrew], *Jewish Studies* 49 (2013), pp. 157–191.

copying and printing effort in order to establish a correct textual version[3] and disseminate it to the entire Jewish Ecumene.

The Sephardi axis turns the story toward another time trajectory, which is the Islamicate context and the rule of Muslims in southern parts of Spain for several centuries. Sephardi heritage thrived for many centuries in the interstice between Spanish Catholicism and Islam. This triple cultural hybridity terminated with the conclusion of the *Reconquista* by the Spanish forces, the expulsion of Muslim rulers and soldiers, and eventually the general expulsion of the remaining Jewish population. The cultural interface between the Jewish and Muslim traditions, by contrast, became even more relevant after the expulsion, and the political and cultural foundation on which both Karo's works took shape was Islamic. This sequence of influences followed the immigration route of Karo's family, like those of many other Sephardi refugees, from the European-Catholic to the Islamicate context. At various points in our exploration, we have returned to the theme of the common cultural and religious language shared by Jewish and Muslim traditions, more extensive and profound than the restricted cultural dialogue between Jews and Catholics in Medieval Europe. Emblematic in this respect is the double face of R. Karo as both legal expert and active mystic. The assertions of Shahab Ahmed in his inspiring book regarding the *Shari'a* proved surprisingly applicable to the *Halakhah*.[4]

Within the Islamicate tradition, the concrete setting in the Ottoman Empire and civilization, where R. Karo spent his entire life (except for his early childhood years prior to the expulsion), is particularly significant. The Sephardi refugees arriving in this new area did not present this change as a decline relative to former times, but expressed a sense of security and continuity in their religious heritage and even an amelioration of the dominant Castilian component. A contemporary rabbi commented that "Right after the sunset of Torah in Castile, due to expulsion tribulations, commenced the sunrise of Torah in the Maghreb, and Egypt, and the Holy Land, and in all the Ottoman Empire thanks to the Sages of Castile, who came from there and established Torah in all lands of the Lord."[5] Following the conquest of Constantinople and its development as the capital city of the Osmanic dynasty, the empire extended to wide territories both in Europe and the Arab lands. No less impressive than its political and military prowess were its cultural achievements, turning Istanbul into a fountain of religious studies,

---

3. Menahem Ben-Sasson, 'Maimonides' Mishneh Torah: Towards Canon-Formation in the Life of an Author' [Hebrew], in: Idem., Robert Brody, Amia Lieblich, Donna Shalev (eds.), *Uncovering the Canon: Studies in Canonicity and Genizah* (Jerusalem: Magnes, 2010), pp. 133–201; Idem., 'The 'Libraries' of Maimonides Family between Cairo and Aleppo' [Hebrew]," in: Yom Tov Assis, Miriam Frenkel, Yaron Harel (eds.), *Aleppo Studies, The Jews of Aleppo*, vol. I – 'Their History and Culture', Jerusalem: Ben-Zvi 2009, pp. 51–105.

4. Ahmed Shahab, *What is Islam. The Importance of Being Islamic*, Princeton and Oxford: Princeton U.P., 2016, passim, as cited in previous chapters.

5. Joseph Hacker, 'The Intellectual Activity among Jews in the Ottoman Empire during the Sixteenth and Seventeenth Centuries' [Hebrew], *Tarbiz* 53, no. 4 (1984), pp. 569–604. Citation from *ibid.*, p. 569.

including the establishment of large mosques, chains of madrasas, and libraries and other public buildings. The destruction in the Islamic world caused by the Mongol invasions was now repaired under the aegis of the Ottomans. Turkish ships and trade competed with the European navies in both the Mediterranean and in South-East Asia.[6] In both geographical domains, international trading networks of Sephardi communities and merchants could also be found. What is the geographical—and hence cultural—extent required for understanding the Ottoman world and its impact on the cultural tradition and life of the Jewish minority, especially in the halakhic domain? This task is hardly possible without taking into consideration the impressive space in which the Ottoman culture flourished, next to the wide continuum on its eastern flank, next to Ilkhanids, Timurids, Ottomans, Safavids, Uzbeks, and Mughals. Each of these polities derived its universalist legitimacy from either the Chingiz Khanids or the Oghuz Turks, while also absorbing Irano-Islamic ideals of kingship and statecraft.[7]

Recent research into Ottoman legal history has highlighted the importance of the common heritage left by the Mongols. The disintegration of the empires established by Chingis Khan and later by Tamerlane left a remarkable vacuum between the Asian steppes and Anatolia. These Mongol empires, probably the largest ones in human history in geographical terms, bequeathed their legal traditions to the smaller succeeding empires. The Turkish tribes and house of Osman, eponymous father of the Ottoman Empire, also shared in this inheritance. Standard Sunni theories of political thought were subjected to Turko-Mongol influences. The study of the eastern Islamic lands in the post-Mongol period as a relatively coherent unit has proven to be illuminating in the fields of political thought, mysticism, art, and architecture. Specific discourses and views concerning the relationship between dynastic and Islamic (Sunni) law circulated across the post-Mongol eastern Islamic lands. The particular structure and discourse of authority, the adoption of specific Sunni school of law (in the Ottoman case the Hanafi *Madhhab*), related to Sunni dynasties, but may equally be applied to Safavid Iran, the major Shi'ite counterpart of the Ottomans.[8]

Is this wide political and cultural horizon from the Balkans in the west to Iran and India in the east relevant at all to the Jewish case? After all, we are dealing with a small minority lacking any autonomous sovereignty or political center and having a

---

6. Jonathan Ray, *After Expusion. 1492 and the Making of Sephardi Jewry*, New York and London: New York U.P., 2013, esp. pp. 4, 66–70; Giancarlo Casale, *The Ottoman Age of Exploration*, Oxford: Oxford U.P. 2010. See further important discussion in Alan Mikhail, *God's Shadow: Sultan Selim, His Ottoman Empire, and the Making of the Modern World*, New York: W.W. Norton, 2020.

7. Sussan Babaie, Kathryn Babayan, Ina Baghdiantz-McCabe, Massumeh Farhad, *Slaves of the Shah. New Elites of Safavid Iran*, London and New York, I.B. Tauris, 2004, passim. See especially *ibid.*, p. 6.

8. Guy Burak, *The Second Formation of Islamic Law. The Hanafi School the Early Modern Ottoman Empire*, Cambridge: Cambridge U.P., 2015, pp. 207–210; Idem., 'Between the Ḳānūn of Qāytbāy and Ottoman Yasaq: A Note on the Ottomans' Dynastic Law', *Journal of Islamic Studies* 26, no. 1 (2015), pp. 1–23. See also David Morgan, 'The "Great Yasa of Chinggis Khan" Revisited', in: Reuven Amitai and Michal Biran (eds.), *Mongols, Turks, and Others. Eurasian Nomads and the Sedentary World*, Leiden and Boston: Brill, 205, pp. 291–308.

limited impact on the Ottoman management of the empire. As in previous phases of Islamicate history, the Jewish minority responded actively and profoundly to its surrounding cultural and political settings, as it did in regard to Ottoman civilization. The Jews acquired a very close acquaintance with the Ottoman culture. Various aspects of Ottoman daily life, culture, and habits infiltrated deeply into Jewish life. They echoed the political ethos and propaganda of the Sultanic rule regarding the role of justice (*adelet*) as a legitimizing factor and the ideal of prosperity and peace (*huzur*), under the Ottomans for all subjects respecting the central control. In general, the members of Eastern Sephardi Diaspora—the communities established in the core lands of the Ottoman Empire after the expulsions—identified with the Ottomans rather than with European states (the Habsburgs, the Italian city-states, and France), during times of military confrontations, and hoped for their victory. The unprecedented rise of Jewish historiographical writing among Ottoman communities around the Mediterranean Basin during the early modern period demonstrated how deep was both the interest and the acquaintance of contemporary Jews with Ottoman history and its political fluctuations, the destiny of various Sultans, and the power mechanisms involved. In short, Jews were deeply exposed to Ottoman civilization in its various aspects, and imperial changes left their mark on Jewish culture and religion.

The search for a time axis began with the individual biography of the composer of *Beit Yosef* and *Shulchan 'Arukh* and ended with a timespan of several centuries, in the open expanses of Asia, the Mongol Empires and their successors, including the Ottoman Empire. The perspective for illuminating the codification project of R. Karo thus proved to be both *global* and *Eurasian*. The micro-history of legal summaries intended to serve a relatively small minority at the same time formed part of global and macrohistorical changes across wide arcs of time and space. In both the Jewish and Islamicate cases, this wide horizon necessitated wide cultural exchanges, transmitted concretely through broad networks of scholars and merchants:

> The boundaries of modern nation-states [...] have tended to obscure both important areas of shared experience and significant systems of connection between the Middle East and South Asia. If this is true of the structural characteristics of the Ottoman, Safavid, and Mughal empires, and if this is also true of their commercial organization and techniques of trade, it is no less true of the content of their systems of formal learning, of the nature of their major sources of esoteric understanding, and of the ways in which they were linked by the connective systems of learned and holy men.[9]

In the parallel Jewish context, this was evident in a paradigmatic shift from the local and fragmentary model to a supra-local model, including the formation of large politico-cultural-religious-legal units, subduing the medieval fragmentary identities of local communities. This process took place in the Ottoman Empire, in Germany (*Ashkenaz* in Jewish terminology), and in Central and Eastern Europe throughout the early modern

---

9. Francis Robinson, 'Ottomans-Safvids-Mughals: Shared Knowledge and Connective Systems', *Journal of Islamic Studies* 8, no. 2 (1997), pp. 151–184. Citation from *ibid.*, p. 151.

period. The crystallization of Sephardi identity was intensified by several factors, such as the print revolution and its universalizing impact on Jewish heritage; economic and familial networks of wide extent from Western Europe to the Indian Ocean, the Mediterranean, and even the "New World;" the interaction between "normative" Jews and *Conversos* living as Catholics; and certainly to life under a single Ottoman Empire. These economic-commercial networks inspired the formation of a parallel chain of communication serving scholars, Talmudic sages, and poets who sent the fruits of their creativity to one another and put them to public test within their milieu.[10] This system functioned as a Jewish-Mediterranean "Republic of Letters," inciting its participants to search for a common "canonical" model. The intellectual networks integrated with the same channels used by Jewish political figures and merchants.[11] The codification of R. Karo should also be read in this light, as an effort to reach legal consensus. This is indicated by the geographical extent of people with whom he engaged in his responsa. Again, this echoed a parallel pattern in the Ottoman Empire, as cogently shown by Helen Pfeifer: informal encounters in literary saloons in the *Bilad a-Sham* area—the same cultural and geographical milieu of Karo and the city of Safed—brought together Ottoman and Arab scholars and *'Ulama* and contributed to the formation of common tastes and cultural consensus.[12]

Another corollary was the functioning of one large community as a virtual center. The Jewish community in Istanbul functioned in late sixteenth century, and even more so throughout the seventeenth century, as a kind of political capital of the Jewish Diaspora under Ottoman rule. It assembled the political petitions of various communities and individuals addressed to the Sultanic court, and later served as a focal agent in concentrating and transferring charity from the entirety of Jewish communities to the poor in the Holy Land, to be divided on a nonethnic basis.[13] The changing balance between the virtual "capital city" and its periphery also affected the Ottoman-Jewish communities and resulted in the formation of several foci of power. Other cities and Jewish communities also bore a typically international character, such as Salonica and Izmir. Safed was unique, however, as it turned into a kind of Jewish microcosm where all the ethnic and cultural traditions met. In the visions of some rabbinical and Kabbalistic authorities in Safed, their city could even stand its own against the historical role and prestige of Jerusalem. Even the construction of an impressive wall around

---

10. Shenhav Bartov, *"Interaction Poems" of the Poets of the Mid-Sixteenth to Early Seventeenth Century in the Ottoman Empire* [Hebrew], M.A. Thesis, submitted at Tel-Aviv University, 2008; Haim Bentov, 'Methods of study of Talmud in the Yeshivot of Salonica and Turkey after the Expulsion from Spain' [Hebrew], *Sefunot: Studies and Sources on the History of the Jewish Communities in the East* 14 (1971–1978), pp. 7–102.

11. On Jewish families connected to Ottoman court, and port merchant, weaving wide network of connections, see Yaron Tzur, *Notables and other Jews in the Ottoman Middle East 1750–1830* [Hebrew], Jerusalem: Bialik Institute, 2016.

12. Helen Pfeifer, 'Encounter after the Conquest: Scholarly Gatherings in 16th Century Ottoman Damascus', *International Journal of Middle East Studies* 47, no. 2 (2015), pp. 219–239.

13. Matthias B. Lehmann, *Emissaries from the Holy Land. The Sephardic Diaspora and the Practice of Pan-Judaism in the Eighteenth Century*, Stanford: Stanford U.P, 2014.

the city of Jerusalem during the period of Süleyman did not halt its declining status in the Jewish context during the sixteenth century. The inhabitants of Safed could hardly ignore the impact of the city of Damascus, a prospering international hub in their vicinity. Thousands of pilgrims passed through the city; estimates vary from about 15,000 to 40,000 in exceptional years. There were also many Turks and eastern Europeans and a smaller number of Persians and central Asians from beyond the Ottoman borders.[14] The Jewish communities in Safed and Damascus maintained strong ties, and voices from Damascus were soon heard in Safed. The encounter between cultural traditions carried by various ethnic Jewish groups left an indelible impact on early modern Jewish culture, as cogently noted by Moshe Idel.[15] One of the results was a constant attempt to form some kind of synthesis of various traditions. The formation of encyclopedic books testified further to the inclination to provide Jewish readers with a universal and comprehensive perspective encompassing the entire Jewish heritage, as a last-word summa. A somewhat younger contemporary of R. Karo, the Sephardi Rabbi Shlomo Almoli (c.1490–1542) composed a "Summa of All the Literary Branches of Knowledge" (*Me'asef le-khol ha-machanot*).[16] This work sought to provide methodological tools enabling the reader to gain a comprehensive understanding of entire human knowledge by summing up the essential content of all existing books "as a set table" (*ve-yimatzu ke-shulchan 'arukh*). Thus, Almoli uses the same expression later employed by R. Karo—*Shulchan 'Arukh*—to characterize the canonization of knowledge. One part is dedicated to an encyclopedic presentation of religious praxis (*mitzvot*), avoiding any legalistic ambiguities, and providing the reader with "the straight and non-false beliefs." It is interesting to note the fusion of legalism, orthodoxy, stricter rules of conduct and belief ("non-false beliefs"), and theology in these sections. Like the processes of *confessionalization* and *Sunnitization* in the Ottoman context, this process was related in the Jewish context not only to "top-down" initiatives or the political control of wide empires but it also related to cultural changes rooted in the local domain, including the response of minorities.

The political and consequently the legal ethos of the Ottoman Empire left its mark on various aspects of R. Karo's work, as shown throughout this book. The work was constructed around the figure of a universal ruler, a vision of renovation (*Tajdid* or *Tecdid* in Arabic and Turkish, respectively), and the reform of religion, alongside the sanctification of the ruler as a saintly figure. The justice mechanism became ever more centralized; it was constructed as a tight hierarchy, with a pre-ordained course of study and

14. Elizabeth Sirriyeh, *Sufi Visionary of Ottoman Damascus. 'Abd al-Ghani al-Nabulusi 1641–1731*, London and New York: Routledge Curzon, 2005, p. 39.

15. Moshe Idel, 'On Mobility, Individuals and Groups: Prolegomenon for a Sociological Approach to Sixteenth-Century Kabbalah', *Kabbalah. Journal for the Study of Jewish Mystical Texts* 3 (1998), pp. 145–173.

16. Shlomo-Solomon Almoli, *Me'asef leKol HaMachanot*, Istanbul: 1535. See also Bartov, *"Interaction Poems" of the Poets of the Mid-Sixteenth to Early Seventeenth Century in the Ottoman Empire*, esp. p. 2, a manuscript bearing the very same title, containing a Summa of contemporary Sephardi poetry composed in the Ottoman Empire.

list of books, a clear preference for the Hanafi school of law (*Madhhab*) at the expense of all the others; a reliance on Ottoman jurists and the marginalization of Arab scholars even within the Hanafi school; a guild and establishment consciousness among jurists affiliated to the state; the formation of a particular *Tabaqat* literature; the state nomination of professional jurists in legal mechanisms across the empire; and, finally, the dominant role of the Grand Mufti in charge of the entire mechanism and responsible for articulating the official legal positions—the *Şeyḫülislâm*. The legal experts functioned alongside a professionalized bureaucracy, in both cases controlled from the center and disseminated to the provinces. These played a definitive role in forming tax policies and surveys of population and land, essential to running the grand empire. Law extended to further domains and integrated with the above-mentioned confessionalization and Sunnitization of Ottoman–Muslim society in the core lands of the empire. Confessional ambiguity gradually gave way to clearer limits between correct and heretical religious positions, with the latter now regarded as dangerous. Broad and popular literature was composed to instruct the believers in regard to their acts and beliefs. The style of writing and the languages used—Turkish and its Arabic translations—clearly indicated the intention to address the public at large. In these tracts, the scholars of religious law (*'Ulama*) enjoyed a prominent place. Paradoxically, the authoritative scholars published texts that made their authority redundant, since their writings provided short and clear-cut statements on religious practices and positions. The fear was that the need for direct and personal contact with religious scholars would eventually wane away.[17] The same dialectical dynamics developed concerning Karo's codes. Contemporary rabbis expressed their concern that people would consult these books rather than address them for halakhic guidance. Nir Shafir characterized the "pietistic turn," achieved through these guiding tracts, next to exerting control on comportment in the public space, the need to memorize the correct phrasing of belief, the missionary effort to disseminate the new "orthodox" messages, the role of law as axial component in correct religious life, and—what is no less important for our discussion—the attempt to extend this confessionalizing policy to the non-Muslim minorities.[18] Cengiz Şişman accurately positioned Jewish confessionalization alongside similar processes in the Ottoman Empire and beyond.[19] Law played a dominant role in this pietistic process, and not only as a

---

17. Nir Shafir, *The Road from Damascus: Circulation and the Redefinition of Islam in the Ottoman Empire, 1620–1720*, Ph.D. submitted at University of California, 2016, esp. p. 139.

18. Derin Terzioğlu, 'Where 'Ilm-I Hal Meets Catechism: Islamic Manuals of Religious Instruction in the Ottoman Empire in the Age of Confessionalization', *Past and Present* 220, no. 1 (2013), pp. 79–114; Tijana Krstić, 'State and Religion, "Sunnitization" and "Confessionalization" in Süleyman's Time', in Pál Fodor (ed.), *The Battle for Central Europe*, Boston and London: Brill, 2019, pp. 65–91. See also Katharina Anna Ivanyi, Virtue, *Piety and the Law: A Study of Birgivi Mehmed Efendi's Al-Tariqa Al-Muhammadiyya*, Ph.D. submitted at Princeton University, 2012. On the 'Pietistic Turn', see Nir Shafir, 'Moral Revolutions: The Politics of Piety in the Ottoman Empire Reimagined', *Comparative Studies in Society and History* 61, no. 3 (2019), pp. 595–623, esp. p. 598.

19. Cengiz Şişman, *Transcending Diaspora: Studies on Sabbateanism and Dönmes*, Istanbul: Libra Kitapçılık ve Yayıncılık, 2016, esp. Ch. II – 'Global Crisis, Puritanism and Prophecy in

regulating factor in political context of public order and domination. The Ottoman codes of law in Arab lands contributed to the Sunnitization effort and began to include ethical sins, not only administrative or political instructions.[20]

Law and legality, then, became an essential element in establishing a wide empire, as part of the political ethos shared in Eurasia and particularly following the Mongol heritage, as a component in religious change and cultural-political control of Muslim population and as a channel for integrating the non-Muslim minorities within the Ottoman state.[21] Again, the question arises to what extent this legal complexity was relevant to the Jewish minority. Despite its clear economic contribution to Ottoman prosperity along the sixteenth century, the Jewish collective enjoyed only very limited political independency, very much like the Armenians or Greek-Orthodox. Jews had no religious leader heading their Diaspora under the Ottomans. Their legal autonomy was even more restricted than that enjoyed by larger minorities, and it faced constant competition from the Ottoman–Muslim courts. Sephardi rabbis constantly complained that many members of Jewish communities preferred the Muslim over the Jewish legal procedure.

Another factor of importance was the interstice between the center and the periphery, the core lands of the Empire—Rumelia and Anatolia—and the conquered Arab lands, where R. Karo finished his codification project, matured as a mystical persona, and acquired his rabbinical fame. The power balance between Ottoman domination, local elites, and the Arab populace was fluid and changed constantly during the early modern period. After the late sixteenth century, local families and elite in the Arab lands played an increasing role in the management of their parts of the empire. This was not necessarily a sign of "Ottoman decline" but rather a changing equilibrium between the center and the periphery. It enabled the Ottomans to control significant aspects of public management within the empire, while leaving a relative liberty to local population and local elites and refraining from direct and protracted violence. This process naturally affected Jewish communities in the eastern Mediterranean and their efforts to maintain their religious, political, and legal autonomy. It was evident in the longing for past glory, when the sacred Temple was still existent and served as focal point of divine presence and assurance of the collective tradition, and no less the validity of the rabbinical tradition. The concrete focus of these longings was the desire to replicate the institution of the Sanhedrin as a prototype of a Supreme Court in vicinity to the religious center of the Holy Temple, assembling the rabbinic elite scholarship, enjoying divine inspiration, and ruling for the entire Jewish Ecumene. These longings and traditions had lain dormant and inactive for centuries, yet they could be awoken in the

---

the Early Modern World. Some Observations on the Apocalyptic Relationship between Christian Salvation, Jewish Conversion and Turkish Doom and Its Impact on the Sabbatean Movement', pp. 23–55.

20. Reem Meshal, 'Antagonistic Shari'as and the Construction of Orthodoxy in Sixteenth Century Ottoman Cairo', *Journal of Islamic Studies*, 21, no. 2 (2010), pp. 183–212, esp. p. 205.

21. See the important discussion in Najwa Al-Qattan, 'Dhimmis in the Muslim Court: Legal Autonomy and Religious Discrimination', *International Journal of Middle East Studies* 31, no. 3 (1999), pp. 429- 444.

appropriate historical circumstances. The new paradigm of the sixteenth century, mentioned previously, toward supra-local political and religious units of Jewish life, whether
in the German, Polish, or Ottoman contexts, led to unification and homogenization
of traditions at the expense of local and ancient heritage.[22] The Sanhedrin ethos was a
component in a rabbinical repertory that could sustain and provide concrete form to
these changes. Karo's vision of establishing a universal and prestigious court of law,
by way of a Jewish response to the universalistic legal systems established around him,
explains his opposition to mediation procedures outside court, his insistence on keeping
rabbinical disagreements away from public knowledge, his participation in the *Semikhah*
initiative, and his fierce rejection of any demand to provide the reasonings of court verdicts, even when this was requested by the litigants. It certainly relates to the sense of an
urgent need for hierarchy within the justice mechanism. Following Guy Burak's lucid
observations, the hierarchy of texts used in Karo's codes of law—as expounded in his
double preambles—enforced and responded to a parallel hierarchy within the rabbin-
ical-legal guilds.[23] Another factor mentioned previously, the print revolution, contributed its part, though it does not deserve the weight attributed to it in modern research.
The eastern branch of Sephardi Diaspora lived under a prosperous civilization that still
relied on an efficient and functioning manuscript tradition. Jews confronted the challenge of cultural unification not only in political, administrative, or religious aspects.
As they travelled in the Ottoman territories, they could not avoid the impressive and
massive constructions projects initiated by the sultanic authorities and family and by the
Ottoman ruling elite in their footsteps. The canonization of esthetic taste was a well-
calculated project of the political center, as persuasively shown by Gülru Necipoğlu, and
was adopted by local Arab elites in the major cities.[24]

In many aspects of R. Karo's life and projects, he was sensitive to the changes
undergone in the Eurasian domain. The interaction of his towering personality and
his sensibility to what happened around him seems to me to be more crucial in understanding his codification project than the legal content and juridical formalities of *Beit
Yosef* and *Shulchan 'Arukh*. Current research almost exclusively focuses on the textual
perspective of positive law and halakhic content and orientation—as a sealed product,
put to print and later disseminated on a massive scale. I chose to present a historical-
contextual perspective of canonization and legal codification as a dynamic process. *Beit
Yosef* and *Shulchan 'Arukh*, an extraordinarily impressive achievement of post-Talmudic
erudition, interacted with political, cultural, and religious changes taking place within

---

22. On these processes of cultural unification in Poland and Germany (Ashkenaz), see Elchanan
    Reiner, 'On the Roots of the Urban Jewish Community in Poland in the Early Modern
    Period' [Hebrew], *Gal-Ed. On the History and Culture of Polish Jewry* 20 (2006), pp. 13–37;
    Joseph Davis, 'The Reception of the *Shulhan 'Aruch* and the Formation of Ashkenazic Jewish
    Identity', *AJS Review* 26:2 (2002), pp. 251–276.
23. Burak, *The Second Formation of Islamic Law*, p. 126.
24. Gülru Necipoğlu, 'A Kanun for the State, a Canon for the Arts: The Classical Synthesis
    in Ottoman Art and Architecture during the Age of Süleyman', in: Gilles Veinstein (ed.),
    Soliman le Magnifique et son temps, Paris: La Documentation Française, 1992, pp. 195–215.

the Jewish Ecumene, as a part of a global and Eurasian context. As seen above, this process also shows surprising similarities with processes of canonization within Islamic tradition.

R. Karo had a very limited capacity to apply and enforce his grand visions. His indelible contribution nevertheless became dominant over the coming centuries, and his religious paradigm won the game. It presents law as the axial element of Jewish tradition and life, next to the rising importance of theological positions of Kabbalistic origins—both serving the task of reforming Jewish religion. The modernization in its first and crucial phase took place in the Ottoman and Islamicate context rather than in the European one as commonly suggested by modern historians. Reformation implied correct and "Orthodox" religious stands, the establishment of pedagogical institutions, control of the body and sexuality, popular guidance literature addressing the public at large, Jewish confessionalization, and the unification of the Jewish Ecumene. All these elements, to which R. Karo contributed significantly, would later erupt and conquer the public sphere in the messianic movement of Sabbatai Zvi fifty years later.[25] Here, too, the Muslim, and particularly Ottoman, contexts are crucial for understanding the Sabbatian adventure and its lasting imprint.

---

25. Roni Weinstein, 'The Ottoman Settings of the Sabbatian Movement' [forthcoming]. On the link between R. Karo and Sabbetai Zvi, see Maoz Kahana, 'Cosmos and Nomos: Sacred Space and Legal Action, from Rabbi Yosef Qaro to Shabbetai Şevi', *El Prezente. Journal for Sephardic Studies* 10 (2016), pp. 143–153.

BIBLIOGRAPHICAL LIST

Primary Sources

Almoli, Shlomo-Solomon, *Me'asef le-Khol Ha-Machanot*, Istanbul, 1535.

Azulai, Yosef-David [HaChidah], *Birkei Yosef*, Livorno 1774, Vol. II, Section – 'Choshen Mishpat'.

Ben Matitya of Arta Binyamin, *Responsa Binyamin Zeev*, Jerusalem, 1959.

Ben Zimrah, David [The *Radbaz*], *Responsa*, Jerusalem, 1972.

Ben-Haviv, Levi [The *Ralbach*], *Responsa*, Jerusalem: Keren Re'em Institute, 2018.

Ben-Haviv, Levi, *Responsa*, Jerusalem: Keren Re'em Institute, 2018.

Conforti, David (1618–1690), *Koreh HaDorot*, Piotrikow, 1895.

Conforti, David, *Koreh Ha-Dorot* [Hebrew], Pietrikow: Solomon Belchotovsky Print House, 1895.

De Medina, Samuel, *Responsa*, New York, 1959.

Di Trani, Moses, *Kiryat Sefer*, Venice: Aldo Bragadin Publishing House, 1551.

Di Trani, Moses, *Responsa*, Jerusalem, 1974.

Gedalya, ibn Yichya, *Shalshelet Ha-Kabbalah* ['*Chain of Transmission*' in Hebrew], Jerusalem: Ha-Dorot Ha-Rishonim ve-Korotam, 1962.

Karo, Joseph, *Magid Meisharim*, Wilnius: Judah Leib Lipman Metz Print, 1875.

Karo, Joseph, *Responsa Avkat Rochel*, Salonica, 1791.

Messer, Leon Yehuda, *Kevod Chakhamim* [Honor of Sages/Rabbis], ed. and introduction by Shimeon Bernfeld, Berlin: H. Itzkowski Print, 1899.

Sirkish, Joel B. Samuel [*HaBach*], *Responsa (The Old Ones)*, [*Shut HaBach HaYeshanot* in Hebrew], New York, 1966.

Zahalon, Yom-Tov, *New Responsa* [*Shut Maharitatz Ha-Chadashot* in Hebrew], Jerusalem: Machon Yerushalayim, 1980–81.

Secondary Sources

Abisaab, Rula Jurdi, *Converting Persia: Religion and Power in the Safavid Empire*, London and New York: I. B. Tauris, 2004.

Abou-El-Haj, Rifa'at Ali, "Aspect of the Legitimation of Ottoman Rule as Reflected in the Preambles to Two Early *Liva Kanunnameler*," *Turcica* 23 (1991), pp. 371–383.

Ahmed, Shahab and Filipovic Nenad, "The Sultan's Syllabus: A Curriculum for the Ottoman Imperial Medreses Prescribed in a Fermān of Qānūnī I Süleymān, Dated 973 (1565)," *Studia Islamica* 98–99 (2004), pp. 183–218.

Ahrend, Aharon, "Mishnah Study and Mishnah Confraternities in the Early Modern Period" [Hebrew], *JSIG* 3 (2004), pp. 19–53.

Akyildiz, Olcay, Kara Halim, and Sagaster Börte (eds.), *Autobiogrpahical Themes in Turkish Literature: Theoretical and Comparative Perspectives*, Würzburg: Ergon Verlag, 2007.

Albeck, Hanoch, "Semichah, Nomination and Court of Law" [Hebrew], *Zion* 8 (1943), pp. 85–93.

Al-Qattan, Najwa, "Dhimmis in the Muslim Court: Legal Autonomy and Religious Discrimination," *International Journal of Middle East Studies* 31, 3 (1999), pp. 429–444.

Al-Tikriti, Nabil, "Ibn-i Kemal's Confessionalism and the Construction of an Ottoman Islam," in: Christine Isom-Verhaaren and Kent F. Schull (eds.), *Living in the Ottoman Realm: Empire and Identity, 13th to 20th Centuries*, Bloomington and Indianapolis: Indiana University Press, 2016, pp. 95–107.

Altshuler, Mor, *The Life of Rabbi Yosef Karo* [Hebrew], Tel-Aviv: Tel-Aviv University Press, 2016.

Andrews, Walter G. and Kapaklı Mehmet, *The Age of Beloveds: Love and the Beloved in Early-Modern Ottoman and European Culture and Society*, Durham: Duke University Press, 2005.

Assis, Yom-Tov and Meyerson Mark, "The Iberian Peninsula," in: Robert Chazan (ed.), *The Cambridge History of Judaism*, Vol. VI: The Middle Ages – The Christian World, Cambridge: Cambridge University Press, 2018, pp. 129–184.

Atcil, Abdurrahman, *Scholars and Sultans in the Early Modern Ottoman Empire*, Cambridge: Cambridge University Press, 2017.

Babaie, Sussan, Babayan Kathryn, Baghdiantz-McCabe Ina, and Farhad Massumeh, *Slaves of the Shah: New Elites of Safavid Iran*, London and New York: I. B. Tauris, 2004.

Barani, Jacob, "R. Yosef Escapa and the Rabbinate of Izmir" [Hebrew], *Sefunot: Studies and Sources on the History of the Jewish Communities in the East* 3 (1985), pp. 53–81.

Bardakjian, Kevork B., "The Rise of the Armenian Patriarchate of Constantinople," in: Bernard Lewis and Benjamin Braude (eds.), *Christians and Jews in the Ottoman Empire: The Functioning of a Plural Society*, New York: Holmes & Meier, 1982, pp. 89–100.

Bar-Ilan, Meir, "Tikkun Leil Shavuot: Its Formation and Precedents" [Hebrew], *Mechkarei Hag* 8 (1997), pp. 28–48.

Barkey, Karen, "Aspects of Legal Pluralism in the Ottoman Empire," in: Lauren Benton and Richard J. Ross (eds.), *Legal Pluralism and Empires, 1500–1850*, New York and London: New York University Press, 2013, pp. 83–107.

Bar-Levav, Avriel, "Between Library Awareness and the Jewish Republic of Letters" [Hebrew], in: Yosef Kaplan and Moshe Sluhovsky (eds.), *Libraries and Book Collections*, Jerusalem: Shazar Center, 2006, pp. 201–224.

Bar-Levav, Avriel, "The Religious Order of Jewish Books: Structuring Hebrew Knowledge in Amsterdam," *Studia Rosenthaliana* 44 (2012), pp. 1–27.

Barnai, Jacob, "The Status of the 'General Rabbinate' in Jerusalem in the Ottoman Period" [Hebrew], *Cathedra: For the History of Eretz Israel and Its Yishuv* 13 (1979), pp. 47–69.

Barnai, Jacob, *Smyrna, the Microcosmos of Europe: The Jewish Community of Smyrna in the 17th and 18th Centuries* [Hebrew], Jerusalem: Carmel, 2014.

Bartov, Shenhav, "'Interaction Poems' of the Poets of the Mid-Sixteenth to Early Seventeenth Century in the Ottoman Empire" [Hebrew], M.A. thesis, submitted at Tel-Aviv University, 2008.

Beinart, Haim (ed.), *Moreshet Sepharad: The Sephardi Legacy*, Jerusalem: Magnes Press, 1992, Vols. I–II.

Bellomo, Manlio, *The Common Legal Past of Europe, 1000–1800*, translated by Lydia G. Cochrane, Washington D.C.: Catholic University of America Press, 1995.

Benayahu, Meir, *R. Hayim Yosef David Azulai* [Hebrew], 2 Vols., Jerusalem: Yad Ben-Zvi and Mosad HaRav Kuk, 1959.

Benayahu, Meir, "The Renovation of Rabbinic Semichah in Safed" [Hebrew], in: S. W. Baron, B. Dinur, S. Ettinger, and I. Halpern (eds.), *Yitzhak F. Baer Jubilee Volume: On the Occasion of his Seventieth Birthday*, Jerusalem: The Historical Society of Israel, 1960, pp. 248–269.

Benayahu, Meir, "Communication of Rabbis of Egypt to Radbaz," "*Sefunot: Studies and Sources on the History of the Jewish Communities in the East* 6 (1962), pp. 125–134.

Benayahu, Meir, "R. Joseph Taitatzak from Salonica, Head of Sephardi Diaspora" [Hebrew], in: Zvi Ankori (ed.), *Then and Now: Annual Lectures on the Jews of Greece (1977–1983)*, Tel-Aviv: The School of Jewish Studies, Tel-Aviv University, 1984, pp. 21–34.

Benayahu, Meir, "The Schools of R. Moses di Trani and Maran Joseph Karo and their Confontations" [Hebrew], in: Meir Benayahu, *Joseph My Chosen One* [Hebrew], Jerusalem: Yad HaRav Nissim, 1991, pp. 9–98.

Benayahu, Meir, *Yosef Bechiri* ['*Joseph, My Chosen One*' in Hebrew], Jerusalem: Yad HaRav Nissim, 1991.

Beneyto, José María and Varela Justo Corti (eds.), *At the Origins of Modernity: Francisco de Vitoria and the Discovery of International Law*, Cham: Springer, 2017.

Ben-Naeh, Yaron, "City of Torah and Study: Salonica as a Torah Center during the Sixteenth and Seventeenth Centuries" [Hebrew], *Pe'amim: Studies in Oriental Jewry*, 80 (1999), pp. 60–82.

Ben-Naeh, Yaron, "The Jewish Community of Istanbul and Eretz Israel Jewry in the Seventeenth Century" [Hebrew], *Cathedra: For the History of Eretz Israel and Its Yishuv* 92 (1999), pp. 65–106.

Ben-Naeh, Yaron, "Honor and Its Meaning among Ottoman Jews," *Jewish Social Studies*, New Series, 11, 2 (Winter, 2005), pp. 19–50.

Ben-Naeh, Yaron, *Jews in the Realm of the Sultans: Ottoman Jewish Society in the Seventeenth Century*, Tübingen: Mohr Siebeck, 2008.

Ben-Naeh, Yaron, "Urban Encounters: The Muslim-Jewish Case in the Ottoman Empire," in: Eyal Ginio and Elie Podeh (eds.), *The Ottoman Middle East: Studies in Honor of Amnon Cohen*, Leiden and Boston: Brill, 2014, pp. 177–197.

Ben-Naeh, Yaron, "Rabbi Joseph Karo and His Time" [Hebrew], in: *Rabbi Joseph Karo: History, Halakhah, Kabbalah*, Jerusalem: Zalman Shazar Center, 2021, pp. 21–127.

Ben-Sasson, Menahem, "The 'Libraries' of Maimonides Family between Cairo and Aleppo" [Hebrew], in: Yom-Tov Assis, Miriam Frenkel, and Yaron Harel (eds.), *Aleppo Studies, The Jews of Aleppo*, Vol. I – 'Their History and Culture', Jerusalem: Ben Zvi, 2009, pp. 51–105.

Ben-Sasson, Menahem, "Maimonides' Mishneh Torah: Towards Canon-Formation in the Life of an Author" [Hebrew], in: Menahem Ben-Sasson, Brody Robert, Lieblich Amia, and Shalev Donna (eds.), *Uncovering the Canon: Studies in Canonicity and Genizah*, Jerusalem: Magnes, 2010, pp. 133–201.

Benton, Lauren, *Law and Colonial Cultures: Legal Regimes in World History, 1400–1900*, Cambridge: Cambridge University Press, 2004.

Bentov, Haim, "Methods of study of Talmud in the Yeshivot of Salonica and Turkey after the Expulsion from Spain" [Hebrew], *Sefunot: Studies and Sources on the History of the Jewish Communities in the East* 14 (1971–1978), pp. 7–102.

Berkey, Karen, "Aspects of Legal Pluralism in the Ottoman Empire," in: Lauren Benton and Richard J. Ross (eds.), *Legal Pluralism and Empires, 1500–1850*, New York and London: New York University Press, 2013, pp. 83–107.

Berkovitz, Jay, *Law's Dominion: Jewish Community, Religion and Family in Early Modern Metz*, Leiden and Boston: Brill, 2020.

Blidstein, Gerald J., "On the Institutionalization of Prophecy in Maimonidean Halakhah" [Hebrew], *Daat: A Journal of Jewish Philosophy & Kabbalah* 43 (1999), pp. 25–42.

Blidstein, Gerald J., "The Suggestion of Maimonides to Renovate the Semichah" [Hebrew], *Dinei Israel: Researches on Halakhah and Jewish Law* 26–27 (2009–2010), pp. 241–252.

Bonfil, Reuven, *Selected Chapters from Sefer Me'or 'Einayim and Matsref la-Kessef* [Hebrew], Jerusalem: Bialik Institute, 1991.

Bonfil, Robert, *Rabbinate in Renaissance Italy* [Hebrew], Jerusalem: Magnes Press, 1979.

Bosbach, Franz, "The European Debate and the Revival of Ghibellinism," David Armitage (ed.), *Theories of Empire, 1450–1800*, London and New York: Routledge, 2016, pp. 81–98.

Breuer, Mordechai, "The Ashkenazi Semichah" [Hebrew], *Zion* 33, 1–2 (1968), pp. 15–46.

Brody, Robert, *The Geonim of Babylonia and the Shaping of Medieval Jewish Culture*, New Haven and London: Yale University Press, 2013.

Brown, Jonathan, *The Canonization of Al-Bukhari and Muslim: The Formation and Function of the Sunni Hadith Canon*, Leiden and Boston: Brill, 2007.

Burak, Guy, "Faith, Law and Empire in the Ottoman 'Age of Confessionalization' (Fifteenth–Seventeenth Centuries): The Case of 'Renewal of Faith,'" *Mediterranean Historical Review* 28, 1 (2013), pp. 1–23.

Burak, Guy, "According to His Exalted Ḳânûn: Contending Visions of the Muftiship in the Ottoman Province of Damascus (Sixteenth-Eighteenth Centuries)," in: Ze'evi Dror and Ehud R. Toledano (eds.), *Society, Law, and Culture in the Middle East: 'Modernities' in the Making*, Berlin and New York: De Gruyter, 2015, pp. 74–86.

Burak, Guy, "Between the Ḳānūn of Qāytbāy and Ottoman Yasaq: A Note on the Ottomans' Dynastic Law," *Journal of Islamic Studies* 26, 1 (2015), pp. 1–23.

Burak, Guy, *The Second Formation of Islamic Law: The Hanafi School the Early Modern Ottoman Empire*, Cambridge: Cambridge University Press, 2015.

Burak, Guy, "Evidentiary Truth Claims, Imperial Registers, and the Ottoman Archive: Contending Legal Views of Archival and Record-Keeping Practices in Ottoman Greater Syria (Seventeenth–Nineteenth Centuries)," *Bulletin of SOAS* 79, 2 (2016), pp. 233–254.

Burak, Guy, "Reliable Books: Islamic Law, Canonization, and Manuscripts in the Ottoman Empire (Sixteenth to Eighteenth Centuries)," in: Grafton Anthony and Most Glenn (eds.), *Canonical Texts and Scholarly Practices: A Global Comparative Approach*, Cambridge: Cambridge University Press, 2016, pp. 14–33.

Burak, Guy, "Madhhab," in: *The [Oxford] Encyclopedia of Islam and Law*, Oxford Islamic Studies Online: http://www.oxfordislamicstudies.com/article/opr/t349/e0094 (accessed November 11, 2017).

Burak, Guy, "'In Compliance with the Old Register': On Ottoman Documentary Depositories and Archival Consciousness," *Journal of the Economic and Social History of the Orient* 62 (2019), pp. 799–823.

Burak, Guy, "Reflections on Censorship, Canonization and the Ottoman Practices of *Imza* and *Takriz*," published on www.acacemia.edu site.

Buzov, Snjezana, "The Lawgiver and His Lawmakers: The Role of Legal Discourse in the Change of Ottoman Imperial Culture," Ph.D. submitted at Chicago University, 2005.

Buzov, Snjezana, *State Law and Divine Law Under the Ottomans: Encounters between Shari'a and the Sultan's Law*, London: I. B. Tauris, 2012.

Carlebach, Elisheva, *The Pursuit of Heresy: Rabbi Moses Hagiz and the Sabbatian Controversies*, New York: Columbia University Press, 1990.

Casale, Giancarlo, *The Ottoman Age of Exploration*, Oxford: Oxford University Press, 2010.

Chajes, Joseph H., "Accounting for the Self: Preliminary Generic-Historical Reflections on Early Modern Jewish Egodocuments," *Jewish Quarterly Review* 95, 1 (2005), pp. 1–15.

Chechik, Moshe Dovid, "The Struggle over Ashkenazi Legacy in Poland: The Printing of Shulhan Aruch in Poland and the Reactions to It" [Hebrew], M.A. thesis submitted at the Hebrew University (Jerusalem), 2018.

Cohen, Marc C., "Systermatizing Gods' Law: Rabbanite Jurisprudence in the Islamic World from the Tenth to the Thirteenth Centuries," Ph.D. submitted at Pennsylvania Univesity, 2016.

Cohen, Mark R., *Maimonides and the Merchants: Jewish Law and Society in the Medieval Islamic World*, University of Pennsylvania Press, 2017.

Çolak, Hasan and Elif Bayraktar-Tellan, *The Orthodox Church as an Ottoman Institution: A Study of Early Modern Patriarchal Berats*, Istanbul: The Isis Press, 2019.

Conte, Emanuele and Ryan Magnus, "Codification in the Western Middle Ages," in: John Hudson and Ana Rodríguez (eds.), *Diverging Paths? The Shapes of Power and Institutions in Medieval Christendom and Islam*, Leiden and Boston: Brill, 2014, pp. 75–97.

Coşgel, Metin M. and Boğaç A. Ergene, "Dispute Resolution in Ottoman Courts: A Quantitative Analysis of Litigations in Eighteenth-Century Kastamonu," *Social Science History* 38, 1–2 (Spring/Summer 2014), pp. 183–202.

Coşgel, Metin M. and Boğaç A. Ergene, *The Economics of Ottoman Justice Settlement and Trial in the Sharia Courts*, Cambridge: Cambridge University Press, 2016.

Crone, Patricia, *God's Caliph: Religious Authority in the First Centuries of Islam*, Cambridge: Cambridge University Press, 1986.

David, Abraham, "New Data on the Biography of R. Joseph Karo" [Hebrew], *Proceedings of the World Congress of Jewish Studies* C, 1 (1989), pp. 201–207.

Davidson, Eyal, "Safed's Sages between 1540–1615, Their Religious and Social Status" [Hebrew], Ph.D. submitted at the Hebrew University, 2009.

Davis, Joseph, "The Reception of the Shulchan 'Arukh and the Formation of Ashkenazic Jewish Identity," *AJS Review* 26, 2 (2002), pp. 251–276.

Dimitrovsky, Haim Z., "A Dispute between Rabbi J. Caro and Rabbi M. Trani" [Hebrew], *Sefunot: Studies and Sources on the History of the Jewish Communities in the East* 6 (1962), pp. 71–123.

Dimitrovsky, Haim Z., "Rabbi Yaakov Beirav's Academy in Safed" [Hebrew], *Sefunot: Studies and Sources on the History of the Jewish Communities in the East* 7 (1963), pp. 41–102.

Dimitrovsky, Haim Z., "New Documents Regarding the Semichah Controversy in Safed" [Hebrew], *Sefunot: Studies and Sources on the History of the Jewish Communities in the East* 10 (1966), pp. 113–192.0

Dinur, Ben-Zion, *People of Israel in Exile* [*Israel baGolah* in Hebbrew], Tel-Aviv: Dvir Publishing House, 1959, Vol. I/1.

Donahue, Charles, *Law, Marriage, and Society in the Later Middle Ages: Arguments About Marriage in Five Courts*, Cambridge: Cambridge University Press, 2007.

Durani, Yaron, "Three Pillars of Guidance in the Halakhic Ruling of R. Joseph Karo" [Hebrew], M.A. thesis submitted at Bar-Ilan University (Ramat-Gan, Israel), 2006.

Dweck, Yaakob, "A Jew from the East Meets Books from the West," in: Richard I. Cohen, Natalie B. Dohrmann, Adam Shear, and Elchanan Reiner (eds.), *Jewish Culture in Early Modern Europe: Essays in Honor of David B. Ruderman*, Pittsburgh and Cincinnati: University of Pittsburgh Press and HUC Press, 2014, pp. 239–249.

Elliot, John H., *Empires of the Atlantic: Britain and Spain in America 1492–1830*, Yale: Yale University Press, 2006.

Elon, Menachem, *Jewish Law: History, Sources, Principles*, translated by Bernard Auerbach and Melvin J. Sykes, Philadelphia and Jerusalem: Jewish Publication Society, 1994, Vols. I–IV.

El-Rouayeb, Khaled, *The Rise of "Deep Reading" in Early Modern Ottoman Scholarly Culture*, Cambridge and London: Harvard University Press, 2015.

El-Shamsy, Ahmed, *The Canonization of Islamic Law: A Social and Intellectual History*, New York: Cambridge University Press, 2013.

Emre, Side, "Crafting Piety for Success: Gülşeniye Literature and Culture in the Sixteenth Century," *Journal of Sufi Studies* 1 (2012), pp. 31–75.

Emre, Side, "A Preliminary Investigation of Ibn 'Arabi's Influence Reflected in the Corpus of İbrahim-i Gulsheni (d.1534) and the Halveti–Gulsheni Order of Dervishes in Egypt," *Journal of the Muhyiddin Ibn 'Arabi Society* 56 (2014), pp. 67–111.

Falk-Moore, Sally, *Law as Process: An Anthropological Approach*, London and Boston: Routledge & K. Paul, 1978.

Falk-Moore, Sally (ed.), *Law and Anthropology: A Reader*, Malden: Blackwell Pub., 2005.

Fenton, Paul B., "Solitary Meditation in Jewish and Islamic Mysticism in the Light of a Recent Archeological Discovery," *Medieval Encounters* 1, 2 (1995), pp. 271–296.

Fenton, Paul B., "Influences soufies sur le dévélopment de la Qabbale à Safed: le cas de la visitation des tombes," in: Paul B. Fenton and Roland Goetschel (eds.), *Expérience et écriture mystiques dans les religions du livre*, Leiden: Brill, 2000, pp. 163–190.

Fenton, Paul B., "Devotional Rites in a Sufi Mode," in: Lawrence Fine (ed.), *Judaism in Practice: From the Middle Ages through the Early Modern Period*, Princeton and Oxford: Princeton University Press, 2001, pp. 364–374.

Fierro, Maribel, "Codifying the Law: The Case of the Medieval Islamic West," in: John Hudson and Ana Rodríguez (eds.), *Diverging Paths? The Shapes of Power and Institutions in Medieval Christendom and Islam*, Leiden and Boston: Brill, 2014, pp. 98–118.

Fine, Lawrence, *Physician of the Soul, Healer of the Cosmos: Isaac Luria and His Kabbalistic Fellowship*, Stanford: Stanford University Press, 2003.

Finkelberg, Margalit, "Homer as a Foundation Text," in: Margalit Finkelberg and Guy G. Stroumsa (eds.), *Homer, the Bible, and Beyond: Literary and Religious Canons in the Ancient World*, Leiden and Boston: Brill, 2003, pp. 75–96.

Fitzgerald, Timothy J., "Murder in Aleppo: Ottoman Conquest and the Struggle for Justice in the Early Sixteenth Century," *Journal of Islamic Studies* 27, 2 (2016), pp. 176–215.

Fitzgerald, Timothy J., "Rituals of Possession, Methods of Control, and the Monopoly of Violence: The Ottoman Conquest of Aleppo in Comparative Perspective," in: Stephan Conermann and Gül Sen (eds.), *The Mamluk-Ottoman Transition Continuity and Change in Egypt and Bilad al-Sham in the Sixteenth Century*, Bonn: Bonn University Press, 2016, pp. 249–273.

Fleischer, Cornell H., *Bureaucrat and Intellectual in the Ottoman Empire: The Historian Mustafa Ali (1541–1600)*, Princeton: Princeton University Press, 1986.

Fleischer, Cornell H., "The Lawgiver as Messiah: The Making of the Imperial Image in the Reign of Süleymân," in: Gilles Veinstein (ed.), *Soliman le Magnifique et son temps*, Paris: La Documentation Française, 1992, pp. 159–177.

Floor, Willem, "The Khlifeh al-kholafa of the Safavid Sufi Order," *Zeitschrift der Deutschen Morgenländischen Gesellschaft* 153, 1 (2003), pp. 51–86.

Galinsky, Yehuda D., "The Four Turim and the Halakhic Literature of 14th Century Spain, Historical, Literary and Halakhic Aspects" [Hebrew], Ph.D. submitted at Bar-Ilan University (Ramat-Gan, Israel), 1999.

Gara, Eleni, "Conceptualizing Interreligious Relations in the Ottoman Empire: The Early Modern Centuries," *Acta Poloniae Historica* 116 (2017), pp. 57–92.

Garcia-Arenal, Mercedes, *Messianism and Puritanical Reform: Mahdis of the Muslim West*, Leiden and Boston: Brill, 2006.

George, Makdisi, *The Rise of Colleges: Institutions of Learning in Islam and the West*, Edinburgh: Edinburgh University Press, 1981.

Ghazzal, Zouhair, "Waqfs and Urban Structures: The Case of Ottoman Damascus by Richard van Leeuwen," *International Journal of Middle East Studies* 33, 4 (2001), pp. 618–620.

Ghazzal, Zouhair, "The 'Ulama: Status and Function," in: Youssef M. Choueiri (ed.), *A Companion to the History of the Middle East*, London: Blackwell, 2005, pp. 71–86.

Ginio, Eyal, "The Administration of Criminal Justice in Selānik (Salonica) during the Eighteenth Century," *Turcica* 30 (1998), pp. 185–209.

Glicksberg, Shlomo and Cassirer Shlomo, "The Halakhah and Meta-Halakhah Codification Debate: Rabbi Chaim ben Bezalel and the Maharal of Prague" [Hebrew], *Jewish Studies* 49 (2013), pp. 157–191.

Goodblatt, David, "The Political and Social History of the Jewish Community in the Land of Israel, C. 235–638," in: Steven T. Katz (ed.), *The Cambridge History of Judaism*, Vol. IV – 'The Late Roman Rabbinic Period', Cambridge: Cambridge University Press, 2008, pp. 404–430.

Goodblatt, Morris S., *Jewish life in Turkey in the XVIth Century: As Reflected in the Legal Writings of Samuel de Medina*, New York: Jewish Theological Seminary of America, 1952.

Gradeva, Rossita, "A Kadi Court in the Balkans: Sofia in the Seventeenth and Early Eighteenth Centuries," in: Christine Woodhead (ed.), *The Ottoman World*, Routledge: London and New York, 2012, pp. 57–71.

Grossman, Avraham and Yosef Kaplan (eds.), *Kehal Yisrael – Jewish Self-Rule through the Ages*, Vol. 2 – 'The Middle Ages and Early Modern Period', Jerusalem: Shazar Center for Jewish History, 2004.

Hacker, Joseph, "The 'Chief Rabbinate' in the Ottoman Empire in the 15th and 16th Century" [Hebrew], *Zion* 49 (1984), pp. 225–263.

Hacker, Joseph, "The Intellectual Activity among Jews in the Ottoman Empire during the Sixteenth and Seventeenth Centuries" [Hebrew], *Tarbiz* 53, 4 (1984), pp. 569–604.

Hacker, Joseph, "The Limits of Jewish Autonomy: Internal Jewish Adjudication in the Sixteenth-Eighteenth Centuries" [Hebrew], in: Shmuel Almog et al. (eds.), *Transition and Change in Modern*

Jewish History: Essays Presented in Honor of Shmuel Ettinger, Jerusalem: Zalman Shazar Center and the Israeli Historical Society, 1987, pp. 349–388.

Hacker, Joseph, "Jewish Autonomy in the Ottoman Empire: Its Scope and Limits. Jewish Courts from the Sixteenth to the Eighteenth Centuries," in: Avigdor Levy (ed.), *The Jews of the Ottoman Empire*, Princeton: Darwin Press in Cooperation with the Institute of Turkish Studies, Washington, D.C, 1994, pp. 153–202.

Hacker, Joseph, "Communal Organization among the Jewish Communities of the Ottoman Empire (1453–1676)" [Hebrew], in: Avraham Grossman and Yosef Kaplan (eds.), *Kehal Yisrael – Jewish Self-Rule through the Ages*, Vol. 2 – 'The Middle Ages and Early Modern Period', Jerusalem: Shazar Center for Jewish History, 2004, pp. 287–309.

Hacker, Joseph, "The Sephardi *Midrash* – A Jewish Public Library" [Hebrew], in: Joseph Hacker, Yosef Kaplan, and Binyamin Z. Kedar (eds.), *From Sages to Savants: Studies Presented to Avraham Grossman*, Jerusalem: Shazar Center, 2010, pp. 263–292.

Hacker, Joseph, "Authors, Readers and Printers of Sixteenth-Century Hebrew Books in the Ottoman Empire," in: Peggy K. Pearlstein (ed.), *The Myron M. Weinstein Memorial Lectures at the Library of Congress*, Washington: Library of Congress, 2012, pp. 17–63.

Hacker, Joseph, "The Rise of Ottoman Jewry," in: Jonathan Karp and Adam Sutcliffe (eds.), *The Cambridge History of Judaism*, Vol. VII – 'The Early Modern World, 1500–1815', Cambridge: Cambridge University Press, 2017, pp. 77–112.

Halbertal, Moshe, *People of the Book: Canon, Meaning, and Authority*, Cambridge and London: Harvard University Press, 1997.

Halbertal, Moshe, "Nahmanides' Conception of the History of Halakhah and the Minhag" [Hebrew], *Zion* 67 (2002), pp. 25–56.

Halbertal, Moshe, "What Is *Mishneh Torah*? On Codification and Ambivalence," in: Jay M. Harris (ed.), *Maimonides after 800 Years: Essays on Maimonides and His Influence*, Cambridge and London: Harvard University Press, 2007.

Halbertal, Moshe, *Maimonides: Life and Thought*, translated by Joel A. Linsider, Princeton: Princeton University Press, 2014.

Hallaq, Wael B., "Was the Gate of Ijtihad Closed," *International Journal of Middle East Studies* 16, 1 (March, 1984), pp. 3–41.

Hallaq, Wael B., *The Origins and Evolution of Islamic Law*, Cambridge and New York: Cambridge University Press, 2004.

Hallaq, Wael B., *Shari'a: Theory, Practice, Transformations*, Cambridge: Cambridge University Press, 2009.

Havlin, Shlomo Zalman, "On Literary Canonization as Constitutive for Time Division in the History of Halakhah" [Hebrew], in: *Studies in the Talmudic Literature: In Honor of Saul Lieberman on His Eightieth Birthday*, Jerusalem: The Israeli Academy of Sciences and Humanities, 1978, pp. 148–192.

Havlin, Solomon, "Rabbi Abraham Halevi (Author of Responsa 'Ginath vradim') and the Scholars of His Time and Place" [Hebrew], Ph.D. submitted at The Hebrew University (Jerusalem), 1983.

Haym, Soloveichik, *Collected Essays*, Oxford: Littman Library of Jewish Civilization, 2013–2014, Vols. I–II.

Headley, John M., "The Habsburg World Empire and the Revival of Ghibellinism," in: David Armitage (ed.), *Theories of Empire, 1450–1800*, London & New York: Routledge, 2016, pp. 45–79.

Hespanha, António Manuel, "Form and Content in Early Modern Legal Books. Bridging the Gap between Material Bibliography and the History of Legal Thought," *Rechtsgeschichte: Zeitschrift des Max-Planck-Instituts für europäische Rechtsgeschichte* 12 (2008), pp. 12–50.

Hidary, Richard, *Dispute for the Sake of Heaven: Legal Pluralism in the Talmud*, Providenc: Braun Judaic Studies, 2010.

Huss, Boaz, *The Zohar: Reception and Impact*, translated by Yudith Naveh, Oxford and Portland: The Littman Library of Jewish Civilization, 2016.

Idel, Moshe, "Inquiries into the Doctrine of 'Sefer ha-Meshiv'" [Hebrew], *Sefunot: Studies and Sources on the History of the Jewish Communities in the East* 2 (1943), pp. 185–266.

Idel, Moshe, "On Mobility, Individuals and Groups: Prolegomenon for a Sociological Approach to Sixteenth-Century Kabbalah," *Kabbalah: Journal for the Study of Jewish Mystical Texts* 3 (1998), pp. 145–173.

Idel, Moshe, "Rabbi Joseph Karo as Kabbalist" [Hebrew], in: *Rabbi Joseph Karo: History, Halakhah, Kabbalah,* Jerusalem: Zalman Shazar Center, 2021, pp. 337–400.

Imber, Colin, *Ebu's-su'ud: The Islamic Legal Tradition*, Edinburgh: Edinburgh University Press, 1997.

Israel, Ta-Shma, *Talmudic Commentary in Europe and North Africa* [Hebrew], Jerusalem: Magnes Press, 2004, Vols. I–II.

Ivanyi, Kathanrina Anna, "Virtue, Piety and the Law: A Study of Birgivi Mehmed Efendi's Al-Tariqa Al-Muhammadiyya," Ph.D. submitted at Princeton University, 2012.

Jacobs, Martin, "An Ex-Sabbatean's Remorse? Sambari's Polemics against Islam," *The Jewish Quarterly Review* 97, 3 (2007), pp. 347–378.

Jensen, Nils, *The Making of Legal Authority: Non-legislative Codifications in Historical and Comparative Perspective*, Oxford: Oxford University Press, 2010.

Jokisch, Benjamin, *Islamic Imperial Law: Harun Al-Rashid's Codification Project*, Berlin and New York: Walter de Gruyter, 2007.

Joseph, Davis, "The Reception of the *Shulhan 'Aruch* and the Formation of Ashkenazic Jewish Identity," *AJS Review*, 26 2 (2002), pp. 251–276.

Kafadar, Cemal, "Self and Others: The Diary of a Dervish in Seventeenth Century Istanbul and First-Person Narratives in Ottoman Literature," *Studia Islamica*, 69 (1989), pp. 121–150.

Kahana, Maoz, "Cosmos and Nomos: Sacred Space and Legal Action, from Rabbi Yosef Qaro to Shabbetai Şevi," *El Prezente: Journal for Sephardic Studies* 10 (2016), pp. 143–153.

Kahana, Maoz, "A Universe Made of Words. The Self-Image of R. Joseph Karo as Composer of Halakhah" [Hebrew], *Hebrew Law Annual [Shnaton Ha-Mishpat Ha-'Ivri* in Hebrew] 30 (2019–2020), pp. 79–127.

Kanarfogel, Ephraim, *'Peering Through the Lattices': Mystical, Magical, and Pietistic Dimensions in the Tosafist Period*, Detroit: Wayne State University Press, 2000.

Karamustafa, Ahmet T., *God's Unruly Friends: Dervish Groups in the Islamic Later Middle Period 1200–1550*, Salt Lake City: University of Utah Press, 1994.

Karateke, Hakan T., "Opium for the Subjects? Religiosity as a Legitimizing Factor for the Ottoman Sultan," in: Hasan T. Karateke and Maurus Reinkowski (eds.), *Legitimizing the Order: The Ottoman Rethoric of State Power*, Leiden and Boston: Brill, 2005, pp. 111–129.

Karateke, Hasan T. and Reinkowski Maurus (eds.), *Legitimizing the Order: The Ottoman Rethoric of State Power*, Leiden and Boston: Brill, 2005.

Katz, Jacob, "The Controversy on the Semichah (Ordination) between Rabbi Jacob Beirav and the Ralbach" [Hebrew], *Zion* 16, 3–4 (1951), pp. 28–45.

Katz, Jacob, *The 'Shabbes Goy': A Study in Halakhic Flexibility*, translated by Yoel Lerner, Philadelphia: JPS, 1989.

Kelman, Tirza Y., "'I Shall Create Halakhic Ruling… for that is the Objective': The Dimension of Halakhic Ruling in Joseph Karo's Beit Yosef" [Hebrew], Ph.D. submitted at Ben-Gurion University (Beer-Shevah, Israel), 2018.

Kermode, Frank, *The Classic*, New York: Viking Press, 1975.

Kiel, Yishai, "Reinventing Yavneh in Sherira's Epistle. From Pluralism to Monism in the Light of Islamicate Legal Culture," in: Michael Satlow (ed.), *Strength to Strength: Essays in Appreciation of Shaye J. D. Cohen*, Providence: Brown Judaic Studies, 2018, pp. 577–598.

Koskenniemi, Martti, "Introduction: International Law and Empire—Aspects and Approaches," in: Martti Koskenniemi, Rech Walter, and Fonseca Manuel Jiménez (eds.), *International Law and Empire Historical Explorations*, Oxford: Oxford University Press, 2016, pp. 1–18.

Kraemer, David, "The Mishnah," in: Katz (ed.), *The Cambridge History of Judaism*, Vol. IV, pp. 299–315.

Krstić, Tijana, "Of Translation and Empire: Sixteenth-Century Ottoman Imperial Interpreters as Renaissance Go-betweens," in: Christine Woodhead (ed.), *The Ottoman World*, London and New York: Routledge, 2012, pp. 130–142.

Krstić, Tijana, "From Shahada to 'Aqida: Conversion to Islam, Catechisation and Sunnitization in Sixteenth Century Ottoman Rumeli," in: A.C.S. Peacock (ed.), *Islamisation: Comparative Perspectives from History*, Edinburgh: Edinburgh University Press, 2017, pp. 296–314.

Krstić, Tijana, "State and Religion, "Sunnitization" and "Confessionalism" in Süleyman's Time," in: Pál Fodor (ed.), *The Battle for Central Europe: The Siege of Szigetvár and the Death of Süleyman the Magnificent and Nicholas Zrinyi (1566)*, Leiden and Boston: Brill, 2019, pp. 65–91.

Lamberton, Robert, "The Neoplatonists and their Books," in: Margalit Finkelberg and Guy G. Stroumsa (eds.), *Homer, the Bible, and Beyond: Literary and Religious Canons in the Ancient World*, Leiden and Boston: Brill, 2003, pp. 95–211.

Lehmann, Matthias B., *Emissaries from the Holy Land: The Sephardic Diaspora and the Practice of Pan-Judaism in the Eighteenth Century*, Stanford: Stanford University Press, 2014.

Libson, Gideon, "Parallels between Maimonides and Islamic Law," in: Ira Robinson, Lawrence Kaplan, and Julien Bauer (eds.), *The Thought of Moses Maimonides: Philosophical and Legal Studies*, Lewiston/Queenston/Lampeter: The Edwin Mellen Press, 1990, pp. 209–248.

Libson, Gideon, *Jewish and Islamic Law: A Comparative Study of Custom in the Geonic Period*, Cambridge: Harvard Law School, 2003.

Libson, Gideon, "Maimonides Halakhic Writings in their Muslim Background" [Hebrew], in: Aviezer Ravitzky (ed.), *Maimonides: Conservatism, Originality, Revolution*, Vol I – 'History and Halakha', Jerusalem: The Zalman Shazar Center for Jewish History, 2009, pp. 247–294.

Libson, Gideon, "The Linkage of Maimonides to the Shari'a in the Context of His Period," in: Aviezer Ravitzky (ed.), *Maimonides: Conservatism, Originality, Revolution*, Vol I – 'History and Halakha', Jerusalem: The Zalman Shazar Center for Jewish History, 2009, pp. 247–294.

Macarena, Crespo Álvarez, "El cargo de Rab Mayor de la corte durante el reinado de Juan II: el camino hacia la centralización," *El Olivo; documentación y estudios para el diálogo entre judíos y cristianos* 61–62 (2005), pp. 51–64.

Mantel, Hugo [=Hayim], *Studies in the History of the Sanhedrin*, Cambridge: Harvard University Press, 1961.

Mantel, Hayim D., "Ordination and Appointment in the Days of the Temple" [Hebrew], *Tarbiz* 32, 2 (1963), pp. 120–135.

Marciano, Yoel, *Sages of Spain in the Eye of the Storm - Jewish Scholars of Late Medieval Spain* [Hebrew], Jerusalem: Bialik Institute, 2019.

Markiewicz, Christorpher, *The Crisis of Kingship in Late Medieval Islam: Persian Emigres and the Making of Ottoman Sovereignty*, Cambridge: Cambridge University Press, 2019.

Masters, Bruce, s.v. "Arabistan," in: Gábor Ágoston and Bruce Masters (eds.), *Encyclopedia of the Ottoman Empire*, n.p.: Fact on Line, 2009, p. 45.

Meier, Astrid, "Patterns of Family Formation in Early Ottoman Damascus: Three Military Households in the Seventeenth and Eighteenth Centuries," in: Peter Sluglett and Stefan Weber (eds.), *Syria and Bilad al-Sham under Ottoman Rule: Essays in honour of Abdul-Karim Rafeq*, Leiden and Boston: Brill, 2010, pp. 347–369.

Menachem, Elon, *Jewish Law*, Philadelphia: Jewish Publication Society, 1994, Vol. III, pp. 1367–1422.

Meri, Josef M., *The Cult of Saints among Muslims and Jews in Medieval Syria*, Oxford: Oxford University Press, 2002.

Meroz, Ronit, "The Circle of R. Moses ben Makhir and its Regulations" [Hebrew], *Pe'amim*, 31 (1987), pp. 40–61.

Meshal, Reem, "Aantagonistic Shari'as and the Construction of Orthodoxy in Sixteenth Century Ottoman Cairo," *Journal of Islamic Studies* 21, 2 (2010), pp. 183–212.

Mikhail, Alan, *God's Shadow: Sultan Selim, His Ottoman Empire, and the Making of Modern World*, New York: Liveright, 2020.

Milhou, Alain, *Colón y su mentalidad mesiánica en el ambiente francicanista español*, Valladolid: Casa-Museo de Colón: Seminario Americanista de la Universidad de Valladolid, 1983.

Moin, A. Azfar, *The Millenial Sovereign: Sacred Kingship and Sainthood in Islam*, New York: Columbia University Press, 2012.

Momen, Moojan, *An Introduction to Shi'i Islam: The History and Doctrines of Twelver Shi'ism*, New Haven and London: Yale University Press, 1985.

Morgan, David, "The 'Great Yasa of Chinggis Khan' Revisited," in: Amitai Reuven and Biran Michal (eds.), *Mongols, Turks, and Others: Eurasian Nomads and the Sedentary World*, Leiden and Boston: Brill, 205, pp. 291–308.

Morsel-Eisenbert, Tamara, "The Organization of Halakhic Knowledge in Early Modern Europe. The Transormation of Scholarly Culture," Ph.D submitted at Pennsylvania University, 2018.

Mutaf, Abdülmecid, "Amicable Settlement in Ottoman Law: *Sulh* System," *Turcica* 36 (2004), pp. 125–140.

Nader, Laura, *Le forze vive del diritto: Un'introduzione all'antropologia giuridica*. Edizioni Scientifiche Italiane, 2003.

Necipoğlu, Gülru, "A Kanun for the State, a Canon for the Arts: The Classical Synthesis in Ottoman Art and Architecture during the Age of Süleyman," in: Gilles Veinstein (ed.), *Soliman le Magnifique et son temps*, Paris: La Documentation Française, 1992, pp. 195–215.

Necipoğlu, Gülru, Crane Howard, and Akin Esra, *Sinan's Autobiographies: Fife Sixteenth-Century Texts*, Leiden and Boston: Brill, 2006.

Niazioğlu, Aslı, "Dreams, Ottoman Biography Writing, and the *Halveti-Sünbüli Şeyh*s of 16th-Century Istnabul," in: Ralf Elger and Yavuz Köse (eds.), *Many Ways of Speaking about the Self: Middle Eastern Ego-Documents in Arabic, Persian and Turkish (14th–20th Century)*, Wiesbabden: Harrassowitz Verlag, 2010, pp. 171–183.

Niazioğlu, Aslı, *Dreams and Lives in Ottoman Istanbul: A Seventeenth-Century biographer's Perspective*, London and New York: Routledge, 2017.

Nizri, Michael, *Ottoman High Politics and the Ulema Household*, London: McMillan and Palgrave, 2014.

Nora, Pierre, (sous la direction de), *Les lieux de la mémoire*, Paris: Gallimard, 1984–1986.

Ohlander, Erik S., *Sufism in an Age of Transition: 'Umar al-Suhrawardi and the Rise of the Islamic Mystical Brotherhoods*, Leiden and Boston: Brill, 2008.

Padoa-Schioppa, Antonio, *A History of Law in Europe: From the Early Middle Ages to the Twentieth Century*, Cambridge: Cambridge University Press, 2018.

Pagden, Anthony, "Introduction: Francisco de Vitoria and the Origins of the Modern Global Order," in: José María Beneyto and Justo Corti Varela (eds.), *At the Origins of Modernity: Francisco de Vitoria and the Discovery of International Law*, Cham (Switzerland): Springer, 2017, pp. 1–17.

Papademetriou, Tom, *Render unto the Sultan: Power, Authority, and the Greek Orthodox Church in the early Ottoman Centuries*, Oxford: Oxford University Press, 2015.

Parker, Geoffrey, "Messianic Visions in the Spanish Monarchy, 1516–1598," *Caliope: Journal of the Society for Renaissance and Baroque Hispanic Poetry* 8, 2 (2002), pp. 5–24.

Pastore, Stefania, *Un'eresia spagnola: Spiritualità conversa, alumbradismo e inquisizione (1449–1559)*, Firenze: Leo S. Olschki Editore, 2004.

Peirce, Leslie, *Morality Tales: Law and Gender in the Ottoman Court of Aintab*, Berkeley, Los Angeles and London: University of California Press, 2003.

Pely, Hagai, "Kabbalah in R. Karo's Halakhic Decisions: A Chapter in the Genealogy of Castilian Halakhic-Ruling until the Sixteenth Century" [Hebrew], *Kabbalah: Journal for the Study of Jewish Mystical Texts* 26 (2012), pp. 243–272.

Pely, Hagai, "The Lurianic Kabbalah: Halakhic and Meta-Halakhic Aspects," Ph.D. submitted at Ben-Gurion University (Beer-Shevah), 2014.

Pely, Hagai, "Halakhah, Pietism, Kabbalah and Revelation in Sixteenth Century Safed: A Study in R. Yosef Karo's Works" [Hebrew], *Jerusalem Studies in Jewish Thought* 24 (2015), pp. 201–234.

Pely, Hagai, "Studies in the Adjudication Project of Rabbi Joseph Karo" [Hebrew], in: *Rabbi Joseph Karo: History, Halakhah, Kabbalah*, Jerusalem: Zalman Shazar Center, 2021, pp. 131–333.

Pfeifer, Helen, "Encounter after the Conquest: Scholarly Gatherings in 16th Century Ottoman Damascus," *International Journal of Middle East Studies* 47, 2 (2015), pp. 219–239.

Plaks, Andrew, "Afterword: Canonization in the Ancient World: The View from Farther East," in: Margalit Finkelberg and Guy G. Stroumsa (eds.), *Homer, the Bible, and Beyond: Literary and Religious Canons in the Ancient World*, Leiden and Boston: Brill, 2003, pp. 267–275.

Prodi, Paolo, *Una storia della giustizia: Dal pluralismo dei fori al moderno dualismo tra coscienza e diritto*, Bologna: Il Mulino, 2000.

Prodi, Paolo, *Una storia della giustizia: Dal pluralismo dei fori al moderno dualismo tra conscienza e diritto*, Bologna: Il Mulino, 2015.

Quaglioni, Diego, *La giustizia nel Medioevo e nella prima età modern*, Bologna: Il Mulino, 2004.

Rachel, Elior, "'Possession' in the Early Modern Period: Speaking Voices, Silent Worlds and Silenced Voices" [Hebrew], *Jerusalem Studies in Jewish Thought* 18–19 (2005), pp. 499–536.

Rafeld, Meir, "The Maharshal and the 'Yam Shel Shlomo'" [Hebrew], Ph.D. submitted at Bar-Ilan University (Ramat-Gan, Israel), 1990.

Rapoport, Yosef, "Royal Justice and Religious Law: *Siyāsah* and Shari'ah under the Mamluks," *Mamluk Studies Review* 16 (2012) pp. 71–102.

Ravitzky, Aviezer (ed.), *Maimonides: Conservatism, Originality, Revolution*, Vol I – 'History and Halakhah', Jerusalem: Zalman Shazar Center, 2008.

Ravitzky, Aviezer and Avinoam Resenak (eds.), *New Streams in Philosophy of Halakhah* [Hebrew], Jerusalem: Magness Press, 2008.

Raz-Krakoztkin, Amnon, "From Safed to Venice: The Shulhan Arukh and the Censor," in: Chanita Goodblatt and Howard Kreisel (eds.), *Tradition, Heterodoxy and Religious Culture: Judaism and Christianity in the Early Modern Period*, Beer Sheva: Ben-Gurion University of the Negev Press, 2007, pp. 91–115.

Raz-Krakotzkin, Amnon, *The Censor, the Editor and the Text: The Catholic Church and the Shaping of Jewish Canon in the Sixteenth Century*, translated by Jackie Feldman, Philadelphia: University of Pennsylvania Press, 2007.

Raz-Krakotzkin, Amnon, "Persecution and the Art of Printing. Hebrew Books in Italy in the 1550s," in: Richard I. Cohen, Natalie B. Dohrmann, Adam Shear, and Elchanan Reiner (eds.), *Jewish Culture in Early Modern Europe: Essays in Honor of David B. Ruderman*, Pittsburgh and Cincinnati: University of Pittsburgh Press and HUC Press, 2014, pp. 97–108.

Reiner, Elchanan, "Rabbi Ya'akov Pollack of Cracow: First and Foremost among Cracow's Scholars" [Hebrew], in: Elchanan Reiner (ed.), *Kroke – Kazimierz – Cracow: Studies in the History of Cracow Jewry*, Tel-Aviv: Publications of the Diaspora Research Institute – Tel-Aviv University, 2001, pp. 43–68.

Reiner, Elchanan, "On the Roots of the Urban Jewish Community in Poland in the Early Modern Period" [Hebrew], *Gal-Ed: On the History and Culture of Polish Jewry* 20 (2006), pp. 13–37.

Reiner, Elchanan, "The Rise of "The Big Community": The Roots of Urban Jewish Community in Early Modern Poland" [Hebrew], *Gal-Ed: History of Polish Jews* 20 (2006), pp. 13–37.

Reiner, Elchanan, "From Joshua to Jesus: Three Chapters of the Galilean Jewish Foundational Myth," Taubman Lectures, Berkeley University, April 2015.

Renard, John, *Friends of God Islamic Images of Piety, Commitment, and Servanthood*, Berkeley, Los-Angeles, London: University of California Press, 2008.

Rey, Jonathan, *After Expulsion 1492 and the Making of Sephardic Jewry*, London and New York: New York University Press, 2013.

Robinson, Francis, "Ottomans-Safavids-Mughals: Shared Knowledge and Connective Systems," *Journal of Islamic Studies* 8, 2 (1997) pp. 151–184.

Rozen, Minna, *A History of the Jewish Community in Istanbul: The Formative Years, 1453–1566*, Leiden: Brill, 2002.

Ruderman, David, *Early Modern Jewry: A New Cultural History*, Princeton and Oxford: Princeton University Press, 2010.

Safrai, Uri, "The Figure and Status of R. Karo in Lurian Circle" [Hebrew], *Sefunot: Studies and Sources on the History of the Jewish Communities in the East* [forthcoming].

Sagi, Avi, "The Dialectic of Decision-Making and Objective Truth in Halakhah: Some Considerations Regarding the Philosophy of Halakhah" [Hebrew], *Dine Israel* 15 (1989–1990), pp. 7–38.

Sagi, Avi, "'Both These Version are Words of Living God' – On the Possibility of Multiple and Contradictory Halakhic Rulings" [Hebrew], in: Moshe Koppel and 'Ali Marzbach (eds.), *Sefer Higayon: On the Thinking Modes of Rabbis*, Alon Shevut: Machon Tzomet, 1995, pp. 113–141.

Sagi, Avi, '*It is not in Heaven': Themes in the Philosophy of Halakah* [Hebrew], 'Ein Tzurim: Jacob Herzog Center, 2003.

Sagi, Avi, *The Open Canon: On the Meaning of Halakhic Discourse*, translated by Batya Stein, London and New York, Continuum, 2007.

Şahin, Kaya, *Empire and Power in the Reign of Süleyman: Narrating the Sixteenth-Century Ottoman World*, Cambridge: Cambridge University Press, 2013.

Salamah-Qudsi, Arin, "The Will to be Unveiled: Sufi Autobiographies in Classical Sufism," *Al-Masaq: Journal of the Medieval Mediterranean* 24 (2012), pp. 199–207.

Savory, Roger M., "The Office of Khalîfat al Khulafâ Under the Safawid," *Journal of American Oriental Society* 85, 4 (1965), pp. 497–502.

Schäfer, Peter, "Research into Rabbinic Literature: An Attempt to Define the Status Quaestionis," *Journal of Jewish Studies* 37, 2 (1986), pp. 139–152.

Schimmel, AnneMarie, *Mystical Dimensions of Islam*, Chapel Hill: The University of North Carolina Press, 1975.

Scholem, Gershom, "The Magid of R. Yosef Taitazak and the Revelations Attributed to Him" [Hebrew], *Sefunot: Studies and Sources on the History of the Jewish Communities in the East* 11 (1969), pp. 69–112.

Seidel-Menchi, Silvana and Quaglioni Diego (eds.), *I processi matrimoniali degli archivi ecclesiastici italiani*, Bologna: Il Mulino, 2000–2006, Vols. I–IV.

Shafir, Nir, "The Road from Damascus: Circulation and the Redefinition of Islam in the Ottoman Empire, 1620–1720," Ph.D. submitted at University of California, 2016.

Shafir, Nir, "Moral Revolutions: The Politics of Piety in the Ottoman Empire Reimagined," *Comparative Studies in Society and History* 61, 3 (2019), pp. 595–623.

Shahab, Ahmed, *What Is Islam? The Importance of Being Islamic*, Princeton and Oxford: Princeton University Press, 2016, p. 192.

Sharon, Avital, "Hidas' Kaballah in his Hallakhic Writings [Hebrew]," Ph.D. submitted at the Hebrew University, 2014.

Shear, Adam, *The Kuzari and the Shaping of Jewish Identity*, Cambridge: Cambridge University Press, 2008.

Shmuelevitz, Aryeh, *Ottoman History and Society: Jewish Sources*, Istanbul: The Isis Press, 1999.

Shochetman, Eliav, "The Obligation to State Reasons for Legal Decisions in Jewish Law" [Hebrew], *Shenaton ha-Mishpat ha-'Ivri: Annual of the Institute for Research in Jewish Law* 6–7 (1980–1981), pp. 319–397.

Simonsohn, Uriel, *A Common Justice: The Legal Allegiances of Christian and Jews under Early Islam*, Philalphia: University of Pennsylvania Press, 2011.

Sirriyeh, Elizabeth, *Sufi Visionary of Ottoman Damascus. 'Abd al-Ghani al-Nabulusi 1641–1731*, London and New York: Routledge Curzon, 2005.

Şişman, Cengiz, *Transcending Diaspora: Studies on Sabbateanism and Dönmes*, Istanbul: Libra Kitapçılık ve Yayıncılık, 2016.

Smail, Daniel L., *The Consumption of Justice: Emotions, Publicity, and Legal Culture in Marseille, 1264–1423*, Ithaca: Cornell University Press, 2003.

Soloveichik, Haym, *Responsa as Historical Source* [Hebrew], Jerusalem: Shazar Center, 1990.

Stepansky, Yosef, "Archeological News regarding the Eastern Galilee" [Hebrew], *Nikrot Zurim* 17 (1991), pp. 21–34.

Stolte, Bernard H., "Codification in Byzantium. From Justinian to Leo VI," in: John Hudson and Ana Rodríguez (eds.), *Diverging Paths? The Shapes of Power and Institutions in Medieval Christendom and Islam*, Leiden and Boston: Brill, 2014, pp. 59–74.

Stroumsa, Sara, *Maimonides in His World: Portrait of a Mediterranean Thinker*, Princeton University Press, 2009.

Tamari, Assaf M., "The Body Discourse of Lurianic Kabbalah [Hebrew]," Ph.D. thesis submitted at Ben-Gurion University (Israel), 2016.

Tamari, Steve, "Biography, Autobiography, and Identity in Early Modern Damascus," in: Mary Ann Fay (ed.), *Auto/Biography and the Construction of Identity and Community in the Middle East*, New York: Palgrave, 2001, pp. 37–49.

Tchernowitz, Chaim (Rav Tzair), *Toldot ha-Poskim* [Hebrew], New York: Jubilee Committee, 1947, Vol. III, pp. 73–137.

Terzioğlu Derin, "Sufi and Dissident in the Ottoman Empire: Niyazî-i Mısrî (1618-1694)," Ph.D. submitted at Harvard University, 1999.

Terzioğlu, Derin, "Man in the Image of God in the Image of the Times: Sufi Self-Narratives and the Diary of Niyāzī-i Mışrī (1618–94)," *Studia Islamica* 94 (2002), pp. 139–165.

Terziğolu, Derin, "Sunna-minded Sufi Preacher in Service of the Ottoman State: The Naşîḥatnâme of Hasan Addressed to Murad IV," *Archivum Ottomanicum* 27 (2010), pp. 241–312.

Terziğolu, Derin, "Sufis in the Age of State-Building and Confessionalization," in: Christine Woodhead (ed.), *The Ottoman World*, Routledge: London and New York, 2012, pp. 86–98.

Terzioğlu, Derin, "How to Conceptualize Ottoman Sunnitization: A Historiographical Discussion," *Turcica* 44 (2012–2013), pp. 301–338.

Terzioğlu, Derin, "Where 'Ilm-I Hal Meets Catechism: Islamic Manuals of Religious Instruction in the Ottoman Empire in the Age of Confessionalization," *Past and Present* 220, 1 (2013), pp. 79–114.

Tezcan, Baki, "The Ottoman *Mevali* as 'Lords of the Law'," *Journal of Islamic Studies* 20, 3 (2009), pp. 383–407.

Tezcan, Baki, *The Second Ottoman Empire: Political and Social Transformation in the Early Modern World*, Cambridge: Cambridge University Press, 2010.

Trivellato, Francesca, *The Familiarity of Strangers: The Sephardic Diaspora, Livorno, and Cross-Cultural Trade in the Early Modern Period*, New Haven: Yale University Press, 2009.

Tucker, Judith E., "Biography as History: The Exemplary Life of Khayr al-Din al-Ramli," in: Mary Ann Fay (ed.), *Auto/Biography and the Construction of Identity and Community in the Middle East*, New York: Palgrave, 2001, pp. 9–17.

Twersky, Isadore, *Introduction to the Code of Maimonides (Mishneh Torah)*, Yale: Yale University Press, 1982.

Tzur, Yaron, *Notables and other Jews in the Ottoman Middle East 1750–1830* [Hebrew], Jerusalem: Bialik Institute, 2016.

Urbach, Efraim E., *The Halakhah – Its Roots and Evolvement* [Hebrew], Jerusalem: Yad LaTalmud, 1983.

Valleriani, Matteo (ed.), *The Structures of Practical Knowledge*, Berlin: Springer, 2017.

Vaya, Ilan, "Moral and Social Aspects in the Doctrine of Rabbi Moses Trani" [Hebrew], M.A. thesis submitted at Bar-Ilan University, 2015.

Weinstein, Roni, *Marriage Rituals Italian Style: A Historical Anthropological Perspective on Early Modern Italian Jews*, Leiden: E. J. Brill, 2003.

Weinstein, Roni, *Juvenile Sexuality, Kabbalah, and Catholic Religiosity among Jewish Italian Communities. "Glory of Youth" by Pinhas Baruch b. Pelatya Monselice (Ferrara, XVII Century)*, Boston and Leiden: E. J. Brill, 2008.

Weinstein, Roni, "L'ethos dell'onore nella vita famigliare e comunitaria della società ebraica italiana all'inizio dell'età moderna," in: Francesco Aspesi, Vermondo Brugnatelli, Anna Linda Callow, and Claudia Rosenzweing (eds.), *Il mio cuore è a oriente. Studi di linguistica, filologia e cultura ebraica dedicati a Maria Modena Mayer*, Quaderni di Acme 101, Milano: Cisalpino Istituto Editoriale Universitario, 2008, pp. 771–790.

Weinstein, Roni, *Kabbalah and Jewish Modernity*, London: Littman Library of Jewish Culture, 2016.

Weinstein, Roni, "Jewish Modern Law and Legalism in A Global Age: The Case of Rabbi Joseph Karo," *Modern Intellectual History* [Cambridge University Publications On-line], (2018), pp. 1–18.

Weinstein, Roni, "The Ottoman Settings of the Sabbatian Movement" [forthcoming].

Werblowsky, R. J. Zvi, *Karo: Lawyer and Mystic*, Philadelphia: Jewish Publication Society of America, 1977.

Wilhelm, Y. D., "Sidrei Tikunim" [Protocols of Kabbalistic Emendations – in Hebrew], in: *'Alei 'Ayin: Homage to Shlomo Zalman Schocken for His Seventieth Birthday*, Jerusalem: n.p., 1948–1952, pp. 125–146.

Wilke, Carsten, "Kabbalistic Fraternities of Ottoman Galilee and their Central European Members, Funders, and Successors," in: Tijana Krstić and Derin Terzioğlu (eds.), *Entangled Confessionalizations? Dialogic Perspectives on the Politics of Piety and Community Building in the Ottoman Empire, 15th – 18th Centuries*, Piscataway (NJ): Gorgias Press, 2022, pp. 255–283.

Winter, Michael, "Egyptian and Syrian Sufis Viewing Ottoman Turkish Sufism: Similarities, Differences, and Interactions," in: Eyal Ginio and Elie Podeh (eds.), *The Ottoman Middle East: Studies in Honor of Amnon Cohen*, Leiden and Boston, Brill, 2014, pp. 93–111.

Yahalom, Yosef, "Hebrew Mystical Poetry and its Turkish Background" [Hebrew], *Tarbiz* 60 (1991), pp. 625–648.

Yılmaz, Hüsein, *Caliphate Redefined: The Mystical Turn in the Ottoman Political Thought*, Princeton: Princeton University Press, 2018.

Yılmaz, Hüseyin, *The Mystical Turn in the Ottoman Political Thought*, Princeton: Princeton University Press, 2018.

Yochanan, Breuer, "Rabbi is Greater than Rav, Rabban is Greater than Rabbi, The Bare Name is Greater than Rabban" [Hebrew], *Tarbiz* 66, 1 (1997), pp. 41–59.

Yuval, Israel, "Rishonim and Aharonim, Antiqui et Moderni (Periodization and Self-Awareness in Ashkenaz)" [Hebrew], *Zion* 57, 4 (1992), pp. 369–394.

Zimmermann, Albert and Vuillemin-Diem Gudrun, *Antiqui und Moderni Traditionsbewusstsein und Fortschrittsbewusstsein im späten Mittelalter*, Berlin and New York: Walter de Gruyter, 1974.

Zinger, Isaac Pesach, *The Life and Compositions of HaMabit* [Hebrew], Jerusalem, 2007.

Zinger, Oded, "Women, Gender and Law: Marital Disputes according to Documents from the Cairo Genizah," Ph.D. submitted at Princeton University, 2014.

INDEX

CPSIA information can be obtained
at www.ICGtesting.com
Printed in the USA
BVHW041301301022
649962BV00001B/25